VIRGINIA GUN LAW

Armed And Educated

A Complete Guide To Gun Law In Virginia

2016-2017 Edition

By Attorneys W. Edward Riley, IV and
Mitchell M. Wells

Written by W. Edward Riley, IV and Mitchell M. Wells and published in the United States of America By U.S. Law Shield, LLP

ISBN 978-0-692-50650-9

To order additional books by phone or for wholesale orders, call (877) 448-6839.

TABLE OF CONTENTS

PREFACE

As lawyers with years of experience defending the constitutional rights of our clients in courts throughout the Commonwealth of Virginia, we have seen how well intended folks can get mixed up in the legal system through a misunderstanding of the law.

For that reason, we published *Virginia Gun Law: Armed And Educated, A Complete Guide To Gun Law In Virginia.* If you are a law abiding gun owner in Virginia, then you need to read this book because the gun laws apply to you. We want people to know and understand the law so that they can properly exercise their constitutional rights. Ignorance of the law is not a valid legal excuse. Therefore, if you want to stay legal, then you must know the law!
The Virginia gun owner has a lot to learn about constitutional rights along with federal and state laws and regulations to stay legal. We understand that much of this information can be overwhelming. Do not panic. This book will provide the law abiding gun owner with a base level of knowledge about gun law in Virginia.

The law can be complicated, overlapping, hard to understand, and in some cases, completely arbitrary to the point of confusion. Laws are often written by lawyers for lawyers or are the result of political compromises that generate confusing laws that the courts are left to interpret. After years of defending criminal law cases involving firearms, we discovered that there was no single book that explained gun law in Virginia in a straightforward simple manner that is easy for everyone to understand. Understanding the law goes far beyond just reading the cases, statutes or regulations. If you do not know either the process by which the law is being administered or how the courts are interpreting the meaning of the law, then you don't understand the full legal story.

That is why we wrote *Virginia Gun Law: Armed And Educated, A Complete Guide To Gun Law In Virginia.* Our collective legal experience has taught us well that anyone can become ensnared in the legal system. Many people firmly believe that "it" cannot happen to them. Even people that have never been in trouble before can find themselves as a criminal defendant through ignorance of the law. Our goal in writing this book was to explain the "law" to law abiding gun owners who wanted to inform and educate themselves. This book will explain what you need to know about gun law in order to stay legal in Virginia. The book contains useful gun law legal analysis and real world applications. Thousands of attorney hours have gone into producing this educational resource.

CHAPTER ONE

BRIEF LEGAL HISTORY OF THE RIGHT TO BEAR ARMS AND THE LAWS REGULATING FIREARMS

I. Introduction and historical overview

The right to own and carry a firearm in Virginia is guaranteed by both the United States Constitution and the Constitution of the Commonwealth of Virginia, but that was not always the case. In May of 1776, the Colony of Virginia, which was the first permanently settled English colony in North America, declared its independence from the British Empire largely over taxation and representation matters to become the independent Commonwealth of Virginia. In June of 1776, the Virginia Declaration of Rights and Constitution of the Commonwealth of Virginia were created. George Mason and James Madison are credited with drafting most of both documents. The Virginia Declaration of Rights proclaimed the inherent rights of man, was the first constitutional protection of individual rights, and was the precursor to the United States Bill of Rights.

The Virginia Constitution was the first written constitution adopted by the people's representatives in the history of the world. The original Virginia Constitution of 1776 was enacted in conjunction with the Declaration of Independence. The Virginia Constitution defines and limits the powers of government and the basic rights of its citizens. The Declaration of Rights was later incorporated within the Constitution of Virginia.

In June of 1788, the Unites States Constitution became the supreme law of the United States of America when it was ratified by thirteen American sovereign and independent states. The original version of the U.S. Constitution did not include any specific enumerated guaranteed individual rights; however, the first Congress of the United States adopted amendments to the U.S. Constitution, ten of which were ratified by the states and are known as the Bill of Rights. Virginian James Madison is hailed as the "Father of the Constitution" for his pivotal role in drafting and promoting the U.S. Constitution and the Bill of Rights. The Second Amendment specifically addresses firearms because it protects the right of the people to keep and bear arms.

II. The right to keep and bear arms in Virginia

The Second Amendment of the U.S. Constitution specifically states that:

> *A well-regulated Militia, being necessary to the security of a free State, the right of the people to keep and bear Arms, shall not be infringed.*

Additionally, the Constitution of the Commonwealth of Virginia in Article I, Section 13 states:

> *The right of the people to keep and bear arms shall not be infringed.*

However, this right is not absolute and it is permissible for there to be regulations that place reasonable restrictions on the use, purchase, possession and carrying of firearms that we will discuss in detail.

A plain reading of the Second Amendment of U.S. Constitution reveals that there are two important parts: first, that a well-regulated militia is necessary to the security of a free state, and second, that there is a right of the people to keep and bear arms. For years, before the issue was decided, gun control advocates tried to argue that the Second Amendment only applied to "militias" and not to individuals, but that is not the law. Nevertheless, despite the U.S. Supreme Court rulings stating otherwise, this myth seems to persist. What do these parts of the Second Amendment of the U.S. Constitution mean?

A. *What is a "Well-Regulated Militia?"*

As we just mentioned, the first part of the Second Amendment references a "well-regulated Militia." What is a well-regulated militia? The U.S. Supreme Court has held what this phrase does and does not mean. In 1939, in the case of *United States v. Miller,* 307 U.S. 174 (1939) (ironically, a ruling that upheld firearms regulation), the U.S. Supreme Court defined a Militia as comprising "all males physically capable of acting in concert for the common defense." Based on how the amendment was drafted, the Court stated, it was clear that the Militia pre-dated Article I of the Constitution, because unlike armies and navies, it did not have to be created by Congress. What does "well-regulated" mean? It is exactly what it sounds like:

the imposition of discipline and training. So, is this just the National Guard? No.

In the case of *District of Columbia v. Heller,* 554 U.S. 570 (2008), the U.S. Supreme Court stated that a well-regulated militia is not a state military force, but a separate entity altogether. The Court also stated that the word "militia" referred to the body of the people, and they—the people—were required to keep a centralized government in check. The Court considered and rejected the position that the National Guard is the current militia under the Second Amendment.

B.   *How has the phrase "right to keep and bear arms" been interpreted by the courts?*
One of the first cases to directly deal with the Second Amendment was *United States v. Miller.* In the *Miller* case, the U.S. Supreme Court found that the National Firearms Act ("NFA"), which imposed registration requirements on machine guns, short-barreled weapons, destructive devices, and other similarly unique firearms, did not violate the Second Amendment. The Court used the reasoning that possession of weapons regulated by the NFA did not reasonably relate to the preservation or efficiency of a well-regulated militia, therefore, the NFA was held constitutional.

Court fight where it all began: *United States v. Miller*
An interesting quirk of history in the *Miller* case is that Miller's attorney never appeared before the U.S. Supreme Court to argue the case because he was court-appointed and had not been paid. There was no legal representation either in the form of a written brief or an oral argument that the National Firearms Act was unconstitutional. The Court only heard the government's argument that the Act was constitutional. Ironically, Miller was shot to death before the decision was rendered.

C. *69 years later, the Supreme Court interprets the Second Amendment again: District of Columbia v. Heller*

It took the U.S. Supreme Court 69 years to again directly address the Second Amendment after the Miller case, except this time the Court would hear both the government's and the gun owner's arguments. In this case, the Court held that individuals have a right to keep and bear arms. It is important to note that the U.S. Supreme Court's decision in the *District of Columbia v. Heller* case was a split 5-4 decision; only one justice away from a different outcome.

> **District of Columbia v. Heller, 544 U.S. 570 (2008)**
> **Facts of the case:**
> Heller had applied for a handgun ownership permit and was denied; without such a permit, the District of Columbia government required that all firearms (including rifles and shotguns) were to be kept unloaded and disassembled, or bound by a trigger lock, even in a person's own home.
>
> **The legal holdings:**
> 1. The U.S. Supreme Court found that the Second Amendment protects an individual right of firearms ownership for purposes of self-defense, not connected with any militia or military purposes; it further elaborated that individual self-defense is "the central component" of the Second Amendment. Further, handguns are the primary defensive weapon of choice and are protected by the Second Amendment.
> 2. A well-regulated militia is not the state's military forces.
> 3. The Court also discussed what the phrase "bear arms" meant: "wear, bear, or carry... upon the person or in clothing or in a pocket, for the purpose... of being armed and ready for offensive or defensive action in a case of conflict with another person."
> 4. The D.C. regulation was held to be unconstitutional.
> 5. The Court concluded that like other rights, the right to bear arms is not completely absolute. Reasonable provisions and restrictions have been upheld.

D. *Can the Second Amendment be ignored? McDonald v. City of Chicago*

The *District of Columbia v. Heller* case was a win for individual gun rights, but there was a slight quirk — the District of Columbia is not a sovereign state, but rather is under the exclusive jurisdiction of Congress. Therefore, the case did not specifically answer the question of what, if anything, can a state do to regulate or ban firearms. *McDonald v. City of Chicago* sought to answer these questions.

> **McDonald v. City of Chicago, 561 U.S. 742 (2010)**
> **Facts of the case:**
> *McDonald v. City of Chicago* was decided in 2010. The case involved a City of Chicago ordinance that banned handgun possession (among other gun regulations). McDonald was a 76-year-old retired maintenance engineer who wanted a handgun for self-defense. Chicago required that all handguns had to be registered, but refused all handgun registration after a 1982 citywide handgun ban.
>
> **The legal holdings:**
> The U.S. Supreme Court held that the Second Amendment is fully applicable to the States and that individual self-defense is "the central component" of the Second Amendment. Therefore, the Second Amendment prohibits states from enacting bans on handguns for self-protection in the home.

E. *Legal limitations of the right to keep and bear arms*

The U.S. Supreme Court has stated: "Of course the right [to keep and bear arms] was not unlimited, just as the First Amendment's right of free speech was not." Courts may have struggled over the years with what the Second Amendment means, but they have been resolute that there is an element of self-defense. The U.S. Supreme Court stated in the *Heller* case that, "The Second Amendment does not protect the right to carry arms for any sort of confrontation," focusing their decision on self-defense.

Further, the Court stated in the *Miller* case that the weapons protected were those "in common use at the time" of the decision. This is supported by historical traditions of prohibiting the carrying of "dangerous and unusual weapons" that are commonly used by criminals for offensive purposes, as opposed to by law-abiding citizens for defensive purposes.

The Second Amendment does not grant felons and the mentally ill the right to possess a firearm. It also does not grant an individual the right to carry a firearm anywhere they want, such as sensitive places like schools and certain government buildings. The U.S. Supreme Court made this point in the *Heller* case. The *Heller* case also made it clear that it was not going to eliminate laws that imposed conditions and qualifications on the commercial sales of firearms.

Additionally, other federal courts have also interpreted the Second Amendment to mean that the right to bear arms is not absolute and that the right can be subject to, "limited narrowly tailored specific exceptions or restrictions for particular cases that are reasonable; it is clear that felons, infants and those of unsound mind may be prohibited from possessing firearms." *U.S. v. Everist,* 368 F.3d 517, 519 (5th Cir. 2004).

PRACTICAL LEGAL TIP

Currently, the two most important court decisions fortifying our gun rights are *Heller* and *McDonald*. But those cases were very, very close to going the other way! Both were decided by a 5-4 majority, meaning that if only one other Supreme Court Justice had decided differently, our individual right to possess and carry firearms could have been severely limited. — *Ed*

III. Major firearms statutes every gun owner needs to know

There are thousands of laws and regulations that concern firearms. This section will mostly focus on some of the more major federal legislative actions that all gun owners need to know, but will also briefly discuss regulation at the state level.

A. *Federal firearms law*
1. Gun Control Act of 1968

The Gun Control Act of 1968 (GCA) was enacted by Congress to "provide for better control of the interstate traffic of firearms." This law is primarily focused on regulating interstate commerce in firearms by generally prohibiting interstate firearms transfers except among licensed manufacturers, dealers, and importers, however, interstate commerce has been held by the courts to include nearly everything. It also contains classes of individuals to whom firearms should not be sold. For the specifics of who can and cannot purchase a firearm, please refer to Chapter 3. Among other things, the GCA mandates the licensing of individuals and companies engaged in the business of selling firearms. This licensing system is called the Federal Firearms License (FFL) system.

2. The Brady Handgun Violence Prevention Act

The Brady Handgun Violence Prevention Act, commonly referred to as the Brady Act, instituted federal background checks for firearms dealer transactions in the United States. The National Instant Criminal Background Check System (NICS) was mandated by the Brady Act. Chapter 3 discusses the NICS in more detail.

3. The Firearm Owners' Protection Act

The Firearm Owners' Protection Act (FOPA) revised many provisions of the original Gun Control Act, including "reforms" on the inspection of FFLs. This same Act updated the list of individuals prohibited from purchasing firearms that was introduced by the GCA. The FOPA also banned the ownership by civilians of any machine gun that was not registered under the National Firearm Act (NFA) as of May 19, 1986. FOPA created what is called a "safe passage" provision of the law, which allows for traveling across states with a firearm provided that the firearms and ammunition are not immediately accessible. Finally, the FOPA prohibits the federal government from keeping a registry that directly links non-NFA firearms to their owners.

4. The Public Safety and Recreational Firearms Use Protection Act

The Public Safety and Recreational Firearms Use Protection Act, commonly referred to as the *Federal Assault Weapons Ban,* was a subsection of the Violent Crime Control and Law Enforcement Act of 1994. It banned outright the manufacture and transfer of certain semi-automatic firearms and magazines. This ban grandfathered-in previously legally owned weapons, but no prohibited firearms could be acquired or manufactured after September 13, 1994. With great foresight, the drafters of this law included a so-called "sunset provision," that stated the ban would expire ten years later unless renewed. The ban expired in 2004, and all attempts to renew have been unsuccessful.

5. The National Firearms Act

The National Firearms Act (NFA) regulates and imposes a statutory excise tax on the manufacture and transfer of certain types of firearms and weapons: machine guns, short-barreled weapons, suppressors, explosive devices, and "any other weapons" (AOWs can range from everyday objects that are actually firearms, such as an umbrella that can fire a round, to other weapons the ATF decides to place in this category). The tax is $200 if you make or transfer an item (other than for the transfer of AOWs); the tax for transferring AOWs is $5. The NFA is also referred to as Title II of the federal firearms laws. For more information on how to navigate the NFA while remaining legal, please see Chapter 14.

B. *Can local governments in Virginia be prohibited from making certain gun laws?*

Yes. The Virginia courts have acknowledged that the Constitution of Virginia allows the legislature to create laws to prohibit certain types of carrying weapons, and have upheld "unlawful carrying" laws and license requirements. Along those lines, the Virginia legislature can and does prohibit local governments from adopting or enforcing certain gun laws. A Virginia locality may not adopt any gun law inconsistent with existing Virginia statutory law.

Va. Code § 15.2-915 states in part that a locality <u>cannot</u> regulate: anything relating to the purchase, possession, transfer, ownership, carrying, storage, or transporting of firearms, ammunition, or combinations of firearms and ammunition other than those expressly authorized by the Code of Virginia.

CHAPTER TWO
WHAT FIREARMS ARE ILLEGAL
OR REGULATED?

I.   Introduction
It is important to first understand how the federal and Virginia laws define a "firearm" and ammunition before discussing topics such as purchase, possession, transportation, concealment and use. In this chapter, we will explain how both the federal and Virginia laws define firearms and their various respective classifications along with types of ammunition. We will be discussing the purchasing, possession, and transferring of firearms and ammunition in Chapter 3.

II.   Types of firearms
A.   *What is a firearm?*
The common definition of a firearm is defined as a portable gun or weapon that launches a projectile, often driven by the action of an explosive force. Understanding what is considered a firearm is usually a simple concept for the law-abiding gun owner; however, sometimes firearm laws and classifications can become complicated and mistakes can trigger consequences. For example, a flare gun that is typically used to launch a distress signal is considered a firearm while a BB gun is not considered a firearm. *See Morris v. Commonwealth*, 269 Va. 127 (2005); *Startin v. Commonwealth*, 281 Va. 374 (2011).

   1.   Federal definition of a firearm
Under the federal law 18 U.S.C. § 921(a)(3), a firearm is defined as "any weapon (including a starter gun) which will or is designed to or may readily be converted to expel a projectile by the action of an explosive." The federal definition of a firearm also includes the frame or receiver of any such weapon, any firearm muffler or silencer, or any "destructive device."

   2.   Virginia definition of a firearm
Under Virginia law, Va. Code § 18.2-433.1, a firearm is defined as, "any weapon that will or is designed to or may readily be converted to expel single or multiple projectiles by the action of an explosion of a combustible material; or the frame or receiver of any such weapon."

Why is it important to know both the federal and the Virginia "firearm" definition? It is important because the federal definition of a firearm will apply if there is an allegation involving a violation of a federal law. Likewise, the Virginia definition of a firearm will apply if there is an allegation involving a violation of the Virginia law. In the next section we will see there are various different classifications of firearms. There are many similarities; however, there are an array of differences that can make violating the law easier than you may think.

B. *Handguns, rifles, and shotguns*
Federal law and Virginia law both classify and define firearms into categories of handguns and long guns (rifles and shotguns). This section will provide an overview of how both federal and Virginia laws classify firearms as well as the physical requirements for a firearm to be legal.

1. What is a handgun?
A handgun is a firearm designed to be handheld. Pistols and revolvers are types of handguns. The essential distinguishing characteristic of a handgun is its facility for one-handed operation although handgun use often includes bracing with a second hand for safety and accuracy purposes. This characteristic differentiates handguns as a general class of firearms from long guns such as rifles and shotguns, which usually can be braced against the shoulder.

Federal definition of a handgun
Federal law in 27 CFR § 478.11 defines a handgun as "(a) any firearm which has a short stock and is designed to be held and fired by the use of a single hand; and (b) any combination of parts from which a firearm described in paragraph (a) can be assembled."

Virginia definition of a handgun
Va. Code § 18.2-307.1 defines a handgun as "any pistol or revolver or other firearm, except a machine gun, originally designed, made, and intended to fire a projectile by means of an explosion of a combustible material from one or more barrels when held in one hand."

2. What is a rifle?

Federal definition of a rifle
Federal law 26 U.S.C. § 5845(c), 27 CFR § 478.11 defines a rifle as "a

weapon designed or redesigned, made or remade, and intended to be fired from the shoulder, and designed or redesigned and made or remade to use the energy of the explosive in a fixed metallic cartridge to fire only a single projectile through a rifled bore for each single pull of the trigger." In addition, a legal rifle must have a barrel length of 16 inches or greater, and includes any weapon made from a rifle which is at least 26 inches overall in length.

<u>Virginia definition of a rifle</u>
Va. Code § 29.1-100 defines a rifle as "a weapon designed or redesigned, made or remade, and intended to be fired from the shoulder, and designed or redesigned and made or remade to use the energy of the explosive in a fixed metallic cartridge to fire only a single projectile through a rifled bore for each single pull of the trigger."

Minimum length of a rifle
The barrel of a rifle must have a length of at least 16 inches and a total length of at least 26 inches overall. If the barrel length of the rifle is shorter than these minimum lengths, then the rifle would be considered short-barreled and be subject to regulation by the National Firearms Act (NFA). The rifle would also be classified as a "sawed off" rifle under Virginia law. *See* Va. Code § 18.2-299, 26 U.S.C. § 5845(a)(c). The Bureau of Alcohol, Tobacco, Firearms and Explosives (ATF) procedure for measuring barrel length is accomplished by measuring from the closed bolt (or breech-face) to the furthermost end of the barrel or permanently attached muzzle device. Below is an example of a rifle that does not meet the minimum barrel length requirement after measurement:

The barrel is measured by inserting a dowel rod into the barrel until the rod stops against the bolt or breech-face. The rod is then marked at the furthermost end of the barrel or permanently attached muzzle device, withdrawn from the barrel, and then measured. Any measurement of less than 16 inches will classify the rifle as being short-barreled under federal law and subject the firearm to the NFA, and being "sawed off" under Virginia law.

Short-barreled rifles and regulation by the NFA is further discussed in Chapter 13. Note: for overall length, rifles with collapsible/folding-stocks are measured from the "extreme ends," unless the stock is "easily detachable," in which case it is measured without the stock.

3. What is a shotgun?
A shotgun is a firearm that is usually designed to be fired from the shoulder. It is generally a smoothbore firearm, which means that the inside of the barrel is not rifled. A shotgun uses the energy of a fixed shell to fire a number of small spherical pellets called shot or a solid projectile called a slug. The shot pellets from a shotgun spread upon leaving the barrel, and the power of the burning charge is divided among the pellets, which means that the energy of any one ball of shot is fairly low.

Federal definition and Virginia definition of a shotgun
The federal and Virginia legal definitions of a shotgun are the same. *See* Va. Code § 29.1-100; 26 U.S.C. § 5845(d), 27 CFR § 478.11. It is a weapon designed or redesigned, made or remade, and intended to be fired from the shoulder, and designed or redesigned and made or remade to use the energy of the explosive in a fixed shotgun shell to fire through a smooth bore either a number of ball shot or a single projectile for each single pull of the trigger. A shotgun must have a minimum barrel length and overall length to be legal.

Minimum lengths of a shotgun
The barrel of a shotgun must be at least 18 inches and must have an overall length of at least 26 inches. If the barrel length is shorter than these minimum lengths, then the shotgun would be considered short-barreled and would be subject to regulation by the National Firearms Act (NFA). The shotgun would also be classified as

a "sawed off" shotgun under Virginia law. *See* Va. Code § 18.2-299; 26 U.S.C. 5845(a)(3). The ATF procedure for measuring the barrel length of a shotgun is the same as it is for a rifle. Below is an example of a shotgun that does not meet the minimum barrel length requirement after measurement:

Short-barreled shotguns and regulation by the NFA is further discussed in Chapter 13. Note: the collapsible/folding-stock rule that applies to rifles applies to shotguns as well.

C. *Antique firearms, curios and relics*
An "antique firearm" is a term that describes a firearm that was designed and manufactured prior to the beginning of the 20th century. "Antique firearms" are usually collected because of their historical interest and/or their monetary value.

The exact legal definition of what constitutes an "antique firearm" is important because an "antique firearm" and a replica firearm are not legally considered a "firearm." The federal law and the Virginia law substantially have the same "antique firearm" legal definition.

    1. Legal definition of "antique firearm"
18 U.S.C. § 921 and Va. Code § 18.2-308.2:2(G) define an "antique firearm" as:
    (A) any firearm (including any firearm with a matchlock,
        flintlock, percussion cap, or similar type of ignition system)

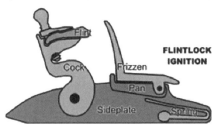

manufactured in or before 1898;

(B) any replica of any firearm described in subparagraph (A) if such replica—

(i) is not designed or redesigned for using rimfire or conventional centerfire fixed ammunition, or

(ii) uses rimfire or conventional centerfire fixed ammunition which is no longer manufactured in the United States and which is not readily available in the ordinary channels of commercial trade; or

Fired rimfire (left) and centerfire cartridges. A rimfire firing pin produces a notch at the edge of the case; a centerfire pin produces a divot in the center of the primer.

(C) any muzzle loading rifle, muzzle loading shotgun, or muzzle loading pistol, which is designed to use black powder, or a black powder substitute, and which cannot use fixed ammunition. For purposes of this subparagraph, the term "antique firearm" shall not include any weapon which incorporates a firearm frame or receiver, any firearm which is converted into a muzzle loading weapon, or any muzzle loading weapon which can be readily converted to fire fixed ammunition by replacing the barrel, bolt, breechblock, or any combination thereof.

"Antique firearms" can be divided into two basic types: muzzleloading and cartridge firing.

Muzzleloading "antique firearms"
Muzzleloading "antique firearms" are not generally owned with the intent of firing. These weapons were designed to be used with black powder. They were limited to low bullet velocities and had

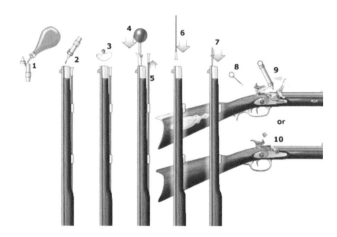

A muzzleloader is any firearm into which the projectile and usually the propellant charge is loaded from the muzzle of the gun (*i.e.*, from the forward, open end of the gun's barrel).

heavily arching "rainbow" bullet trajectories. Most own this type of "antique firearm" as either a display piece or for their historic value.

Cartridge-firing "antique firearms"
Cartridge-firing "antique firearms" are more commonly encountered as shooting pieces due to advancements in steel metallurgy and the advent of mass-produced smokeless powder in the early 1890s.

    2. Legal definition of "curio or relic"
"Curios" or "relics" mean firearms that are of special interest to collectors by reason of some quality other than is associated with firearms. Virginia law defines "curios" and "relics" as "antique firearms" in Va. Code § 18.2-308.2:2(G). A firearm must fall within one of the below categories in order for it to be recognized as a "curio" or "relic" under federal or Virginia law:
    a. Firearms that were manufactured at least 50 years prior to the current date, which use rimfire or conventional centerfire fixed ammunition that is no longer manufactured in the United States and that is not readily available in the ordinary channels of commercial trade, but not including replicas thereof;

b. Firearms that are certified by the curator of a municipal, state, or federal museum that exhibits firearms to be curios or relics of museum interest; and

c. Any other firearms that derive a substantial part of their monetary value from the fact that they are novel, rare, bizarre, or because of their association with some historical figure, period, or event. Proof of qualification of a particular firearm under this category may be established by evidence of present value and evidence that like firearms are not available except as collectors' items, or that the value of like firearms available in ordinary commercial channels is substantially less.

The federal law is a bit more complex with respect to "curios" and "relics." Federal law and Virginia law both have the same definition for "curio" or "relic," but the federal law does not specifically define a "curio" or "relic" as an "antique firearm."

The ATF will determine what firearms are "curios" or "relics" as defined in 27 CFR § 478.11. Such determination merely classifies the firearm as a "curio" or "relic" and thereby authorizes licensed collectors to acquire, hold or dispose of them as "curios" or "relics" subject to the provisions of 18 U.S.C. Chapter 44 and the regulations of 27 CFR § 478. They are still "firearms" as defined in 18 U.S.C. Chapter 44.

In addition to "curios" or "relics" being defined as "firearms," they may also be regulated under the National Firearms Act (NFA). However, the ATF may also remove the "curio" or "relic" from the NFA and classify the "curio" or "relic" as an "antique firearm," which would no longer subject the weapon to the Gun Control Act. It is recommended that the lawful gun owner consult the ATF's Firearms "Curios or Relics" List to determine the proper classification that can be found on the ATF's website. If your "curio" or "relic" is a NFA firearm and you desire removal of the NFA status, then you must submit it to the ATF's Firearms and Ammunition Technology Division (FATD) for evaluation and a formal classification.

D. _What firearms are illegal or regulated?_
The Virginia Code & the National Firearms Act have banned, regulated or restricted certain firearms. See Chapter 13 for more information on the NFA.

1. Plastic firearms

Va. Code § 18.2-308.5 defines a "plastic firearm" as any firearm, including machine guns and sawed-off shotguns, as containing less than 3.7 ounces of electromagnetically detectable metal in the barrel, slide, cylinder, frame or receiver which does not generate an image that accurately depicts its shape when subjected to X-ray machine inspection. It is unlawful for any person to manufacture, import, sell, transfer or possess any plastic firearm. A violation is a felony punishable by up to 10 years in prison!

2. Striker 12

Va. Code § 18.2-308.8 makes it unlawful to possess the Striker 12 also known as a "streetsweeper," or any semi-automatic folding stock shotgun of like kind with a spring tension drum magazine capable of holding twelve shotgun shells. The Striker 12 is a 12-gauge shotgun with a revolving cylinder that was designed for riot control and combat. It is unlawful to import, sell, possess or transfer the Striker 12 or any firearm of like kind. A violation is a felony punishable by up to 5 years in prison.

3. Assault firearms

Va. Code § 18.2-308.2:01 defines an "assault firearm" as any semi-automatic center-fire rifle or pistol which expels single or multiple projectiles by action of an explosion of a combustible material and is equipped at the time of the offense with a magazine which will hold more than 20 rounds of ammunition or designed by the manufacturer to accommodate a silencer or equipped with a folding stock.

4. Machine guns

Virginia definition of a machine gun

Virginia's Uniform Machine Gun Act regulates machine guns in Virginia. Va. Code § 18.2-288 defines any weapon which shoots or is designed to shoot automatically more than one shot, without manual reloading, by a single function of the trigger as a machine gun.

Federal definition of a machine gun
Federal law, in 26 U.S.C. § 5845 and 27 CFR § 478.11, defines a machine gun as "any weapon which shoots, is designed to shoot, or can be readily restored to shoot, automatically more than one shot, without manual reloading, by a single function of the trigger. The term shall also include the frame or receiver of any such weapon, any part designed and intended solely and exclusively, or combination of parts designed and intended, for use in converting a weapon into a machine gun, and any combination of parts from which a machine gun can be assembled if such parts are in the possession or under the control of a person."

III. Ammunition
No discussion concerning firearms laws would be complete without an understanding of the ammunition that goes into a firearm. Modern ammunition is a combination of the bullet or projectile, the propellant, the primer, the rim, and the cartridge case. Just like firearms, the federal and Virginia laws thoroughly define ammunition, which we will discuss now. Chapter 3 will explain the laws regarding the purchase, possession, and use of ammunition.

> **PRACTICAL LEGAL TIP**
>
> Even with firearms, having the right tool for the job is important. Practically speaking, you should choose the firearm and ammo that you feel most comfortable using. At the end of the day, why you started shooting is always more important than what you chose to shoot with. — *Mitch*

A. *Ammunition Types*
Ammunition types are categorized by their construction and assembly, not by use.

1. Fixed ammunition
Fixed ammunition is characteristically used in most small arms such as handguns and rifles. Fixed ammunition is also called a cartridge. This type of ammunition consists of a container for the propel-

lant charge (cartridge case) and a projectile that flies downrange at the target. The propellant charge, priming, and ignition system are assembled inside the cartridge case and are not alterable. The cartridge case is firmly attached to the projectile by crimping or cement. The cartridge case remains in the weapon after firing and is ejected near it or is consumed during firing.

Centerfire ammunition
A centerfire cartridge is a cartridge with a primer located in the center of the cartridge case head. The primer is a separate and replaceable component. Centerfire cartridges are the most popular variety of ammunition in almost all cartridge sizes.

Rimfire ammunition
Rimfire is a method of ignition for metallic firearm cartridges as well as the cartridges themselves. It is called rimfire because the firing pin of a gun strikes and crushes the base of the cartridge's rim to ignite the primer. This is in contrast to the more common centerfire method, where the firing pin strikes the primer cap at the center of the base of the cartridge. The rim of the rimfire cartridge is essentially an extended and widened percussion cap which contains the priming compound, while the cartridge case itself contains the propellant powder and the projectile (bullet). Once the rim of the cartridge has been struck and the bullet discharged, the cartridge cannot be reloaded, because the head has been deformed by the firing pin impact.

2. Separable ammunition
Separable ammunition also consists of the cartridge case and projectile, but the case is not attached firmly to the projectile and can be removed in the field and altered. The projectile may either consist of "shot" or a "slug." This type of ammunition is used in shotguns.

B. *Ammunition size*
Ammunition is generally expressed in a measurement. Most of the world uses a metric rating, while the commercial market in the United States uses a U.S. standard measurement. Handgun and rifle ammunition is measured by the caliber, which is simply a measurement of

the internal diameter of the barrel measured in millimeters or inches and is approximately equal to the diameter of the projectile that is fired. The larger the caliber, the bigger in diameter the ammunition.

Different calibers of handgun ammunition, left to right: Shotgun shell; (2) AA Battery; (3) .454 Casull; (4) .45 Winchester Magnum; (5) .44 Remington Magnum; (6) .357 Magnum; (7) .38 Special; (8) .45 ACP; (9) .38 Super; (10) 9mm Luger; (11) .32 ACP; and (12) .22 LR.

Different calibers of rifle ammunition, left to right: .22 Long Rifle (LR), .30 Carbine, .300 Blackout, 7.62x39mm, 5.56x45mm (.223 Remington), 7.62x51mm (.308 Winchester), 7.62x54mmR (Rimmed), .30-06 Springfield, .50 BMG (Browning Machine Gun).

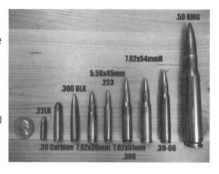

Shotgun ammunition, on the other hand, comes in self-contained cartridges loaded with some form of shot or slug which is designed to be fired from a shotgun. Shotgun shells are generally measured by "gauge." The gauge of a firearm is a unit of measurement used to express the diameter of the barrel.

Different shotshell sizes, left to right: .410 bore, 28 gauge, 20 gauge, 16 gauge, 12 gauge, and 10 gauge.

C. _Bullet type_

There are numerous styles of bullets that can be put into a cartridge of any caliber of ammunition. Different types of bullets have different effects when they strike a target. For example, the hollow-point round design causes the bullet to expand (or mushroom) rapidly when it hits soft tissue and therefore, to stop in soft-tissue targets. More of the energy of the bullet is deposited in the intended target because of the

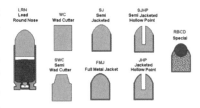

mushrooming and the bullet is more likely to stop a perpetrator from doing what he is doing. Some manufacturers have further developed the hollow-point rounds to make them more lethal such as the R.I.P. ammunition, Black Talons, *etc.,* which star outward upon impact in order to do more internal damage.

D. *How does the law define ammunition?*
    1. Federal definition of ammunition
Under federal law 18 U.S.C. § 921(a)(17)(A), the term ammunition means "ammunition or cartridge cases, primers, bullets, or propellant powder designed for use in any firearm." Thus, the federal definition of ammunition includes the finished product and all of the components in making a round of ammunition. However, the federal definition of ammunition neither includes (1) any shotgun shot or pellet not designed for use as the single, complete projectile load for one shotgun hull or casing, nor (2) any unloaded, non-metallic shotgun hull or casing not having a primer. *See* 27 CFR § 478.11. In other

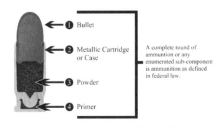

words, individual ammunition components are legally defined as ammunition themselves, even if they are simply parts, except that shotgun ammunition components, if not completely assembled, are not ammunition.

    2. Virginia definition of legal ammunition
Va. Code § 18.2-308.2 defines "ammunition for a firearm" as "the combination of a cartridge, projectile, primer, or propellant designed for use in a firearm other than an antique firearm..."

E. *Regulated ammunition defined*
    1. Federal armor-piercing ammunition definition

What is armor-piercing ammunition? According to federal law 18 U.S.C. § 921(a)(17)(b) it is "[1] a projectile or projectile core which may be used in a handgun and which is constructed entirely (excluding the presence of traces of other substances) from one or a combination of tungsten alloys, steel, iron, brass, bronze, beryllium copper, or depleted uranium; or [2] a full jacketed projectile larger than .22 caliber designed and intended for use in a handgun and whose jacket has a weight of more than 25 percent of the total weight of the projectile." The production, sale, importation, delivery, and possession of armor-piercing ammunition is discussed in Chapter 3.

2. Virginia restricted firearm ammunition definition
Va. Code § 18.2-308.3 makes it a felony offense to possess "restricted firearm ammunition." Restricted firearm ammunition includes bullets, projectiles or other types of ammunition that are: (i) coated with or contain, in whole or in part, polytetrafluoroethylene or a similar product, (ii) commonly known as "KTW" bullets or "French Arcanes"; or (iii) any cartridges containing bullets coated with a plastic substance with other than lead or lead alloy cores, jacketed bullets with other than lead or lead alloy cores, or cartridges of which the bullet itself is wholly comprised of a metal or metal alloy other than lead." However, this definition does not include shotgun shells or solid plastic bullets.

Our discussion of the National Firearms Act and Virginia Uniform Machine Gun Act is discussed in more detail in Chapter 13.

CHAPTER THREE
PURCHASING AND POSSESSING
FIREARMS AND AMMUNITION

I. Introduction

The federal and Virginia laws regarding the purchase and possession of firearms and ammunition are extensive, and sometimes
confusing. In general, if it is lawful for a person to purchase a firearm and ammunition, then it is lawful for that person to possess a
firearm and ammunition. However, the reverse is not always true.
In some instances, it may be legal for someone to "possess" a firearm, yet illegal for them to "purchase" a firearm.

The purchase of a firearm by an individual from a firearm dealer is
the most common form of firearm transfer; however, transfers do
not always involve a dealer and can include gifting a firearm. The
Bureau of Alcohol, Tobacco, Firearms and Explosives (ATF), is the
primary federal agency charged with regulating, investigating and
enforcing various firearm laws including the transfer and sale of
firearms through Federal Firearms Licensees (FFLs or firearm dealers). There is no direct state-level equivalent to the ATF in Virginia,
but the Department of State Police (VSP) plays a significant role
with respect to criminal background record checks, investigation
and enforcement of firearm sales and transfers by firearm dealers.
Local law enforcement agencies typically have little to no role regarding the sale or transfer of firearms, but will routinely investigate and enforce firearm possession and use offenses.

II.   Minimum age to possess vs. minimum age to purchase?

Under federal law, 18 U.S.C. § 922(x), a person must be at least 18
years of age in order to possess a handgun or ammunition for a
handgun. A violation of this section is a misdemeanor punishable
by no more than 1 year of imprisonment. *See* 18 U.S.C. § 924(a)
(6). There is no federal age requirement for the possession of long
guns such as a rifle or a shotgun. *See* 18 U.S.C. § 922(x). Va. Code §
18.2-308.7 makes it unlawful for anyone under the age of 18 (also
defined as a minor/child/juvenile) to knowingly or intentionally
possess or transport any handgun or assault firearm. A violation
of this section is a misdemeanor punishable by up to 12 months

in jail. Note: there are exceptions to this minimum age to possess requirement, which we will discuss later. There is no Virginia age requirement for the possession of long guns such as a rifle or a shotgun unless the shotgun comes with a magazine which will hold more than seven rounds. Virginia law does not have a minimum age for the possession of ammunition.

According to federal law, a person must be 21 years of age or older before they may purchase a handgun or ammunition for a handgun from a firearm dealer. *See* 18 U.S.C. § 922(a)(6). Additionally, a person must be 18 years of age or older before they may purchase a long gun or ammunition for a long gun from a firearm dealer. However, a handgun or long gun may be purchased in a private sale by a person who is 18 years of age. *See* 18 U.S.C. § 922(b)(1). Firearm dealer transactions, private sales and ammunition are discussed later in this chapter.

Required Age To Purchase Firearms	From Dealer	Private Sale
Handgun	21	18
Long Gun	18	18

III. The Federal Firearm License System

The Federal Firearm License System (FFL) regulates those engaged in the business of selling, importing and manufacturing firearms in the United States. The lawful transfer of firearms in the United States is almost entirely conducted by persons or companies holding a Federal Firearms License. A federal firearms licensee is often called an "FFL" or "dealer." An FFL is a license in the United States that is required by an individual or a company that engages in a business pertaining to the manufacture or importation of firearms and ammunition or the interstate and intrastate sale of firearms.

When an individual purchases, sells, or transfers a firearm through a firearm dealer, the dealer and the individual must both comply with specific legal requirements, paperwork, and procedures concerning the buying, selling, or transferring of those firearms.

NOTE: There are various exceptions to firearm transactions that are not regulated by the Federal Firearm License System. The purpose of this overview is to explain the most common transaction between an individual and a firearm dealer.

A. *Who must obtain an FFL?*
Federal law requires a federal firearms license if a person is engaged in business as a firearms dealer, manufacturer, or importer. For the purposes of our discussion in this chapter, a person is engaged in the business when the person "devotes time, attention, and labor to dealing in firearms as a regular course of trade or business with the principal objective of livelihood and profit through the repetitive purchase and resale of firearms, but such term shall not include a person who makes occasional sales, exchanges, or purchases of firearms for the enhancement of a personal collection or for a hobby, or who sells all or part of his personal collection of firearms." *See* 18 U.S.C. § 921(a)(21)(C).

B. *FFL firearm transaction overview*
Any attempted purchase or transfer of a firearm from an FFL dealer will trigger legal requirements imposed by both federal and Virginia law. Such an event will require a firearm transaction record. These requirements will include processing federal and Virginia forms to ensure that the purchaser is neither prohibited from making the purchase nor from possessing a firearm under federal and Virginia law.

The first thing that a prospective purchaser will typically do is select a firearm to purchase from the firearm dealer. After a selection has been made, the prospective purchaser is required to show proper identification and complete ATF Form 4473 and Virginia Department of State Police Form SP-65. *See* Va. Code § 18.2-308.2:2. These forms require the applicant purchaser, under penalty of law, to provide accurate identifying information, as well as answer certain questions in order to establish whether the applicant purchaser may legally purchase and possess a firearm.

In Virginia, the FFL firearm dealer submits the executed forms along with a criminal background check request to the Virginia Department of State Police's Firearms Transaction Program (VFTP). The VFTP was created by the Virginia Department of State Police to provide a timely, point-of-sale, approval or disapproval decision regarding the sale or transfer of all firearms (except antiques) based upon the results of a criminal history record information check and purchaser answers to potentially disqualifying questions. The criminal background check requirement is further explained in section III of this chapter.

C.   *What is ATF Form 4473?*

ATF Form 4473 is the ATF's form known as a Firearms Transaction Record which must be completed when a person purchases a firearm from an FFL. ATF Form 4473 requires the applicant to provide their name, address, birth date, state of residence, and other information including government issued photo identification. The form also contains information blanks to be filled-in including the NICS background check transaction number, the make, model, and serial number of the firearm to be purchased, and a series of questions that a person must answer. *See* 27 CFR § 478.124. This series of questions and the corresponding answers help determine a purchaser's eligibility under federal law to purchase a firearm. Once the form is completed, the prospective purchaser will sign the form and attest that the information provided thereon is truthful and accurate under penalty of federal law. VSP Form SP-65 is the Virginia equivalent form that is required by Va. Code § 18.2-308.2:2.

Additionally, the dealer must also sign ATF Form 4473 and retain it for at least 20 years. The ATF is permitted to inspect, as well as receive a copy of Form 4473 from the dealer both during audits and during the course of a criminal investigation. An FFL dealer's ATF Form 4473 records must be surrendered to the ATF in the event the FFL dealer retires or ceases business.

D.   *Sale of multiple handguns must be reported to the ATF*

Under federal law, firearm dealers are required to report to the ATF any sale or transfer of two or more pistols, revolvers, or any combination of pistols and revolvers to an unlicensed (non-FFL) individual that takes place at one time or during any five consecutive business days. This report is made to the ATF on Form 3310.4 and is completed in triplicate with the original copy sent to the ATF, one sent to the VSP, and one retained by the dealer and held for no less than five years. *See* 18 U.S.C. § 923(g)(3). In 1993, Virginia passed a law that limited handgun purchases to one a month, but that law was repealed in 2012.

E. *Special duty of firearms dealers involving minors*
Federal law requires that firearm dealers who deliver handguns to non-licensees display at their licensed premises (including temporary business locations at gun shows) a sign that customers can readily see. These signs are provided by the ATF and contain the following language:

(1)   The misuse of handguns is a leading contributor to juvenile violence and fatalities.

(2)   Safely storing and securing firearms away from children will help prevent the unlawful possession of handguns by juveniles, stop accidents, and save lives.

(3)   Federal law prohibits, except in certain limited circumstances, anyone under 18 years of age from knowingly possessing a handgun, or any person from transferring a handgun to a person under 18.

(4)   A knowing violation of the prohibition against selling, delivering, or otherwise transferring a handgun to a person under the age of 18 is, under certain circumstances, punishable by up to 10 years in prison.

In addition to the displayed sign, federal law requires firearm dealers to provide non-licensee customers with a written notification containing the same four points as listed above as well as sections 922(x) and 924(a)(6) of Title 18, Chapter 44 of the United States Code. This written notification is available as a pamphlet published by the ATF entitled "Youth Handgun Safety Act Notice" and is sometimes referred to as ATF information 5300.2. Alternatively, this written notification may be delivered to customers on another type of written notification, such as a manufacturer's brochure accompanying the handgun or a sales receipt or invoice applied to the handgun package. Any written notification delivered to a customer other than the one provided by the ATF must include the language described here, and must be "legible, clear, and conspicuous, and the required language shall appear in type size no smaller than 10-point type." *See* 27 CFR § 478.103.

F. *What is a private sale?*
A private sale or transfer of a firearm in Virginia is a sale or transfer of a firearm by individual private parties that are not licensed firearm dealers. No Firearm Transaction Record is required. ATF Form 4473 & VSP Form SP-65 are not required. A private sale or transfer

is lawful as long as the parties meet the legal requirements. Private sales will be discussed later in this chapter. *See* 18 U.S.C. § 922.

IV. National Instant Criminal Background Check System
The National Instant Criminal Background Check System (NICS) is the system for determining if a prospective firearm purchaser is eligible to purchase a firearm. Virginia also uses a state-based background check system. In Virginia, after a prospective purchaser completes ATF Form 4473 and VSP Form SP-65, the firearms dealer initiates the NICS background check process with the VSP Firearms Transaction Center. The VSP is the point of contact between the FFL firearm dealers and the NICS.

The NICS and Virginia background check systems will check the applicant purchaser against multiple different databases containing various types of records. The NICS searches the National Crime Information Center (NCIC) consisting of the Wanted Persons File, Protection Order File, Interstate Identification Index (III), Deported Felons File, US Secret Service Protective File, Foreign Fugitive File, Bureau of Alcohol, Tobacco, and Firearms' Violent Felon File, and NICS indexes: Illegal/Unlawful Aliens File, Mental Defectives/Commitments File, Dishonorable Discharges, Citizenship Renunciants, Controlled Substance Abuse File and Denied Persons File. The Virginia search is accessed through the Virginia Criminal Information Network (VCIN), which includes Virginia's wanted and missing persons files and protective orders, Virginia's criminal history record files, and Virginia's database of adjudications of legal incompetence and incapacity, as well as involuntary commitments to mental institutions for inpatient or outpatient treatment.

The response to background check requests come in three basic forms: approved, delayed, or denied. According to the Federal Bureau of Investigation (FBI), NICS checks are usually determined within minutes of initiation. The Brady Handgun Violence Prevention Act of 1993 states that the FBI has three business days to make its decision to approve or deny the transfer; however, according to Va. Code § 18.2-308.2:2, the VSP has until the end of the firearm dealer's next business day to advise the firearm dealer of the decision to either approve or deny the transfer.

If an identification is not made in one or more of the background check files, the computer responds "APPROVED" and a unique computer-generated approval number is provided to the firearm dealer for the transaction. The firearm may be transferred upon the dealer's receipt of the approval number. The "DENIED" response means that the transfer may not take place. The "DELAYED" response means that the purchase or transfer may not legally proceed. If a possible identification is made during the background checks, then the computer responds "DELAYED" and a review of the information/record is conducted to determine probable identification and lawful eligibility of the prospective firearms purchaser. The firearm dealer is notified immediately upon a final determination of eligibility. In the case of electronic failure or other circumstances beyond the control of the VSP, the firearm dealer shall be advised immediately of the reason for such delay and be given an estimate of the length of such delay. After such notification, the VSP shall, as soon as possible but in no event later than the end of the firearm dealer's next business day, inform the requesting firearm dealer if the purchaser is disqualified. Exception: The VSP has up to 10 days to inform the firearm dealer of a background check response in instances involving non-resident background checks for the purchase or transfer of a rifle or shotgun. *See* Va. Code § 18.2-308.2:2.

A.   *What transactions require background checks?*
A background check is required before any sale, rental, trade or transfer between any person and an FFL-licensed firearm dealer can be complete unless an exception is provided under the law. *See* Va. Code § 18.2-308.2:2(A)(B)(C).

B.   *What transactions do not require a background check?*
Under Va. Code § 18.2-308.2:2(I)(J) the VSP is not required to conduct a NICS background check under the following circumstances:

i.   Transactions between persons who are licensed as firearms importers or collectors, manufacturers or dealers pursuant to 18 U.S.C. § 921 *et seq*;
ii.   Purchases by or sales to any law enforcement officer or agent of the United States, the Commonwealth or any local government, or any campus police officer; or
iii. Transactions of antique firearms, curios or relics.

V.   Disqualifications for purchasing & possessing a firearm
As we previously discussed, an individual who attempts to purchase a firearm from a firearm dealer is required to execute ATF Form 4473 and VSP Form SP-65. Federal and Virginia law make it illegal for certain individuals to purchase a firearm. Admissions to certain questions on these forms can disqualify the applicant purchaser from completing an attempted purchase.

A.   *Firearm purchase disqualifications*
   1)   if the person is not the actual purchaser of the firearm—also known as a "straw man purchaser;"
   2)   if the person is under indictment or information in any court for a felony or any other crime for which the judge could imprison the person for more than one year;
   3)   if the person has ever been convicted in any court for a felony or other crime for which the judge could imprison the person for more than one year or found guilty or adjudicated delinquent as a juvenile 14 years of age or older at the time of the offense of a delinquent act that would be a felony if committed by an adult;
   4)   if the person is a fugitive from justice;
   5)   if the person is an unlawful user of, or addicted to, marijuana, or any depressant, stimulant, narcotic drug, or controlled substance; (The Federal Gun Control Act defines an addicted person, or unlawful user, as a person who has a conviction for use or possession of a controlled substance within the past year or persons found through a drug test to use a controlled substance unlawfully, provided that the test was administered within the past year.)
   6)   if the person has, within a 36-consecutive-month period, been convicted of two misdemeanor drug offenses;
   7)   if the person has ever been adjudicated as mentally defective or has been committed to a mental institution, has ever been acquitted by reason of insanity and prohibited from purchasing, possessing or transporting a firearm pursuant to Va. Code § 18.2-308.1:1 or any substantially similar law of any other jurisdiction, been adjudicated legally incompetent, mentally incapacitated or adjudicated an incapacitated person and prohibited from purchasing a firearm pursuant to Va. Code § 18.2-308.1:2 or any substantially similar law of any other jurisdiction, or been

involuntarily admitted to an inpatient facility or involuntarily ordered to outpatient mental health treatment and prohibited from purchasing a firearm pursuant to Va. Code § 18.2-308.1:3 or any substantially similar law of any other jurisdiction;

8) if the person has been dishonorably discharged from the Armed Forces;

9) if the person is subject to an active protective order restraining the person from harassing, stalking, or threatening the person's child, or an intimate partner or child of such partner;

10) if the person has been convicted in any court for a misdemeanor crime of domestic violence;

11) if the person has ever renounced their United States citizenship;

12) if the person is an alien illegally in the United States;

13) if the person is admitted under a non-immigrant visa and does not qualify for an exception; and

14) if the applicant is subject to a court order restraining the applicant from harassing, stalking, or threatening the applicant's child or intimate partner, or a child of such partner, or if the applicant is subject to a protective order.

The purchaser must legally affirm that they are not subject to any of the criteria listed above to complete the purchase transaction. If a prospective purchaser answers any question on the form in a manner that indicates they are legally disqualified, it is illegal for the firearm dealer to sell that person the firearm, and it is illegal for the purchaser to complete the transaction or possess the firearm. It is also illegal and a felony to make any false oral or written statement with respect to ATF Form 4473 and/or VSP Form SP-65 and to exhibit any false or misrepresented identification with respect to the transaction. Certain violations of the Gun Control Act pursuant to 18 U.S.C. § 921 are punishable by up to 10 years in prison and/or up to a $250,000 fine. Va. Code § 18.2-308.2:2(K) makes any willful and intentional materially false statement on the consent form or on such firearm transaction records as may be required by federal law a felony punishable by up to ten years in prison.

B. *Firearm purchase & possession disqualifications*
   1. Can I buy a firearm for another person?

No. This would be a "straw man" purchase. Purchases for third persons are often called "straw man" purchases and are illegal. If you are not the actual purchaser, beware! In order to legally purchase a firearm from a firearm dealer, you must be the "actual purchaser" or "actual buyer." If you are not the "actual purchaser" or "actual buyer," then it is illegal for you to complete the transfer or sale under federal and Virginia law.

In fact, the ATF has a campaign called "Don't Lie for the Other Guy" that is targeted at (as they term it on their website) detection and deterrence of "straw man" purchases. The ATF website lists numerous examples of prosecutions for "straw man" purchases and a U.S. Supreme Court case examined and upheld federal law on this matter. *See Abramski v. United States,* 134 S.Ct. 2259, 2264 (2014).

So who is the "actual" buyer or transferee so as not to be a "straw man?" The ATF states that you are the actual "transferee/buyer if you are purchasing the firearm for yourself or otherwise acquiring the firearm for yourself (*e.g.,* redeeming the firearm from pawn/ retrieving it from consignment, firearm raffle winner)." The U.S. Supreme Court ruled in the *Abramski* case that gifting a firearm was not a "straw man" purchase. Additionally, the ATF also states that "you are the actual buyer if you are legitimately purchasing the firearm as a gift for a third party."

Example:

> *Bobby asks John to purchase a firearm for Bobby. Bobby gives John the money for the firearm. John then buys the firearm with Bobby's money and gives Bobby the firearm.*

John is not the "actual buyer" (he is legally a "straw man") of the firearm and if John indicates that he is the "actual buyer" of the firearm on ATF Form 4473, then he has committed a felony punishable by imprisonment.

Therefore, a firearm purchaser cannot check the "yes" box on ATF Form 4473 when asked if he is the "actual purchaser," when he previously engaged in a separate transaction to sell or transfer the firearm privately. NOTE: The U.S. Supreme Court's ruling in the

Abramski case also held that a person cannot legally purchase a firearm on behalf of another even if the person receiving the firearm was able to make the purchase himself. Do not buy a firearm for another person no matter how good a friend, relative, or person they are—it is a crime!

FREQUENTLY ASKED QUESTIONS FROM ATF WEBSITE

Q: May I buy a firearm from an FFL firearm dealer as a "gift" for another person?
A: Yes.

Editor's note: Instead of the previous example where Bobby paid John to purchase a firearm for him, if John decides to buy a firearm with his own money and then give the firearm to Bobby as a present, then John is the actual buyer/transferee of the firearm. Since John is the actual buyer, no sham or "straw man" exists and the purchase is legal.

Q: May a parent or guardian purchase a firearm as a gift for a juvenile?
A: Yes, however with certain exceptions, possession of handguns by juveniles is generally unlawful under federal and Virginia law. For more information, please visit ATF.gov.

Va. Code § 18.2-308.2:2(L1) states that any person who attempts to solicit, persuade, encourage, or entice any dealer to transfer or otherwise convey a firearm other than to the actual buyer, as well as any other person who willfully and intentionally aids or abets such person, is guilty of a felony punishable by up to five years in prison.

Va. Code § 18.2-308.2:2(M) states that any person who purchases a firearm with the intent to (i) resell or otherwise provide such firearm to any person who he knows or has reason to believe is ineligible to purchase or otherwise receive from a dealer a firearm for whatever reason or (ii) transport such firearm out of the Commonwealth to be resold or otherwise provided to another person who the transferor knows is ineligible to purchase or otherwise receive a firearm, shall be guilty of a felony punishable by up to ten years in prison with fines of up to $100,000. A mandatory minimum term of imprisonment of five years applies if more than one firearm is transferred. NOTE: This section shall not apply to the purchase of a firearm by a person for the lawful use and possession for his child, grandchild, or individual for whom he is the legal guardian if such child, grandchild, or individual is ineligible to purchase a firearm solely because of his age pursuant to Va. Code § 18.2-308.7.

Va. Code § 18.2-308.2:2(N) also makes it illegal for any person who is ineligible to purchase or otherwise receive or possess a firearm in Virginia to solicit, employ or assist any person in violating Va. Code § 18.2-308.2:2(M). A violation of this section is a felony punishable by up to ten years in prison with fines of up to $100,000, and with five years of the prison sentence being a mandatory minimum term of imprisonment.

Va. Code § 18.2-308.2:1 makes it illegal for any person to sell, barter, give or furnish, or have in his possession or under his control with the intent to sell, barter, give or furnish, any firearm to any person he knows is prohibited from possessing or transporting a firearm pursuant to Va. Code §§ 18.2-308.1:1, 18.2-308.1:2, 18.2-308.1:3, 18.2-308.2, subsection B of Va. Code § 18.2-308.2:01, or Va. Code § 18.2-308.7 such a person shall be guilty of a felony punishable by up to ten years in prison with a fine of up to $100,000. However, this prohibition shall not be applicable when the person convicted of the felony, adjudicated delinquent or acquitted by reason of insanity has (i) been issued a permit pursuant to subsection C of Va. Code § 18.2-308.2 or been granted relief pursuant to subsection B of Va. Code §§ 18.2-308.1:1, 18.2-308.1:2 or 18.2-308.1:3; (ii) been pardoned or had his political disabilities removed in accordance with subsection B of Va. Code § 18.2-308.2; or (iii) obtained a permit to ship, transport, possess or receive firearms pursuant to the laws of the United States.

> ### PRACTICAL LEGAL TIP
>
> Thinking about buying a gun on behalf of your buddy? Not a good idea! One of the purposes of ATF Form 4473 is to conduct a background check on individuals who want to purchase firearms in order to make sure they are legally allowed to do so. Acting as a "straw man" by purchasing it for your buddy circumvents this process and is a crime. — *Ed*

2. A person cannot purchase a firearm if they have been convicted or are under "indictment or information" for a felony or certain misdemeanors

If a person has been convicted of a felony or other crime for which a judge may sentence, or could have sentenced the person to more than one year imprisonment, that person may not legally purchase a firearm (unless the crime was a state misdemeanor punishable by imprisonment of two years or less). Likewise, if a person is under "indictment" or "information" for a felony, or any other crime for which a judge may sentence the person to more than one year imprisonment, that person is disqualified from purchasing a firearm. An "indictment" or "information" is a formal accusation of a crime punishable by imprisonment for a term exceeding one year. It is important to point out that the actual sentence received is not the determining factor for disqualification, rather, it is the possible maximum sentence. A person may have only been sentenced to 30 days imprisonment, but if the crime for which they were charged allowed a maximum penalty of five years, then that person is disqualified. *See* 18 U.S.C. § 921(a)(20)(B); Schrader v. Holder, 831 F. Supp.2d 304 (D.D.C. 2011, aff'd 704 F3d 980 (D.C. Cir. 2013)).

Va. Code § 18.2-308.2 states that it is unlawful for any person to knowingly and intentionally possess or transport any firearm or ammunition for a firearm to someone:

(i) who has been convicted of a felony;

(ii) who was adjudicated delinquent as a juvenile 14 years of age or older at the time of the offense of murder in violation of Va. Code § 18.2-31 or Va. Code § 18.2-32, kidnapping in violation of Va. Code § 18.2-47, robbery by the threat or presentation of firearms in violation of Va. Code § 18.2-58, or rape in violation of Va. Code § 18.2-61;

(iii) who is under the age of 29 and who was adjudicated delinquent as a juvenile 14 years of age or older at the time of the offense of a delinquent act which would be a felony if committed by an adult, other than those felonies set forth in clause (ii), whether such conviction or adjudication occurred under the laws of the Commonwealth, or any other state, the District of Columbia, the United States or any territory.

NOTE: Any of the above persons may possess in his residence or the curtilage thereof a stun weapon as defined by Va. Code § 18.2-308.1.

Any person who violates Va. Code § 18.2-308.2 shall be guilty of a felony punishable by up to 5 years in prison. However, this section shall not apply to:

    (i)   any person who possesses a firearm or ammunition for a firearm while carrying out his duties as a member of the Armed Forces of the United States or of the National Guard of Virginia or of any other state;

    (ii) any law-enforcement officer in the performance of his duties;

    (iii) any person who has been pardoned;

    (iv) any person whose right to possess firearms or ammunition has been restored under the law of another state;

    (v) any person adjudicated delinquent as a juvenile who has completed a term of service of no less than two years in the Armed Forces of the United States or if such person received an honorable discharge from the Armed Forces of the United States after such term of service.

3. <u>What does it mean to be a "fugitive from justice" so as to be disqualified from purchasing a firearm?</u>

A "fugitive from justice" is a person who, after having committed a crime, flees from the jurisdiction of the court where the crime was committed. A fugitive from justice may also be a person who goes into hiding to avoid facing charges for the crime of which he or she is accused. Such individuals are not eligible to purchase or possess firearms.

4. <u>Unlawful users of or persons addicted to drugs are disqualified from purchasing firearms</u>

Federal law is very broad in that it disqualifies persons from the purchase of firearms if they are either users of or addicted to marijuana or any depressant, stimulant, narcotic drug, or any controlled substance. Under federal law, an "addict" is defined as a person that "habitually uses any narcotic so as to endanger the public morals, health, safety, or welfare, or who is so far addicted to the use of narcotic drugs as to have lost the power of self-control with reference to his addiction." *See* 21 U.S.C. § 802(1). However, in using the terms "users of," no such frequency or dependence seems contemplated in the words, nor did Congress give further guidance. Illegal users and addicts are prohibited from purchasing firearms from any person under federal law, and are likewise prohibited from possessing firearms. *See* 18 U.S.C. §§ 922(d) and (g).

Va. Code § 18.2-308.1:5 makes it illegal for any person to purchase or transport a handgun who, within a 36-consecutive-month period, has been convicted of two misdemeanor drug offenses under former Va. Code § 18.2-248.1:1, Va. Code § 18.2-250 or Va. Code § 18.2-250.1. However, the ineligibility shall be removed upon expiration of a period of five years from the date of the second conviction, provided the person has not been convicted of any such offense within that period.

5. <u>A person can't legally buy or possess firearms if they are "mentally defective"</u>

What does "mentally defective" mean? According to 27 CFR § 478.11, a person is considered to have been adjudicated as "mentally defective" if there has been a "determination by a court, board, commission, or other lawful authority that a person, as a result of marked subnormal intelligence, or mental illness, incompetency, condition, or disease: is a danger to himself or others, or lacks the mental capacity to contract or manage his own affairs." The term "mentally defective" includes "a finding of insanity by a court in a criminal case, and those persons found incompetent to stand trial or found not guilty by reason of insanity or lack of mental responsibility."

"Mentally defective," as defined in 18 U.S.C. § 922(g)(4), also includes a person who has been committed to a mental institution by a court, board, commission, or other lawful authority or committed to a mental institution involuntarily. The term includes commitment for mental defectiveness or mental illness, and also includes commitment for other reasons, such as drug use. However, it does not include a person in a mental institution for observation or a voluntary admission to a mental institution. Individuals who have been adjudicated as mentally defective are also prohibited from possessing firearms under federal law.

Va. Code § 18.2-308.1:1 makes it unlawful for any person to knowingly and intentionally purchase, possess, or transport any firearm after having been acquitted by reason of insanity and committed to the custody of the Commissioner of Behavioral Health and Developmental Services for any felony or select misdemeanors pursuant to statute. A violation of this section is a misdemeanor offense punishable up to 12 months in jail.

Va. Code § 18.2-308.1:2 makes it unlawful for any person to purchase, possess, or transport any firearm that has been adjudicated legally incompetent, mentally incapacitated or incapacitated. A violation of this section is a misdemeanor offense punishable up to 12 months in jail.

Va. Code § 18.2-308.1:3 makes it unlawful for any person to purchase, possess or transport a firearm who has been involuntarily admitted to a facility or ordered to mandatory outpatient treatment pursuant to Va. Code § 19.2-169.2, involuntarily admitted to a facility or ordered to mandatory outpatient treatment as the result of a commitment hearing pursuant to Va. Code § 37.2-814 or who was the subject of a temporary detention order pursuant to Va. Code § 37.2-809 and subsequently agreed to voluntary admission pursuant to Va. Code § 37.2-805. A violation of this section is a misdemeanor offense punishable up to 12 months in jail.

6. A person subject to a protective or restraining order may not purchase or possess a firearm

Under 18 U.S.C. § 922(g)(8), firearms may not be sold to or received by a person subject to a court order that: (a) was issued after a hearing which the person received actual notice of and had an opportunity to participate in; (b) restrains the person from harassing, stalking, or threatening an intimate partner or child of such intimate partner or person, or engaging in other conduct that would place an intimate partner in reasonable fear of bodily injury to the partner or child; and (c) includes a finding that such person represents a credible threat to the physical safety of such intimate partner or child; or by its terms explicitly prohibits the use, attempted use, or threatened use of physical force against such intimate partner or child that a person would reasonably be expected to cause bodily injury. An "intimate partner" of a person is the spouse or former spouse of the person, the parent of a child of the person, or an individual who cohabitates with the person.

Va. Code § 18.2-308.1:4(A) makes it unlawful for any person to purchase or transport any firearm while a protective order is in effect that was entered subject to (i) Va. Codes §§ 16.1-253.1, 16.1-253.4, 16.1-278.2, 16.1-279.1, 19.2-152.8, 19.2-152.9, or 19.2-152.10; (ii) an order issued pursuant to subsection B of Va. Code § 20-103; (iii) an order entered pursuant to subsection E of Va. Code § 18.2-60.3; (iv) a preliminary protective order entered pursuant to subsection F of Va. Code § 16.1-253 where a petition alleging abuse or neglect has been filed; or (v) an order issued by a tribunal of another state, the United States or any of its territories, possessions, or commonwealths, or the District of Columbia pursuant to a statute that is substantially similar to those cited in clauses (i), (ii), (iii), or (iv). Any person with a concealed handgun permit shall be prohibited from carrying any concealed firearm, and shall surrender his permit to the court entering the order, for the duration of any protective order referred to herein. A violation of this section is a misdemeanor offense punishable by up to 12 months in jail.

Va. Code § 18.2-308.1:4(B) makes it unlawful for any person subject to a family abuse protective order to knowingly possess any firearm while the protective order is in effect pursuant to Va. Code § 16.1-279.1 or an order issued by a tribunal of another state, the United States or any of its territories, possessions, or commonwealths, or the District of Columbia pursuant to a statute that is substantially similar to Va. Code § 16.1-279.1, provided that for a period of 24 hours after being served with a protective order in accordance with subsection C of Va. Code § 16.1-279.1 such person may continue to possess and, notwithstanding the provisions of subsection A, transport any firearm possessed by such person at the time of service for the purposes of selling or transferring any such firearm to any person who is not otherwise prohibited by law from possessing such firearm. A violation of this section is a felony punishable by up to five years in prison.

Additionally, any protective order will disqualify an individual from obtaining a concealed handgun permit (Va. Code § 18.2-308.09) and shall also prohibit one from carrying any concealed firearm with a previously issued permit. A previously issued concealed handgun permit shall be surrendered to the court entering the order for the duration of any protective order.

7.   Domestic violence issues and disqualifications
A person who has ever been convicted of the crime of domestic violence may not purchase or possess firearms under federal law.

These restrictions were passed in what is known as the Violence Against Women Act in 1994 and amended in 1996. This is an often misunderstood law, and, in fact, the ATF has numerous "Frequently Asked Questions" concerning this disqualification on its website: www.atf.gov. The ATF does a good job of explaining the scope of this subject in their FAQs. Due to the complexity of this issue, the ATF examples are included on the following pages.

FREQUENTLY ASKED QUESTIONS FROM ATF WEBSITE

Q: What is a "misdemeanor crime of domestic violence?"
A: A "misdemeanor crime of domestic violence" means an offense that:

1. is a misdemeanor under federal or State law;
2. has, as an element, the use or attempted use of physical force, or the threatened use of a deadly weapon; and
3. was committed by a current or former spouse, parent, or guardian of the victim, by a person with whom the victim shares a child in common, by a person who is cohabiting with or has cohabited with the victim as a spouse, parent, or guardian, or by a person similarly situated to a spouse, parent, or guardian of the victim.

However, a person is not considered to have been convicted of a misdemeanor crime of domestic violence unless:

1. the person was represented by counsel in the case, or knowingly and intelligently waived the right of counsel in the case; and
2. in the case of a prosecution for which a person was entitled to a jury trial in the jurisdiction in which the case was tried, either-
    1. the case was tried by a jury, or
    2. the person knowingly and intelligently waived the right to have the case tried by a jury, by guilty plea or otherwise.

In addition, a conviction will not be disabling if it has been expunged or set aside, or is an offense for which the person has been pardoned or has had civil rights restored (if the law of the jurisdiction in which the proceedings were held provides for the loss of civil rights upon conviction for such an offense) unless the pardon, expunction, or restoration of civil rights expressly provides that the person may not ship, transport, possess, or receive firearms, and the person is not otherwise prohibited by the law of the jurisdiction in which the proceedings were held from receiving or possessing firearms. *See* U.S.C. 921(a)(33) 27 CFR 478.11.

FREQUENTLY ASKED QUESTIONS FROM ATF WEBSITE

[Editor's note: A significant number of people make the mistake of overlooking or forgetting about a court issue or family law judicial proceeding. However, if you meet the above criteria, you are federally disqualified from possessing a firearm. The fact that it may have happened a long time ago, or that you did not understand the ramifications, is legally irrelevant.]

Q: What is the effective date?
A: The law was effective September 30, 1996. However, the prohibition applies to persons convicted of such misdemeanors at any time, even if the conviction occurred prior to the law's effective date.

[Editor's note: For those wondering why this is not an unconstitutional ex-post facto law, multiple federal appeals courts have ruled against that argument and the Supreme Court has consistently declined to review any of those cases, effectively accepting the ruling of the courts of appeals and upholding the law.]

Q: X was convicted of misdemeanor assault on October 10, 1996, for beating his wife. Assault has as an element the use of physical force, but is not specifically a domestic violence offense. May X lawfully possess firearms or ammunition?
A: No. X may not legally possess firearms or ammunition. *See* 18 U.S.C. 922(g)(9); 27 CFR 478.32(a)(9).

[Editor's note: In this situation because X's conviction for assault was against a person in the statute's protected class, the conviction would be, for purposes of firearms purchasing disqualification, a domestic violence conviction.]

Q: X was convicted of a misdemeanor crime of domestic violence on September 20, 1996, 10 days before the effective date of the statute. He possesses a firearm on October 10, 2004. Does X lawfully possess the firearm?
A: No. If a person was convicted of a misdemeanor crime of domestic violence at any time, he or she may not lawfully possess firearms or ammunition on or after September 30, 1996. *See* 18 U.S.C. 922(g)(9); 27 CFR 478.32(a)(9).

FREQUENTLY ASKED QUESTIONS FROM ATF WEBSITE

Q: In determining whether a conviction in a State court is a "conviction" of a misdemeanor crime of domestic violence, does Federal or State law apply?

A: State law applies. Therefore, if the State does not consider the person to be convicted, the person would not have the Federal disability. See 18 U.S.C. 921(a)(33); 27 CFR 478.11.

Q: Is a person who received "probation before judgment" or some other type of deferred adjudication subject to the disability?

A: What is a conviction is determined by the law of the jurisdiction in which the proceedings were held. If the State law where the proceedings were held does not consider probation before judgment or deferred adjudication to be a conviction, the person would not be subject to the disability. See 18 U.S.C. 921(a)(33); 27 CFR 478.11.

Q: What State and local offenses are "misdemeanors" for purposes of 18 U.S.C. 922(d)(9) and (g)(9)?

A: The definition of misdemeanor crime of domestic violence in the GCA (the Gun Control Act of 1968) includes any offense classified as a "misdemeanor" under Federal or State law. In States that do not classify offenses as misdemeanors, the definition includes any State or local offense punishable by imprisonment for a term of 1 year or less or punishable by a fine. For example, if State A has an offense classified as a "domestic violence misdemeanor" that is punishable by up to 5 years imprisonment, it would be a misdemeanor crime of domestic violence. If State B does not characterize offenses as misdemeanors, but has a domestic violence offense that is punishable by no more than 1 year imprisonment, this offense would be a misdemeanor crime of domestic violence. See 18 U.S.C. 921(a)(33); 27 CFR 478.11.

Q: Are local criminal ordinances "misdemeanors under State law" for purposes of sections 922(d)(9) and (g)(9)?

A: Yes, assuming a violation of the ordinance meets the definition of "misdemeanor crime of domestic violence" in all other respects.

FREQUENTLY ASKED QUESTIONS FROM ATF WEBSITE

Q: In order for an offense to qualify as a "misdemeanor crime of domestic violence," does it have to have as an element the relationship part of the definition (e.g., committed by a spouse, parent, or guardian)?
A: No. The "as an element" language in the definition of "misdemeanor crime of domestic violence" only applies to the use of force provision of the statute and not the relationship provision. However, to be disqualifying, the offense must have been committed by one of the defined parties. *See* 18 U.S.C. 921(a)(33); 27 CFR 478.11.

[Editor's note: This basically means that if illegal force was used against another person, regardless of the language in the underlying statute, if the illegal force was used against a member of the protected class under the statute, federal law will deem this as satisfying the requirements and disqualify the individual from purchasing and possessing firearms.]

Q: What should an individual do if he or she has been convicted of a misdemeanor crime of domestic violence?
A: Individuals subject to this disqualification should immediately dispose of their firearms and ammunition. ATF recommends that such persons transfer their firearms and ammunition to a third party who may lawfully receive and possess them, such as their attorney, a local police agency, or a Federal firearms dealer. The continued possession of firearms and ammunition by persons under this disability is a violation of law and may subject the possessor to criminal penalties. In addition, such firearms and ammunition are subject to seizure and forfeiture. *See* 18 U.S.C. 922(g)(9), 924(d)(1); 27 CFR 478.152.

Q: Does the disqualification apply to law enforcement officers?
A: Yes. The Gun Control Act was amended so that employees of government agencies convicted of misdemeanor crimes of domestic violence would not be exempt from disqualifications with respect to their receipt or possession of firearms or ammunition. Thus, law-enforcement officers and other government officials who have been convicted of a disqualifying misdemeanor may not lawfully possess or receive fire-

FREQUENTLY ASKED QUESTIONS FROM ATF WEBSITE

arms or ammunition for any purpose, including performance of their official duties. The disqualification applies to firearms and ammunition issued by government agencies, purchased by government employees for use in performing their official duties, and personal firearms and ammunition possessed by such employees. *See* 18 U.S.C. 922(g)(9), 925(a)(1); 27 CFR 478.32(a)(9), 478.141.

Q: Is an individual who has been pardoned, or whose conviction was expunged or set aside, or whose civil rights have been restored, considered convicted of a misdemeanor crime of domestic violence?
A: No, as long as the pardon, expungement, or restoration does not expressly provide that the person may not ship, transport, possess, or receive firearms.

PRACTICAL LEGAL TIP

If you or a loved one are going through court proceedings involving family issues and a restraining or protective order is entered in your case, it can suspend your ability to purchase or possess firearms. Language in the court order prohibiting any acts of family violence whether or not family violence actually occurred, make it so the person whom the other impacts is legally barred from the purchase or possession of any firearm. — *Ed*

8. <u>Illegal aliens or aliens admitted under a nonimmigrant visa</u> Persons who are illegally in the United States may not legally purchase, possess, or transport firearms. Generally, nonimmigrant aliens are also prohibited from legally purchasing, possessing, or transporting firearms.

Exceptions for nonimmigrant aliens
However, a nonimmigrant alien who has been admitted under a nonimmigrant visa is not prohibited from purchasing, receiving, or possessing a firearm if the person falls within one of the following exceptions:

- if the person was admitted to the United States for lawful hunting or sporting purposes or is in possession of a hunting license or permit lawfully issued in the United States;
- if the person is an official representative of a foreign government who is accredited to the United States Government or the Government's mission to an international organization having its headquarters in the United States;
- if the person is an official representative of a foreign government who is en route to or from another county to which that alien is accredited;
- if the person is an official of a foreign government or a distinguished foreign visitor who has been so designated by the Department of State;
- if the person is a foreign law enforcement officer of a friendly foreign government entering the United States on official law enforcement business; or
- if the person has received a waiver from the prohibition from the Attorney General of the United States. *See* 18 U.S.C. § 922(y).

Va. Code § 18.2-308.2:2(B) states that no firearm dealer shall sell, rent, trade, or transfer from his inventory any assault firearm to any person who is not a citizen of the United States or who is not a person lawfully admitted for permanent residence.

Va. Code § 18.2-308.2:01 makes it unlawful for any person who is not a citizen of the United States or who is not a person lawfully admitted for permanent residence to knowingly and intentionally possess or transport any firearm or assault firearm or to knowingly and intentionally carry about his person, hidden from common observation, an assault firearm. A violation of this section is a felony punishable by up to five years in prison with a $2,500 fine.

C. *What if my gun purchase from a firearm dealer is denied?*
Any individual that is denied the purchase, trade, exchange or pawn redemption of a firearm shall be provided a Virginia Firearms

Transaction Program Brochure that explains options the individual may pursue if he believes he is not prohibited by federal or Virginia law from purchasing or possessing a firearm.

A denied individual may:

- Contact the VSP Firearms Transaction Center (FTC) to discuss the ineligible determination and/or to provide additional information deemed pertinent to the final determination of eligibility. Fingerprint comparison may be necessary in some instances, and may support the issuance of a Unique Firearms Identification Number (UFIN) to facilitate future purchase approvals.
- Review the criminal history record and request correction of the record if the record is found to be in error, pursuant to Va. Code § 9.1-132, provided that any such action is initiated within 30 days of the denial. Obtain a copy of the Virginia criminal history record by completing a Criminal History Record Request on VSP Form SP-167.
- Exercise the right to institute a civil action pursuant to Va. Code § 9.1-135, provided that any such action be initiated within 30 days of the denial.
- Elect to direct the challenge to the accuracy of a record, in writing, to: FBI, NICS Operations Center, Criminal Justice Information Services Division, 1000 Custer Hollow Road, Module C-3, Clarksburg, West Virginia 26306. Electronic appeal requests can be made through the NICS Appeal Website: fbi.gov/nics-appeals. This appeal process is authorized by 28 CFR § 25.10.

D. *Criminal liability for allowing a minor access to firearms*
Va. Code § 18.2-309 states that it is illegal for any person to sell, barter, give or furnish a handgun to any minor. A violation of this section is a felony punishable by up to five years in prison; however, this law does not apply to any transfer made between family members or for the purpose of engaging in a sporting event or activity. The federal law also makes it illegal to sell, transfer or deliver a handgun and handgun ammunition to a minor, but there are some exceptions, which we will discuss momentarily. *See* 18 U.S.C. § 922(x). A violation of the federal version of this law is punishable by up to ten years in prison. *See* 18 U.S.C. § 924(A)(6)(B)(ii).

Va. Code § 18.2-56.2 states that it is unlawful for any person to recklessly leave a loaded, unsecured firearm in such a manner as to endanger the life or limb of any child under the age of 14. A violation of this section shall be a misdemeanor punishable only by a fine. However, it is unlawful to knowingly authorize a child under the age of 12 to use a firearm except when the child is under the supervision of an adult. A violation of this section is also a misdemeanor, but punishable up to 12 months in jail. *See* Va. Code § 18.2-56.2(a).

E.   *When may a minor legally possess a handgun?*
As we discussed, Va. Code § 18.2-308.7 states that "it is unlawful for anyone under the age of 18 to knowingly or intentionally possess or transport any handgun or assault firearm." A violation of this statute is a misdemeanor and is punishable by up to 12 months in jail. However, this law does not apply to the following:

"1) Any minor (i) while in his home or on his property; (ii) while in the home or on the property of his parent, grandparent, or legal guardian; or (iii) while on the property of another who has provided prior permission, and with the prior permission of his parent or legal guardian if the minor has the landowner's written permission on his person while on such property;

2) Any minor who, while accompanied by an adult, is at, or going to and from, a lawful shooting range or firearms educational class, provided that the weapons are unloaded while being transported;

3) Any minor actually engaged in lawful hunting or going to and from a hunting area or preserve, provided that the weapons are unloaded while being transported; and

4) Any minor while carrying out his duties in the Armed Forces of the United States or the National Guard of this Commonwealth or any other state." *See* Va. Code 18 § 18.2-308.7.

Additionally, the federal law in 18 U.S.C. § 922(x)(2) similarly states that it is unlawful for a minor to knowingly possess a handgun or handgun ammunition. A violation of this statute is punishable by no more than one year of imprisonment. However, this law does not apply to a minor possessing a firearm, according to 18 U.S.C. § 922(x)(3):

1) in the course of employment,
2) in the course of ranching or farming, target practice, hunting, or a course of instruction in the safe and lawful use of a handgun,
3) with the prior written consent of the minor's parent with exceptions,
4) as a member of the Armed Forces of the United States or the National Guard who possess or are armed with a handgun in the line of duty,
5) in self-defense or defense of others against a residential intruder.

VI. Private sales in Virginia
The firearms transaction forms and background checks we previously discussed that are required for firearm dealer transactions do not apply to private transfers conducted in Virginia among Virginia residents. The ATF website has an informative pamphlet entitled "Best Practices: Transfers of Firearms by Private Sellers" located on its website. This pamphlet is a must-read before entering into a "private sale" transaction involving a firearm.

A. *Private Sale disqualifications under federal & Virginia law*
The federal law does require a Virginia resident seller transferring a firearm to a Virginia resident buyer to believe that the buyer is not prohibited from possessing firearms. *See* 18 U.S.C. § 922(g). The federal law makes it illegal for any person to possess or receive any firearm or ammunition if he:

(1) has been convicted in any court of a crime punishable by imprisonment for a term exceeding one year;
(2) is a fugitive from justice;
(3) is an unlawful user of or addicted to any controlled substance (as defined in section 102 of the Controlled Substances Act (21 U.S.C. § 802));
(4) has been adjudicated as a mental defective or who has been committed to a mental institution;
(5) is an illegal or unlawful alien—except as provided in subsection (y)(2), and has been admitted to the United States under a nonimmigrant visa (as that term is defined in section 101(a)(26) of the Immigration and Nationality Act (8 U.S.C. § 1101(a)(26)));

(6) has been discharged from the Armed Forces under dishonorable conditions;

(7) was a citizen of the United States that renounced his citizenship;

(8) is subject to a court order that—

(A) was issued after a hearing of which such person received actual notice, and at which such person had an opportunity to participate;

(B) restrains such person from harassing, stalking, or threatening an intimate partner of such person or child of such intimate partner or person, or engaging in other conduct that would place an intimate partner in reasonable fear of bodily injury to the partner or child; and

(C) (i) includes a finding that such person represents a credible threat to the physical safety of such intimate partner or child; or

(ii) by its terms explicitly prohibits the use, attempted use, or threatened use of physical force against such intimate partner or child that would reasonably be expected to cause bodily injury; or

(9) has been convicted in any court of a misdemeanor crime of domestic violence;

(10) is under indictment for a crime punishable by imprisonment for a term exceeding one year to ship or transport in interstate or foreign commerce any firearm or ammunition or receive any firearm or ammunition which has been shipped or transported in interstate or foreign commerce. *See* 18 U.S.C. § 922(s).

Va. Code § 18.2-308.2:1 states that no person may sell, barter, give or furnish, or have in his possession or under his control with the intent of selling, bartering, giving or furnishing, any firearm to any person he knows:

1. has been acquitted by reason of insanity and committed to the custody of the Commissioner of Behavioral Health and Developmental Services, on a charge of treason, any felony or any offense punishable as a misdemeanor under Title 54.1 or a Class 1 or Class 2 misdemeanor under Title 18.2, except misdemeanor violations of:

(i) Driving under the influence pursuant to Va. Code § 18.2-266,

    (ii) Disorderly conduct pursuant to Va. Code § 18.2-415,
    (iii) Trespass pursuant to Va. Code § 18.2-119, or
    (iv) An ordinance of any county, city, or town similar to the offenses specified in (i), (ii), or (iii);

2. has been adjudicated
    (i)   legally incompetent,
    (ii)   mentally incapacitated, or
    (iii) incapacitated.

3. was involuntarily admitted to a facility or ordered to mandatory outpatient treatment pursuant to Va. Code § 19.2-169.2, involuntarily admitted to a facility or ordered to mandatory outpatient treatment as the result of a commitment hearing pursuant to Va. Code § 37.2-814, or who was the subject of a temporary detention order pursuant to Va. Code § 37.2-809 and subsequently agreed to voluntary admission pursuant to Va. Code § 37.2-805;

4. (i) has been convicted of a felony;
    (ii) has been adjudicated delinquent as a juvenile 14 years of age or older at the time of the offense of murder in violation of Va. Codes § 18.2-31 or 18.2-32, kidnapping in violation of Va. Code § 18.2-47, robbery by the threat or presentation of firearms in violation of Va. Code § 18.2-58, or rape in violation of Va. Code § 18.2-61; or
    (iii) was under the age of 29 when adjudicated delinquent as a juvenile 14 years of age or older at the time of the offense of a delinquent act which would be a felony if committed by an adult, other than those felonies set forth in clause (ii), whether such conviction or adjudication occurred under the laws of the Commonwealth, or any other state, the District of Columbia, the United States or any territory thereof;

5. is not a citizen of the United States and who is not lawfully present in the United States;

6. is under 18 years of age but only if the firearm is a handgun, assault firearm, or shotgun with a magazine that will hold more than seven rounds of the longest ammunition for which it is chambered.

A violation of this Virginia law is a felony punishable up to ten years in prison with a maximum $100,000 fine; however, this prohibition does not apply if the purchaser has had his eligibility to purchase or possess a firearm restored under Va. Code § 18.2-308.2:1.

Va. Code § 54.1-4201.2 requires the Department of State Police to be available at every Virginia gun show in order to facilitate voluntary background checks requested by either party to a transaction if the seller is an unlicensed individual.

B. *Residency requirements*
In order for the private transfer, sale, trade, gift or delivery of a firearm to be legal in Virginia, both parties must be Virginia residents. This means that a Virginia resident is prohibited from selling or transferring a firearm to a resident of another state. It is a violation of the federal law if the seller or transferor knows or has reasonable cause to believe that the purchaser does not reside in the same state as the seller/transferor. *See* 18 U.S.C. § 922(a)(5). NOTE: A private individual may complete a firearm transfer to a resident of another state, but the seller must follow a procedure that requires the use of a federal firearm dealer. *See* 18 U.S.C. § 922(a) (3), 922(b)(3); 27 CFR 478.29. The federal law also makes it illegal for a non-firearm dealer individual to transport into or receive in his state of residence a firearm purchased or otherwise obtained from a resident of another state. *See* 18 U.S.C. § 922(a)(3).

How does the law determine a person's residence when buying or selling a firearm?

1. State of residence
An individual resides in a state if he or she is present in a state with the intention of making a home in that state. If an individual is on active duty as a member of the Armed Forces, the individual's state of residence is the state in which his or her permanent duty station is located, as stated in 18 U.S.C. § 921(b). *See* 27 CFR § 478.11.

The following are examples that illustrate this definition:
Example:
> *A maintains a home in State X. A travels to State Y on a hunting, fishing, business, or other type of trip. A does not become a resident of State Y by reason of such trip.*

2. What if a person maintains a home in two states?

If a person maintains a home in two (or more) states and resides in those states for periods of the year, he or she may, during the period of time the person actually resides in a particular state, purchase a firearm in that state. However, simply owning property in another state does not qualify a person as a resident of that state so as to purchase a firearm in that state. To meet the residency requirements, a person must actually maintain a home in a state which includes an intention to make a particular state a residence. This issue may ultimately be a fact question with evidence of residency being things like a driver's license, insurance records, recurring expenses in the state, as well as other things related to making a particular state a person's residence.

Example:

> *A maintains a home in State X and a home in State Y. A resides in State X except for weekends or the summer months of the year and in State Y for the weekends or the summer months of the year. During the time that A actually resides in State X, A is a resident of State X, and during the time that A actually resides in State Y, A is a resident of State Y.*

3. Members of the armed forces

A member of the Armed Forces on active duty is a resident of the state in which his or her permanent duty station is located. If a member of the Armed Forces maintains a home in one state and the member's permanent duty station is in a nearby state to which he or she commutes each day, then the member has two states of residence and may purchase a firearm in either the state where the duty station is located or the state where the home is maintained. *See* 18 U.S.C. § 921(b). *See also* ATF FAQs on residency at ATF.gov.

4. Non-citizen resident aliens

Persons who are legally present in the United States are residents of the state in which they reside and where they intend to make a home. Such persons, provided they meet all other requirements are not otherwise prohibited from purchasing a firearm and are lawfully permitted to purchase a firearm.

Example A:

> *A, an alien, travels to the United States on a three-week*

vacation to State X. A does not have a state of residence in State X because A does not have the intention of making a home in State X while on vacation. This is true regardless of the length of the vacation.

Example B:
A, an alien, travels to the United States to work for three years in State X. A rents a home in State X, moves his personal possessions into the home, and his family resides with him in the home. A intends to reside in State X during the 3-year period of his employment. A is a resident of State X. (Though A must still meet all other requirements to purchase.)

C.   *Private Sale Examples*

Example A:
Bob and Jim were best friends and attended high school in Virginia Beach. After high school, Bob moved to North Carolina. Bob is visiting Jim for the summer. One night, Bob and Jim decide to go to the shooting range during Bob's vacation, and Bob borrows one of Jim's handguns. After shooting at the range, impressed with both the feel and action of Jim's handgun, Bob asks Jim if he could buy it from him. Since they've been friends for so many years, Jim says yes, and even offers him a good price for the transaction. Before leaving at the end of his vacation to go home to North Carolina, Bob pays Jim and packs his new handgun.

Has Jim committed a crime in selling the handgun to Bob? Has Bob committed a crime in purchasing the handgun from Jim? The answer to both questions is yes! Under federal law, Bob is not allowed to privately purchase a handgun in another state and transport it back to his home state. Likewise, Jim is not allowed to sell a firearm legally to a person he knows lives in another state. In this example, both Bob and Jim know that Bob is not a Virginia resident—the place where Jim has sold his firearm. Bob has committed the crime of willful receipt of a firearm from an out-of-state unlicensed person while Jim has committed the federal crime of willful sale of a firearm to an out-of-state resident. The penalties for these crimes include imprisonment. *See* 18 U.S.C. § 924.

What if the situation is less obvious? Let's take a look at an example where the federal provision of "reasonable cause to believe" comes into play.

> Example B:
> *Frank, a Virginia resident, recently posted his Glock 19 for sale on an internet message board in Southwest Virginia. Frank receives an email from a person named Ted who would like to buy the handgun. Frank and Ted agree, via email, on a purchase price and arrange to meet at a place in Virginia one week later to facilitate the transfer. When Ted pulls up in his 1978 Ford LTD Wagon, Frank notices the car's Tennessee license plates. Nevertheless, Frank shrugs and sells Ted the gun anyway without going through any of the formalities of a bill-of-sale, or asking for identification. Two weeks later, Frank finds himself at an FBI field office in Bristol, VA answering questions about a shooting that took place with his (former) Glock 19.*

Is Frank in trouble? Possibly. Although Frank is not the center of the shooting investigation, Frank is probably the center of an investigation for illegally selling a firearm to an out-of-state resident under federal law.

> Example C:
> *Gordon and Josh are friends and Josh tells Gordon that he has just attempted to buy a gun from a local firearms dealer and that he was denied because he was disqualified for some reason under federal law (something about a conviction or restraining order or drug use or psychiatric problems—Josh was too mad to remember!). Gordon says, "no problem, I'll just sell you one of mine," and he does.*

Gordon has just committed a federal and Virginia criminal offense because he now knows that Josh was prohibited from purchasing a firearm due to various disqualifying reasons.

D.   *Private sale documentation suggestions*
Protect yourself! Exercise a little due diligence and use good common sense when transferring a firearm. This is practical advice that

should not be ignored. Below are some practical tips if you engage in the private sale or transfer of a firearm:

- Ask for identification whether you are the buyer/transferee or seller/transferor to establish residency
- Get and/or give a "bill of sale" for the transfer and keep a copy—identify the firearm including make, model, and serial number, as well as the date and place of transfer
- Put the residency information on the "bill of sale" including names, addresses, and phone numbers
- Do not sell or transfer a firearm or ammunition if you think the person may not be permitted or is prohibited from receiving the firearm
- Take advantage of the Virginia State Police optional background check process at all Virginia gun shows for $2.

Why do this? There are several reasons. First, you will want to make sure that the other party is a Virginia resident. Second, you will want to ensure that the other party is at least 18 years old. Finally, you will want to document the transaction to establish that the firearm is not in your possession during certain times in the event the firearm is used in the commission of crime when not in your possession.

Additionally, it is also a good idea for private sellers to ask prospective buyers "is there any reason you cannot own a firearm?" or ask the prospective buyer the same questions posed on ATF Form 4473 and VSP Form SP-65. Why? So that if there is an issue later, you can at a minimum say that you had no reason to know the buyer could not legally possess or purchase the firearm. Do not overlook behavior that may indicate the buyer is not telling you the truth because law enforcement will not overlook facts that show you did know or should have had reasonable cause to believe that the buyer could not own a firearm at the time of the transfer if a legal issue arises later.

VII. Additional considerations in firearms purchasing and possession laws

A. Can I purchase a firearm via the Internet?

Maybe, but the answer will depend on who and where the seller is located. As we have previously discussed, there are numerous provisions within the GCA and the Code of Virginia that govern the transfer or sale of a firearm between a FFL firearm dealer and a non-licensed individual and the private transfer or sale of a firearm between Virginia residents.

For private sales, a Virginia resident who is not otherwise prohibited from receiving, possessing, or purchasing a firearm may legally purchase a firearm from another Virginia resident whether the transaction is in person or on-line.

An individual who is not otherwise prohibited from receiving, possessing, or purchasing a firearm may purchase a firearm from either a Virginia or out–of–state FFL firearm dealer, provided the transfer takes place through an FFL firearm dealer in Virginia, which will require the necessary paperwork, background checks and presentation of photo identification that we previously discussed. *See* 18 U.S.C. § 922(a)(3); 18 U.S.C. § 922(b)(3); 27 CFR § 478.29; Va. Code § 18.2-308.2:2.

The shipment of the firearm as a result of an internet transaction is another matter.

B.   *Shipping firearms*
Whether or not you can ship a firearm will depend on the parties of the shipment, whether the firearm is a handgun or a long gun, and what service is used for the shipping. Firearms cannot be shipped loaded and ammunition may not be shipped in the same box as the firearm. Only long guns can be shipped through the U.S. Postal Service (USPS). A non-licensee may mail a shotgun or rifle to a resident of his or her own state or to an FFL firearm dealer in any State. The USPS recommends that long guns be mailed via registered mail and that the packaging used to mail the long gun be ambiguous so as to not identify the contents.

Handguns must be shipped using a common or contract carrier. In addition, Federal law requires that the carrier be notified that the shipment contains a firearm or ammunition, prohibits common or contract carriers from requiring or causing any label to be placed on any package indicating that it contains a firearm and requires obtaining written acknowledgement of receipt.

1.   Can I ship my firearm to myself for use in another state?
Yes. In accordance with the law as described in the preceding sec-

tion, a person may ship a firearm to himself or herself in care of another person in another state where he or she intends to hunt or engage in other lawful activity. The package should be addressed to the owner and persons other than the owner should not open the package and take possession of the firearm.

2. Can the moving company move my firearms?
Yes, a person who lawfully possesses firearms may transport or ship the firearms interstate when changing the person's state of residence so long as the person complies with the requirements for shipping and transporting firearms as outlined earlier. *See* 18 U.S.C. § 922(e) and 27 CFR § 478.31. However, certain NFA items such as destructive devices, machine guns, short-barreled shotguns or rifles, and so forth require approval from the ATF before they can be moved interstate. *See* 18 U.S.C. § 922(a)(4) and 27 CFR § 478.28. It is important that the person seeking to move the firearms also checks state and local laws where the firearms will be relocated to ensure that the movement of the firearms into the new state does not violate any state law or local ordinance. Va. Code § 18.2-295 requires every machine gun in Virginia to be registered with the Department of State Police within twenty-four hours after its acquisition.

C. *May I loan my firearm to another person?*
There is no prohibition on loaning a firearm to another person, so long as the person receiving the firearm may lawfully possess one.

D. *What happens to my firearms when I die?*
Depending on the manner in which a person leaves his or her estate behind, firearms may be bequeathed in a customary manner like other personal property. However, firearms held in an estate are still subject to the laws of transfer and possession. Thus careful consideration needs to be given in estate planning with consideration for firearms law of both the jurisdiction in which the estate is located as well as consideration of who is to receive the firearms.

VIII. Ammunition: purchase, possession and use
In Chapter 2 we defined ammunition and its various types. This section will discuss when it is legal to purchase, possess, transport and use ammunition or regulated ammunition under both the federal and Virginia laws.

A. *Federal law*
Federal law prohibits the sale and/or transfer of ammunition for certain purchaser categories just like it prohibits the sale and/or transfer of firearms to certain categories of purchasers. However, ammunition sellers are not required to conduct background checks or verify that a prospective purchaser is of legal age to purchase or possess ammunition when trying to determine if a prospective purchaser falls into a prohibited category. Federal law requires any person engaged in importing or manufacturing ammunition to obtain an FFL license; but there is no FFL license requirement to sell ammunition. *See* 18 U.S.C. § 923(a). The reality is that almost all ammunition sellers will be FFL firearm dealers and will thus be licensed FFL dealers as a result of their firearm business.

Ammunition may not be sold or otherwise transferred to any person who:
- Is underage;
- Has been convicted of, or is under indictment for, a crime punishable by imprisonment for more than one year;
- Is a fugitive from justice;
- Is an unlawful user of or addicted to a controlled substance;
- Has been adjudicated as a mental defective or committed to a mental institution;
- Is an illegal alien;
- Has been dishonorably discharged from the military;
- Has renounced his or her U.S. citizenship;
- Is subject to a court order restraining him or her from harassing, stalking or threatening an intimate partner, his or her child or a child of a partner; or
- Has been convicted of a misdemeanor offense of domestic violence. *See* 18 U.S.C. § 922(b)(1), (d), (x)(1).

1. Minimum age to purchase or possess ammunition
FFL firearm dealers are prohibited from selling or transferring ammunition for a shotgun or rifle to any person the FFL firearm dealer knows or has reasonable cause to believe is under the age of 18. *See* 18 U.S.C. § 922(b)(1), (c)(1). Federal law does not provide a minimum age requirement for the sale of long gun ammunition by an unlicensed person.

The minimum age that permits an FFL firearm dealer to sell or transfer handgun ammunition is 21. Unlicensed persons may not sell, deliver or otherwise transfer handgun ammunition to any person the transferor knows or has reasonable cause to believe is under the age of 18.

Federal law prohibits, with certain exceptions, the possession of handgun ammunition by any person under the age of 18, but there is no minimum age for the possession of long gun ammunition according to federal law. *See* 18 U.S.C. § 922(x).

2. Armor piercing ammunition

Federal law makes it illegal to possess, carry and/or use armor piercing ammunition during and in relation to any crime of violence or drug trafficking crime. *See* 18 U.S.C. § 924(c)(5). A violation of this law carries a minimum term of imprisonment of not less than 15 years and can be punishable by death if a death results from the use of such ammunition. The federal law does not otherwise criminalize the possession of armor piercing ammunition; however, it is so highly regulated that it is almost impossible to possess.

Federal law prohibits the manufacture, importation, sale or delivery of armor-piercing ammunition, unless manufactured for certain federal and state government divisions, exportation, testing, or if primarily intended for sporting or industrial purposes. *See* 18 U.S.C. §§ 921(a)(17)(C), 922(a)(7), 922(a)(8); 27 C.F.R. § 478.37, 27 C.F.R. § 478.148.

FFL dealers are prohibited from "willfully" transferring armor-piercing ammunition unless the ammunition was received and maintained by the FFL dealer as business inventory prior to August 28, 1986, and then, it may only be transferred to federal, state or local law enforcement. *See* 27 C.F.R. § 478.99(e). Finally, FFL firearm dealers must keep a record of any transfer in the event such transfer is permissible. *See* 18 U.S.C. § 922(b)(5).

B. *Virginia law*

Virginia law does not require a license to purchase, possess or sell ammunition nor is there a minimum age for possessing ammunition; however, federal law imposes a minimum age. Virginia law does make it illegal for certain classes of individuals to possess and transport ammunition. Va. Code § 18.2-308.2(A) makes it illegal to knowingly and intentionally possess or transport ammunition by any person:

- convicted of a felony;
- adjudicated delinquent as a juvenile 14 years of age or older at the time of the offense of murder, kidnapping, robbery by the threat or presentation of firearms, or rape; or
- who is under the age of 29 and was found guilty as a juvenile (14 years of age or older) of a delinquent act which would be a felony if committed by an adult.

A violation of this statute is a felony punishable by up to 5 years in prison and a $2500 fine. However, Virginia law does not prohibit other individuals ineligible to possess firearms under state law from possessing ammunition.

The prohibitions of this section shall not apply to:

(i) any person carrying out his duties as a member of the Armed Forces of the United States or of the National Guard of Virginia or of any other state;

(ii) any law enforcement officer in the performance of his duties;

(iii) any person who has been pardoned or whose political disabilities have been removed pursuant to Article V, Section 12 of the Constitution of Virginia provided the Governor, in the document granting the pardon or removing the person's political disabilities, may expressly place conditions upon the reinstatement of the person's right to ship, transport, possess or receive firearms;

(iv) any person whose right to possess firearms or ammunition has been restored under the law of another state subject to conditions placed upon the reinstatement of the person's right to ship, transport, possess, or receive firearms by such state; or

(v) any person adjudicated delinquent as a juvenile who has completed a term of service of no less than two years in the Armed Forces of the United States and, if such person has been discharged from the Armed Forces of the United States, received an honorable discharge and who is not otherwise prohibited.

In addition to ammunition in general, Va. Code § 18.2-308.3 makes it unlawful for any person to knowingly use or attempt to use restricted firearm ammunition such as KTW bullets or French Arcanes while committing or attempting to commit a crime. A violation of this law is a felony punishable by up to 10 years in prison.

CHAPTER FOUR

WHEN CAN I LEGALLY USE MY GUN
FOR SELF-DEFENSE IN VIRGINIA?

I.   Introduction and overview

When a person can legally use a gun for self-defense in Virginia is a critically important legal issue for every law abiding gun owner. A failure to understand or properly apply the Virginia self-defense law can get a lot of good folks in serious trouble! The purpose of this chapter is to educate the gun owner on when a gun may and may not be legally used for self-defense in Virginia.

II.   Ignorance of the law is NO excuse!

The Virginia self-defense law is a law of necessity that provides excellent protection for those that need to use force to defend themselves from an attacker, including deadly force. The amount of force used to defend oneself must not be excessive. It must be proportional and reasonable in relation to the perceived threat. *See Diffendal v. Commmonwealth,* 8 Va. App. 417, 421 (1989). Thus, you cannot use deadly force to shoot and kill someone for starting a fight by punching you in the face and call it self-defense. You can certainly defend yourself but your self-defense must always be proportional to your attacker's actions. If you know and follow the law, then you have put yourself in the best possible situation to preserve your legal rights and to defend yourself. Remember, ignorance of the law holds no weight in a courtroom!

III.   Force versus Deadly Force

The use of force is permitted for self-defense. Force can be defined as "[t]he impetus of power; physical power or strength exerted against a person or thing" (*See Force, Ballentine's Law Dictionary* (2010).) and deadly force is any force that endangers human life or causes great bodily harm. *See Commonwealth v. Alexander*, 260 Va. 238, 241, 531 S.E.2d 567, 568 (2000). It is very important to know and understand the difference between force and deadly force because an individual's right to self-defense "begins where the necessity begins and ends where it ends." *See Caison v. Commonwealth,*

52 Va. App. 423, 440, 663 S.E.2d 553, 561 (Va. App. Ct. 2008) (quoting *Thomason v. Commonwealth,* 178 Va. 489, 498, 17 S.E.2d 374, 378 (1941). Going on the offensive with excessive force is no longer self-defense.

If a person uses force when no force is legally allowed, then that use of force will not be legally justified. Likewise, if a person uses deadly force when the law only allows for the use of force, then that use of deadly force will not be legally justified. Justification is a sufficient or acceptable legal excuse or explanation for an act that is otherwise unlawful.

Force and deadly force can be applied with or without the use of a weapon. The weapon could be a gun, a knife, or items not originally intended to be a weapon such as a baseball bat, a hammer or a lead pipe. Many items can be used to cause injury or death under certain circumstances. How the weapon or item is being used is the key.

A.   *Deadly weapon defined*
A deadly weapon is any tool likely to produce death or great bodily harm from the manner in which it is used. In determining whether a weapon is regarded as deadly, more weight is given to the manner in which the weapon is used than to the inherent character of the instrument. *See Pritchett v. Commonwealth, 219 Va. 927, 929, 252 S.E.2d 352, 353 (1979).*

Any firearm is by design a tool that has the ability to deliver deadly force. The firing of a gun is considered a use of deadly force because it endangers human life and can cause great bodily harm. Death is not a requirement for the use of deadly force to be lawful. Additionally, a gun may be used without being fired.

The two most common other uses are displaying a gun in self-defense to scare off an attacker or using the butt of a pistol in self-defense to strike and fight off an attacker. These other uses would be considered force but not necessarily deadly force. Thus, it is critically important for the gun owner to understand both when and how he or she may legally use a gun for self-defense.

B.   *Use of force continuum*
A use of force continuum is a standard that provides guidelines as

to how much force may be used in a specific situation. The purpose of a use of force continuum model is to clarify the complex subject of use of force. Any use of force continuum generally has many levels of force. The circumstances of the attack or altercation will determine what level of force, if any, would be appropriate. Keep in mind that an altercation can quickly change and that one may move from one part of the continuum to another in a matter of seconds.

There is no one single universally accepted use of force continuum model; however, we have provided an example use-of-force continuum that can assist gun owners in understanding the various levels of force. Understanding various levels of acceptable force is naturally crucial because some circumstances will justify the use of deadly force where others may only justify either no force or a lower level of force. The use of excessive force or the unlawful use of force can get a lot of good folks into trouble with the law.

1. Verbal communication – Force does not have to be physical. Use of calm, nonthreatening language, such as "Stop," "Get off me," "Don't touch me" "Leave me alone," "Get off my property" or "I do not want to get into a fight with you" would likely be the first step of any use of force continuum. Increasing the volume and repeating the command may be necessary to gain compliance.
2. Bodily force — Using bodily force would be considered more force than a verbal command but would generally be considered less force than using a weapon.
3. Empty hand control — The use of hands
    a   Soft technique. Use of grabs, holds, joint locks or "come along" escort techniques. A good example of the "come along" escort technique might involve situations to escort a trespasser off of one's property when the command to "get off my property" is either ignored or not properly followed.
    b   Hard technique. Use of punches and kicks. Human fists ordinarily are not considered deadly weapons. *See Thurston v. Commonwealth,* 2008 Va. App. 443, 6 (2008). Punching and kicking another person, while generally not considered the use of deadly force, could transition into the use deadly force depending on the circumstances. A black belt martial artist's use of his

hands and feet in some cases or a series of repeated severe kicks to the head of another person could be a use of deadly force.
4. Less than deadly force — Use of less-lethal technologies.
   a Blunt impact. Use of a baton, club, and stick/staff. There are countless objects that can be used to fight off an attacker. Some objects are considered non-deadly weapons and are specifically designed for such a purpose, while in other cases an object can become improvised from its intended use and become a weapon. CAUTION: Consider how the object or weapon is being used because it is possible for virtually any item to become a deadly weapon based on its use.
   b Chemical. Use of pepper spray. Pepper spray, also known as oleoresin capsicum or OC, is made from the same naturally-occurring chemical that makes chili peppers hot, but at concentrations much higher. Pepper spray is legal in Virginia and can be used to disable an attacker long enough for you to get to safety if you are in a threatening situation where you need to defend yourself.
   c Conducted electrical devices. Use of a taser. The use of a taser is not intended to be fatal, but that does not mean the weapon cannot cause death.
   d Brandishing of a firearm. The pointing or holding of any firearm in a manner to reasonably induce fear in the mind of another is a threat to use deadly force. If the use of self-defense is justified or excused then you can brandish your gun to defend yourself. *See* Va. Code § 18.2-282; Harper v. Commonwealth, 196 Va. 723, 733 85 S.E.2d 249, 255 (1955). Justifiable and excusable self-defense will be discussed in the next section.
5. Deadly Force – Firing of a gun. The firing of a gun is only permitted where there is imminent danger of death or serious bodily harm.

> ## PRACTICAL LEGAL TIP
>
> If you carry a handgun in your vehicle, don't allow yourself to be drawn into a road-rage incident, no matter how minor. Someone who calls 911 to report that you pointed a gun at them, even though it was really just your middle finger, may get you arrested and charged with a crime. So, if you carry a gun in the car, forget how to flip the bird! — *Mitch*

IV. Self-defense must be either "justified" or "excused"

Under what circumstances is it lawful to use deadly force against another person in Virginia for self-defense? In Virginia, the legal use of self-defense can either be justifiable self-defense or excusable self-defense.

A. *Justifiable self-defense: not at fault*

If you are without fault in provoking or bringing on the fight, and you reasonably fear that you are in imminent danger of being killed or in imminent danger of great bodily harm, and you use no more force than is reasonably necessary to protect yourself from the perceived harm under the circumstances as they appear to you, then your use of deadly force in self-defense is legally justified. *See* Virginia Model Jury Instruction 33.800. Self-Defense – Defendant Without Fault.

1. Stand your ground

"Stand Your Ground" is a common term that means a person has no legal duty to retreat before using self-defense if legally justified. Virginia is a stand your ground state, which means that if you did not start the fight or provoke the incident in any way, then you can stand your ground and defend yourself against your attacker without having to retreat. *See Foote v. Commonwealth,* 11 Va. App. 61, 67 (App. Ct. 1990).

On the other hand, if you are partially at fault in starting the fight or confrontation, then Virginia law requires you to retreat as far as you safely can before you are permitted to use what is called excusable self-defense, which we will discuss later.

2. Is your fear sufficiently reasonable?

The test of whether your fear was sufficiently reasonable to justify acting in self-defense is based upon your subjective point-of-view rather than the reaction of an ordinary person to similar circumstances. Additionally, the perceived danger must be imminent and must be manifested by an overt act. *See Commonwealth v. Sands,* 262 Va. 724 (2001). Compare: Many other states require that your fear must be both subjectively real and objectively reasonable before a killing will be justified or excused; however, the Supreme Court of Virginia has expressly rejected any objective component in Virginia's test. *See Peeples v. Commonwealth,* 28 Va. App. 360, 367 (1998). Nevertheless, it is critically important that your fear is reasonable because there have been cases where the accused in fact feared death or serious bodily harm, but the fear was unreasonable. Unreasonable fear will not entitle you to your claim of self-defense, rather it would merely reduce the killing from murder to manslaughter. *See Thomason v. Commonwealth,* 178 Va. 489 (1941).

3. Imminent danger

The existence of imminent danger is determined from your point of view at the time you used deadly force to defend yourself. Whether imminent danger existed or not will depend on the facts and circumstances of each particular case. Threats or words alone by one to take the life of another will not justify the taking of a life prior to an overt act. The "bare fear" of serious bodily injury, or even death, however well-grounded, will not justify the taking of human life. There must also be some overt act indicative of imminent danger at the time. In other words, you must wait until some overt act is done until the danger becomes imminent. Additionally, you must be able to articulate in as much detail as possible that the assailant acted in a manner that either threatened your life or safety – you cannot simply say that you feared the assailant, you must be able to describe the threatening conduct.

In the context of a self-defense plea, "imminent danger" is defined as an immediate, real threat to one's safety. There must be some menacing act presenting peril and the act must be of such a character as to afford a reasonable ground for believing there is a design to do some serious bodily harm, and imminent danger of carrying such design into immediate execution. The requirement of an overt act indicative of imminent danger ensures that the most extreme recourse, the killing of another human being, will be used only in situations of necessity. The plea of self-defense is a plea of necessity, and the necessity must be shown to exist or there must be shown such reasonable apprehension of the immediate danger, by some overt act, as to amount to the creation of necessity." *See Commonwealth v. Sands*, 262 Va. 724 (2001).

4. Justifiable self-defense examples

Reading about the law can be confusing. Below are some examples that demonstrate the concept of justifiable self-defense. Note: These are general examples. In the real world, there will likely be numerous detailed factors under the totality of the circumstances that will be considered when determining whether self-defense was justified.

Example:
One busy day at his job, David is working quietly at his desk when he hears an angry voice yell out, "I hate this company, and I'm going to kill every one of you!" About that time, David spots a machete in a deranged-looking stranger's hand. The stranger turns toward David with an evil look. David, fearing he is about to be struck with a machete and be killed, draws a gun from his desk, points it at the attacker and shouts "Stop, drop the weapon, or I will shoot." As the man rushes toward David with the machete raised, David fires two shots at the attacker, killing him.

Will David's use of deadly force be justified? It is important to not forget that any killing will be thoroughly investigated by the law enforcement community. The prosecution will be gathering evidence, which will include considering various questions as follows:

- Was David's fear reasonable?
- Was David in imminent danger of being killed or suffering a serious bodily injury?
- Was David required to try and escape the office first before using force against the attacker?
- Was David required to first use non-lethal force before using deadly force?
- Was David's use of force proportional and reasonable under the circumstances?

If the prosecution had sufficient evidence to believe that David's use of force was unlawful, then David could find himself accused of murder in this hypothetical. In that case, it would be up to the judge or jury hearing the case and sitting in judgment to determine if David's claim of self-defense was justified. However, in this example, it is unlikely that David would be arrested and stand trial for the murder of the stranger.

The facts demonstrate that David was in fear and was in imminent danger from the crazy stranger who was a second away from seriously injuring or killing David with a machete while yelling "I am going to kill every one of you" and ignoring David's demand to "Stop, drop the weapon, or I will shoot." David does not appear to be at fault here in any way, thus, he can stand his ground and defend himself. David first used force with his verbal command then quickly transitioned to the use of deadly force by firing his gun. Remember, the type of force that is justified can change quickly along the use of force continuum and it is permissible to skip lower levels of force and immediately use deadly force if the circumstances permit. Therefore, David would likely be legally justified in using deadly force to defend himself.

> Example:
> *Jane is out jogging one evening. A white van pulls up alongside her and a masked man pointing a gun at her jumps out of the van, grabs Jane and is attempting to drag her into his van. A freaked out Jane manages to pull out her Glock pistol and fire two shots at the attacker, who is killed.*

- Was Jane's use of deadly force justified?
- Was her fear of death or serious bodily injury reasonable?
- Was she in imminent danger of being killed or suffering a serious bodily injury?
- Was she required to try and escape her attacker first before using force against the attacker?
- Was she required to first use some type of non-lethal force before using deadly force?
- Was her use of force proportional and reasonable under the circumstances?

Under these circumstances, Jane became the victim of an attempted abduction by an armed attacker. Jane can stand her ground and defend herself because she was without fault in provoking the incident. Her fear or being "freaked out" would likely be viewed as reasonable. The masked man pointing a gun while attempting to abduct Jane created an imminent danger of Jane either being killed or suffering great bodily harm. Jane immediately used deadly force to defend herself without first attempting to use less than lethal force. Was Jane required to first use a lower level of force before using deadly force? No. Jane's use of deadly force to defend herself would likely be considered justified.

> Example:
> *Billy is walking to his car after leaving the grocery store when three individuals with baseball bats confront him in the parking lot and surround him in an aggressive manner. Billy fears that he is about to get beat up by the individuals with bats. Billy draws his gun and clearly demands that the aggressors leave him alone, at which point they all flee from the scene.*

Has Billy used deadly force by showing his gun? No. The display of the gun is a use of force but not a use of deadly force. It is pretty clear that Billy is the victim of an assault that is about to get worse. Billy's production of a weapon was a use of force in self-defense to scare off his attackers. A person can legally "display" a gun in self-defense when the use of force is legally justified—not just when the use of deadly force is justified! CAUTION: If a self-defense claim involving the display of a gun is not valid and the use of force is not justified, then the gun owner could be charged with the criminal violation of brandishing a firearm according to Va. Code 18.2-282.

> Example:
> *Tina is on her way home from work. She stops by a local convenience store for some bread and milk. As she enters the store, a masked man suddenly approaches her with a knife, grabs her by the arm, places the knife alongside her body, and demands all of her money. Tina, scared, shaken, fearing for her life and remembering her training, opens her purse and manages to pull out her .357 revolver. She fires her gun and kills the masked robber.*

Remember, every killing will be thoroughly investigated by the authorities. Ideally, Tina would not even be arrested under these circumstances. She was permitted to stand her ground and defend herself. Her fear was more than reasonable that she was in imminent danger of being killed or suffering great bodily harm from the masked robber who held her at knifepoint and she used no more force than was reasonably necessary to protect herself. What if the altercation is less clear?

Example:
Hank, a sixty-six year old disabled man, works downtown. He has to park four blocks from his company's office building and walk through some rough parts of town in order to get to work. One day on his walk to work after parking his car, a panhandler suddenly appears in front of him and says, "Hey man—give me some money!" Hank, feeling very frightened and intimidated, ignores the panhandler and keeping walking. The panhandler gets louder and more aggressive demanding, "Hey! Man! I said give me some money!" Hank now becomes extremely concerned for his safety. About that time, Hank makes a wrong turn into an alley where he is cornered. He again hears, "HEY! MAN! I SAID GIVE ME SOME MONEY!" When Hank turns around, he sees the panhandler, now very aggressive, with something in his hand.

Is the panhandler just being annoying or is Hank about to be attacked? The panhandler neither verbally threatened Hank nor did he ever physically touch him. All the panhandler said was "give me some money;" he didn't even demand all of Hank's money—just some. Do robbers ever demand just some money? What if Hank took out his legally concealed carry pistol and fired it at the panhandler to defend himself? Would Hank be justified in his use of deadly force against the panhandler for self-defense under these circumstances? Would Hank's claim that he was fearful of the panhandler and that he believed he was in imminent danger of being killed or suffering serious bodily harm be reasonable? Would it be reasonably necessary for Hank to use deadly force to protect himself under the circumstances?

The authorities might believe that Hank used excessive force against the panhandler and charge him with a crime regardless of whether the panhandler was struck by the bullet or not. What if the object in the panhandler's hand was actually a weapon and he raised it up in the air as he was moving aggressively toward Hank? What if the panhandler out-weighed Hank by 75 pounds and was a foot taller? What if Hank's sworn testimony was that he was in fear for his safety, had seen the panhandler acting violently on the same street many times in the past, and was about to be robbed? Hank would certainly be able to claim self-defense, but as we have said repeatedly now, it would be up to the judge or jury to decide if Hank's use of deadly force for self-defense was justified.

The point of this example is not to answer the question of whether Hank's use of deadly force was justified. The point is to demonstrate that it can sometimes be difficult to assess a situation and that the circumstances of an encounter can quickly change. Always remember, if you are without fault in provoking the fight, and (1) you reasonably fear, under the circumstances as they appear to you, that you are in imminent danger of being killed or that you are in imminent danger of great bodily harm; and (2) you use no more force, under the circumstances as they appear to you, than was reasonably necessary to protect yourself from the perceived harm, then the use of deadly force for self-defense is legally justified.

5.   "Castle Doctrine"

The castle doctrine concept originated in England where it was said that an Englishman's home is his castle and that if you are attacked in your own home, you need not retreat, but may stand your ground and defend yourself. Many people think that the castle doctrine means that you can legally shoot any stranger you find in your house. That is not the case in Virginia and to do so could likely be a use of excessive deadly force.

In Virginia, **there is no statutory castle law that has been created by the legislature.** The Supreme Court of Virginia discussed the Defense of Castle in the 1922 case of *Fortune v. Commonwealth, 139 Va. 669,687 (1922),* a case that did not even involve an attack inside the home.

The Virginia Supreme Court went on to explain that you are not required to retreat if assaulted in your house or on the curtilage, but you may stand your ground and use such means as are absolutely necessary to repel your assailant from your house or to prevent your attacker's forcible entry. The curtilage of a house is the land immediately surrounding it. This is essentially an example of justifiable self-defense, which we previously discussed to mean that if you reasonably fear that you are in imminent danger of being killed or in imminent danger of great bodily harm, then you may use no more force that was reasonably necessary to protect yourself from the perceived harm under the circumstances as they appeared to you. Remember, you are actually defending yourself and your family and not merely defending your real estate. Defense of others will be discussed in the next chapter.

The defense does not apply to ejecting visitors, guests, or those who have an implied license. In those instances, you are limited to reasonable force in ejecting the visitor, guest or implied licensee. On the other hand, if your visitor attacks you and you are without fault, then you may stand your ground and use justifiable self-defense. However, if you are at fault in starting or provoking the fight in your home, then you would only be able to claim excusable self-defense, which we discuss in the next section. Excusable self-defense requires that you retreat before you can claim self-defense.

Example:
Harry the homeowner and his family live in a peaceful Richmond neighborhood. One night after everyone has gone to bed and all the lights have been turned down, Harry hears a strange noise downstairs at his back door. He grabs his 12 gauge Remington shotgun and goes to the back door to investigate. At his backdoor, he finds a large man, 6 foot 5, 275 pounds, with an angry look on his face, with a crowbar wedged within the door frame of the back door in the process of prying open the door. Harry, with his Remington shotgun pointed at the man making his presence known by repeatedly shouting "Stop. Get out of here. I have already called the police. I am going to shoot you if you come any closer." The man ignores Harry and within seconds breaks the door open. Harry fires off two blasts from his Remington shotgun at the man. The man dies instantly.

Was Harry's use of deadly force absolutely necessary? Would Harry's use of force be justified? As we previously explained, any killing will be thoroughly investigated by the law enforcement community and any dispute regarding the lawfulness of his actions will be determined by the judge or jury. However, if Harry reasonably feared that he was in imminent danger of being killed or suffering great bodily harm from the intruder, then it seems pretty clear that he would be justified in his use of deadly force in this example. Harry used lower levels of force when he verbally commanded multiple times "Stop. Get out of here. I have already called the police. I am going to shoot you if you come any closer" along with pointing his shotgun at the attacker. What else could Harry have reasonably done to protect himself from the perceived harm presented by a large angry man intruding into his house that failed to heed his warning and kept charging an armed Harry? Note: Every situation is different and the circumstances are critically important to every use of force in self-defense.

> Example:
> Harriett is a student and lives alone in busy Northern Virginia in an apartment complex. She works part time as a lifeguard at the local swimming pool. One afternoon Harriett comes home to her apartment after her lifeguard shift at the pool to find a strange looking man jumping out of her apartment window holding her new expensive flat screen television. Harriett quickly runs to the window, draws her .380 pistol and fires it at the fleeing man running through the apartment parking lot because she cannot afford to buy a new television. Harriett's shot strikes and injures the man, but Harriett recovers her expensive television.

Is Harriett's use of deadly force justified? Probably not. As we previously discussed, the firing of a gun is considered the use of deadly force even if nobody dies. The castle doctrine allows for the use of deadly force if absolutely necessary to keep out aggressors, which would include Harriett's apartment. In this example, the man holding Harriett's television is more of a thief than an aggressor, besides – he was in the apartment parking lot when Harriett fired her gun.

Additionally, the facts are clear that Harriett was neither fearing for her life in any way nor was she in imminent danger of being killed or suffering serious bodily injury. Harriett seemed pretty focused on saving her expensive television. A person has no right to use deadly force solely to defend personal property. In Chapter 6, we discuss defense of personal property in more detail.

B. *Excusable self-defense: At fault*
The self-defense law is different if you are partially at fault for starting the fight or confrontation. Excusable self-defense requires that you must retreat before you can legally use deadly force to defend yourself.

If you are at least some degree at fault in provoking or bringing on the fight, but you:

1. retreat as far as you safely can under the circumstances in a good faith attempt to abandon the fight;
2. you make known your desire for peace by word or act;
3. you reasonably fear, under the circumstances as they appear to you, that you are in imminent danger of being killed or that you are in imminent danger of great bodily harm; and
4. you use no more force, under the circumstances as they appear to you, than was reasonably necessary to protect yourself from the perceived harm,

then your use of deadly force in self-defense is legally excused. *See Bailey v. Commonwealth,* 200 Va. 92, 96 (1958); Virginia Model Jury Instruction 33.810. Self-Defense – Defendant With Fault – Retreat to Wall.

1. Provocation – retreat
What does it mean to provoke an attack? One who uses provoking language or incites a fight or follows the other combatant from a prior altercation has lost his claim of justifiable self-defense. In essence, a person cannot effectively "bait" another person into a violent confrontation and then claim justifiable self-defense.

The accused must be without fault "in the minutest degree" to claim justifiable self-defense. *See Smith v. Commonwealth,* 165 VA. 776,

785 (1935). However, what if a person who started or provoked a fight soon realizes they bit off more than they can chew? Under the law, that person may be able to claim excusable self-defense if that person can retreat and communicate his or her desire to abandon the encounter. If, after a person abandons or attempts to abandon the encounter he or she started or provoked, and the other combatant who was provoked pursues and uses unlawful force against the provocateur, then the provocateur would be permitted to use force in self-defense.

2. Excusable self-defense examples

These are general examples. In the real world, there will likely be numerous detailed factors under the totality of the circumstances that the judge or jury sitting in judgment will consider when determining whether the use of self-defense was excused.

> Example:
> Dave is at a bar when he notices another man checking out his girlfriend. Dave tells the other man, "take a hike or you'll regret it" and slightly shoves the admirer. The other man responds by punching Dave in the face. Dave, who didn't really want a confrontation, holds both his hands up in surrender and says, "I don't want any more trouble!" as he starts to exit the bar. However, the other man pulls out a knife and lunges at Dave just as he is exiting through the bar's front door and shouts "take that!"

Would Dave be legally permitted to fight back and defend himself? What if Dave pulled out a pistol, and shot and killed the knife-wielding attacker as he was exiting the bar? Would this use of deadly force be excusable self-defense?

In this scenario, Dave clearly started or provoked the encounter. Dave would not be permitted to stand his ground and claim self-defense. The law of excusable self-defense would require that Dave retreat.

Would Dave's use of deadly force at the end of the encounter be legally excused? Possibly. Dave's walking away from the admirer while attempting to exit the bar while stating "I don't want any more trouble!" would likely be sufficient as a retreat to abandon the fight and to communicate that Dave's desire was for peace. The remaining questions deal with whether Dave reasonably feared he was in imminent danger of being killed or suffering great bodily injury and whether he used no more force than was reasonably necessary to protect himself. Again, as always, any killing will be thoroughly investigated by the authorities, and in the event of a trial, it will be up to the judge or jury hearing the case to decide whether Dave's fear and use of deadly force were reasonable under the circumstances to accept his self-defense claim and legally excuse the killing.

> Example:
> *Police respond to a two-car collision in a parking lot. When the police arrive on the scene, they discover that the collision sparked a violent road-rage incident between the two drivers. At the scene, one of the drivers is lying dead on the ground from bullet wounds with a tire iron beside him. The other driver was Stan the shooter. Stan claimed that the other driver became irate after the collision, was verbally abusive, threatened him, and aggressively came toward him with the tire iron raised in his hand. Stan made a statement to the police, which included an admission that he was in fear for his life and that he fired two shots at the other driver in self-defense. Stan is a 45 year-old man with no previous criminal record. The physical evidence recovered at the scene of the collision makes it unclear who was the true victim of the encounter, but one investigator thinks Stan is lying. There are no other witnesses. Stan is now a suspect in a murder investigation.*

In some instances, it can be unclear if a person can stand their ground and defend themselves or if they are required to first retreat before using force in self-defense. Assume Stan is ultimately arrested, indicted, and stands trial for murder and claims self-defense. Will Stan's use of deadly force be justified or excused? Was he entitled to stand his ground and defend himself or was he required to retreat because he was at least partially at fault in bringing on the fight? Was his fear reasonable? Was he in imminent danger of being killed or suffering a serious bodily injury? Was his use of force proportional and reasonable under the circumstances?

At trial, the prosecution's case would be strongest if they could prove that Stan was at least partially at fault in starting the road rage altercation and that he was not entitled to stand his ground and claim self-defense without first retreating. There seems to be no indication of an attempt by Stan to retreat. The prosecution will also likely present the physical evidence at the scene, which will include testimony from investigators. The prosecution may also argue that Stan's claimed fear was unreasonable and that his use of deadly force was excessive and unnecessary. In Stan's defense, his lawyers will have the burden of producing at least "some evidence" at trial to support his self-defense claim that he was not at fault in provoking the fight and that he reasonably feared he was in imminent danger of being killed or suffering great bodily harm and that he used no more force under the circumstances as reasonably necessary to protect himself from the other driver's attack in order for the court to consider his claim of self-defense. Either way, it would be up to the judge or jury hearing the case to determine if Stan's use of deadly force was justified. If the court were to determine that Stan was partially at fault in provoking the fight and that he did not retreat before using deadly force, then the killing would not be excused and Stan would be found guilty of killing the other driver.

C.   *Federal self-defense laws*
Virginia is home to several national parks, national forests and national wildlife refuges. Federal law determines what amount of force, if any, is permitted for self-defense on federal property. Federal law recognizes the common law defense of self-defense. Under federal law, the use of force is justified when a person reasonably believes that force is necessary for self-defense against the immediate use of unlawful force. However, a person must use no more force than appears reasonably necessary under the circumstances. Force likely to cause death or great bodily injury is justified in self-defense only if a person reasonably believes such force is necessary to prevent death or great bodily harm. *See Brown v. United States*, 256 U.S. 335 (1921); U.S. Fifth Circuit Pattern Jury Instructions, 1.36A Criminal, 2015; *Dixon v. United States*, 548 U.S. 1, 126 S. Ct. 2437 (2006).

V. Warning shots

A warning shot is an intentional gunshot often made with the firearm pointed in the air with the intent not to harm one's adversary, but to subdue or scare off an attacker. The purpose of firing warning shots is to warn or intimidate an opponent and to showcase one's capability or will to act if provoked. They are intended to convince a potentially hostile force to withdraw or cease its actions. This is a sufficiently aggressive act to demand attention and alert those nearby that they might be shot if directions are not followed.

Warning shots are not recommended and will almost always get you in trouble because a shot fired into the air or in some other direction has the ability to strike an unintended target or ricochet. Warning shots are commonly portrayed in movies and television as a good idea and people like to mimic what they see in movies and on TV!

As we have previously discussed, the firing of a gun is considered the use of deadly force, thus, you better make sure that the use of deadly force is lawful under the circumstances. Every law abiding gun owner needs to know that willfully discharging a firearm in a public place in Virginia can lead to criminal prosecution unless such firing is considered justifiable or excusable self-defense. *See* Va. Code § 18.2-280.

VI. Mutual combat

Mutual Combat is a fight wherein both parties mutually fight upon equal terms. In some instances, mutual combat can lead to death. Killing another during such an activity is manslaughter. If you agree to a fight then you cannot claim justifiable self-defense because you are at fault in entering into the fight. *See Jones v. Commonwealth,* 196 Va. 10 (1954). Likewise, you cannot claim excusable self-defense because you did not abandon the fight and retreat. *See Ballard v. Commonwealth,* 156 Va. 980 (1931).

Example:
Andy and Dwight are at the local sports bar watching NFL football on television. The two strike up a conversation about their favorite teams making it to the Super Bowl. After a few minutes, the two become engaged in a heated argument about whose favorite football team will win the Super Bowl. In the heat of the argument, Andy calls Dwight a derogatory name and Dwight asks if Andy wants to take

it outside. Andy agrees, and they both begin fist fighting in the parking lot. Shortly after they begin fighting, the police show up and arrest both of them for assault and battery.

Will either Andy or Dwight be able to defend against their assault and battery criminal cases with a claim of self-defense?

Not likely. Both appear to be at fault in starting or provoking the fight, neither attempted to retreat, and both parties agreed to the fight. If a person agrees to engage in using force against another person, then that person cannot later claim that they fought back in self-defense!

VII. Right to resist unlawful arrest
Unfortunately, there are instances where police officers exceed their authority and attempt to make an unlawful arrest. If this is the case, the use of reasonable force in self-defense is justified. However, it is important to note that it can be extremely difficult to know at the time of the arrest whether the arrest is lawful or unlawful. *See Foote v. Commonwealth,* 11 Va. App. 61, 69, 396 S.E.2d 851, 856 (Va. App. Ct. 1990). CAUTION: If you use force to resist an arrest by police and the courts later determine that the arrest was lawful, then you may find yourself in violation of the resisting arrest and/or obstruction of justice laws. Questioning a policeman's authority to arrest during the actual arrest is a very slippery slope.

VIII. The Virginia criminal trial
Virginia uses a two-tiered trial court system comprised of trial courts "not of record" and trial courts "of record." Courts "not of record" are called District Courts and courts "of record" are called Circuit Courts. Misdemeanor trials are typically held in the District Courts unless the defendant appeals a District Court conviction to the Circuit Court or if there is a direct indictment by the prosecuting attorney. The defendant has an automatic right to appeal any District Court misdemeanor conviction to the Circuit Court for a new trial. There is no right to a trial by jury in the District Courts. A District Court judge hears the case and imposes the sentence in the event of a conviction.

Felony trials must be held in the Circuit Court. The right to trial by jury can only be carried out in the Circuit Court. Virginia is one of the few jurisdictions in the United States in which the jury recommends the sentence in the event of a conviction. In a Virginia jury trial, the jury must first decide if the defendant is guilty or not guilty. If the jury finds the defendant not guilty, then the defendant is set free. If the jury finds the defendant guilty, then the jury will immediately begin the sentencing phase of the trial where the jury will recommend a sentence. The judge must ratify or affirm the jury's sentence.

In Virginia, a judge can lower or reduce a jury's sentence if appropriate, but the judge cannot increase the jury's sentence. In most instances, judges do not view it as their role to impede or step on the toes of a jury's sentence and jury sentences are often ratified.

A. *Defendant's right to testify at trial*
The Fifth Amendment to the U.S. Constitution provides that no person shall be compelled in any criminal case to be a witness against himself. At trial, the prosecution can neither call the defendant as a witness, nor comment on the defendant's failure to testify. The decision to testify or not is exclusively the privilege of the defendant. In many cases, the defendant will have to testify in his trial about his fear and that he had no other choice but to act the way he did when he used force to defend himself. However, in some cases, it may be a trial tactic for the defendant not to testify because it prevents the prosecution from examining the defendant under oath and on the witness stand. Once the defendant takes the witness stand, he will be subject to cross-examination by the prosecuting attorney, which can severely alter the outcome of the trial based on the circumstances of the case and the credibility of the defendant.

B. *Burden of Proof*
The prosecution has the burden to prove the defendant's guilt in every criminal trial. This means that it is the prosecutor's responsibility to present enough evidence to prove every element of the offense beyond a reasonable doubt that the defendant committed the crime alleged. This burden of proof that the prosecutor bears is a standard called "beyond a reasonable doubt." It is the highest level of proof used in the American justice system.

Self-defense is an affirmative defense. An affirmative defense is a set of facts or some evidence produced by the defendant after the prosecution rests its case, which if believed by the judge or jury sitting in judgment, defeats or mitigates the legal consequences of the defendant's otherwise unlawful conduct. However, in self-defense cases, the defendant has the burden of coming forward with or producing self-defense evidence. The prosecution is required to prove the alleged offense beyond a reasonable doubt but is not required to disprove self-defense beyond a reasonable doubt. The defendant should be acquitted only if the self-defense evidence raises a doubt as to his guilt by justifying or excusing his actions under the circumstances.

C.   *Necessary Evidence & Jury Instruction*
The defendant must put forth "some evidence" at trial that he reasonably feared he was in imminent danger of being killed or suffering serious bodily injury, and that he used no more force than necessary to defend himself under the circumstances as they appeared to him. In a jury trial, if there is evidence in the record to support the defendant's theory of self-defense, then the trial judge must properly instruct the jury on the law. If the evidence is in conflict, then the judge is to instruct the jury on the law as it relates to theories of the case for both the prosecution and the defense. *See Delacruz v. Commonwealth*, 11 Va. App. 335, 338, 398 S.E.2d, 103, 105 (Va. App. Ct. 1990). Thus, the judge must instruct the jury on both theories of the case to guide the jury in their deliberations as to the law applicable to the case, depending upon how the jury decides the facts. The jury, as the finder of fact, has the right to reject evidence they believe to be untrue and accept evidence they believe to be true. *See Id*. Finally, it is up to the judge or jury hearing the case to decide whether the defendant is either guilty of the crime alleged or should be found not guilty because the use of force in self-defense was either justified or excused. *See Hodge v. Commonwealth,* 217 Va. 338, 341, 228. S.E. 2d 692, 695 (1976) (stating "Neither the Due Process Clause nor case law prohibits the use of presumptions or inferences as procedural devices to shift to the accused the burden of producing some evidence contesting the otherwise presumed or inferred fact.").

CHAPTER FIVE
WHEN CAN I LEGALLY USE MY GUN TO DEFEND ANOTHER PERSON?

I.   Introduction and overview

In addition to self-defense, every law abiding gun owner needs to also know when they can use their gun to defend another person. Failure to understand the law can quickly get good folks in serious trouble!

II.   Defense of others in Virginia

Defense of others is an affirmative defense, just like self-defense; the concept of an affirmative defense is discussed in the previous chapter. *See* Smith v. Commonwealth, 2013 Va. App. 29 (Va. App. Ct. 2013). In Virginia, you may defend another person, even a stranger. *See Foster v. Commonwealth,* 13 Va. App. 380, 386 (1991); Va. Prac. Jury Instruction § 63:3. However, generally there is no duty to render aid unless there is some special relationship such as a business proprietor and an invitee or an innkeeper and a guest. *See Bosworth v. Vornado Realty L.P.,* 83 Va. Cir. 549, 551 (19th Cir. 2010) (citing *Holles v. Sunrise Terrace, Inc.,* 257 Va. 131, 136, 509 S.E.2d. 494, 497 (1999)). The amount of force used to defend another must not be excessive and must be reasonable in relation to the harm threatened. The defense of another against an aggressor also includes the use of deadly force, if necessary under the circumstances. Deadly force is justified in the defense of another party when you reasonably believe that the person you are defending is not at fault in provoking the conflict and is in imminent danger of being killed or suffering great bodily harm based on the circumstances. However, if you reasonably believe that the party you are defending was at fault in provoking the conflict but sufficiently retreated, and that they are still in imminent danger of being killed or suffering great bodily harm based on the circumstances, then your use of deadly force in defense of another would be excusable.

It is important to note that whether the defended person was in fact free from fault is legally irrelevant to the defense. The reason is based on the principle that one should not be convicted of a crime for attempting to protect another perceived to be a faultless victim from a violent assault. The policy of the law is to encourage individuals to come to the aid of perceived victims of assault. *See Foster v. Commonwealth,* 13 Va. App. 380, 386 (1991).

> Example:
> *Elliott is taking a stroll one evening in the downtown sec-*
> *tion of Richmond when he hears cries for help emanating*
> *from a nearby alley. Elliott runs to the alley and finds a*
> *masked man beating Drew's head with a baseball bat and*
> *yelling repeatedly "give me all your money!" Elliott runs up*
> *closer to find blood everywhere as the man standing over*
> *Drew continues the beat down. Drew is not armed with a*
> *weapon. Elliott draws his holstered pistol and shouts re-*
> *peatedly "Stop, drop the bat!" Elliott believes that Drew*
> *is about to be killed. Elliott fires two shots into the back of*
> *the masked man, killing him instantly. Elliott neither knew*
> *the masked man nor Drew, and had never seen either one*
> *of them in his life. There were no other witnesses.*

Was Elliott justified in using deadly force to defend Drew? As we have previously stated, any death will be thoroughly investigated by the law enforcement community and any dispute as to what happened will be determined by a judge or jury hearing the case.

It seems pretty clear here that Elliott would be justified in his use of deadly force to defend Drew. First, did Elliott reasonably believe that Drew was not at fault? There are no facts to suggest that Elliott could have possibly believed Drew was in any way at fault in provoking this incident. It is irrelevant whether Drew was at fault or not in how the confrontation with the masked man started. It is likely that Elliott's reasonable belief that Drew was not at fault would be determined as lawful. Second, was Drew in imminent danger of being killed or suffering serious bodily injury? Drew was being severely beaten in the head with a baseball bat, and as any reasonable person would know, being beaten in the head with a baseball bat is a sure-fire way to either suffer serious bodily injury or even die. Additionally, it seemed as if Drew had already suffered serious bodily injuries to the head and that according to Elliott it looked like he would die if Elliott did not do something.

> Example:
> *Mark is walking up to the entrance of his favorite local bar*
> *when he sees Spencer pointing a gun at Eric's face at close*

> *range, yelling "I told you not to mess with me!" Mark, thinking Eric may get shot, quickly rushes up to Spencer, and demands that he put the gun down. When Spencer fails to do so after a second request, Mark shoots and kills him. Mark has never seen either Spencer or Eric in his life.*

In this example, Eric has a gun pointed in his face. As we previously discussed, this is considered a threat of deadly force by Spencer. Eric is in imminent danger of being killed or suffering serious bodily injury. This example becomes less clear than the last example with respect to whether Mark, the defender, reasonably believed that the person being defended, Eric, was free from fault.

Was Eric at fault in instigating the incident? Maybe. Maybe not, but it does not matter because Eric's fault or not is legally irrelevant to Mark's defense of others claim. Was there any way for Mark to reasonably believe that Eric was at fault in any way in bringing about the conflict? Mark really has no way of knowing whether Eric was in any way at fault in this example except for one clue when Spencer yelled "I told you not to mess with me!" However, just because Spencer yelled this does not necessarily put Mark on notice that Eric was at fault in starting the incident. Spencer's statement could have been a result of a misunderstanding, or an overreaction to something Eric did that Spencer did not like inside the bar.

In this example, the judge or jury may have difficulty determining Mark's defense of others claim based on his reasonable belief regarding Eric's fault or lack of fault. Some might be satisfied that Mark reasonably believed that Eric was free from fault while others may disagree.

As we mentioned in Chapter 4, the federal law determines what amount of force, if any, is permitted for self-defense on federal property such as a national park, forest or wildlife refuge. Federal law also recognizes the common law defense of defense of others. Under federal law, the use of force is justified when a person reasonably believes that force is necessary for the defense of another against the immediate use of unlawful force. However, a person must use no more force than appears reasonably necessary under the circumstances. Force likely to cause death or great bodily injury is justified in the defense of another only if a person reasonably believes such force is necessary to prevent death or great bodily harm. *See Brown v. United States, 256 U.S. 335 (1921); U.S. Fifth Circuit Pattern Jury Instructions, 1.36A Criminal, 2015; Dixon v. United States, 548 U.S. 1, 126 S. Ct. 2437 (2006).*

CHAPTER SIX

WHEN CAN I LEGALLY USE MY GUN TO DEFEND MY PROPERTY?

The defense of property is completely different than self-defense or defense of others because this defense does not involve the protection of human life. This defense only applies where you are only defending your property and not defending yourself or another person.

I.   Can I use deadly force to protect my property?

You can never use deadly force to solely defend your property. An easy example would be that you cannot shoot someone in the back while they are running across your yard with your television. Likewise, you can never threaten the use of deadly force, such as brandishing a firearm, solely to defend your property. *See Commonwealth v. Alexander,* 260 Va. 238, 241 (2000).

On the other hand, you may use as much force as reasonably necessary, such as using your hands in a proper manner so as to protect your property as long as you do not commit an assault & battery or a breach of the peace. *See Swilling v. Commonwealth,* 2011 Va. App. 169; *Montgomery v. Commonwealth*, 99 Va. 833 (1901). In trespassing cases, the landowner has the right to order a trespasser to leave his property, and, if the trespasser refuses to leave, then the landowner may lay hands on the trespasser in a proper manner solely to expel him from the property. The landowner cannot commit an assault and battery for the purpose of expelling the trespasser.

If the landowner does commit an assault and battery, then the trespasser has the right to strike in defense. A good recommendation is to always call the authorities anytime your property is in jeopardy.

How much force is reasonably necessary to protect my property?

Example 1:
Harry the homeowner lives on a busy street in the ocean-front area of Virginia Beach. Harry looks out his window and sees a person standing in the middle of his front lawn. Harry yells at the fellow to get out of his yard. The fellow

on the lawn does not respond. Harry rushes out to confront the fellow and demands that he immediately leave his lawn.

What degree of force may Harry use to remove the trespasser? This fellow does not belong on the property and is clearly a trespasser! Harry can issue multiple orders that this fellow is trespassing and that he must immediately exit the property. Harry may also make use of a "come-along" escort technique with his hands to remove this trespasser from his lawn. Both of these actions would be considered lower levels of force, which we discussed in the example use of force continuum in Chapter 4, that the law allows. Harry would not be permitted to assault the fellow or commit a breach the peace by doing something like starting a fight. Sometimes the best thing may be to call the police for assistance.

Example 2:
Mike sees Todd taking a walk on his farm land. Mike immediately runs up to Todd with a shotgun in his hands and yells at Todd to get off his property. Todd is startled and freezes in his tracks. Mike then shoots Todd and kills him.

Mike was neither permitted to threaten the use of deadly force or actually use deadly force to defend his farm land from a trespasser. However, Mike would have been able to use proper force as a landowner to order Todd the trespasser to leave and to employ proper force if Todd the trespasser refused to leave, provided no breach of the peace or assault is committed. The brandishing of the firearm is an assault. It is highly likely that Mike will be charged with a crime for killing Todd.

Example 3A:
One day, looking for a shortcut through the neighborhood, Tom hops a fence and is walking across open property to reach the street on the other side of the property. Tom is now a trespasser. Phil the property owner verbally confronts Tom. Tom tries to explain that he meant no harm and was just taking a shortcut. However, Phil becomes irate and cocks his gun, aims it at Tom, and says "I'm going to kill you!"

Is Phil's brandishing of his gun and his threat to use deadly force permissible? No. As we previously discussed, Virginia law considers brandishing a firearm an assault and an excessive use of force solely to defend property. Now let us take the example one step further:

> Example 3B:
> *Tom is scared out of his mind as he looks down the barrel of Phil's shotgun. The two are about 20 feet apart. Tom, hearing Phil's threat to kill him, draws his own firearm and fires two shots, killing Phil.*

Is Tom justified to use deadly force to defend against Phil's brandishing of a firearm and threat to kill? Yes, if Tom reasonably fears that he is in imminent danger of being killed or suffering serious bodily injury and he uses no more force than as is necessary under the circumstances as they appear to him, then he can defend himself from Phil's threat to use deadly force. Tom was not at fault in provoking the fight, thus he can stand his ground and defend himself from Phil's illegal brandishing of a gun. *See Commonwealth v. Alexander,* 260 Va. 238 (2000) (permitting one to threaten to use deadly force leads in dangerous progression to an unacceptable conclusion. The victim of a brandishing in this case would have been entitled to use deadly force to repel the perceived threat).

Here, Phil is threatening deadly force against Tom, who appears to be a non-threating trespasser. As previously discussed, brandishing a firearm is illegal if it is done solely for the purpose of defending property.

In some instances, the defense of property can quickly become self-defense.

> Example 3C:
> *Assume that when Phil verbally confronts Tom about Tom's trespassing, it is done in a very calm non-threatening manner without the display of weapons of any kind. It is Tom who becomes irate and hostile. Subsequently, it is Tom in a rage who pulls out a knife and attempts to stab Phil in the chest. Phil then draws his gun, and fires it at Tom, killing him instantly.*

Was Phil's use of force justified? Phil's verbal confrontation ordering Tom to exit the property is lawful in his defense of his property. Tom's reaction and use of force with the knife changes the encounter. Phil can now use more force for self-defense than the law would have allowed if he were merely protecting property. Remember the justified self-defense requirements we discussed in the previous chapter. If you are without fault in provoking the fight, and you reasonably fear that you are in imminent danger of being killed or in imminent danger of great bodily harm, and you use no more force than is reasonably necessary to protect yourself from the perceived harm, under the circumstances as they appear to you, then you can stand your ground and use deadly force.

Was Phil at fault in any way? Was his fear reasonable? Was he in imminent danger of being killed or suffering serious bodily injury? Did Phil use more force than was reasonably necessary?

As we have said many times, any death will be fully investigated by the law enforcement community and it would ultimately be up to the judge or jury hearing the matter to decide, in the event of a trial. However, it seems pretty clear that Phil was well within the law to defend his property and a verbal request asking Tom to leave would not be viewed as an excessive use of force. Additionally, it seems pretty clear that Tom's actions triggered Phil's self-defense rights. Phil's use of his gun was for self-defense not to defend his property. Phil was not at fault in provoking the incident so he is entitled to stand his ground and defend himself. It also seems clear that Phil's use of his gun against an irate knife wielding attacker would be viewed as reasonable under the circumstances.

CHAPTER SEVEN
UNDERSTANDING WHEN DEADLY FORCE
CAN BE USED AGAINST ANIMALS

I.   Defense against animals
The Virginia cruelty to animals law pursuant to Va. Code § 3.2-6570 states in part that it is a criminal offense to cruelly or unnecessarily beat, maim, mutilate or kill any animal; however, there are many exceptions to this law where you can kill an animal if the killing is in self-defense, is in defense of others or is to defend property from an attacking or nuisance animal.

A.   *Self-defense against an animal attack & defense of others against an animal attack*
The law of self-defense and defense of others applies when defending against an animal attack. *See Smith v. Commonwealth,* 2013 Va. App. 29 (Va. App. Ct. 2013). We previously discussed the law of self-defense in Virginia at length in Chapter 4.

Example:
Wendy the walker is taking a casual afternoon walk by herself near her home in her friendly suburban retirement community. Suddenly, a pit bull dog manages to escape its fenced property and is aggressively running toward Wendy. The dog is aggressively barking, growling, and showing its teeth as it is directly approaching Wendy in a very rapid pace with its ears pulled back. Wendy quickly starts to distance herself from the dog's property attempting to create as much space as possible, but it is impossible to "outrun" the dog. The dog is now 2-3 seconds from Wendy's position as she begins to frantically scream at the dog to stay away. Wendy is 65 years old, weighs 110 pounds, and legally carries a pistol with her concealed handgun permit.

What is Wendy to do? Does the dog have to actually bite Wendy before she can use deadly force to defend herself? What would you do?

Example continued:
Wendy fires two quick shots at the dog at the last second

based on her training from her local self-defense instruc-
tor. The dog later dies from the gunshot wound.

Was Wendy's use of deadly force in self-defense justified? As we have said, events like this will be thoroughly investigated by the law enforcement community. If the law enforcement community believes that Wendy used excessive force, then they may charge her with a cruelty to animals or firearm offense. It would then be up to the judge or jury hearing the case to determine if Wendy's fear was reasonable, under the circumstances as they appeared to her, that she was in imminent danger of being killed or that she was in imminent danger of great bodily harm. Also that she used no more force, under the circumstances as they appeared to her, than was reasonably necessary to protect herself from the perceived harm.

Every case is different. Some judges, jurors and prosecutors may take the position that Wendy's fear was unreasonable. Some may take the position that Wendy's force was excessive and that she should have tried kicking the dog first before using deadly force. Others may believe that what Wendy did was justified. The purpose of this example is to bring awareness to an all too common scenario and educate the law abiding gun owner that they are permitted to use deadly force to defend against an animal attack, just like defending against an attack from a person, however, the use of force must still be justified.

As we previously discussed, federal law determines what amount of force, if any, is permitted in self-defense and defense of others regarding attacks on federal property such as national parks, forests and wildlife refuges. In accordance with the principles of self-defense, deadly force can only be used against animals while on federal land when you reasonably believe that the animal poses an imminent threat of death or serious bodily injury to yourself or another. This remains true even when the animal is protected by federal law. Federal statutes expressly allow for the use of deadly force against endangered species and other protected classifications when such force is used in self-defense and defense of others. *See* 16 U.S.C. § 1540(b)(3) (threatened or endangered species); 50 CFR 17.21(c)(2) (endangered species); 50 CFR 17.31(a) (threatened species).

B. *Defense of property against an animal attack*
Property can be categorized as real property or personal property. Land and any improvements on the land would be considered real property. Personal property is generally considered to be movable, as opposed to real property. Livestock, such as cattle and fowl, and domestic animals, such as cats and dogs, are considered personal property. *See* Va. Code § 3.2-6585.

1. Defending personal property from an animal attack
The Supreme Court of Virginia has stated that the owner of personal property in the form of livestock, domestic animals or fowl, has the right to defend them from injury or destruction from an animal attack, but the extent of the defense will depend on the circumstances and necessities of the particular case. The use of force in defense must be reasonably or properly exercised to make it lawful and justifiable. *See Willeroy v. Commonwealth,* 181 Va. 779, 782 (1943).

Each disputed incident involving the killing of an attacking animal will be a question for the judge or jury sitting in judgment to decide. Would a man of ordinary prudence reasonably be led to believe that it was necessary for him to kill the attacking animal to protect his property? There is no hard and fast rule, but such a killing is illegal if the property can be reasonably protected without a killing. *See Breedlove v. Hardy,* 132 Va. 11 (1922).

The Code of Virginia Section 3.2-6552 has further defined what action may be taken against dogs that are endangering livestock or poultry. Any person who finds a dog in the act of killing or injuring livestock or poultry shall have the right to kill such dog on sight as shall any owner of livestock or his agent who finds a dog chasing livestock on land utilized by the livestock when the circumstances show that such chasing is harmful to the livestock.

It is important to exercise caution when using force against any animal because an excessive use of force under the circumstances against any animal resulting in an unnecessary beating or death could trigger a cruelty to animals arrest under Va. Code § 3.2-6570. Along those lines, there is one very important provision of the cruelty to animals law that all property owners must know. The homeowner is entitled to a rare presumption in defense of his dog or cat. If a dog or cat is attacked on its owner's property by a dog so as to cause injury or death, the owner of the injured dog or cat may use all reasonable and necessary force against the dog at the time of the attack to protect his dog or cat. Such owner may be presumed to have taken necessary and appropriate action to defend his dog or cat and shall therefore be presumed not to be in violation, pursuant to Va. Code § 3.2-6570(F).

Federal law does not allow for the use of deadly force against a federally protected animal in order to defend property. If a protected animal is harming your property, including livestock, you may not use deadly force to prevent such harm. The appropriate measure is to either contact the Virginia Department of Game & Inland Fisheries or the U.S. Fish & Wildlife Service, which we discuss in more detail momentarily. Under federal regulations, permits authorizing the killing of the protected animal causing property damage may be issued. *See* 50 CFR 17.22 (endangered animals) and 50 CFR 17.32 (threatened wildlife). If no such permits are issued, the property owner may not kill the animal. The killing of a protected animal, when not in self-defense or pursuant to a lawful permit, is a violation of federal law which carries both civil and criminal penalties. *See* 16 U.S.C. § 1540.

PRACTICAL LEGAL TIP

Beware! Using deadly force against a dog or cat that is only digging into your flowerbed or getting into your garbage may not be justified even under the doctrine of necessity. —*Mitch*

2.   Defending real property from animals

In some instances, various kinds of wildlife animals can either cause damage to, become a nuisance to, or interfere with the enjoyment of a residential homeowner's real property. This can often be seen with wild animals digging through one's garden, trash or banging and pecking into the side of the home to name a few examples. Commercial businesses, agricultural entities and other various types of property owners can also experience animals that cause damage to real property.

The cruelty to animals law pursuant to Va. Code § 3.2-6570(D) shall not prohibit authorized wildlife management activities or hunting, fishing or trapping as regulated under the Code of Virginia.

Caution: There are various wildlife animals that are protected from wildlife management activities, hunting, or fishing under federal and state law.

The best recommendation for the Virginia property owner experiencing wildlife animal nuisance issues to property that are not posing a direct threat to human life, livestock, fowl or domestic animals that we have previously discussed in detail would be to contact the Virginia Department of Game & Inland Fisheries (VDGIF).

The Virginia Department of Game & Inland Fisheries (DGIF.virginia.gov) and the U.S. Fish & Wildlife Service (FWS.gov) investigate, enforce, and regulate wildlife among other responsibilities. Law enforcement officers of VDGIF carry the official title of Conservation Police Officer (formerly known as Game Warden) and are also cross-designated as Deputy U.S. Fish & Wildlife Special Agents to investigate violations of federal wildlife laws.

The VDGIF publishes a list of wildlife animals on its website with detailed instructions on how to prevent and resolve issues with wildlife animals. There are too many wildlife animals with exceptions to go into great detail ranging from bears to groundhogs. Some animals like groundhogs and coyotes are considered nuisance species and can be killed by the property owner at any time. Other animals are considered endangered species that are protected by law and a killing of one would be illegal, as we discussed in the last section. Contact the VDGIF to make sure you understand the law relative to the animal you are having an issue with before you decide to kill the animal.

In some instances, the wildlife animal at issue may be damaging fruit trees, crops, livestock, personal property, or creating a hazard. In cases like this, you should contact your local Conservation Police Officer at the VDGIF and apply for a kill permit to be issued. The Conservation Police Officer will come and investigate to determine if the wildlife animal is responsible for the alleged damage. The Conservation Police Officer may issue the landowner a kill permit that will allow the landowner to kill the wildlife animal when found on the property where the damage occurred. The Virginia Department of Game & Inland Fisheries has created a form called the "Commercial Nuisance Animal Permit." Individuals with a permit must fill out an annual report form, due January 10th of each year, of animals that they have captured, euthanized, released on site, or relocated. Note that the permit does allow for immediate dispatch or killing of these animals when necessary.

However, there are exceptions, and the permit does not apply to all animals. For example, the permittee may not capture, possess, transport, or kill companion animals, including domestic dogs and cats that are owned or feral. Further, the permit does not apply to state or federal threatened or endangered species, protected bird species, black bears, white-tailed deer, and wild turkeys.

For more in-depth information about the permit and the animals it does and does not apply to, please visit DGIF.virginia.gov/forms-download/PERM/PERM-nuisance.pdf.

PRACTICAL LEGAL TIP

It is possible that you may be authorized to kill select animals on your private property without a permit if you have a hunting license and the animal is killed during hunting season. Still, be sure to consult with the Department of Game and Inland Fisheries to ensure that your actions are legal. — *Ed*

CHAPTER EIGHT

THE CONCEALED HANDGUN PERMIT (CHP)

Virginia is a "shall issue" state, which means that a Virginia concealed handgun permit (CHP) shall be issued upon application unless the applicant is otherwise disqualified. *See* Va. Code § 18.2-308.04(C); Va. Code § 18.2-308.09. An issued CHP or *de facto* CHP (a certified pending application) must be carried by the CHP holder if he is carrying a concealed handgun and must be displayed with a photo-identification issued by a government agency of the Commonwealth or by the United States Department of Defense or United States State Department upon demand by a law enforcement officer. *See* Va. Code § 18.2-308.05; Va. Code 18.2-308.01.

PRACTICAL LEGAL TIP

A Concealed Handgun Permit can make you feel safer as you are out and about. But remember, a CHP is a license to protect against trouble—not a license to go looking for it! — *Mitch*

Virginia has two types of CHPs: a CHP for residents and a CHP for nonresidents. Virginia resident CHPs are issued by the circuit court of the county or city in which the applicant resides. Nonresident CHPs are issued by the Virginia State Police (VSP).

Va. Code § 18.2-308.016 grants retired law enforcement an exception to the CHP requirement, which allows for concealed carry without a CHP if certain procedures are followed.

I.   Application for resident CHP process
Any person 21 years of age or older may apply in writing to the clerk of the circuit court of the county or city in which he or she resides, or if he is a member of the United States Armed Forces, the county or city in which he is domiciled, for a five-year permit to carry a concealed handgun. There is no requirement as to the length of time an applicant for a CHP must have been a resident or domiciliary of

the county or city where he or she resides. *See* Va. Code § 18.2-308.02. It is suggested that the applicant check with the Circuit Court where they reside for any local procedures. Questions specific to completion of the application, residency, or acceptable proof of handgun competency should be directed to the court.

PRACTICAL LEGAL TIP

Va. Code §18.2-308.06 allows non-residents who are otherwise qualified to obtain a Virginia nonresident Concealed Handgun Permit . — *Ed*

A. *Documentation of proof of handgun competency*
The court shall require proof that the applicant has demonstrated competence with a handgun and the applicant may demonstrate such competence by one of the following:

- Completing any hunter education or hunter safety course approved by the Department of Game & Inland Fisheries or a similar agency of another state;
- Completing any National Rifle Association firearms safety or training course;
- Completing any firearms safety or training course or class available to the general public offered by a law enforcement agency, junior college, college, or private or public institution or organization or firearms training school utilizing instructors certified by the National Rifle Association or the Department of Criminal Justice Services;
- Completing any law enforcement firearms safety or training course or class offered for security guards, investigators, special deputies, or any division or subdivision of law enforcement or security enforcement;
- Presenting evidence of equivalent experience with a firearm through participation in organized shooting competition or current military service or proof of an honorable discharge from any branch of the armed services;
- Obtaining or previously having held a license to carry a firearm in this Commonwealth or a locality thereof, unless

such license has been revoked for cause;

- Completing any firearms training or safety course or class, including an electronic, video, or on-line course, conducted by a state-certified or National Rifle Association-certified firearms instructor;
- Completing any governmental police agency firearms training course and qualifying to carry a firearm in the course of normal police duties; or
- Completing any other firearms training which the court deems adequate. *See* Va. Code § 18.2-308.2.

A photocopy of a certificate of completion of any of the courses or classes; an affidavit from the instructor, school, club, organization, or group that conducted or taught such course or class attesting to the completion of the course or class by the applicant; or a copy of any document which shows completion of the course or class or evidences participation in firearms competition, shall constitute evidence of qualification under this subsection.

No applicant shall be required to submit to any additional demonstration of competence, nor shall any proof of demonstrated competence expire.

B. *Fees and issuance of the CHP*
The court shall charge a fee of $10 for the processing of an application or issuing of a permit. Local law enforcement agencies may charge a fee not to exceed $35 to cover the cost of conducting an investigation pursuant to Va. Code § 18.2-308.03. The VSP may charge a fee not to exceed $5 to cover the cost associated with processing the application. The total amount of the charges may not exceed $50, and payment may be made by any method accepted by the court. Certain classes of individuals are exempt from this fee. The court shall issue the permit within 45 days of receipt of the completed application unless it appears that the applicant is disqualified. *See* Va. Code § 18.2-308.03; Va. Code §18.2-308.04.

C. *Application is not complete within 45 days*
If the court has not issued the permit or determined that the applicant is disqualified within 45 days of the date of receipt noted on the application, then the clerk shall certify on the application that the 45-day period has expired, and send a copy of the certified ap-

plication to the applicant. The certified application shall serve as a *de facto* permit, which shall expire 90 days after issuance, and shall be recognized as a valid concealed handgun permit when presented with a valid government-issued photo identification until the court issues a five-year permit or finds the applicant to be disqualified. If the applicant is found to be disqualified after the *de facto* permit is issued, the applicant shall surrender the *de facto* permit to the court and the disqualification shall be deemed a denial of the permit and a revocation of the *de facto* permit. If the applicant is later found by the court to be disqualified after a five-year permit has been issued, the permit shall be revoked. *See* Va. Code § 18.2-308.05.

D. *CHP renewal*
Persons who previously have held a Virginia resident permit shall be issued, upon application, a new five-year permit unless there is good cause shown for refusing to reissue a permit. The same fees and time constraints apply in the instance of renewal. Persons who previously have been issued a concealed handgun permit are not required to appear in person to apply for a new five-year permit; the application for the new permit may be submitted via the United States mail. The circuit court that receives the application shall promptly notify the applicant if the application is incomplete or if the fee submitted is incorrect. *See* Va. Code § 18.2-308.10.

If the new five-year permit is issued while an existing permit remains valid, the new five-year permit shall become effective upon the expiration date of the existing permit, provided that the application is received by the court at least 90 days but no more than 180 days prior to the expiration of the existing permit.

If a permit holder is a member of the Virginia National Guard, Armed Forces of the United States, or the Armed Forces Reserves of the United States, and his five-year permit expires during an active-duty military deployment outside of the permittee's county or city of residence, such permit shall remain valid for 90 days after the end date of the deployment.

In order to establish proof of continued validity of the permit, such a permittee shall carry with him and display, upon request of a law enforcement officer, a copy of the permittee's deployment orders or other documentation from the permittee's commanding officer that order the permittee to travel outside of his county or city of residence and that indicate the start and end date of such deployment.

E.   *Change of address and replacement CHPs*
The clerk of a circuit court who issued a valid CHP shall, upon presentation of the valid CHP and proof of a new address of residence by the CHP holder, issue a replacement CHP specifying the CHP holder's new address. The total amount assessed for processing a replacement CHP due to a change of address shall not exceed $10, with such fees to be paid in one sum to the person who accepts the information for the replacement CHP. *See* Va. Code § 18.2-308.11.

The clerk of a circuit court who issued a valid CHP shall, upon submission of a notarized statement by the CHP holder who the CHP was lost or destroyed or that the CHP holder has undergone a legal name change, issue a replacement CHP. The replacement CHP shall have the same expiration date as the CHP that was lost, destroyed, or issued to the CHP holder under a previous name. The clerk shall issue the replacement CHP within ten business days of receiving the notarized statement and may charge a fee not to exceed $5.

F.   *Denied CHP applications*
Only a circuit court judge may deny issuance of a CHP to a Virginia resident or domiciliary who has applied for a CHP pursuant to Va. Code § 18.2-308.04. Any order denying issuance of a CHP shall state the basis for the denial of the CHP and shall provide notice in writing to the applicant that the CHP application was denied along with notice that the applicant may request a hearing to appeal the decision to deny issuance of the CHP. *See* Va. Code § 18.2-308.08.

The applicant may appeal a denied CHP application within 21 days. The court shall place the matter on the docket for a hearing. The applicant may be represented by counsel, but counsel shall not be appointed, and the rules of evidence shall apply. The final order of the court shall include the court's findings of fact and conclusions of law.

Any applicant denied a CHP may present a petition for review to the Virginia Court of Appeals. The petition for review shall be filed within 60 days of the expiration of the time for requesting a hearing pursuant to Va. Code § 18.2-308.08(C) or if a hearing was requested, then within 60 days of the entry of the final order of the circuit court following the hearing. The petition shall be accompanied by a copy of the original papers filed in the circuit court, including a copy of the order of the circuit court denying the CHP. According to Va. Code § 17.1-410, the decision of the Virginia Court of Appeals shall be final. If the decision to deny the CHP is reversed on appeal, then taxable costs incurred by the applicant shall be paid by the Commonwealth.

G. _Revocation or suspension of a CHP_
Pursuant to Va. § Code 18.2-308.013 any CHP holder convicted of an offense that would disqualify that person from obtaining a CHP or who makes a materially false statement in a CHP application shall forfeit his CHP and surrender it to the court. Persons disqualified from obtaining a CHP are discussed later in section III of this chapter. _See_ also Va. Code § 18.2-308.09; Va. Code § 18.2-308.02(C).

Any CHP holder who has a felony charge pending or a charge of any assault, assault and battery, sexual battery, discharging a firearm, brandishing a firearm, or stalking may have the CHP suspended by the court before which such charge is pending or by the court that issued the CHP.

The court shall revoke the CHP of any individual who has been adjudicated legally incompetent, mentally incapacitated, incapacitated, or any individual who has been involuntarily admitted to a facility or ordered to mandatory outpatient treatment as explained in Va. Code § 18.2-308.1:3 or to any individual who was the subject of a temporary detention and subsequently agreed to voluntary admission. Virginia Code § 64.2-2000 defines an "incapacitated person" as an adult who has been found by a court to be incapable of receiving and evaluating information effectively or responding to people, events, or environments to such an extent that the individual lacks the capacity to meet the essential requirements for his health, care, safety, or therapeutic needs without the assistance or protection of a guardian, or to manage property or financial affairs or provide for his support or for the support of his legal dependents without the assistance or protection of a conservator. _See_ Va. Code §37.2-809; Va. Code § 37.2-805.

Any CHP holder who becomes subject to a protective order pursuant to Va. Code § 18.2-308.1:4 shall be prohibited from carrying any concealed firearm and shall surrender his CHP to the court entering the order for the duration of any protective order.

Pursuant to Va. Code § 18.2-308.012, any CHP holder who is convicted of being under the influence of alcohol or illegal drugs while carrying such handgun in a public place shall have his CHP revoked. Such person shall be ineligible to apply for a CHP for a period of five years.

II. Application for nonresident CHP process

Nonresidents of Virginia who are 21 years of age or older may apply in writing to the VSP for a five-year permit to carry a concealed handgun. The application shall be made under oath before a notary or other person qualified to take oaths on a form provided by the VSP requiring only that information necessary to determine eligibility for the permit. Every applicant for a nonresident CHP shall submit two photographs of a type and kind specified by the VSP for inclusion on the CHP and shall submit fingerprints on a card provided by the VSP for the purpose of obtaining the applicant's state or national criminal history record. The applicant shall submit to fingerprinting by his local or state law enforcement agency using the provided VSP fingerprint cards. The applicant must provide a legible photocopy of a valid photo ID issued by a governmental agency. The VSP may charge a fee not to exceed $100 to cover the cost of the background check and issuance of the CHP.

A Virginia nonresident CHP may be necessary for residents of other states who have a CHP issued from a state that Virginia law does not recognize as valid for purposes of carrying a concealed firearm in Virginia. We will discuss the reciprocity of the CHP later in this chapter.

A. *Documentation of proof of handgun competency*
Proper documentation regarding proof of handgun competency was previously discussed in Section I of this chapter. The same documentation applies to nonresident applicants as Virginia resident applicants except that the VSP, as opposed the court, may deem other training as adequate. *See* Va. Code §18.2-308.06(B).

B. *CHP renewal*
The renewal process is identical to the processes and costs associated with the original permit with the exception of proof of compe-

tence with a handgun. New photos and fingerprint impressions will be required. It is suggested that all renewal application packages be submitted at least 60 days prior to expiration of the existing permit. Request a packet for the renewal process by contacting the VSP Firearms Transaction Center (FTC) at nonrespermit@vsp.virginia.gov.

C. *Change of address*
Nonresident CHP holders are requested to notify the VSP Firearms Transaction Center of changes of address. Notification may be made in writing to the FTC at P.O. Box 85141, Richmond, VA, 23285-5141 or nonrespermit@vsp.virginia.gov, and must include the CHP file number or a photocopy of the CHP. A change of address card will be provided to the CHP holder to be retained with the original CHP.

D. *Replacement CHP*
A replacement CHP may be requested in writing addressed to the FTC at P.O. Box 85141, Richmond, VA, 23285-5141. All requests for replacement must include a cashier's check or money order in the amount of $5 made payable to the VSP, a photograph and one of the following:

- the CHP file number
- a photocopy of the CHP
- a photocopy of a valid photo-ID issued by a governmental agency

A replacement CHP will have the same expiration date as the permit originally issued.

E. *CHP revocation*
If the applicant is later found by the VSP to be disqualified, then the CHP shall be revoked and the CHP holder shall return the CHP after being so notified by the VSP. *See* Va. Code § 18.2-308.06(A).

F. *Appeal procedure*
If you are denied a nonresident concealed handgun permit and do not believe that you have a previous conviction or other disqualification that renders you ineligible, you may contact the VSP Firearms Transaction Center to discuss the ineligible determination and/or to provide additional information deemed pertinent to the final determination of eligibility.

Any person denied a permit and not satisfied with the explanation provided by the Firearms Transaction Center may appeal such denial to the Superintendent of the VSP provided that any such action is initiated within 30 days of the denial by the State Police. Such appeal must be in writing setting forth any grounds that the applicant wishes to be considered. The Superintendent of VSP shall consider each such appeal, and will notify the applicant in writing of his decision within five business days after the day on which the appeal is received.

III. Disqualified individuals ineligible to obtain a CHP

Virginia Code § 18.2-308.09 lists individuals who are disqualified from obtaining either a Virginia resident CHP or a Virginia nonresident CHP as follows:

1. An individual who was acquitted of any felony and most misdemeanor criminal offenses as explained in Va. Code § 18.2-308.1:1 by reason of insanity and committed to the custody of Behavioral Health and Developmental Services, or who has been adjudicated legally incompetent, mentally incapacitated, incapacitated, or has been involuntarily admitted to a facility or ordered to mandatory outpatient treatment as explained in Va. Code § 18.2-308.1:3 or who was the subject of a temporary detention and subsequently agreed to voluntary admission. *See* Va. Code § 37.2-809; Va. Code § 37.2-805. These disqualifications also apply to substantially similar laws of the United States or any other state.

2. An individual who was acquitted of any felony and most misdemeanor criminal offenses as explained in Va. Code § 18.2-308.1:1 by reason of insanity and committed to the custody of Behavioral Health and Developmental Services and was discharged from custody less than five years before the date of his CHP application.

3. An individual who was has been adjudicated legally incompetent, mentally incapacitated, or incapacitated and whose competency or capacity was restored less than five years before the date of his CHP application.

4. An individual who was involuntarily admitted to a facility or ordered to mandatory outpatient treatment as explained in Va. Code § 18.2-308.1:3, or who was the subject of a temporary detention and subsequently agreed to voluntary admission and who was released from commitment

less than five years before the date of his CHP application.

5. An individual who is subject to a restraining order or to a protective order and is prohibited from purchasing or transporting a firearm pursuant to Va. Code § 18.2-308.1:4.

6. An individual who has been convicted of a felony; or an individual who was once adjudicated delinquent as a juvenile at 14 years of age or older at the time of the offense for the offenses of either murder, kidnapping, robbery by the threat or presentation of a firearm, or rape; or an individual under the age of 29 who was once adjudicated delinquent as a juvenile at 14 years of age or older at the time of the offense for a delinquent act which would be a felony if committed by an adult, whether such conviction or adjudication occurred under the laws of Virginia, another state, the District of Columbia, or the United States or any territory thereof unless such individual may now lawfully possess or carry a firearm after successfully petitioning the applicable circuit court.

7. An individual who has been convicted of two or more misdemeanors within the five-year period immediately preceding the CHP application, if one of the misdemeanors was a Class 1 misdemeanor, but the judge shall have the discretion to deny a CHP for two or more misdemeanors that are not Class 1 misdemeanors. Traffic infractions and misdemeanors set forth in the Motor Vehicle Code pursuant to Title 46.2, such as reckless driving, shall not be considered for purposes of this disqualification.

8. An individual who is addicted to, or is an unlawful user or distributor of, marijuana, synthetic cannabinoids, or any controlled substance.

9. An individual who has been convicted of driving under the influence or a substantially similar local ordinance, or of public drunkenness, or of a substantially similar offense under the laws of any other state, the District of Columbia, the United States, or its territories within the three-year period immediately preceding the CHP application, or who is a habitual drunkard as determined pursuant to Va. Code § 4.1-333.

10. An alien other than an alien lawfully admitted for permanent residence in the United States.

11. An individual who has been discharged from the Armed

Forces of the United States under dishonorable conditions.

12. An individual who is a fugitive from justice.

13. An individual who the court finds, by a preponderance of the evidence, based on specific acts by the CHP applicant, is likely to use a weapon unlawfully or negligently to endanger others. The sheriff, chief of police, or attorney for the Commonwealth may submit to the court a sworn, written statement indicating that, in the opinion of such sheriff, chief of police, or attorney for the Commonwealth, based upon a disqualifying conviction or upon the specific acts set forth in the statement, the CHP applicant is likely to use a weapon unlawfully or negligently to endanger others. The statement of the sheriff, chief of police, or the attorney for the Commonwealth shall be based upon personal knowledge of such individual or of a deputy sheriff, police officer, or assistant attorney for the Commonwealth of the specific acts, or upon a written statement made under oath before a notary public of a competent person having personal knowledge of the specific acts.

14. An individual who has been convicted of any assault, assault and battery, sexual battery, discharging of a firearm or brandishing of a firearm within the three-year period immediately preceding the CHP application.

15. An individual who has been convicted of stalking.

16. An individual whose previous convictions or adjudications of delinquency were based on an offense that would have been at the time of conviction a felony if committed by an adult under the laws of any state, the District of Columbia, the United States or its territories. For purposes of this disqualifier, only convictions occurring within 16 years following the later of the date of (i) the conviction or adjudication or (ii) release from any incarceration imposed upon such conviction or adjudication shall be deemed to be "previous convictions." Disqualification under this subdivision shall not apply to an individual with previous adjudications of delinquency who has completed a term of service of no less than two years in the Armed Forces of the United States and, if such person has been discharged from the Armed Forces of the United States, received an honorable discharge.

17. An individual who has a felony charge pending or a charge of

any assault, assault and battery, sexual battery, discharging of a firearm, brandishing of a firearm, or stalking pending.

18. An individual who has received mental health treatment or substance abuse treatment in a residential setting within five years prior to the date of his CHP application.

19. An individual who was found guilty of any criminal offense set forth in Title 18.2, Chapter 7, Article 1 of the Code of Virginia, which include drug and drug related offenses, or of a criminal offense of illegal possession or distribution of marijuana or any controlled substance, under the laws of any state, the District of Columbia, or the United States or its territories within the three-year period immediately preceding the CHP application.

20. An individual whose first offense or drug offense was disposed of pursuant to Va. Code § 18.2-251 or the substantially similar law of any other state, the District of Columbia, or the United States or its territories within the three-year period immediately preceding the CHP application.

IV. CHP reciprocity

CHP reciprocity is the recognition or honoring of a concealed carry license or permit that was issued by another state. In 2015, the Virginia Attorney General announced that Virginia would be terminating CHP reciprocity agreements with 25 states. This caused quite a stir to say the least. In the end, Virginia did not terminate its CHP reciprocity agreements. We mention this because CHP reciprocity agreements are subject to change at any time due to the nature of politics. The VSP website maintains a CHP reciprocity and recognition list for convenience, but it is always a good idea to confirm the other state's recognition or lack thereof regarding your Virginia resident or nonresident CHP if you will be travelling through another state and expect that the other state will recognize your Virginia CHP.

Effective July 1, 2016, the holder of a valid CHP issued by another state may carry a concealed handgun in Virginia provided:
- the holder of such permit or license is at least 21 years of age;
- the permit or license holder carries a photo identification issued by a government agency of any state or by the U.S. Department of Defense or U.S. Department of State;
- the holder displays the permit or license and such identifi-

cation upon demand by a law enforcement officer;

- the issuing authority maintains the means for instantaneous verification of the validity of all such permits or licenses issued within that state accessible 24 hours a day; and
- the permit or license holder has not previously had a Virginia concealed handgun permit revoked. *See* Va. Code § 18.2-308.014.

Jurisdiction	Limitations
Alabama	
Alaska	
Arizona	
Arkansas	
Colorado	Virginia Resident Permits Only
Florida	Virginia Resident Permits Only
Idaho	
Indiana	
Iowa	
Kansas	
Kentucky	
Louisiana	
Maine	Virginia Resident Permits Only
Michigan	Virginia Resident Permits Only
Mississippi	
Missouri	
Montana	
Nebraska	
Nevada	
New Hampshire	Resident Permits Only
New Mexico	
North Carolina	
North Dakota	
Ohio	
Oklahoma	
Pennsylvania	Virginia Resident Permits Only
South Carolina	
South Dakota	
Tennessee	
Texas	
Utah	
West Virginia	
Wisconsin	Virginia Nonresident Permits Only
Wyoming	

States that recognize Virginia CHP permits effective 7/1/2016.

CHAPTER NINE

LAW OF OPEN CARRY AND CONCEALED CARRY & PROHIBITIONS

I. Introduction

We have previously discussed that the constitutional right to bear arms is not an absolute right, that certain classes of individuals are prohibited from purchasing and possessing firearms, and that the government has the authority to regulate firearms under certain circumstances. In this chapter, we discuss the law of open carry, concealed carry, and where the federal and Virginia law regulates the possession, carrying, and transportation of firearms on certain premises.

II. Virginia is an open carry state

A person's right to carry a firearm openly is considered universal in Virginia, subject to definite and limited restrictions upon certain locations and classifications of individuals. *See* 43 Op. Att'y Gen. 4 (2008). If you are at least 18 years old and not otherwise prohibited from possessing a firearm, then you may openly carry a loaded firearm in public without a license or a concealed handgun permit (CHP); however, there are exceptions. *See* also Schaaf v. Commonwealth, 220 Va. 429, 433 (1979).

Open carry on private property is different. Any private party can either regulate or ban firearms on their property, even property leased from the government. *See* 23 Op. Att'y Gen. 4 (2011); 9 Op. Att'y Gen. 1,3 (2010). If a private property owner or responsible person asks an open carry individual to leave, then that individual must leave or he may be prosecuted for trespassing pursuant to Va. Code § 18.2-119, which is punishable by up to 12 months in jail and a $2,500 fine. A firearm may also be openly carried in either a personal, private motor vehicle or vessel if the firearm is openly and plainly visible.

Virginia Code § 15.2-915.2 creates an open carry exception for loaded shotguns and rifles in vehicles traveling on public highways. This law allows for any county or city to pass an ordinance that makes it unlawful for any person to transport, possess or carry a loaded shotgun or loaded rifle in any vehicle on any public street, road, or highway within such locality. However, this section shall neither apply to law enforcement or military personnel in the performance of their lawful duties nor to any person who reasonably believes that a loaded rifle or shotgun is necessary for his personal safety in the course of his employment or business. Any violation of such ordinance shall be punishable by a fine of not more than $100.

Virginia Code § 18.2-287.4 creates another open carry exception regarding the carrying of a loaded assault firearm in public in certain jurisdictions. Virginia Code § 18.2-308.7 states that it is unlawful for any person to carry a loaded assault firearm on or about his person on any public street, road, alley, sidewalk, public right-of-way, or in any public park or any other place of whatever nature that is open to the public in the Cities of Alexandria, Chesapeake, Fairfax, Falls Church, Newport News, Norfolk, Richmond, or Virginia Beach or in the Counties of Arlington, Fairfax, Henrico, Loudoun, or Prince William. A violation of this section is a misdemeanor punishable by up to 12 months in jail and a $2,500 fine; however, this does not apply to any person having a valid CHP, law enforcement, licensed security guards, military personnel in the performance of their lawful duties, or to any person actually engaged in lawful hunting, or lawful recreational shooting activities at an established shooting range or shooting contest.

There are other exceptions that limit a person's ability to open carry that we will also discuss in this chapter along with firearm restrictions that prohibit all firearms from various premises.

III.   Law of concealed carry of a firearm
Concealed carry of a firearm is significantly more restrictive than open carry of a firearm. Concealed carry of a firearm refers to the practice of carrying a firearm in a concealed or hidden manner, either on one's person or in close proximity. Virginia Code § 18.2-308(A) defines concealed carry, as it relates to a firearm, as any person who carries about his person any pistol, revolver, or other weapon designed or intended to propel a missile of any kind by action of an explosion of any combustible material, hidden from common observation. Hidden from common observation includes when the firearm is observable, but is of such a deceptive appearance as to disguise the firearm's true nature. A first violation of this law is a misdemeanor punishable by up to 12 months in jail and/or a $2,500

fine. Second and third violations of this law are felonies and are punishable by up to 5 and 10 years in prison, respectively, both with fines of up to $2,500. Law enforcement will also confiscate the firearm for a violation.

Concealed carry of any firearm is permissible for a limited number of very specific reasons as determined by the Virginia State Legislature. *See* Va. Code § 18.2-308(B)(C). If one of these specific reasons to carry a concealed firearm does not apply to you, then you may only carry a concealed handgun with a CHP if not otherwise prohibited by law or the owner of private property. *See* Va. Code § 18.2-308.1(C).

The following are allowed to carry any concealed firearm without a CHP if not otherwise prohibited by law:

- any person while in his own place of abode or on the curtilage;
- any person while in his own place of business;
- any person who may lawfully possess a firearm and is carrying a handgun while in a personal, private motor vehicle or vessel and such handgun is secured in a container or compartment in the vehicle or vessel; *See* also Doulgerakis v. Commonwealth, 61 Va. App. 417 (2013); 11-111 Op. Att'y Gen. 3 (2012);
- any law enforcement officer or retired law enforcement officer pursuant to Va. Code § 18.2-308.016;
- any person who is at, or going to or from, an established shooting range, provided that the weapons are unloaded and securely wrapped while being transported;
- any enrolled participant of a firearms training course who is at, or going to or from, a training location, provided that the weapons are unloaded and securely wrapped while being transported;
- any regularly enrolled member of a weapons collecting organization who is at, or going to or from, a bona fide weapons exhibition, provided that the weapons are unloaded and securely wrapped while being transported;
- any person carrying such weapons between his place of abode and a place of purchase or repair, provided the weapons are unloaded and securely wrapped while being transported;

- any person actually engaged in lawful hunting, as authorized by the Department of Game & Inland Fisheries, under inclement weather conditions necessitating temporary protection of his firearm from those conditions, provided that possession of a handgun while engaged in lawful hunting shall not be construed as hunting with a handgun if the person hunting is carrying a valid concealed handgun permit;
- any attorney for the Commonwealth or assistant attorney for the Commonwealth;
- any judge of the Commonwealth;
- certain individuals while in the discharge of their official duties or while in transit to or from such duties as follows:
  o carriers of the United States mail;
  o officers or guards of any state correctional institution;
  o conservators of the peace; or
  o noncustodial employees of the Department of Corrections designated to carry weapons by the Director of the Department of Corrections pursuant to Va. Code § 53.1-29.

IV. Firearm prohibitions by premises

Federal law and Virginia law prohibit firearms from being possessed on certain premises. Generally, premises are land and buildings together considered as a property; however, the legal definition of premises can vary based on the law that is restricting or banning the firearm. As we will see, the law completely bans the possession of all firearms on certain premises, but there are some exceptions where it is lawful to either open carry or conceal carry a handgun with a CHP.

A. *Private property*

As we previously discussed, any private party can ban the open carry of firearms on its property. *See also* 23 Op. Att'y Gen. 4 (2011); 9 Op. Att'y Gen. 1,3 (2010). A private party can also ban the carrying of a concealed handgun with a CHP. *See* Va. Code § 18.2-308.01 (C). The Second Amendment acts as a restraint on government, not private parties. *See* Op. Att'y Gen. 4 (2011).

B. *Restaurants and clubs that serve alcoholic beverages*

Virginia Code § 18.2-308.012 states that no person who carries a concealed handgun with a CHP onto the premises of any restaurant or club as defined in Va. Code § 4.1-100 that has an Alcoholic Beverage Control license to sell and serve alcoholic beverages on-premises may consume an alcoholic beverage while on the premises. A violation of this section is a misdemeanor punishable by six months in jail and/or a $1,000 fine. This law does not apply to law enforcement.

Remember, as we previously discussed in Chapter 8, any CHP holder who is convicted for being under the influence of alcohol or illegal drugs while carrying such handgun in a public place shall have his CHP revoked. Such person shall be ineligible to apply for a CHP for a period of five years under Va. Code § 18.2-308.012.

C. *Place of employment*
A private employer may prohibit firearms in the workplace and may ban firearms on its private property. Such a prohibition includes storing a firearm in one's vehicle at a place of employment if there is a company policy or signage prohibiting firearms on the premises. It is recommended that all gun owners understand their employer's position on firearms before taking any firearm into their place of employment. *See* Op. Att'y Gen. 1 (May 25, 2012).

Federal and state employees are prohibited from possessing firearms in their government building workplaces unless an exception applies.

A local government employer may adopt workplace rules that restrict or prohibit firearms; however, no local government employer shall adopt any workplace rule that prevents an employee of that local government from storing at that local government's workplace a lawfully possessed firearm and ammunition in a locked private motor vehicle. *See* Va. Code § 15.2-915.

D. *Courts and government buildings*
   1. Courthouses
Virginia Code § 18.2-283.1 states that it is unlawful for any person to possess a firearm or to transport a firearm into any courthouse. A violation of this section is a misdemeanor punishable up to 12 months in jail and a $2,500 fine. However, this section shall not apply to law enforcement and other officials, any police officer, sheriff, law enforcement agent or official, conservation police officer, conservator of the peace, magistrate, court officer, judge, or city or county treasurer while in the conduct of such person's official

duties. Under federal law, it is unlawful to knowingly possess a firearm or cause a firearm to be present in a federal court facility. A violation of the federal law is punishable by imprisonment of up to two years. *See* 18 U.S.C. § 930.

2. Government buildings
    Federal buildings
Federal law prohibits anyone from knowingly possessing a firearm or causing a firearm to be present in a federal facility, such as a prison, VA hospital, post office or military installation. A violation is punishable by imprisonment of no more than one year. If the firearm is used in the commission of a crime or is intended to be used in the commission of a crime in a federal facility, then the violation is punishable by imprisonment of up to five years. *See* 18 U.S.C. § 930.

Veterans Affairs Hospitals

> *"No person while on property shall carry firearms, other dangerous or deadly weapons, or explosives, either openly or concealed, except for official purposes."* See 38 CFR § 1.218(a)(13).

One place where many law-abiding CHP holders fall victim is at the VA Hospital. The VA Hospital system is governed by federal law which prohibits the carrying of any firearm while on VA property. This includes the parking lot, sidewalk, and any other area which is the property of the VA.

The "official purposes" specified above refers specifically to the VA Hospital Police. The area where this specific law gets good people in trouble is that the Department of Veterans Affairs has its own set of laws and guidelines and is not controlled strictly by the Gun Control Act and the general provisions regarding the prohibition of firearms on federal property. The VA law is much more restrictive, and many veterans have found themselves in trouble when they valet-park their vehicle and the valet discovers a concealed handgun in the console or concealed in the door storage area. How rigidly this law is enforced is determined by the individual hospital administrators as described in 38 CFR § 1.218(a). However, regardless of how strictly the law is enforced, firearms are still prohibited under the federal law and the VA police can be very aggressive with enforcement.

United States Post Offices

"Notwithstanding the provisions of any other law, rule or regulation, no person while on postal property may carry firearms, other dangerous or deadly weapons, or explosives, either openly or concealed, or store the same on postal property, except for official purposes." See 39 CFR § 232.1(l).

Under this federal regulation, firearms are prohibited on postal property which includes not only the building, but all property surrounding the building where a post office is located. This includes the parking lot (*e.g.,* a person's vehicle where a firearm may be stored), as well as the sidewalks and walkways.

Military bases and installations
Military bases and installations are treated much like the VA Hospital and U.S. Post Offices in that they have and are governed by a separate set of rules and regulations with respect to firearms on the premises of an installation or base and are generally prohibited. Military installations are governed by the federal law under Title 32 of the Code of Federal Regulations. Moreover, the sections covering the laws governing and relating to military bases and installations are exceedingly numerous. There are, in fact, sections which are dedicated to only certain bases or installations.

Virginia buildings
Firearms are prohibited in Virginia state government executive branch offices and workplace facilities, such as the Department of Motor Vehicles (DMV), Alcohol Beverage Control (ABC) retail stores, and any Department of Corrections facility. This prohibition does not apply to law enforcement officers, authorized security personnel, or military personnel, when such individuals are authorized to carry a firearm in accordance with their duties, and when they are carrying the firearm within that authority. It also does not apply to state employees where the employee's position requires carrying a concealed firearm. *See* Exec. Order No. 50 (Oct. 15, 2015); 1VAC30-105. This concealed-carry regulation also does not apply to individuals who are on public hunting lands and are engaged in lawful hunting according to the Department of Game and Inland Fisheries' Hunting and Trapping regulations found in 4VAC15. A state institution of higher education is exempt from this regulation if the insti-

tution has implemented its own policies or regulations governing firearms under 1VAC30-105.

However, it is important to note that the concealed carry prohibition pursuant to 1VAC30-105 is effective from December 3, 2015, through June 3, 2017, and that the open carry prohibition pursuant to Governor Terry McAuliffe's Executive Order 50 may be reversed by future administrations.

Firearms are prohibited in Virginia General Assembly buildings except for legislators, law enforcement, and CHP holders pursuant to a Joint Rules Committee rule. The state Senate also bars a variety of weapons in the gallery, whether or not the owner has a CHP.

As we previously discussed, a locality may adopt workplace rules that restrict or prohibit firearms at the workplace. Additionally, any local or regional jail or juvenile detention facility may adopt and enforce a firearms ordinance. *See* Va. Code § 15.2-915.

E.   *Elementary, middle and high schools*
Firearms are restricted in public, parochial and private schools according to federal and Virginia law. Virginia Code § 18.2-308.1 prohibits anyone from knowingly possessing any firearm while such person is upon:

    i.   any public, private or religious elementary, middle, or high school, including buildings and grounds;
    ii.   that portion of any property open to the public and then exclusively used for school-sponsored functions or extra-curricular activities while such functions or activities are taking place; or
    iii.   any school bus owned or operated by any such school.

A violation of this section is a felony punishable by up to five years in prison and a $2,500 fine. However, this section does not apply to:

    i.   a person who has a valid CHP and possesses a concealed handgun while in a motor vehicle in a parking lot, traffic circle, or other means of vehicular ingress or egress to the school;
    ii.   any law enforcement officer;

iii. an unloaded firearm that is in a closed container in or upon a motor vehicle;

iv. unloaded shotguns or rifles in or upon a motor vehicle in a firearms rack in or upon a motor vehicle;

v. an armed security officer hired by a private or religious school for the protection of students and employees as authorized by such school.

The Gun-Free School Zones Act (GFSZA) prohibits any person from knowingly possessing a firearm that has moved in or otherwise affects interstate or foreign commerce at a place the individual knows, or has reasonable cause to believe, is a school zone. The GFSZA also prohibits any person from knowingly, or with reckless disregard for the safety of another, discharging or attempting to discharge a firearm that has moved in or otherwise affects interstate or foreign commerce at a place the person knows is a school zone. *See* 18 U.S.C. § 922(q)(2)(A). The GFSZA defines "school zone" as: 1) in, or on the grounds of, a public, parochial or private school; or 2) within a distance of 1,000 feet from the grounds of a public, parochial or private school. *See* 18 U.S.C. § 921(a)(25). Exceptions to the possession prohibition include:

- if the individual possessing the firearm has a Virginia-issued CHP (*see* 18 U.S.C. § 922(q)(2)(B)(ii)); or
- where the firearm is:
  o unloaded and in a locked container or locked firearms rack on a motor vehicle (*see* 18 U.S.C. § 922(q)(2)(B)(iii)); or
  o unloaded and possessed while traversing school premises for the purpose of gaining access to public or private lands open to hunting, if the entry on school premises is authorized by school authorities. *See* 18 U.S.C. § 922(q)(2)(B)(vii).

Exceptions to both the possession and discharge bans include:

- possession of a firearm on private property not part of school grounds (*see* 18 U.S.C. § 922(q)(3)(B)(i); 18 U.S.C. § 922(q)(2)(B)(i));
- where the firearm is possessed for use in a program approved by a school held in the school zone, or in accordance

with a contract entered into between a school and the individual or an employer of the individual (*see* 18 U.S.C. § 922(q)(3)(B)(ii)(iii); 18 U.S.C. § 922(q)(2)(B)(iv)(v)); or

- where the firearm is possessed or used by a law enforcement officer acting in his or her official capacity. *See* 18 U.S.C. § 922(q).

The Virginia Gun-Free Schools Act (GFSA) requires each local elementary or secondary educational agency requesting financial assistance from the state educational agency charged with receiving and distributing federal funds to expel any student for bringing a firearm to school or possessing a firearm at school, to include school-sponsored events and activities, even those held off school grounds. The chief administering officer of a local educational agency is allowed to modify an expulsion for a student, in writing, on a case-by-case basis. *See* 21 U.S.C. § 7151.

Furthermore, the GFSA provides that a state may allow a local educational agency that has expelled a student from the student's regular school setting to provide an alternative educational setting, but a referral to the criminal justice or juvenile delinquency system is required. The exception to the GFSA permits firearm possession where the firearm is lawfully stored inside a locked vehicle on school property, or where the gun is possessed for an activity approved and authorized by the local educational agency, if the agency has adopted appropriate safeguards to ensure student safety.

F.   *Universities and colleges*
Private universities, like any other owner of private property, may restrict or ban the carrying of weapons onto their property. The Second Amendment acts as a restraint on government, not private parties. *See* 23 Op Att'y Gen. 4 (2011). It is recommended that all gun owners review a private university's firearm policy before taking any firearm onto any private university's property.

Most of the public universities and colleges in Virginia have very similar firearm regulations, which include prohibitions to the carrying of firearms in school buildings and at school events. Each university or college's weapon policy is published in the Virginia Administrative Code under Title 8 by the respective agency. According to Virginia Attorney General Opinion 78 (2006), a public university cannot generally prohibit firearms on campus. However, a public university can prohibit students and university employees from carrying firearms on campus, even if those individuals hold a CHP, since specific statutes grant a public university authority to regulate the conduct of students and university employees.

The Supreme Court of Virginia has held that a public university can regulate and restrict the possession and carrying of firearms inside public campus buildings and at campus events. The court pointed out that such a regulation was tailored, restricting weapons only in those places where people congregate and are most vulnerable. Individuals could still carry or possess weapons on the open grounds of the university, and in other places on campus not enumerated in the regulation. *See Digiacinto v. The Rector & Visitors of George Mason University,* 281 Va. 127 (2011)

1. George Mason University
Virginia Administrative Code, Title 8, Agency 35, Chapter 60, cited as 8VAC35-60, states that it is prohibited for any person, except law enforcement, to possess or carry any firearm on university property in academic buildings, administrative office buildings, student residence buildings, dining facilities, or while attending sporting, entertainment or educational events.

2. Virginia Tech
8VAC105-20 states that university employees, students, and volunteers are prohibited from carrying, maintaining, or storing a firearm or weapon on any university property. Any visitor or other third party attending a sporting, entertainment, or educational event or visiting an academic or administrative office building, dining facility, or residence hall is prohibited from carrying, maintaining, or storing a firearm or weapon on any university facility, even if the owner has a valid CHP. This prohibition also applies to all events on campus where people congregate in any public or outdoor areas. Virginia Administrative Code 8VAC105-20-30 outlines various exceptions such as for law enforcement purposes and for those employees who reside in university owned houses. These types of employees are permitted to keep personal firearms on these premises; however, this exception does not extend to employees living in university residence halls.

3. College of William and Mary
8VAC115-20 states that it is prohibited for any person, except law enforcement or authorized personnel, to possess or carry any firearm on university property in academic buildings, administrative buildings, student residence and student life buildings, dining or athletic facilities, or while attending an official university event, such as an athletic, academic, social, recreational or educational event, or on vessels that are university property.

4. James Madison University
8VAC45-10 states that it is prohibited for any person, except law enforcement, to possess or carry any firearm on university property in any buildings or any outdoor area to which access is restricted to members of the university community and invited guests, or while attending any university events or university sanctioned events.

5. Longwood University
8VAC50-20 states that it is prohibited for any person, except law enforcement, to possess or carry any firearm on university property in academic buildings, administrative office buildings, student resident buildings, or dining facilities, or while attending sporting, entertainment, or educational events.

6. Old Dominion University
8VAC65-10 states that it is prohibited for any person, except law enforcement, to possess or carry any firearm on university property in academic buildings, administrative office buildings, student residence buildings, or dining facilities, or while attending sporting, entertainment, or educational events.

7. Radford University
8VAC75-20 states that university employees, students, and volunteers are prohibited from carrying, maintaining, or storing a firearm or weapon on any university property. Any visitor or other third party attending a sporting, entertainment, or educational event, or visiting an academic or administrative office building, dining facility, or residence hall, is prohibited from carrying, maintaining, or storing a firearm or weapon on any university facility, even if the owner has a valid CHP. This prohibition also applies to all events on campus where people congregate in any public or outdoor areas. Virginia Administrative Code 8VAC75-20-30 outlines various excep-

tions that include the Chief of the Radford University Police Department authorizing a student or employee on a case-by-case basis in writing to store a firearm that would normally be prohibited.

8. Richard Bland College
8VAC115-30 states that it is prohibited for any person, except law enforcement, to possess or carry any firearm on college property in academic buildings, administrative buildings, student residence and student life buildings, or dining or athletic facilities, or while attending an official college event, such as an athletic, academic, social, recreational, or educational event, or on vessels that are college property.

9. University of Mary Washington
8VAC55-10 states that it is prohibited for any person, except law enforcement, to possess or carry any firearm on university property in academic buildings, administrative office buildings, student residence buildings, dining facilities, or athletic facilities or while attending sporting, entertainment or educational events.

10. University of Virginia
8VAC85-20 states that it is prohibited for any university student, faculty, employee, trainee, or volunteer, except law enforcement, to possess, store, or use any firearm on university property. The possession, storage, or use of any firearm is prohibited by the general public or visitors, except law enforcement, on university property in academic, administrative, athletic, entertainment, or student residence buildings, child care or dining facilities, or the University Medical Center, or while attending sporting, entertainment, or educational activities. Exceptions can be made in various circumstances as outlined in Va. Admin. Code 8VAC85-20-30(D).

11. Virginia Commonwealth University
8VAC90-60 states that it is prohibited for any person, except law enforcement, to possess or carry any firearm on university property in academic buildings, administrative office buildings, medical venues, clinics, laboratories, research facilities, student residence buildings, and dining facilities or while attending sporting, entertainment, or educational events.

12. Virginia Military Institute
8VAC100-10 states that it is prohibited for any person, except law

enforcement, to possess or carry any firearm on institute property, to include academic buildings, administrative office buildings, support buildings, military training facilities, athletic facilities, barracks or any structure designated for cadet housing, or dining facilities, or while attending sporting, entertainment, or educational events. The prohibition would not apply to those activities falling under the Reserve Officer Training Corps programs, NCAA rifle teams, Trap and Skeet Club, VMI Firing Range(s) or Marksmanship Club, or other official institute club or other activities.

13. Virginia State University
8VAC110-10 states that it is prohibited for university employees, students, and volunteers to carry, maintain, or store a firearm on any university property. Any visitor or other third party attending a sporting, entertainment, or educational event, or visiting an academic or administrative office building, dining facility, or residence hall is prohibited from carrying, maintaining, or storing a firearm or weapon on any university facility, even if the owner has a valid CHP. This prohibition also applies to all events on campus where people congregate in any public or outdoor areas. 8VAC110-10-30 outlines exceptions to this prohibition, which states that an employee may possess or carry a firearm if the employee is residing in university owned houses and is permitted to keep personal firearms on the premises; however, this exception does not extend to employees living in university residence halls.

14. Christopher Newport University
Unauthorized possession, storage, or control of a firearm and ammunition by students on university property is prohibited. This includes storage in vehicles on campus as well as in the residence halls.

15. Norfolk State University
The unauthorized possession, carrying, maintaining, storage, control, brandishing, or use of firearms and weapons, or any reasonable facsimiles thereof, by students, faculty, staff, transient personnel, invitees or any other third parties, except law enforcement, while on university property or on university controlled sites, and at university-sponsored activities, services or programs, even if the owner has a valid CHP is prohibited.

This prohibition includes the unauthorized storage of firearms and weapons in vehicles on campus and in residential halls. This policy prohibits all concealed weapons and unauthorized possession of realistic replicas of weapons. There are various narrow exceptions to this policy. *See* nsu.edu/Assets/websites/policy-library/policies/03/Administrative-Policy-47-10-Weapons-Policy.pdf.

16. Virginia Community Colleges

8VAC95-10 states that it is prohibited for any person to possess or carry any firearm on college property in academic buildings, administrative office buildings, student centers, child care centers, dining facilities and places of like kind where people congregate, or while attending any sporting, entertainment, or educational events; however this prohibition neither applies to law enforcement nor to possession of a weapon when stored securely inside the vehicle of properly permitted students and employees.

G.   *Airports and commercial air travel as a passenger*

Traveling with a firearm on a commercial airline can be legal as long as the firearms transported are unloaded and in a locked, hard-sided container as checked baggage. Anyone traveling with firearms and/or ammunition should always check with every airport being used, their commercial airline, and any other state being visited with firearms to verify any applicable firearm laws, regulations or policies before traveling. Lawful conduct in one state may be a felony criminal offense in another state.

Every year, hundreds of firearms are confiscated in airports across the country by the Transportation Security Administration (TSA), a federal agency within the U.S. Department of Homeland Security. The majority of these confiscated firearms are found loaded in the traveler's carry-on luggage. Despite many of these cases being accidental, there are nevertheless consequences that accompany being found with a handgun in your carry-on luggage or a firearm that has not been properly processed in accordance with TSA policies, and federal, state, and local law.

Virginia Code § 18.2-287.01 states that it is unlawful for any person to possess a firearm inside or transport a firearm into any air carrier airport terminal in Virginia. A violation of this section is a misdemeanor punishable by up to 12 months in jail, a $2,500 fine, and forfeiture of the firearm.

This section shall not apply to law enforcement or to any passenger of an airline who, to the extent otherwise permitted by law, transports a lawful firearm, or ammunition into or out of an air carrier airport terminal for the sole purposes, respectively, of (i) presenting such firearm or ammunition to U.S. Customs agents in advance of an international flight, in order to comply with federal law, (ii) checking such firearm, weapon, or ammunition with his luggage, or (iii) retrieving such firearm or ammunition from the baggage claim area.

The TSA has a number of rules which must be followed in order to carry a firearm and/or ammunition aboard a commercial airliner or in the sterile area of an airport. These rules follow federal statutory law, and complying with them will prevent you from violating federal laws which carry harsh penalties. *See* TSA.gov/travel/transporting-firearms-ammunition.

Firearms must be unloaded, stored in a locked, hard-sided container, and in checked baggage. NOTE: Some jurisdictions define "loaded firearm" differently, thus make sure you know the law of the other state you are traveling to before you arrive in the other state.

The TSA allows plastic or metal hard-sided cases, as long as the case completely secures the firearm from being accessed and you are the only person who has the key or combination to the lock. TSA approved locks are recommended on checked firearms and ammunition. No tag is required on the outside of the case and an airline is prohibited from requiring any label or tag on your checked luggage indicating that a firearm is inside. *See* 18 U.S.C. § 922(e). Any magazines or clips, whether loaded or empty, must be securely boxed or included within the hard-sided case. Realistic replicas of firearms are also prohibited in carry-on bags and must be packed in checked baggage. Rifle scopes are permitted in carry-on and checked bags.

No firearms, firearms parts or ammunition are allowed in carry-on baggage. They must be declared and checked with the airline. Different airlines and airports have varying policies on how they want you to declare your firearms and/or ammunition. It is recommended to verify any policy with your airline and airport.

All ammunition must be securely packed in cardboard, wood, or metal boxes, or in other packaging specifically designed to carry small amounts of ammunition. It can also be loaded into magazines that are securely boxed or placed in the hard-sided, locked container holding the firearm. Additionally, airlines may have their own preferences as to how they want ammunition packaged and the amount you may have in checked baggage. Contact your airline for more details regarding ammunition.

Gunpowder and black powder are prohibited from commercial flights by the TSA. If your firearm or ammunition is not properly declared or packaged, then the TSA will give the checked bag to law enforcement for resolution with the airline. This may lead to a delay that could prevent you from making your flight, so it is very important to properly declare all firearms and ammunition with the airline.

Carrying of a concealed handgun onto an aircraft or in a sterile area is a very serious criminal offense, even with a CHP. Federal law prohibits both open carry and concealed carry onto an aircraft or in a sterile area. *See* 14 CFR § 135.119; 49 CFR § 1544.201(d); 49 CFR § 1540.111. Carrying a concealed handgun on an aircraft or attempting to get on an aircraft while carrying concealed is punishable by up to 10 years in prison and/or a fine of up to $250,000! Additionally, attempting to place or having placed a loaded firearm in property that is inaccessible to passengers in flight is also punishable by up to 10 years in prison and/or a fine of up to $250,000. A violation can also trigger civil penalties of up to $10,000 for each violation regardless of whether there is a criminal prosecution. *See* 49 U.S.C. § 46303A.

PRACTICAL LEGAL TIP

Most people say that the reason they forgot to remove a firearm from their baggage at the airport is because they were in such a hurry to not miss their flight. But, if you do accidentally leave it in your carry-on bags, you can be assured that you will miss your flight! At a very minimum, if TSA finds a gun in your baggage, you will not only cause a scene and miss your flight, but you will also incur a fine from the TSA and possibly be subjected to prosecution by local law enforcement. — *Ed*

H. *Place of religious worship*

Virginia Code § 18.2-283 states that it is illegal for any person to carry any firearm without a good and sufficient reason to a place of worship while a meeting for religious purposes is being held at such place. A violation of this section is a misdemeanor punishable by a maximum $250 fine. Personal protection is considered to be a good and sufficient reason to carry a firearm; however, a place of worship can choose to ban guns on its property. *See* 23 Op. Att'y Gen. 4 (2011). It is recommended that all gun owners understand their place of worship's position on firearms before taking any firearm into their place of worship.

I. *Child-care facilities*

Child-care facilities must be licensed by the Department of Social Services under 22 VAC40-111. Firearms shall be stored unloaded in a locked container, compartment, or cabinet, and apart from ammunition. Ammunition shall be stored in a locked container, compartment, or cabinet during the family day home's hours of operation. If a key is used to lock the container, compartment, or cabinet, the key shall be inaccessible to children. *See* 22 VAC40-111-270.

Virginia Code § 15.2-914 states that certain localities based on their form of government may regulate the possession and storage of firearms, ammunition, or components or combination thereof at child-care facilities so long as such regulation remains no more extensive in scope than comparable state regulations applicable to family day homes. It is recommended that all gun owners understand their child-care facility's position on firearms before taking any firearm into their child-care facility.

J. *National forests, parks and wildlife refuges, and state lands*

1. National Parks & Wildlife Refuges and Virginia State Parks

Possession of a firearm in a National Park or National Wildlife Refuge is lawful if in compliance with the law of the state in which the federal land is located. *See* 16 U.S.C. § 1a–7b 23; Op. Att'y Gen. 4 (2011). Thus, an individual can open carry a firearm on these federal lands located in Virginia because open carry is lawful. NOTE: this does not grant an individual the ability to possess a firearm inside a federal building. *See* 18 U.S.C. § 930. The law of open carry applies to Virginia State Parks just like any other public location that is not otherwise restricted. *See* 43 Op. Att'y Gen. 4 (2008). Concealed carry is also permissible on these lands with a CHP if the person is not otherwise prohibited from possessing a firearm.

2. National forests and land owned or managed by the Department of Game & Inland Fisheries

4VAC15-40-60 states that it shall be unlawful to possess any firearm that is not unloaded and cased or dismantled on all National Forest lands statewide, and on Department of Game & Inland Fisheries (DGIFS) owned lands, and on other lands managed by DGIFS under a cooperative agreement. It is also unlawful to possess or transport any loaded firearm in or on any vehicle at any time on DGIFS owned lands. However, this prohibition shall neither prohibit the possession, transport and use of loaded firearms by employees of the DGIFS while engaged in the performance of their authorized and official duties, nor shall it prohibit possession and transportation of loaded concealed handguns where the individual possesses a CHP, nor at archery and shooting ranges. Hunting regulations differ, thus it is recommended that hunters refer to all applicable hunting laws and regulations.

3. Hog Island Wildlife Management Area

4VAC15-40-120 states that it is unlawful to possess at any time a gun which is not unloaded and cased or dismantled on that portion of the Hog Island Wildlife Management Area bordering on the James River and lying north of the Surry Nuclear Power Plant, except while hunting deer or waterfowl in conformity with a special permit issued by the department.

4. Buggs Island

4VAC15-40-140 states that it is unlawful to possess a loaded gun on Buggs Island or to shoot over or have a loaded gun upon the water on Gaston Reservoir (Roanoke River) from a point beginning at High Rock and extending to the John H. Kerr Dam.

V. Traveling across state lines with firearms

Most states have different firearm laws, which can make traveling across state lines with a firearm complicated. The question that is often asked is, "What do I do with my firearm when traveling through a state that either has different or more restrictive laws than my state?" The answer: safe-passage legislation.

A. *Federal law: Qualifying for firearms "Safe Passage"*
Traveling across state lines with a firearm means that a person may need to use the provisions of the federal law known as the "Safe Passage" provision. Federal law allows individuals who are legally in possession of firearms in their state (the starting point of traveling) to travel through states that are not as friendly. This protection is only available under federal law to transport such firearms across state lines for lawful purposes, as long as they comply with the requirements of the Firearm Owners Protection Act, 18 U.S.C. § 926A, nicknamed the "Safe Passage" provision. The first requirement to qualify for the federal "Safe Passage" provision is that throughout the duration of the trip through the anti-firearm-state, the firearm must be unloaded and locked in the trunk, or locked in a container that is out of reach or not readily accessible from the passenger compartment. The ammunition also must be locked in the trunk or a container. Note that for the storage of both firearms and ammunition, the glove box and center console compartment are specifically not allowed under the statute.

B. *"Safe Passage" requires legal start to legal finish*
To get protection under federal law, a gun owner's journey must start and end in states where the traveler's possession of the firearm is legal. For instance, a person traveling with their Glock 17 starting in Virginia and ending in Vermont. Even though a person must drive through New York or Massachusetts to get to Vermont, as long as the person qualifies under the "Safe Passage" provision then they may legally pass through. However, if the start point was Virginia and the end point was New York (a place where the handgun would be illegal), there is no protection under the federal law. Safe passage requires legal start and legal finish.

Although traveling across state lines naturally invokes federal law, it is important to remember that whenever a person finally completes their journey and reaches their destination state, the laws of that state control the possession, carrying, and use of the firearm. Federal law does not make it legal or provide any protection for possession of a firearm that is illegal under the laws of the destination state (*i.e.*, the end state of your travels).

C. *What is the definition of "traveling" for "Safe Passage" provisions?*
The final requirement for protection under the federal law is that individuals MUST be "traveling" while in the firearm hostile state. The legal definition of "traveling" is both murky and narrow. The "Safe Passage" provision protection has been held in courts to be limited to situations that strictly relate to traveling and nothing more. Traveling is a term that is not defined in the federal statute; however, it has received treatment in the courts that is indicative of what one can expect. Generally speaking, if a person stops somewhere for too long they cease to be "traveling" and, therefore, lose their protection under the "Safe Passage" provision. How long this time limit is has not been determined either statutorily or by case law with any definitiveness.

While stopping for gas or restroom breaks may not disqualify a person from the "traveling" protection, any stop for an activity not directly related to traveling could be considered a destination and thus you would lose the legal protection. For example, in Chicago anyone in the city for more than 24 hours is not considered to be traveling under local policy. In an actual case, stopping for a brief nap in a bank parking lot in New Jersey caused a Texan driving back home from Maine to lose the "traveling" protection. He received five years in prison for possession of weapons that are illegal under New Jersey law. Of course, if the driver would have made it to Allentown, Pennsylvania, he would have been safe. The moral of the story is to travel through these gun-unfriendly states as fast as you can (without breaking the speed limit, of course)!

D. *Protection under federal law does not mean protection from prosecution in unfriendly states*
To make matters even worse for firearms travelers, even if a person qualifies for protection under the federal "Safe Passage" provision, New Jersey and New York seem quite proud to treat this protection as an affirmative defense. This means that someone can be arrested even though he or she met all of the requirements of the federal statute. Then, they would have to go to court to assert this defense. In other words, while a person could beat the rap, they will not beat the ride! This becomes even more troublesome in the instance of someone who is legally flying with their firearm and

then due to flight complications, must land in New Jersey or New York, as travelers in this position have been arrested or threatened with arrest.

Once again, the "Safe Passage" provision only applies while a person is traveling; as soon as they arrive at their destination and cease their travels, the laws of that state control a person's actions. Remember: check all applicable state firearms laws before you leave for your destination!

A good recommendation is to carry a copy of 18 USC § 926A of the Federal Code with you because not all law enforcement officers may be familiar with this law.

VI. Frequently asked questions
A.   *Can I carry my gun in a hospital or polling place?*
Virginia has no laws prohibiting firearms in these places; however, some hospitals are operated by public university institutions and many polling places are held on elementary, middle or high school properties. Additionally, many hospitals are private and some polling places may be located on private property, and the private property owner has the authority to ban firearms from their property.

B.   *Can I keep a loaded handgun in my glove box even if I do not have a CHP?*
Yes. Virginia Code § 18.2-308(C)(8) states that it is lawful for any person to carry a handgun while in a personal, private motor vehicle that is secured in a container or compartment in the vehicle, provided that person may lawfully possess a firearm. *See* Doulgerakis v. Commonwealth, 61 Va.App. 417 (2013); 11-111 Op. Att'y Gen. 3 (2012).

C.   *Can I carry my gun into a nightclub or bar?*
It depends. An owner of private property may ban firearms from its property. If there is no private property weapons ban, then an individual may open carry a firearm. If a handgun is lawfully being carried concealed by a CHP holder, and there is no private property weapons ban, then the handgun may be lawfully carried while concealed as long as CHP holder does not consume alcohol. It is important to note that guns and alcohol don't mix.

D. *Can I carry my handgun concealed with my CHP to a professional or collegiate sporting event or an amusement park?*

It depends. An owner of private property may ban firearms from its property. Most public universities and colleges ban open carry and concealed carry by CHP holders at sporting events. Make sure you understand the public university or college firearm policy before you attempt to carry a firearm to a collegiate sporting event. The policy for students and employees is sometimes different than the policy for visitors.

E. *Must I tell a police officer that I have a concealed handgun in the car if pulled over for a traffic violation?*

No, Virginia Code § 18.2-308.01 only requires that you provide your CHP along with proper identification to law enforcement upon demand. However, sometimes it may be wise to advise the police officer of a firearm being in the vehicle for safety reasons. It is important to note that the CHP files are linked to the Department of Motor Vehicles database, thus an alert police officer may be aware of a possible firearm being in the vehicle during the traffic stop. If the police officer locates a firearm during the traffic stop, then expect a brief investigation into the lawfulness of your firearm possession before being released from the traffic stop.

F. *Can I carry my handgun while in a local county or city park?*

Yes, you can either open carry or carry concealed with a CHP, assuming the handgun is not an assault firearm. Virginia Code § 15.2-915 states that no locality shall adopt or enforce any ordinance, resolution or motion governing the possession or carrying or transporting of firearms except workplace rules relating to employment.

G. *May I keep a handgun in my vehicle if there are children in the vehicle?*

Firearm safety is very important, especially when children are involved. However, there is no simple answer to this question. The answer will depend on various circumstances. Virginia Code § 18.2-56.2 states that it is unlawful for any person to recklessly leave a loaded, unsecured firearm in such a manner as to endanger the life or limb of any child under 14 years old. Additionally, it is also unlawful for any person to knowingly authorize a child under 12 years old to use a firearm except when the child is under the supervision of an adult.

H.   *May I travel with a firearm in the cabin of a private aircraft and air carrier terminal?*
It depends. First, it is important to note that an "air carrier terminal" as defined in Va. Code §18.2-287.01 usually refers to a commercial airport with commercial airlines not to airports that engage in general aviation with non-commercial private aircraft. Nevertheless, private pilots and their passengers typically access the aircraft in or near the hanger and never enter a terminal. Confirm with your airports to make sure you are not in violation.

Second, the law of open carry and concealed carry with or without a CHP would apply if traveling in Virginia.

The final issue deals with travel where the aircraft is taking off from one state and landing in another. It is important to know ahead of time what the firearm laws are in the state where the aircraft is to land. Individuals can avail themselves of the Firearm Owners Protection Act we discussed earlier in this chapter for instances of traveling through a state with more restrictive firearm laws. The "Safe Passage" provision of that act allows for transportation of a firearm through the anti-firearm state, but the firearm must be unloaded and neither the firearm nor any ammunition being transported can be readily accessible or directly accessible from the passenger compartment. If the aircraft is without a separate compartment, then the firearm or ammunition shall be contained in a locked container other than the glove compartment or console. *See* 18 U.S.C. § 926A.

CHAPTER TEN
RESTORATION OF FIREARMS RIGHTS:
THE LAW OF PARDONS AND EXPUNGEMENTS

I.   Can a person's right to bear arms be restored?
An individual who has been convicted of a felony, or adjudicated insane, incompetent or incapacitated will lose their firearm rights; however, there is a procedure to have firearm rights later restored. This chapter will explain how a person, under very limited circumstances, can regain firearm rights once lost, and in some instances, the arrest and criminal conviction can be removed from the record or nullified. The federal government and each state have their own procedures for such a process. NOTE: Success in this area due to a disqualifying criminal conviction is *very* rare.

A.   *What is clemency?*
Clemency is an action by the chief executive of the executive branch of the government that either reduces or eliminates certain penalties for a particular criminal conviction without actually clearing the arrest record or public record. The President is the chief executive of the federal government and the Governor is the chief executive of the respective state government.

Clemency can come in the form of a pardon, which is forgiveness of a sentence; a commutation, which is a reduction of a sentence; or a reprieve, which is a temporary putting off of punishment while the situation is analyzed further. It is important to note that no form of clemency overturns or removes the criminal conviction from either the arrest record or public record. Those seeking to remove either a criminal arrest or a conviction from either the criminal arrest record or public record will need to pursue an expungement.

1.   Pardon
A pardon is when the chief executive forgives a certain criminal offense. A pardon is meant to indicate forgiveness of a particular crime, either because a person was wrongfully convicted or the punishment was not appropriate for the crime committed or for political reasons. A pardon also cancels any penalty associated with

that crime. The record of the criminal conviction would remain, but no further restrictions or criminal penalties would be imposed.

2. Commutation

A commutation is a merciful act offered by the chief executive in instances where the penalty or sentence imposed by the courts was too harsh. A common use of commutation is to either reduce a death penalty verdict to life in prison or to reduce or eliminate the remaining active prison sentence of a prison inmate.

3. Reprieve

A reprieve may be given when more information is needed to determine the appropriate course of action. This is often used in death penalty situations.

B. *What is an expungement?*

An expungement is a legal proceeding that can be used to destroy, purge or erase a case from both the arrest and public records. The qualifications for expungement vary from state to state.

II. Virginia law

How an individual will restore his right to purchase, possess or transport a firearm will depend on how the right to purchase, possess or transport a firearm was lost in the first place. As we discussed in Chapter 3, it is unlawful to purchase, possess, or transport a firearm as follows, if an individual:

- was convicted of a felony;
- was adjudicated delinquent of an offense which would be a felony if committed by an adult;
- was either acquitted of a felony or almost any class 1 or class 2 misdemeanor as outlined in Va. Code § 18.2-308.1:1 by reason of insanity and committed to the custody of the Commissioner of Behavioral Health and Developmental Services;
- was adjudicated incompetent or incapacitated; or,
- was involuntarily admitted to a facility or ordered to mandatory outpatient treatment or who was the subject of a temporary detention order and subsequently agreed to voluntary admission as outlined in Va. Code § 18.2-308.1:3.

An individual adjudicated delinquent as a juvenile of an offense which would be a felony if committed by an adult who has served for at least two years in the U.S. Armed Forces, and received an honorable discharge if no longer serving, is not required to seek a pardon from the Governor or petition the circuit court for restoration because they are not prohibited from possessing a firearm or ammunition pursuant to Va. Code § 18.2-308.2(A).

Individuals serving in law enforcement, the Armed Forces of the United States, the National Guard of Virginia or of any other state who would otherwise not be permitted to possess or transport a firearm or ammunition are not required to petition the circuit court for restoration or seek a pardon from the Governor if their possession or transportation of a firearm or ammunition is in the performance of their duties. *See* Va. Code § 18.2-308.2.

If a felony conviction from another state disqualified an individual from possessing or transporting a firearm, but that other state restored that individual's firearm rights, then that individual does not need to also have firearm rights restored in Virginia.

A. *Petition the court*
    1. Criminal convictions
In cases involving a felony conviction or a juvenile's adjudication of delinquency for an offense which would have been a felony if committed by an adult, the Governor must first restore the individual's civil rights before a petition to restore firearm rights can be filed with the circuit court. *See* Va. Code § 18.2-308.2. Virginia residents file their petition in the circuit court where they reside and non-residents file their petition in the circuit court where the individual was last convicted of a felony or adjudicated delinquent for an offense which would have been a felony if committed by an adult.

The circuit court shall conduct a hearing if requested. The circuit court may, in its discretion and for good cause shown, grant such petition and issue a permit that would allow the convicted felon or adjudicated delinquent the right to possess, transport or carry a firearm or ammunition. The statute does not state specific factors for the circuit court to consider, but the circuit court "may" grant the petition for "good cause shown."

2. Insanity, incompetence, incapacitation, treatment

The following individuals can petition the general district court in the city or county in which they reside to restore firearm rights:

- any individual acquitted of a criminal offense by reason of insanity upon discharge from custody;
- any individual whose competency or capacity has been restored; or
- any individual following release from involuntary admission to a facility, or release from an order of mandatory outpatient treatment, or release from voluntary admission.

The general district court shall conduct a hearing if requested. Any individual denied relief by the general district court may petition the circuit court for a *de novo* review of the denial.

B. *Governor pardon*

Pardons by Virginia governors in criminal cases are considered for exceptional situations because governors are reluctant to substitute their judgment for that of the courts. However, any individual may submit a petition for a pardon, but such petition must provide substantial evidence of such exceptional circumstances in order to justify a pardon. All petitions for a pardon are processed by the Secretary of the Commonwealth and require a Virginia Pardon Petition Questionnaire.

A Governor's pardon is not necessarily a victory for the individual applicant's restoration of firearm rights because the Governor may expressly place conditions upon the reinstatement of the person's right to ship, transport, possess or receive firearms. *See* Va. Code § 18.2-308.2.

There are 3 types of Governor pardons: simple, conditional, and absolute.

1. A simple pardon is a statement of official forgiveness. It does not expunge or remove a criminal conviction from the record, but it often serves as a means for the petitioner to advance in employment, education, and self-esteem.
2. A conditional or medical pardon is available only to people who are currently incarcerated. It is usually granted for

early release and involves certain conditions. There must be extraordinary circumstances for an inmate to be considered for such a pardon.

3. An absolute pardon is rarely granted because it is based on the belief that the petitioner was unjustly convicted and is innocent. An absolute pardon is the only form of executive clemency that would allow for a petition to the circuit court to have the underlying conviction expunged or removed from both the criminal record and public record.

If the petition is denied, then the petitioner has no right of appeal, but may reapply after a two-year period.

Special Note: An individual convicted of a Virginia misdemeanor domestic violence offense cannot possess a firearm according to 18 U.S.C. § 922(g)(9). This is an instance where a state conviction has triggered a loss of firearm rights under federal law. Such an individual cannot petition a Virginia circuit court for restoration of firearm rights according to Virginia Code § 18.2-308.2(C). Such an individual cannot be pardoned by the President of the United States. The only remedy for such an individual would be a pardon from the Governor.

C. *Expungement of a Virginia criminal case*
Criminal convictions in Virginia cannot be expunged from the criminal record, unless there is an absolute pardon from the Governor. Other states allow for a criminal conviction to be expunged from the record under certain circumstances. Consult the state where the felony conviction occured to determine eligibility. The following instances allow for a Virginia expungement:

- individuals who have been found innocent of the alleged offense;
- individuals whose criminal cases were later dropped, not prosecuted, *nolle prosequi* by the Commonwealth Attorney, or were otherwise disposed of without a finding of guilt; or
- individuals who were granted an absolute pardon by the Governor.

A petition to expunge the criminal record is filed in the circuit court that disposed of the case. *See* Va. Code § 19.2-392.2.

III. Federal law

A. *The Presidential pardon*

A presidential pardon is currently the only means by which a person convicted of a federal felony offense may have his federal right restored to bear arms again. The President of the United States has the power "to grant reprieves and pardons for offenses against the United States, except in cases of impeachment, under Article II, Section 2 of the United States Constitution. The U.S. Supreme Court has also noted that the President's pardoning power "may be exercised at any time after the commission of the offense, either before legal proceedings are taken, or during their pendency, or after conviction and judgment." *See Ex parte Garland*, 71 U.S. 333, 380 (1866). A pardon "blots out of existence the guilt," and makes the offender "as innocent as if he had never committed the offense." Example: President Gerald Ford granted a full and unconditional pardon to former President Richard Nixon prior to any indictment or charges being filed related to his involvement in a break-in at the Democratic National Committee headquarters at the Watergate office complex in Washington, D.C.

Under the Gun Control Act of 1968 (GCA), a person who has received a presidential pardon is not considered convicted of a crime preventing the purchase and possession of firearms subject to all other federal laws. In addition, persons who had a conviction expunged or set aside, or who have had their civil rights restored are not considered to have been convicted for purposes of the GCA "unless the pardon, expungement, or restoration of civil rights expressly provides the person may not ship, transport, possess, or receive firearms." *See* 18 U.S.C. §§ 921(a)(20) & (a)(33). Compare: Restoration of civil rights under Virginia law does not restore firearm rights. Restoration of civil rights by the Governor under Virginia law is a prerequisite to petition the circuit court for restoration of firearm rights. *See* Va. Code § 18.2-308.2(c).

A presidential pardon will restore various rights lost as a result of the pardoned offense; however, it will not expunge the conviction from either the criminal record or the public record. This means that even if a person is granted a presidential pardon, the person must still disclose the conviction on any form where such information is required. The presidential pardon power only applies to offenses recognizable under federal law.

Under federal law, a person requesting a presidential pardon must petition for executive clemency. The petition must be submitted to the Office of the Pardon Attorney in the Department of Justice. The Office of the Pardon Attorney can provide petitions and other required forms necessary to complete the application for clemency. *See* 28 CFR § 1.1. All petitions for executive clemency are reviewed by the Office of the Pardon Attorney. A non-binding recommendation on an application is made to the President. Federal regulations also provide for guidelines and requirements to notify victims of the crimes, if any, for which a pardon is sought. The President will either grant or deny a pardon. There are no hearings and there is no appeal of the President's decision.

A presidential pardon for military offenses has a separate process. A petitioner applying for executive clemency with respect to military offenses should submit his or her petition directly to the Secretary of the military department that had original jurisdiction over the court-martial trial and conviction of the petitioner. In such a case, a form furnished by the Pardon Attorney may be used, but should be modified to meet the needs of the particular case.

The Code of Federal Regulations requires an applicant to wait five years after the date of the release of the petitioner from confinement, or in a case where no prison sentence was imposed, an applicant is required to wait five years after the date of conviction prior to submitting a petition for executive clemency. The regulation further states that "generally, no petition should be submitted by a person who is on probation, parole, or supervised release." *See* 28 CFR § 1.2.

There is another means under federal law to have the right to bear arms restored after a federal felony conviction, but such procedure has not been funded by Congress since 1992. The GCA also provides the U.S. Attorney General with the authority to grant relief from a disqualifying federal felony conviction and restore the right to bear arms "if it is established to his satisfaction that... the applicant will not be likely to act in a manner dangerous to public safety and that the granting of the relief would not be contrary to the public interest." *See* 18 U.S.C. § 925(c).

The Bureau of Alcohol, Tobacco, Firearms and Explosives (ATF) is the federal agency responsible for processing such requests for the Attorney General; however, Congress has prohibited the ATF from spending any appropriated funds to investigate or act upon applications for such relief. Therefore, a presidential pardon is the only means by which a person convicted of a federal felony may restore the right to bear arms.

B. *Expungement of federal convictions*
    1. No law exists for general federal expungement
Congress has not provided federal legislation that offers any comprehensive authority or procedure for expunging federal criminal offenses. There exist only statues that allow expungement in certain cases for possession of small amounts of controlled substances (see below) and interestingly, a procedure to expunge DNA samples of certain members of the military wrongfully convicted. Because there is no statutory guidance, federal courts have literally made up the rules and procedures themselves, often coming to different conclusions. Some federal court circuits have stated they have no power to expunge records, while other federal courts have indicated that they do have the power to expunge. *See Sealed Appellant v. Sealed Appellee,* 130 F.3d 695 (5th Cir. 1997). The U.S. Supreme Court has passed on hearing cases that would have resolved the split between the circuits. This issue remains legally murky.

    2. Possible procedure for federal expungement
There are no statutory guidelines for how to seek an expungement under federal law. The place to start would be to file a motion with the federal court that entered the conviction; however, federal judges very rarely grant these types of motions. Some circuits have adopted a balancing test to decide if a record held by the court may be expunged: "if the dangers of unwarranted adverse consequences to the individual outweigh the public interest in maintenance of the records, then expunction is appropriate." *See United States v. Flowers,* 389 F.3d 737 (7th Cir. 2004). Further, these same courts have freely stated that this balancing test "rarely tips in favor of expungement," and that expungement should be granted in only the most extreme cases. Some of the areas where expungement has worked are in incidents of extreme police misconduct, or where the conviction is being misused against the person. Unless there exist compelling reasons, a federal judge is highly unlikely to grant expungement.

3. Expungement for drug possession: statutory authority

Under a federal law entitled "Special Probation and Expungement Procedures for Drug Possessors," certain persons are allowed to request a federal court to issue an expungement order from all public records. *See* 18 U.S.C. § 3607. Congress intended this order to restore the person to the status he or she "occupied before such arrest or institution of criminal proceedings." *See* 18 U.S.C. § 3607(c).

In order to qualify for this type of expungement, you must have been under the age of 21 when you were convicted, you must have no prior drug offenses, and your conviction must have been for simple possession of a small amount of a controlled substance.

C. *Adjudicated as a mental defective or committed to a mental institution*

Any individual who has been "adjudicated as a mental defective" or "committed to a mental institution" is prohibited under federal law from shipping, transporting, receiving, or possessing any firearm or ammunition; however, such individuals may receive relief from such disqualifications. *See* 18 U.S.C. § 922(g)(4). The federal law does not call such relief a restoration of firearm rights like the Virginia mental health counterpart, but there are similarities.

The affected individual can receive relief from either the ATF pursuant to 18 U.S.C. § 925(c) or from a proper federal or state authority under a relief from disabilities program that meets the requirements of the NICS Improvement Amendments Act of 2007, Public Law 110-180. Additionally, the affected individual can also seek relief as follows:

- the adjudication or commitment was set aside or expunged;
- the individual was fully released from mandatory treatment, supervision or monitoring;
- the individual was found to no longer suffer from the disabling mental health condition;
- the individual has otherwise been found to be rehabilitated; or
- adjudication or commitment was based solely on a medical finding without opportunity for hearing by the federal department or agency with proper jurisdiction.

CHAPTER ELEVEN
I'M BEING SUED FOR WHAT?
CIVIL LIABILITY IF YOU HAVE USED YOUR GUN

I. Introduction

Every law-abiding gun owner knows that a firearm is a dangerous weapon that must be responsibly handled with care. A failure to either handle or use a firearm responsibly can result in an injury and create liability. Liability is defined as the state of being legally responsible for something. Unfortunately, there are instances where an individual may become injured or harmed due to the irresponsible or wrongful actions of another's handling of a firearm. The individual or party responsible for the harm caused may be civilly liable or financially responsible to the aggrieved individual or party.

In the event that the parties cannot resolve their differences, then a civil lawsuit may be filed. A civil lawsuit is a cause of action that is filed with the courts for adjudication or judgment where it would ultimately be up to a judge or jury hearing the case to determine liability and the legal responsibilities of the parties. Civil lawsuits involving a firearm are almost exclusively about one party seeking to be monetarily compensated for damages caused by the wrongful acts of another party. In Virginia, a civil lawsuit is called a Motion for Judgment or Complaint.

It is important to note that an individual's irresponsible or wrongful conduct can result in both criminal liability and civil liability. In general, civil liability differs from criminal liability in that a civil wrong does not subject the responsible or liable party to incarceration or punishment for a crime. The so-called trial of the century involving O.J. Simpson is a prime example. Mr. Simpson was arrested for murder and prosecuted criminally, but was found not to be criminally liable or found to be not guilty of the crimes alleged because the jury believed that the prosecution did not prove its case "beyond a reasonable doubt." However, Mr. Simpson was later sued civilly for wrongful death. The civil jury found him to be civilly liable for his wrongful actions by the "preponderance of the evidence" and awarded money damages to the plaintiffs. "Beyond a reasonable doubt" and "preponderance of the evidence" are the standards of proof that determine criminal liability and civil liability, respectively.

II.   Criminal liability versus civil liability

Criminal liability is the responsibility for a crime or an offense against the state. An individual will be criminally liable for a crime if the prosecution proves beyond a reasonable doubt that the individual committed the alleged criminal act with the required intent. Criminal liabilty and the use of a firearm for self-defense were discussed in Chapter 4. Justifiable and excusable self-defense negate criminal liability.

A criminal prosecution is an action brought by the government to punish an individual for committing a crime against the public or the state, and to deter others from committing similar crimes. The public policy is that a violation of any criminal law harms the public in general and not just a particular person or victim. Therefore, it is generally the government's job and not the individual victim's job to prosecute a criminal case. The victim will of course always be a key witness to the prosecution's case. The lawyer for the government is called the prosecutor and the individual alleged to have committed the crime is called the defendant. Penalties for criminal liabilty may include a criminal conviction, incarceration, court fines, and victim restitution. Restitution in the criminal justice system means payment by the defendant to the victim for the harm caused by the defendant's wrongful acts. Courts have the authority to order the convicted defendant to pay restitution to the victim as part of their sentence.

A civil lawsuit may be filed by any individual, corporation, or trust. The person or entity that files the civil lawsuit with the court is called the plaintiff. The plaintiff or the plaintiff's lawyer files an action or civil lawsuit against the defendant. The government can also initiate a civil lawsuit. For example, if an individual were to shoot a county propane tank and cause a fire, then the county could sue that individual civilly to recover for those damages. The party being sued is called the defendant; however, the defendant is permitted to file either cross-claims or counterclaims against the plaintiff. There is no criminal prosecutor in a civil case and there are no criminal penalites associated with a civil lawsuit.

A. *Standards of proof*

The level of certainty and the degree of evidence necessary to establish proof in either a criminal case or a civil lawsuit is referred to as the standard of proof. In a criminal case, the standard of proof is "beyond a reasonable doubt." This is the highest standard of proof that must be met in any trial. The prosecution's evidence in a criminal case must prove the defendant's guilt beyond a reasonable doubt such that no other logical explanation can be derived from the facts except that the defendant committed the alleged crime. If there is any reasonable uncertainty of guilt based on the evidence presented, then the defendant cannot be convicted. Legal authorities who venture to assign a numerical value to "beyond a reasonable doubt" place it in the certainty range of 98 or 99 percent.

In a civil lawsuit, the standard of proof is "preponderance of the evidence." A preponderance of the evidence is a much lower standard than the criminal standard of beyond a reasonable doubt. Legal authorities who venture to assign a numerical value to a "preponderance of the evidence" place it in the certainty range of as little as 51 percent. This means that the party who presents the greater weight of credible evidence or whose evidence demonstrates that something "more likely occurred than not" will prevail. It does not mean the party with the most exhibits or greater number of witnesses will prevail. One highly credible witness can prevail over the testimony of a dozen biased, shady witnesses.

> Example:
> *John mistakes a utility meter reader in the back alley of his Northern Virginia condo for a burglar. The meter reader has a disheveled appearance, a tool bag, and looks to be snooping around John's condo. John fires a shot without warning and injures the meter reader.*

Possible criminal liability: Virginia prosecutors could bring various criminal charges against John for his shooting and injuring the meter reader. Any criminal case would have to be proved "beyond a reasonable doubt." A conviction could trigger imprisonment, a fine, and/or restitution to the meter reader for the injuries sustained.

Possible civil liability: The meter reader could file a civil lawsuit against John alleging that John was responsible for the harm caused and damages suffered due to his civil wrong. The meter reader would be required to prove his civil lawsuit allegations by a "preponderance of the evidence." A civil lawsuit could be filed whether or not there was a criminal case.

B.   *Parallel proceedings*
As a general rule, parallel proceedings is a term that can refer to two actions, one civil and one criminal, both arising out of the same set of facts that proceed either simultaneously or successively against the same party.

> Example 1:
> *Phil and Jeremy become involved in a road rage incident, and a physical altercation follows. Phil shoots and wounds Jeremy. Can Phil be criminally prosecuted by the government and sued civilly by Jeremy at the same time?*

Yes. Virginia criminal prosecutions and civil cases arising out of the same set of facts can proceed simultaneously although it is rare. Typically, the Virginia criminal prosecution proceeds first and the civil case, if one is filed at all, is filed after the criminal case is finalized; however, there is no bar to pursing a civil action during a pending criminal prosecution.

> Example 2:
> *Phil and Jeremy become involved in a road rage incident, and a physical altercation follows. Phil shoots and wounds Jeremy. Phil is criminally prosecuted by the government for assaulting Jeremy. Phil pleads not guilty, but is convicted for assaulting Jeremy. After the criminal case, Jeremy sues Phil civilly for his injuries in an attempt to collect money damages. Can Phil's guilty verdict be used as evidence in the civil trial?*

No. In Virginia, a criminal verdict of either guilt or innocence cannot be used as evidence in a later civil trial. *See Ayala v. Aggressive Towing and Transport,* 276 Va. 169 (2008). However, Phil's plea in the criminal case and any statements or testimony he made about the incident could be used in the civil trial.

Example 3:
Phil and Jeremy become involved in a road rage incident, and a physical altercation follows. Phil shoots and wounds Jeremy. Phil is arrested and criminally prosecuted for assaulting Jeremy. Phil pleads guilty.

In Example 3, Phil's admission of guilt by way of his guilty plea may be used as evidence to prove liability in a later civil action brought by Jeremy.

CAUTION: The primary area where a civil case can impact a criminal case and vice versa is the potential for overlapping use of evidence and testimony. A party's statement or under oath admission in one case can almost always be used in the other case.

C.   *Res Judicata & Collateral Estoppel*

Res judicata is latin for the legal doctrine that bars "claims" that have been previously finally adjudicated by a trial court from being pursued further by the same parties in a subsequent trial court. *See Arkansas Best Freight Sys. v. H.H. Moore Trucking,* 244 Va. 304 (1992). Collateral estoppel is the doctrine that bars "issues" that have been finally adjudicated by a trial court from being further pursued by the same parties in a subsequent trial court. *See Scales v. Lewis,* 261 Va. 379 (2001). However, the truth of any facts or disposition determined in a previous criminal trial are neither admissible in a subsequent civil trial nor does it bar a later civil trial. *See Ayala v. Aggressive Towing and Transport,* 276 Va. 169 (2008). In layman's terms, the government and the civil plaintiff are not the same "person," which is why two legal actions, one civil and one criminal, against the same defendant for actions arising from the same act are permissible.

PRACTICAL LEGAL TIP

Criminal cases must be proved with evidence "beyond a reasonable doubt," which is the highest standard of proof in the land. Civil actions for money damages only need to be proved with a "preponderance of the evidence," which is a much lower standard of proof. — *Ed*

Note: An appeal from a trial court to an appellate court neither violates the doctrine of *res judicata* nor the doctrine of collateral estoppel. The purpose of the appellate court is to review the prior trial and to determine if the trial court correctly applied the law.

III. Intentional torts and negligence

Civil liability involving a firearm can occur as the result of either an intentional, unintentional, or accidental shooting. A wrongful shooting that creates civil liability due to either an intentional or unintentional wrongful act is commonly referred to as a tort. A tort is nothing more than a civil wrong.

An intentional tort is a category of torts that results from an intentional, purposeful and/or deliberate wrongful act. There is no requirement that the wrongful act be done with either a hostile intent or a desire to do serious harm. An unintentional or accidental shooting due to carelessness is called a negligent tort.

A. *Intentional torts*

An intentional tort that results in an injury after the use of a firearm may range from a minor assault to a wrongful death. An assault is an act intended to cause either harmful or offensive contact with another person or apprehension of such contact that creates a reasonable apprehension of an imminent battery in another person's mind. *See Koffman v. Garnett,* 265 Va. 12 (2003). A battery is an unwanted touching that is neither consented to, excused, nor justified. *See* Model Jury Instruction Nos. 36.080 & 36.081. There are many instances where the law abiding gun owner's use of a firearm can be classified as an intentional tort of assault and battery; however, it is important to note that justified self-defense negates civil liability arising from intentional tort allegations. **Caution:** Intentional tort conduct that creates civil liability may also be a crime.

> Example 1:
> *Bill is driving through an unfamiliar part of downtown Richmond and comes to a stop at a red light. Martha is standing next to his passenger window at the traffic light screaming that he cut her off in traffic, but taking no action to indicate she intends to harm Bill or do anything besides verbally lodge her complaints. In response, Bill points*

his gun at Martha, says "You're dead!" and fires his gun but misses.

In Example 1, Bill has likely committed an intentional tort of civil assault. Bill may also face a criminal prosecution. He knowingly threatened Martha with imminent bodily injury with no legal justification.

Example 2:
Bill is driving through an unfamiliar part of downtown Richmond and comes to a stop at a red light. Martha is standing next to his passenger window at the traffic light screaming that he cut her off in traffic, but taking no action to indicate she intends to harm Bill or do anything besides verbally lodge her complaints. A startled Bill fires a shot at Martha to make her go away and hits her in the leg.

In Example 2, Bill has likely committed an intentional tort of assault and battery. Bill may also face a criminal prosecution. He intended to and did cause serious bodily injury to Martha with an insufficient legal justification. Martha's mere words are not enough justify Bill's use of deadly force. Therefore, a civil jury would likely find Bill liable and financially responsible for Martha's injuries.

Example 3:
Bill is driving through an unfamiliar part of downtown Richmond and comes to a stop at a red light. Martha is standing next to his passenger window at the traffic light screaming that he cut her off in traffic, but taking no action to indicate she intends to harm Bill or do anything besides verbally lodge her complaints. A startled Bill fires a shot at Martha to make her go away, but this time Martha is hit in the head and dies.

In Example 3, Martha's heirs or surviving family members will be able to bring a wrongful death civil lawsuit against Bill for his intentional tort of battery that killed Martha. Bill will also likely face a criminal prosecution for killing Martha. In Virginia, an individual is civilly liable for his wrongful acts if they caused an individual's death. *See* Va. Code § 8.01.50.

Example 4:
Emily fears she is about to be attacked in a grocery store parking lot by Randall. Randall follows her step-by-step through the parking lot and stops right next to Emily's car. Emily draws her .380, points it directly at Randall and tells him to "stay right there while I call the police." Randall does not move. Emily keeps the gun pointed at Randall until the police arrive. When the police arrive, they determine that Randall was an out-of-uniform grocery store employee tasked with rounding up the grocery carts in the parking lot and was no threat to Emily.

In Example 4, Emily has likely committed an intentional tort of false imprisonment when she held Randall at gun point. Emily may also be criminally prosecuted. False imprisonment occurs when an individual is willfully detained or restrained without consent by another, and without the legal right to do so. *See Zayre of Va., Inc. v. Gowdy,* 207 Va. 47 (1966).

B.   *Negligence*
An unintentional or negligent tort is called negligence. Negligence is the legal term for careless behavior that causes or contributes to an accident. In the context of firearms, an individual has a duty to exercise reasonable or ordinary care with their firearms; however, reasonable or ordinary care is a relative term, and varies with the nature and character of the situation to which it is applied. There are various types of firearm discharges that could create civil liability due to the law abiding gun owner's negligence. Hunting accidents, cleaning accidents and the mishandling of a gun are common events associated with a civil liability negligence lawsuit. It is important to note that the mere discharge of a firearm is not automatically negligent. The amount or degree of diligence and caution which is necessary to constitute reasonable or ordinary care depends upon the circumstances and the particular surroundings of each specific case, which is ultimately decided by the judge or jury if there is a dispute. The test is that degree of care which an ordinarily prudent person would exercise under the same or similar circumstances to avoid injury to another. *See Perlin v. Chappell,* 198 Va. 861 (1957); Model Jury Instruction No. 4.0. An individual may be considered negligent and civilly liable whenever he had a duty to act carefully and failed to do so.

In Virginia, there are three levels of negligence. The first level, sometimes called "simple negligence," was just described above. The second level is "gross negligence." The difference between simple negligence and gross negligence is one of degree; however, gross negligence is not typically relevant to a civil lawsuit alleging negligent use of a firearm unless there is a special legal relationship. *See* Model Jury Instruction No. 4.030. The third level of negligence is "willful and wanton negligence," which is conduct defined as acting consciously in disregard of another person's rights or acting with reckless indifference to the consequences, with the defendant aware, from his knowledge of existing circumstances and conditions, that his conduct probably would cause injury to another. *See Cowan v. Hospice Support Care, Inc.,* 268 Va. 482, 487 (2004); Model Jury Instruction No. 9.080.

If the plaintiff establishes willful and wanton negligence, then the plaintiff may be entitled to an additional monetary award not available in simple negligence cases.

Example 1:
Jessica has practiced her target shooting at a private range on her country property in Southwest Virginia for 20 years, without incident. Jessica shoots towards an area where she has never seen another person, and she believes the range of her guns cannot reach her property line. One day, a neighbor is hit by a shot and injured as he is strolling through the woods just along the other side of Jessica's property. The neighbor later files a civil lawsuit against Jessica for his injuries.

In Example 1, Jessica might be civilly liable for simple negligence if a jury determines, for example, that a reasonably prudent person would have acted differently, tested the range of her guns, or built a different type of back stop or berm, *etc.*

Example 2:
Jessica has received several complaints over the years about bullets leaving her property from the private shooting range and hitting her neighbor's property. She received other reports that neighbors often walked in the area. Nevertheless, Jessica ignores the complaints and

*continues her target practice as usual. One day while tar-
get shooting, her bullet leaves her property, and hits her
neighbor causing an injury. The neighbor files a civil lawsuit against Jessica for the injuries.*

In Example 2, Jessica may very well be civilly liable for willful and wonton negligence if the jury finds she consciously disregarded another person's rights or was acting with reckless indifference to the consequences, being aware, from her knowledge of existing circumstances and conditions, that her conduct would probably cause injury to another. She continued to shoot in the same area without taking any safety measures such as building a backstop or berm after she was advised multiple times that her shots were reaching the neighbor's property and that there were people in the same area.

Example 3:
*Jessica's shot in either Example 1 or Example 2 killed the
neighbor. The neighbor's surviving family members or
heirs file a civil lawsuit against Jessica for wrongful death.*

In Example 3, Jessica did not intend to shoot anyone, but if the jury hearing the case believed that the killing was due to her negligence, then she may be liable for damages caused by the neighbor's wrongful death. *See* Va. Code § 8.01-50.

1. Negligent entrustment

Civil liability under the doctrine of negligent entrustment requires that the owner of the firearm used to inflict the injury knew, or had reasonable cause to know, that he was entrusting the firearm to a third person who was likely to use it in a manner that would cause injury to others. *See Kingrey v. Hill*, 245 Va. 76 (1993).

Example:
*Steve lost his way in Craig County and drove his car onto
property belonging to Betty and Frank. Frank fired a rifle
at Steve's vehicle and injured Steve when a bullet fragment
grazed his head. Betty had previously received the rifle
that Frank used from her grandfather five years before the
incident of Frank shooting Steve. Betty placed the rifle with
other possessions upon receiving it and never touched it
thereafter. Betty was not present when Frank fired the rifle*

at Steve. Frank was prohibited from possessing a firearm due to a prior incident ten years earlier that resulted in a felony conviction. Betty knew about Frank's prior incident and conviction, but never instructed Frank not to use the rifle and did not keep the rifle in a manner which would prevent Frank from having access to it. There was no evidence that Betty either permitted Frank to use the rifle or prohibited him from doing so. Frank had a previous altercation with trespassers, but no firearms were involved in that incident. Steve files a civil lawsuit against Betty, the owner of the rifle, for negligent entrustment of a firearm.

Did Betty negligently entrust her rifle to Frank? Will Betty be civilly liable to Steve in his negligent entrustment of a firearm lawsuit? The answer to both of these questions is no. Betty did not negligently entrust her firearm to Frank and will not be civilly liable to Steve for negligent entrustment of a firearm according to the Supreme Court of Virginia.

Negligent entrustment cases require evidence of express permission, evidence of a pattern of conduct supporting implied permission, or evidence of knowledge that the firearm would be used notwithstanding explicit instructions to the contrary to establish that entrustment occurred.

In this example, the evidence that Betty "entrusted" the rifle to Frank is insufficient. There is no evidence that Betty expressly permitted Frank to use the rifle. There is no affirmative act or pattern of action establishing implied permission. Nor is the evidence sufficient to show that Betty knew, or should have known, that regardless of her actions, if Frank had access to the rifle, he would use it to harm others. Betty's knowledge of a single incident a decade ago involving Frank's use of a firearm is insufficient as a matter of law to support a finding that she should have known that Frank would take the rifle and injure another. The rifle was on the premises for five years without incident. The prior altercation with trespassers did not involve a firearm. There was no habit or pattern of conduct which supports a finding that Betty knew or should have known that Frank would engage in dangerous or reckless handling of her rifle. Betty's failure to keep a gun under lock and key, or failure to otherwise prohibit Frank from using the rifle, does not support a finding that she negligently entrusted the rifle to him under the facts of this example.

2. Parental liability

Educated and responsible gun owning parents understand that they have a duty to supervise their children and to take proper measures in order to safeguard firearms from their children. Unfortunately, there may be instances where a child is able to access a parent's firearm and cause an injury. If such an event were to happen, then the parent would generally not be civilly liable for the civil wrong or tort of the minor child. *See Bell v. Hudgins,* 232 Va. 491 (1987); *Hackley v. Robey,* 170 Va. 55 (1938)(unless there is an employer-employee or principal-agent relationship between the parent and minor child). This is also true even if the parent is careless or negligent in his supervision of the child who engages in the tortious conduct. An exception may be in situations involving negligent entrustment as discussed above. However, the minor child is civilly liable for his own civil wrongs or torts. *See Midkiff v. Midkiff,* 201 Va. 829 (1960). There is a statutory exception that provides for parental civil liability for up to $2,500 in damages to public or private property when the child's destruction of or damage to property was willful or malicious. *See* Va. Code §§ 8.01-43 and 8.01-44.

Parents also need to be aware of Va. Code § 18.2-56.2, which is a criminal law that punishes those who allow children access to firearms. This statute makes it a misdemeanor criminal offense for any person to recklessly leave a loaded, unsecured firearm in such a manner as to endanger the life or limb of any child under the age of fourteen. A violation is punishable by a fine not to exceed $500. It is also a misdemeanor criminal offense for any person to knowingly authorize a child under the age of twelve to use a firearm except when the child is under the supervision of an adult. A violation is punishable with a maximum fine of $2,500 and incarceration of up to 12 months.

A violation of Va. Code § 18.2-56.2 may create civil liability on a negligence *per se* theory. The violation of a statute constitutes negligence *per se*, and if such negligence is the cause of an injury, then it will support a recovery for damages for such injury. The question of whether such conduct is negligence *per se* and was the cause of an injury is usually a question of fact for the judge or jury hearing the case to determine. *See Standard Oil Co. v. Williams,* 202 Va. 362 (1960).

Example:
Jon and his father go bird hunting in the Virginia countryside. Jon, 17-years-old, has been hunting since he was 11-years-old and has taken several firearms training courses. Jon accidentally discharges his rifle and injures another person.

Note: There is no minimum age to possess a rifle in Virginia.

In this example, it is highly unlikely that Jon's father will be civilly liable for the injury in the accidental discharge of Jon's rifle.

Example:
Gordon, 12-years-old, and his father, Glen, go to the firing range together for the first time to shoot Glen's Glock. Gordon has never handled a gun or taken a firearms training course. Gordon repeatedly fires the Glock into the ceiling and the floor. The firing range asks Glen and Gordon to leave the range. Glen and Gordon leave the first firing range and immediately go to a second firing range across the street with no additional instruction or training for Gordon. Gordon shoots and injures another person with Glen's Glock at the second firing range. The injured person files a civil lawsuit for negligent entrustment of a firearm against Glen.

Did Glen negligently entrust his Glock to Gordon? Will Glen be civilly liable for his negligent entrustment of his Glock to Gordon?

Glen expressly permitted Gordon to use his Glock at both firing ranges. It is likely that a jury hearing a case like this example would find that Glen should have known that Gordon was engaging in dangerous and reckless conduct at the first range and that to immediately keep shooting at the second range without any training would likely injure another person. Glen will likely be civilly liable for the injuries caused at the second firing range due to his negligent entrustment of the Glock to Gordon.

Note: Va. Code § 18.2-309 states that it is illegal for anyone to furnish a handgun to any minor and that Va. Code § 18.2-308.7 states that it is illegal for anyone under the age of 18 to knowingly and intentionally possess a handgun; however, there is an exception to such possession by a minor if he is accompanied by an adult at a lawful shooting range.

Example:
Bobby, a 14-year-old boy, does not like his neighbor. One day, he retrieves the family 12-gauge shotgun and decides to shoot the neighbor's fence. Bobby's parents know nothing about this behavior and Bobby has never had trouble with a firearm in the past. As a result of the shooting, a number of pickets from the fence were destroyed, three windows were broken, and numerous pockmarks were left in the brick façade of the home. Can the neighbor file a civil lawsuit against Bobby's parents and seek recovery for the damages from Bobby's parents?

The neighbor can file a civil lawsuit against Bobby's parents pursuant to Va. Code § 8.01-44 for the damage to their private property. The owner of any private property may institute a civil action and recover from the parents of a minor who is living with his parents for damages suffered by reason of the willful or malicious destruction of, or damage to, such property by the minor, but no more than $2,500 may be recovered from the parents. Any recovery from the parents of the minor shall not preclude the neighbor from full recovery from the minor except to the amount of the recovery already paid by the parents.

3. Contributory negligence

Virginia is known as a "pure contributory negligence" state, which means that plaintiffs who are contributorily negligent or contributed to the accident at all are completely barred from any recovery. This means that if the jury thinks the plaintiff is even 1% at fault, then the plaintiff cannot recover. Technically, contributory negligence is considered an affirmative defense to the plaintiff's negligence lawsuit, but it requires the defendant to present evidence and prove by a preponderance of the evidence that the plaintiff contributed to the accident. Alabama, North Carolina, Maryland, Virginia, and Washington D.C., are the only jurisdictions that still have "pure" contributory negligence. The plaintiff may also assert alternative facts and theories of recovery in his lawsuit so long as all the claims arise out of the same event. This means that a plaintiff may assert both intentional tort and negligence claims. *See* Va. Code §8.01-281; *Berry v. Klinger* 225 Va. 201, 207 (1983).

IV. The Virginia civil trial: An overview
A civil lawsuit in the context of an incident involving the use of a firearm is typically a plaintiff's attempt to secure financial compensation for injuries allegedly caused by the wrongful actions of the defendant. As we have discussed, any use of a firearm creates the possibility of civil liability, regardless of what happens with any criminal case. If a civil plaintiff alleges to have been injured as the result of the defendant's wrongful actions in the use of a firearm, then a civil lawsuit can be filed against the defendant upon the payment of a filing fee. The filing of a civil lawsuit by the plaintiff, no matter how frivolous, must still be taken seriously and defended by the defendant. The process can take significant time, money, and legal energy, even for the most frivolous of cases. It is important to understand that the mere filing of a civil lawsuit by the plaintiff does not mean the plaintiff will succeed. The plaintiff must prove his case by a preponderance of the evidence in order to win his lawsuit.

A. *Statute of limitations*
The statute of limitations is a doctrine in Virginia (and almost every other jurisdiction) that requires a civil lawsuit to be filed within a certain period of time after the incident. If the plaintiff does not file his civil lawsuit within the statute of limitations period, then he is forever barred from bringing that civil case against the defendant. There are a number of issues relating to when the statute of limitations period begins, but for the most part, the time period will start to run immediately after the incident. The statute of limitations can vary by legal claim, but most limitation periods range between one and four years. In Virginia, the statute of limitations period that will apply to a civil lawsuit involving a firearm is going to be two years. Assault and battery, negligence, wrongful death, and false imprisonment claims all provide two-year statutory limitation periods.

B. *Causation*
Causation or proximate cause is the legal causal relationship or connection between either the alleged intentional tort or negligent tort and the resulting injury. Proximate cause must be established in every case. The civil plaintiff must prove that his damages from

the injury were proximately caused by the defendant's wrongful act. Damages are discussed in the next section.

In a case involving the firing of a gun, the most obvious proximate cause would be pulling the trigger on a firearm and hitting your intended target. The law will hold that your action proximately caused whatever physical damage was caused by that bullet. However, there are circumstances where the use of the firearm is far removed from the alleged damages. This is where the doctrine of proximate cause will cut off civil liability. If the damages are too far removed from the act, then the act cannot be a proximate cause of those damages.

> Example:
> *Anthony is cleaning his AR-15 one night in his apartment and is negligent in his handling of the rifle. The firearm discharges, the bullet goes through the wall of his apartment and strikes his neighbor Ray in the leg. Ray, obviously in pain, received prompt medical care from his wife, Gail, and made a speedy recovery. Ray and Gail both file civil lawsuits against Anthony to recover money damages.*

In this example, it is clear that Anthony's negligence "proximately caused" damages for things like Ray's medical bills, hospital stay, and perhaps even lost wages. However, has Gail suffered any damages? What if Gail claims that she missed a big job interview, lost out on a big raise in pay, and that she wants Anthony to pay that as a component of damages because of her treating Ray's wounds? The law would hold that Gail likely could not recover damages for her lost raise in pay because the loss was not "proximately caused" by Anthony's negligence in carelessly firing the rifle. To put it another way, it is reasonably foreseeable that the negligent discharge of a firearm will cause medical bills for someone struck by a bullet, but the loss of a possible job opportunity for the wife who treated the person who was actually shot is not a reasonably foreseeable consequence of negligently discharging a firearm.

C. *Damages*
Damages are awarded by the judge or jury deciding the case. Damages typically come in the form of money to be paid to the plaintiff as compensation for a loss or injury if the plaintiff proves his case;

however, the plaintiff is required to also prove his damages. It is possible that the defendant is 100% at fault or liable for the plaintiff's injury, but no damages are awarded to the plaintiff because the plaintiff failed to prove damages by a preponderance of the evidence. For example, a plaintiff who seeks reimbursement for medical expenses, but has no evidence that they ever went to a doctor or hospital will unlikely be able to recover those medical expenses.

Damages are categorized into compensatory (or actual) damages, and punitive damages. Compensatory damages are further categorized into special damages and general damages. Special damages are economic losses such as loss of earnings, property damage, and medical expenses. General damages are noneconomic damages such as pain and suffering and emotional distress. Punitive damages are not awarded in order to compensate the plaintiff, but are awarded to punish the defendant and warn others. Punitive damages are recoverable if the plaintiff pleads and proves either an intentional tort or willful and wanton negligence. *See Shaw v. Titan Corp.,* 255 Va. 535 (1998).

V. Insurance
A firearm is personal property and can be insured against theft and damage, but this section will focus on how insurance relates to the law abiding gun owner's use of a firearm. Every law abiding gun owner should take the time to consult their insurance companies to understand the coverage their policies offer in the event they use a firearm.

A. *Homeowners' insurance*
Many homeowner insurance policies will provide coverage for accidental firearm discharges, which may likely include legal representation if necessary. Coverage for instances involving the careless or negligent use of a firearm are less clear, while insurance companies almost never provide coverage for intentional torts involving a firearm. Thus, it is always important for the lawful gun owner to understand what coverage is provided by any homeowner's insurance policy.

As we previously discussed, self-defense is a defense to civil liability for intentional torts, but it is up to the judge or jury hearing the case to make that determination if there is a dispute. The act of using a firearm in self-defense is almost always an intentional act because it was fired with an intention to stop the threat. In instances like these, the insurance company would not be required to provide coverage assuming the policy does not cover intentional torts. The gun owner would then be responsible for his own legal defense because he would not be receiving any assistance from his insurance company due to lack of coverage. Furthermore, if the judge or jury found that the firing of the gun was not self-defense and awarded damages to the plaintiff, then the defendant will be subject to a judgment for money damages without assistance from the insurance company.

B. *Automobile insurance*
Scores of cases exist where the parties allege that a gun incident is covered by an automobile insurance policy because the use of the firearm either occurred in an automobile or involved an automobile. However, these incidents are not covered by the insurance company merely because the discharge occurred in a motor vehicle or involved a motor vehicle.

In order for automobile insurance coverage to apply, the injury must arise from the "use" of a motor vehicle as a motor vehicle. There must be a causal connection between the use of the motor vehicle and the injury. This connection is shown if the injury is the natural and reasonable consequence of the motor vehicle's use. There is no coverage if the injury results from something wholly disassociated from, independent of, and remote from the motor vehicle's normal employment. *See Lexie v. State Farm Mut. Auto. Ins. Co.,* 251 Va. 390 (1996).

> Example:
> *Justin is cleaning his 9mm handgun in his car. Justin has an automobile insurance policy. Justin's gun discharges and severely injures his passenger.*

In this example, Justin's automobile insurance policy will not likely cover the injuries of the passenger.

PRACTICAL LEGAL TIP

Most people have no idea how a civil lawsuit works. Just about anyone can file a civil action against another person if they can pay the filing fee. In Virginia, the courts have no mechanism of sifting through the thousands of lawsuits filed every year to determine which are frivolous and which are meritorious and should go forward. The civil justice system is "user driven," meaning that unless one side or the other asks the judge to rule on a particular issue (usually called a "motion"), no one at the courthouse, including the judge, is going to take any action to examine the merit, or lack thereof, of a lawsuit. — *Ed*

CHAPTER TWELVE

BEYOND FIREARMS: KNIVES, BLACKJACKS, NUN CHUCKS, THROWING STARS & TASERS

I. Introduction

A person's right to carry a firearm openly is considered universal in Virginia, subject to definite and limited restrictions upon certain premises and classifications of individuals. *See* 43 Op. Att'y Gen. 4 (2008). The right to open carry a different weapon is no different just because it is not a firearm. The Code of Virginia's weapon regulation deals primarily with certain weapons it deems dangerous when either carried concealed or taken upon certain premises. As we have previously discussed, it is always important to remember that a private party is free to regulate or ban weapons on its property. *See* 23 Op. Att'y Gen. 4 (2011); 9 Op. Att'y Gen. 1, 3 (2010).

II. Weapons regulated by Va. Code § 18.2-308

Va. Code § 18.2-308 makes it unlawful for any person to carry certain weapons about his person if hidden from common observation. A weapon shall be deemed to be hidden from common observation when it is observable, but is of such deceptive appearance as to disguise the weapon's true nature. Note: The same concealed carry exceptions for handguns with no CHP we discussed in Chapter 9, section III, also apply to the specifically regulated weapons as listed in Va. Code § 18.2-308. There is no prohibition to open carry any of these listed weapons unless otherwise prohibited by law. The weapons that are illegal to carry concealed are as follows:

- any dirk, bowie knife, switchblade knife, ballistic knife, machete, razor, slingshot, spring stick, metal knucks, or blackjack;
- nun chahka, nun chuck, nunchaku, shuriken, fighting chain or any flailing instrument consisting of two or more rigid parts connected in such a manner as to allow them to swing freely;
- throwing star, oriental dart, or any disc, of whatever configuration, having at least two points or pointed blades which is designed to be thrown or propelled; or
- any weapon of like kind as enumerated above.

From left: brass knuckles, Bowie Knife, throwing star or Shuriken, dirk, and nun chucks.

A violation is a misdemeanor punishable by 12 months in jail and/or a $2,500 fine. A violation by a convicted felon or person adjudicated delinquent of a delinquent act which would be a felony if committed by an adult is a felony punishable up to five years in prison and/or a $2,500 fine. A second violation is a felony punishable up to five years in prison and/or a $2,500 fine. A third or subsequent violation is also a felony, but punishable up to ten years in prison.

The Code of Virginia Sec. 18.2-307.1 only defines the following weapons in Va. Code § 18.2-308:

- a "ballistic knife" is any knife with a detachable blade that is propelled by a spring-operated mechanism; and
- a "spring stick" is a spring-loaded metal stick activated by pushing a button that rapidly and forcefully telescopes the weapon to several times its original length.

Left to right: Ballistic Knife and Blackjack

The following weapons listed in Va. Code § 18.2-308 are not defined by the Code of Virginia, but have been defined by the courts as follows:

- a "dirk" is a long straight-bladed dagger formerly carried by Scottish Highlanders or is a short sword formerly worn by British junior naval officers;
- a "bowie knife" is a large hunting knife adapted for knife-fighting and common in western frontier regions and having a guarded handle and a strong single-edge blade typically 10 to 15 inches long with its back straight for most of its length and then curving concavely and sometimes in a sharpened edge to the point; and
- a "switchblade knife" is a pocketknife having the blade

spring-operated so that pressure on a release catch causes it to fly open. *See Thompson v. Commonwealth,* 277 Va.
280 (2009).

The remaining weapons listed below from Va. Code § 18.2-308 are
not defined by the Code of Virginia, but have been defined by either
Merriam-Webster or the Oxford Dictionary, sources the courts often
refer to when the Code of Virginia is silent on a weapon definition:

- a "machete" is a broad, heavy knife used as an implement
  or weapon, originating in Central America and the Carib-
  bean;
- a "razor" is a tool or device with a sharp edge that is used
  to shave or cut hair from the face, body, or head;
- a "slingshot" is a Y-shaped stick or piece of metal with an
  elastic strip between the prongs for shooting stones and
  other small missiles;
- "metal knucks" also called brass knuckles, is a metal weapon that is worn over the knuckles and is intended to increase the injuries caused when hitting a person;
- a "blackjack" is a short, leather-covered, typically lead-
  filled club with a flexible handle; and
- a "shuriken" is a weapon in the form of a star with project-
  ing blades or points, used as a missile in some martial arts.

Caution: Virginia has a law that makes the sale or distribution of
certain weapons illegal. Va. Code § 18.2-311 makes it illegal to sell,
give, exhibit for sale or possess with an intention to sell a blackjack,
brass or metal knucks, a throwing star, a switchblade knife or ballistic knife. A violation is a misdemeanor punishable by a maximum
fine of $250.

It is not unlawful to simply possess a blackjack or other weapon
listed in the statute, but *it is unlawful to possess such weapons
with an intent to sell them.* The law is made more complicated for
lawful possessors of such weapons due to language in the statute
that makes possession *prima facie* evidence of an intent to sell the
weapon. This essentially means that the mere possession of such
weapon proves that you had an intent to sell the weapon.

Does that mean an individual is in violation of this law that appears intended to stop the sale and/or distribution of such weapons for mere possession? No. Such an individual would have various valid defenses to such an allegation as long as the possession was not otherwise unlawful. Still mere possession could trigger a law enforcement officer lawfully charging you with a violation under Va. Code § 18.2-311.

On a related note, Va. Code § 18.2-309 makes it unlawful to sell, barter, give or furnish any dirk, switchblade knife or bowie knife to a minor. Such an offense is a misdemeanor punishable by 12 months in jail and/or a $2500 fine.

PRACTICAL LEGAL TIP

The simple possession of a blackjack, brass knuckles, throwing star, switchblade knife or ballistic knife, while legal, can still trigger an arrest or criminal charge by the police because the wording of the law presumes that possession includes an intention to sell. Note: An arrest is not a conviction. A person simply possessing any of these enumerated weapons would have valid defenses. — *Ed*

III. Stun weapons

Va. Code § 18.2-308.1 defines a stun weapon as any device that emits a momentary or pulsed output, which is electrical, audible, optical or electromagnetic in nature and which is designed to temporarily incapacitate a person. Stun weapons are also commonly referred to as stun guns, stun batons, or tasers. It is legal to open carry

Above left: Handheld "Stun Gun," above right, Cartridge Taser

and conceal carry a stun weapon unless otherwise prohibited by law due to premises prohibitions or a felony conviction.

It is unlawful for any person convicted of a felony or adjudicated delinquent of a delinquent act which would be a felony if committed by an adult to knowingly and intentionally possess or transport any stun weapon. A violation is a felony punishable up to five years in prison and/or a $2500 fine. However, there is an exception that allows such persons to possess a stun weapon in his residence or on the curtilage. *See* Va. Code § 18.2-308.2.

Note: Use of a stun weapon would be considered a use of force and the same standards of self-defense as discussed in Chapter 4 would apply.

IV. Other weapons
A. *Chemical weapons*
As a general rule, pepper spray may be carried in Virginia. However, federal property is governed by federal law. It is recommended to contact either the federal agency or property you may visit if you will be carrying pepper spray to ensure you are in compliance with any federal regulations. Additionally, there are two chemical weapon sections in the Code of Virginia that you should be aware of when carrying pepper spray.

Va. Code § 18.2-312 states that it is unlawful to release tear gas, mustard gas, phosgene gas or other noxious or nauseating gases or mixtures of chemicals designed to produce vile or injurious or nauseating odors or gases that results in bodily injury. A violation is a felony punishable up to five years in prison and/or a $2,500 fine. A violation if done maliciously is a felony punishable by five to 20 years in prison and a maximum fine of $100,000. Law enforcement are exempt if used in the performance of their duties.

Va. Code § 18.2-52 states that it is unlawful to cause any other person bodily injury by means of any acid, lye or other caustic substance or agent or use of any explosive or fire. A violation is a felony punishable up to five years in prison and/or a $2,500 fine. A violation if done maliciously is punishable by five to 30 years in prison and a maximum fine of $100,000.

B. *Crossbow and bow and arrow*
It is unlawful to discharge a crossbow or bow and arrow in or across any road, or within the right-of-way thereof, or in a street of any city or town. A violation is a misdemeanor punishable by a fine of up to $250. Military personnel and law enforcement officers are exempt if in performance of their lawful duties. *See* Va. Code § 18.2-286.

C. *Spring gun*
It is unlawful for any person to set or fix in any manner any firearm or other deadly weapon so that it may be discharged or activated by a person coming in contact with any string, wire, spring, or any other contrivance attached thereto or designed to activate such weapon remotely. A violation is a felony punishable up to 5 years in prison and/or a $2,500 fine. *See* Va. Code § 18.2-281.

D. *Nails, tacks, etc. on a highway*
No person shall throw or deposit or cause to be deposited upon any highway any glass bottle, glass, nail, tack, wire, can, or any other substance likely to injure any person or animal, or damage any vehicle upon such highway. A violation is a misdemeanor punishable by up to 12 months in jail and/or a $2,500 fine. This law does not apply to law enforcement in the discharge of official duties while using any device designed to deflate tires. *See* Va. Code § 18.2-324.

> Example:
> *A caltrop is a weapon made up of two or more sharp*
> *nails arranged in a way that one always points up*
> *from a stable base. In ancient times, caltrops were* **Caltrops**
> *used as a way to slow the advance of horses, war*
> *elephants, camels, and human troops and were used as*
> *early as 331 BC. Today, caltrops (pictured right) are used*
> *to deflate automobile tires.*

E. *Pointing a laser at law enforcement*
It is unlawful for any person to intentionally project a point of light from a laser or a beam of light from any device that simulates a laser at a law enforcement officer engaged in the performance of his public duties. A violation is a misdemeanor punishable by 6 months in jail and/or a $1,000 fine. *See* Va. Code § 18.2-57.01.

F. *Bricks, bottles, rocks and ball bearings*
The Code of Virginia also states that it is illegal to unlawfully or maliciously throw or shoot any "missile" against any motor vehicle, dwelling house, building, train, vessel, watercraft, or other vehicle when occupied by one or more persons. The Code of Virginia does not define missile; however, the courts have defined a missile to be various items such as: bricks, bottles, rocks and ball bearings. Es-

sentially, any object that can be hurled can meet the definition of a missile for purposes of these laws. *See Thomas v. Danville,* 207 Va. 656 (1967); *Lamb v. Commonwealth,* No. 1262-02-2, 2003 Va. App. 252 (Ct. App. Apr. 29, 2003); *Kim v. Commonwealth,* No. 1090-13-4, 2014 Va. App. 145 (Ct. App. Apr. 22, 2014). A violation is a felony punishable by incarceration and a fine. The amount of incarceration and any fine depends upon whether the missile was thrown or shot unlawfully or maliciously, and whether any person died. *See* Va. Code § 18.2-154; Va. Code § 18.2-279.

V.   Prohibitions on regulated weapons at certain premises
A.   *Public and private elementary, middle and high schools*
Va. Code § 18.2-308.1 permits a pocket knife with a folding metal blade of less than 3 inches on school property; however, it is unlawful to knowingly possess any of the regulated weapons from Va. Code § 18.2-308 and/or a stun weapon upon:

   a) the property of any public, private or religious elementary, middle or high school, including buildings and grounds;
   b) that portion of any property open to the public and then exclusively used for school-sponsored functions or extra-curricular activities while such functions or activities are taking place; or
   c) any school bus owned or operated by any such school.

A violation is a misdemeanor punishable by up to 12 months in jail and/or a $2,500 fine. Exceptions include:

- persons who possess such weapon or weapons as a part of the school's curriculum or activities;
- a person possessing a knife customarily used for food preparation or service and is using it for such purpose;
- persons who possess such weapon or weapons as a part of any program sponsored or facilitated by either the school or any organization authorized by the school to conduct its programs either on or off the school premises;
- law enforcement and licensed security officers;
- any person who possesses a knife or blade which he uses customarily in his trade;
- a person who possesses a knife having a metal blade, in or upon a motor vehicle.

B. *Virginia courthouses*

Va. Code § 18.2-283.1 makes it unlawful for any person to possess in a courthouse or transport into a courthouse any of the regulated weapons from Va. Code § 18.2-308 and/or a stun weapon. A violation is a misdemeanor, will result in the weapon being seized by law enforcement, and is punishable up to 12 months in jail and/or a $2500 fine. The provisions of this law do not apply to law enforcement, a magistrate, a court officer, judge, or city/county treasurer while in the conduct of such person's official duties.

C. *Place of worship*

Va. Code § 18.2-283 states that a person may not carry any bowie knife, dagger or other dangerous weapon, without good and sufficient reason, to a place of worship while a meeting for religious purposes is being held at such place. A violation is a misdemeanor punishable by a maximum $250 fine. Personal protection is considered to be a good and sufficient reason to carry a weapon; however, a place of worship can choose to ban weapons on its property. *See* 23 Op. Att'y Gen. 4 (2011). It is recommended to understand the place of worship's position on weapons before taking any weapon into a place of worship.

D. *Airports*

Va. Code § 18.2-287.01 states that it is unlawful for any person to possess or transport into any air carrier airport terminal any of the regulated weapons from Va. Code § 18.2-308, stun weapons, and other dangerous weapons or explosives. A violation is a misdemeanor, results in forfeiture of the weapon, and is punishable up to 12 months in jail and/or a $2,500 fine.

E. *Federal courts, buildings and facilities*

18 U.S.C. § 930 states that it is unlawful to knowingly possesses a dangerous weapon in a federal facility or federal courthouse or to cause a dangerous weapon to be present in a federal facility or federal courthouse. A "dangerous weapon" is defined as a weapon, device, instrument, material, or substance, animate or inanimate, that is used for, or is readily capable of, causing death or serious bodily injury, except that such term does not include a pocket knife with a blade of less than 2½ inches in length.

A violation involving federal facilities can result in imprisonment for up to 1 year and/or a fine and a violation involving federal courthouses can result in imprisonment for up to 2 years and/or a fine. The penalties increase if such an act was done in the commission of a crime or resulted in the killing of a person.

Exceptions are permitted for those in the lawful performance of official duties by an officer, member, agent, or employee of the United States, a state, or a political subdivision thereof, or the lawful carrying of other dangerous weapons in a federal facility incident to hunting or other lawful purposes.

F.   _Universities and colleges_
Private universities, like any other owner of private property, may restrict or ban weapons on their property. The Second Amendment acts as a restraint on government, not private parties. It is recommended to review a private university's weapons policy before taking any weapon onto any private university's property.

Most of the public universities and colleges in Virginia have very similar weapons regulations, which include prohibitions on the carrying of firearms and weapons in school buildings and at school events. Each university or college's weapons policy is published in the Virginia Administrative Code under Title 8, which we discuss below.

   1.   George Mason University
Virginia Administrative Code, Title 8, Agency 35, Chapter 60, cited as 8VAC35-60, states that it is prohibited for any person, except law enforcement, to possess or carry any weapon on university property in academic buildings, administrative office buildings, student residence buildings, dining facilities, or while attending sporting, entertainment or educational events.

A "weapon" is defined as any pistol, revolver, or other weapon designed or intended to propel a missile of any kind, or any dirk, bowie knife, switchblade knife, ballistic knife, razor, slingshot, spring stick, metal knucks, blackjack, or any flailing instrument consisting of two or more rigid parts connected in such manner as to allow them to swing freely, which may be known as nun chahka, nun chuck, nunchaku, shuriken, or fighting chain, or any disc, of whatever configuration, having at least 2 points or pointed blades that is designed to be thrown or propelled and that may be known as throwing star or oriental dart.

2. Virginia Tech

8VAC105-20 states that university employees, students, and volunteers are prohibited from carrying, maintaining, or storing a firearm or weapon on any university property. Any visitor or other third party attending a sporting, entertainment, or educational event or visiting an academic or administrative office building, dining facility, or residence hall is prohibited from carrying, maintaining, or storing a firearm or weapon on any university facility, even if the owner has a valid CHP. This prohibition also applies to all events on campus where people congregate in any public or outdoor areas.

8VAC105-20-30 outlines various exceptions such as for law enforcement purposes and for those employees who reside in university owned houses. These types of employees are permitted to keep personal firearms on these premises; however, this exception does not extend to employees living in university residence halls.

A "weapon" is defined as any instrument of combat, or any object not designed as an instrument of combat but carried for the purpose of inflicting or threatening bodily injury. Examples include but are not limited to (i) firearms; (ii) knives with fixed blades or pocket knives with blades longer than 4 inches; (iii) razors or metal knuckles; (iv) blackjacks, foils, or hatchets; (v) bows and arrows; (vi) nun chahkas; (vii) stun weapons or (viii) any explosive or incendiary device. "Stun weapon" is defined as any device that emits a momentary or pulsed output that is electrical, audible, optical, or electromagnetic in nature and that is designed to temporarily incapacitate a person.

3. College of William and Mary

8VAC115-20 states that it is prohibited for any person, except law enforcement or authorized personnel, to possess or carry any weapon on university property in academic buildings, administrative buildings, student residence and student life buildings, or dining or athletic facilities, or while attending an official university event, such as an athletic, academic, social, recreational or educational event, or on vessels that are university property.

A "weapon" is defined as any firearm or any other weapon listed in Va. Code § 18.2-308.

4. James Madison University

8VAC45-10 states that it is prohibited for any person, except law enforcement, to possess or carry any weapon on university property in any buildings or any outdoor area to which access is restricted to members of the university community and invited guests, or while attending any university events or university-sanctioned events.

A "weapon" is defined as any firearm or any other weapon listed in Va. Code § 18.2-308.

5. Longwood University

8VAC50 20 states that it is prohibited for any person, except law enforcement, to possess or carry any weapon on university property in academic buildings, administrative office buildings, student resident buildings, or dining facilities or while attending sporting, entertainment, or educational events.

A "weapon" is defined as (i) any pistol, revolver, shotgun, bow and arrow, or other weapon designed or intended to propel a missile of any kind; (ii) any dirk, bowie knife, switchblade knife, ballistic knife, razor, slingshot, spring stick, metal knucks, or blackjack; (iii) any flailing instrument consisting of 2 or more rigid parts connected in such manner as to allow them to swing freely, which may be known as nun chahka, nunchaku, shuriken, or fighting chain; or (iv) any disc, of whatever configuration, having at least 2 points or pointed blades that is designed to be thrown or propelled and that may be known as throwing star or oriental dart.

6. Old Dominion University

8VAC65-10 states that it is prohibited for any person, except law enforcement, to possess or carry any weapon on university property in academic buildings, administrative office buildings, student residence buildings, or dining facilities, or while attending sporting, entertainment, or educational events.

"Weapon" means (i) firearms; (ii) knives, machetes, straight razors, spring sticks, metal knucks, or blackjacks; (iii) any flailing instrument consisting of 2 or more rigid parts connected in such a manner as to allow them to swing freely, which may be known as a nun chahka, nun chuck, nunchaku, shuriken, or fighting chain; (iv) any disc, of whatever configuration having at least 2 points or pointed blades, that is designed to be thrown or propelled and that may be known as a throwing star or oriental darts; and (v) any electrical conduction weapon including tasers.

"Weapon" does not mean knives used for domestic purposes, pen or folding knives with blades less than 3 inches in length, or box cutters and utility knives kept or carried for use in accordance with the purpose intended by the original seller.

7. Radford University
8VAC75-20 states that university employees, students, and volunteers are prohibited from carrying, maintaining, or storing a firearm or weapon on any university property. Any visitor or other third party attending a sporting, entertainment, or educational event, or visiting an academic or administrative office building, dining facility, or residence hall, is prohibited from carrying, maintaining, or storing a firearm or weapon on any university facility, even if the owner has a valid CHP. This prohibition also applies to all events on campus where people congregate in any public or outdoor areas. Exceptions include the Chief of the Radford University Police Department authorizing a student or employee on a case-by-case basis in writing to store a firearm that would normally be prohibited.

"Firearms" are defined as any gun, rifle, pistol, or handgun designed to fire any projectile including but not limited to bullets, BBs, pellets, or shots, including paint balls, regardless of the propellant used.

"Weapons" are defined as any instrument of combat, or any object not designed as an instrument of combat but carried for the purpose of inflicting or threatening bodily injury. Examples include but are not limited to firearms, knives with fixed blades or pocket knives with blades longer than 4 inches, razors, metal knuckles, blackjacks, hatchets, bows and arrows, nun chahkas, foils, stun weapons, or any explosive or incendiary device. Stun weapon is defined as any device that emits a momentary or pulsed output that is electrical, audible, optical, or electromagnetic in nature and that is designed to temporarily incapacitate a person.

8. Richard Bland College

8VAC115-30 states that it is prohibited for any person, except law enforcement, to possess or carry any weapon on college property in academic buildings, administrative buildings, student residence and student life buildings, or dining or athletic facilities, or while attending an official college event, such as an athletic, academic, social, recreational, or educational event, or on vessels that are college property.

A "weapon" is defined as any firearm or any other weapon listed in Va. Code § 18.2-308.

9. University of Mary Washington

8VAC55-10 states that it is prohibited for any person, except law enforcement, to possess or carry any weapon on university property in academic buildings, administrative office buildings, student residence buildings, dining facilities, or athletic facilities or while attending sporting, entertainment or educational events.

A weapon is defined as any (i) pistol, revolver, or other weapon designed or intended to propel a missile of any kind; (ii) any dirk, bowie knife, switchblade knife, ballistic knife, razor, slingshot, spring stick, metal knucks, or blackjack; (iii) any flailing instrument consisting of 2 or more rigid parts connected in such manner as to allow them to swing freely, which may be known as nun chahka, nun chuck, nunchaku, shuriken, or fighting chains; or (iv) any disc, of whatever configuration, having at least 2 points or pointed blades that is designed to be thrown or propelled and that may be known as a throwing star or oriental dart.

10. University of Virginia

8VAC85-20 states that it is prohibited for any university student, faculty, employee, trainee, or volunteer, except law enforcement, to possess, store, or use any weapon on university property. The possession, storage, or use of any weapon is prohibited by the general public or visitors, except law enforcement, on university property in academic, administrative, athletic, entertainment, or student residence buildings, child care or dining facilities, the University Medical Center, or while attending sporting, entertainment, or educational activities. Exceptions can be made in various circumstances as outlined in Va. Admin Code 8VAC85-20-30(D).

A "weapon" is defined a (i) any firearm including any pistol, revolver, rifle, shotgun, air-pistol, paintball gun, or other instrument designed or intended to propel a bullet, cartridge, or other missile of any kind including a bow or cross-bow; (ii) any dirk, bowie knife, switchblade knife, ballistic knife, butterfly knife, sword, machete, or other bladed weapon with a blade longer than 4 inches in length; (iii) any razor, slingshot, spring stick, metal or lexan knucks, or blackjack; (iv) any flailing instrument consisting of 2 or more rigid parts connected in such manner as to allow them to swing freely, which may be known as nun chahka, nun chuck, nunchaku, shuriken, or fighting chain, or (v) any disc, of whatever configuration, having at least 2 points or pointed blades that is designed to be thrown or propelled and that may be known as throwing star or oriental dart.

11. Virginia Commonwealth University
8VAC90-60 states that it is prohibited for any person, except law enforcement, to possess or carry any weapon on university property in academic buildings, administrative office buildings, medical venues, clinics, laboratories, research facilities, student residence buildings, and dining facilities; or while attending sporting, entertainment, or educational events.

A "weapon" is defined as (i) any pistol, revolver, or other weapon designed or intended to propel a missile of any kind; (ii) any dirk, bowie knife, switchblade knife, ballistic knife, razor, slingshot, spring stick, metal knucks, blackjack; (iii) any flailing instrument consisting of two or more rigid parts connected in such manner as to allow them to swing freely, which may be known as nun chahka, nun chuck, nunchaku, shuriken, or fighting chain, or (iv) any disc, of whatever configuration, having at least 2 points or pointed blades that is designed to be thrown or propelled and that may be known as throwing star or oriental dart.

12. Virginia Military Institute
8VAC100-10 states that it is prohibited for any person, except law enforcement, to possess or carry any weapon on institute property, to include academic buildings, administrative office buildings, support buildings, military training facilities, athletic facilities, barracks or any structure designated for cadet housing, or dining facilities, or while attending sporting, entertainment, or educational events. The prohibition would not apply to those activities falling under the

Reserve Officer Training Corps programs, NCAA rifle teams, Trap and Skeet Club, VMI Firing Range(s) or Marksmanship Club, or other official institute club or other activity.

A "weapon" is defined as (i) any pistol, revolver, or other weapon designed or intended to propel a missile of any kind; (ii) any dirk, bowie knife, switchblade knife, ballistic knife, razor, slingshot, sprint stick, metal knucks, or blackjack; (iii) any flailing instrument consisting of 2 or more rigid parts connected in such manner as to allow them to swing freely, which may be known as nun chahka, nun chuck, nunchaku, shuriken, or fighting chain, or (iv) any disc, of whatever configuration, having at least 2 points or pointed blades that is designed to be thrown or propelled and that may be known as throwing star or oriental dart.

13. Virginia State University
8VAC110-10 states that it is prohibited for university employees, students, and volunteers to carry, maintain, or store a firearm or weapon on any university property. Any visitor or other third party attending a sporting, entertainment, or educational event, or visiting an academic or administrative office building, dining facility, or residence hall is prohibited from carrying, maintaining, or storing a firearm or weapon on any university facility, even if the owner has a valid CHP. This prohibition also applies to all events on campus where people congregate in any public or outdoor areas.

8VAC110-10-30 outlines exceptions to this prohibition, which states that an employee may possess or carry a firearm if the employee is residing in university-owned houses and is permitted to keep personal firearms on the premises; however, this exception does not extend to employees living in university residence halls.

"Firearms" are defined as any gun, rifle, pistol, or handgun designed to fire any projectile including but not limited to bullets, BBs, pellets, or shots, including paint balls, regardless of the propellant used.

"Weapons" are defined as any instrument of combat, or any object not designed as an instrument of combat but carried for the purpose of inflicting or threatening bodily injury. Examples include but are not limited to firearms, knives with fixed blades or pocket knives with blades longer than 4 inches, razors, metal knuckles, blackjacks, hatchets, bows and arrows, nun chahkas, foils, stun weapons, or any explosive or incendiary device. "Stun weapon" is defined as any device that emits a momentary or pulsed output that is electrical, audible, optical, or electromagnetic in nature and that is designed to temporarily incapacitate a person.

14. Christopher Newport University
Unauthorized possession, storage, or control of weapons, firearms and ammunition by students on University property is prohibited. This includes storage in vehicles on campus as well as in the residence halls.

A "firearm" is defined as any gun, rifle, pistol, or handgun designed to fire bullets, BBs, pellets, or shot regardless of the propellant used. Other weapons include any instrument of combat, or any object not designed as an instrument of combat but carried for the purpose of inflicting or threatening bodily injury. Examples include, but are not limited to, knives with fixed blades or pocket knives with blades longer than 4 inches, razors, metal knuckles, blackjacks, hatchets, bows and arrows, nunchakus, foils, or explosives and incendiary devices.

15. Norfolk State University
The unauthorized possession, carrying, maintaining, storage, control, brandishing, or use of firearms and weapons, or any reasonable facsimiles thereof, by students, faculty, staff, transient personnel, invitees or any other third parties, except law enforcement, while on University property or on University controlled sites, and at University-sponsored activities, services or programs, even if the owner has a valid CHP is prohibited.

This prohibition includes the unauthorized storage of firearms and weapons in vehicles on campus and in residential halls. This policy prohibits all concealed weapons and unauthorized possession of realistic replicas of weapons. There are various narrow exceptions to this policy.

A firearm is defined as any device that can be used as a weapon, and that is designed to fire either single or multiple projectiles propelled at high velocity regardless of the type of propellant used. A firearm includes, but is not limited to any gun, rifle, air-gun, pistol, cannon, or handgun designed to fire bullets, BBs, pellets, balls, air, spears, flares, tranquilizers, darts, shots (including paintballs), or any other projectile, whether loaded or unloaded, and the ammunition for any such device.

A "weapon" is defined as, but is not limited to, any instrument of combat or any object that is used, designed to be used or intended to be used by the possessor to inflict death or bodily injury to any person, or for the purpose of threatening or intimidating any person with death or bodily injury. Examples of weapons include, but are not limited to, knives with fixed blades, pocket knives, dirks, switchblades, butterfly knives, firearms, ammunition, explosives or other incendiary devices, box cutters, razors, broken bottles, metal knuckles, blackjacks, bows and arrows, billy clubs, night sticks, bludgeons, slingshots, machetes, hatchets, nun chukkas, foils, chains, swords, ice picks, stun weapons, acid and other corrosive chemicals. The unauthorized possession of realistic replicas of weapons is prohibited. The possession, carrying, use and brandishing of a potentially harmful object(s) in a situation where there is no reasonable use for it and/or when such object(s) is used to intimidate, cause death or serious bodily injury, or to threaten another with death or serious bodily injury will be considered a violation of this policy. Examples include, but are not limited to, steak knives, butcher knives, tools, hammers, shovels and any other potentially harmful object or implement.

16. Virginia Community Colleges
8VAC95-10 states that it is prohibited for any person to possess or carry any weapon on college property in academic buildings, administrative office buildings, student centers, child care centers, dining facilities and places of like kind where people congregate, or while attending any sporting, entertainment, or educational events. However this prohibition neither applies to law enforcement nor to possession of a weapon when stored securely inside the vehicle of properly permitted students and employees.

A "weapon" is defined as (i) any pistol, revolver, or other weapon designed or intended to propel a missile of any kind by action of an explosion of any combustible material; (ii) any dirk, bowie knife, switchblade knife, ballistic knife, machete, razor, slingshot, spring stick, metal knucks, or blackjack; (iii) any flailing instrument consisting of 2 or more rigid parts connected in such a manner as to allow them to swing freely, which may be known as a nun chahka, nun chuck, nunchaku, shuriken, or fighting chain; (iv) any disc, of whatever configuration, having at least 2 points or pointed blades that is designed to be thrown or propelled and that may be known as a throwing star or oriental darts; or (v) any weapon of like kind, to include but not limited to, tasers.

"Weapon" does not mean knives or razors used for domestic purposes, pen or folding knives with blades less than 3 inches in length, or knives of like kind carried for use in accordance with the purpose intended by the original seller.

Chapter Thirteen

What Firearms Are Regulated by the NFA?

The National Firearms Act (NFA) and the Virginia Uniform Machine Gun Act regulate machine guns. The NFA also regulates silencers or suppressors, short-barreled shotguns & rifles, and destructive devices. These firearms and devices are legal to purchase and/or possess, but there are certain specific requirements that must be followed for such purchase, transfer and/or possession to be lawful. In this chapter, we will discuss both Acts, the purpose behind the NFA, what firearms and other items are regulated, as well as the process and procedure for legally possessing weapons that are subject to each Act's provisions.

I.   Virginia Uniform Machine Gun Act

A.   *Registration of a machine gun*

Virginia Code § 18.2-295 requires every machine gun in Virginia to be registered with the Virginia State Police (VSP) within 24 hours after its acquisition. A certificate of registration is issued upon receipt of a completed machine gun registration application and is valid as long as the registrant information remains the same. The transferor of the machine gun is required to immediately notify the VSP Superintendent of the transfer in writing with the name and address of the transferee along with the date of the transfer.

The VSP must be notified promptly of any change of information pertaining to the registration, such as change of address, telephone number, *etc.*, to initiate receipt of an updated registration. Failure to either give the required notification to the VSP or to keep and/or produce a certificate of registration for inspection is a misdemeanor punishable by a fine of up to $500.

B.   *Possession or use of a machine gun*

The possession of a machine gun for a purpose manifestly not aggressive or offensive, for scientific purposes, or possessed as a curiosity, ornament, or keepsake is lawful. *See* Va. Code § 18.2-293.1. Possession or use of a machine gun shall be presumed to be for an offensive or aggressive purpose when:

(1) the machine gun is on premises not owned or rented as a bona fide permanent residence or business occupancy by the possessor of the machine gun;

(2) the machine gun is in the possession of, or used by, a person who has been convicted of a crime of violence in any federal or state court of record;

(3) the machine gun has not been registered as required by Va. Code § 18.2-295; or

(4) empty or loaded shells which have been or are susceptible of use in the machine gun are found in the immediate vicinity. *See* Va. Code § 18.2-291.

Unlawful possession or use of a machine gun for an offensive or aggressive purpose is a felony punishable by up to ten years in prison and a fine of up to $100,000. Possession or use of a machine gun in the perpetration or attempted perpetration of a crime of violence is a felony punishable by up to life imprisonment and a fine of up to $100,000. *See* Va. Code § 18.2-290; Va. Code § 18.2-289.

Caution: The language of Va. Code § 18.2-292 has a presumption that merely being in the same room or vehicle where a machine gun is located would be sufficient evidence for the prosecution that an individual was in possession of said machine gun. Additionally, Va. Code § 18.2-292 presumes certain types of conduct to meet the legal definition of possessing or using a machine gun for an offensive or aggressive purpose. Legal presumptions can be rebutted with defense motions, evidence and arguments, but make no mistake, the language of the Uniform Machine Gun Act is written to greatly favor the prosecution in any case involving a machine gun.

II.   The National Firearms Act

The NFA was enacted in 1934 in response to gangster crimes. Prior to the Act's passage, any person could go to the local hardware store and purchase a Thompson Submachine Gun or shorten the barrel on their rifle or shotgun. President Franklin D. Roosevelt pushed for the passage of the NFA in an attempt to diminish a gangster's ability to possess and carry dangerous and/or easily concealable firearms, such as machine guns and short-barreled rifles and shotguns. The constitutionality of the NFA was subsequently challenged five years later. The U.S. Supreme Court in the case of *United States v. Miller,* 307 U.S. 174 (1939), held that the Constitution does guarantee a right to bear arms, but that right does not extend to every firearm.

The NFA regulates certain firearms and requires the manufacture and transfer of such firearms to be registered along with the payment of a tax. The law created a tax of $200 on the transfer of the following firearms: short-barreled shotguns, short-barreled rifles, machine guns, silencers, and destructive devices. Back in 1934, a $200 tax was the approximate equivalent to about $3,500 today! The tax is only $5 for firearms that are classified as "Any Other Weapons" or AOWs.

III. What firearms are regulated by the NFA?
A. Short-barreled or "sawed-off" rifles and shotguns
Shotguns and rifles are classified based on length, which was discussed in Chapter 2. Short-barreled rifles and shotguns are regulated by the NFA. A short-barreled shotgun is a shotgun with either a smoothbore barrel less than 18 inches long or a minimum overall length under 26 inches. A short-barreled rifle is any rifle with a butt-stock and either a rifled barrel less than 16 inches long or an overall length under 26 inches. *See* 27 CFR § 478.11; 18 U.S.C. § 921(a)(6); 18 U.S.C. § 921(a)(8); 26 U.S.C. § 5845. The Virginia definition of a short-barreled rifle or shotgun is essentially the same, but the firearms are referred to as being "sawed-off." *See* Va. Code § 18.2-299.

In order to be legal under the NFA, short-barreled shotguns and rifles must be registered, and a tax paid on the firearm. Short-barreled shotguns and rifles are typically purchased from an FFL firearms dealer that deals in NFA items; however, such firearms are very popular for individuals to build and/or modify on their own. This is legal if the individual has properly registered the firearm to be modified into a short-barreled firearm with the ATF and paid the tax before it is modified. Once approved, an individual may alter or produce a short-barreled firearm and must engrave legally required information on the receiver of the firearm such as manufacturer, location, *etc.*

Virginia Code § 18.2-303.1 states that possession of a "sawed-off" shotgun or "sawed-off" rifle is lawful if possessed in compliance with federal law, for scientific purposes, or not usable as a firing weapon but possessed as a curiosity, ornament, or keepsake; however, unlawful possession or use of a "sawed-off" rifle or shotgun is a felony punishable by up to 10 years or life in prison depending on whether such firearm is used in a crime of violence. Law enforcement and military are exempt from this provision. *See* Va. Code § 18.2-300; Va. Code § 18.2-303.

B. *Machine guns*

The machine gun is also regulated by the NFA. It is important to make sure that you are in compliance with the legal requirements of the NFA to ensure that your machine gun possession is lawful under federal law. *See* 26 U.S.C. § 5845. It is lawful to possess or transfer only certain machine guns. Such machine guns must have been lawfully possessed before May 19, 1986, which means they were manufactured and registered before May 19, 1986. Machine guns manufactured after May 19, 1986, may only be transferred to or possessed by the federal and state governments or their political subdivisions. *See* 18 U.S.C. § 922(o). Machine guns available for lawful private ownership are limited.

C. *Firearm suppressors*

Firearm suppressors are regulated by the NFA. Generally, a firearm suppressor is a muffler for a firearm and is legal if all NFA requirements are met. According to federal law, a firearm suppressor, silencer or muffler is defined as "any device for silencing, muffling, or diminishing the report of a portable firearm, including any combination of parts, designed or redesigned, and intended for use in assembling or fabricating a firearm silencer or firearm muffler, and any part intended only for use in such assembly or fabrication." *See* 27 CFR § 478.11; 18 U.S.C. § 921(a)(24).

Firearm suppressors are very practical instruments. They are great for hunting and recreational shooting because they suppress gunshots in a way so as to not alarm other animals being hunted, while lessening the impact on the shooter's ears. However, firearm owners should be carefully aware that the definition of a suppressor is very broad. Suppressors do not need to be items manufactured specifically for use as a suppressor. There are some ordinary, every-day items that could be easily converted into a suppressor such as a water bottle or an automotive oil filter. Possession of otherwise legal items when used or modified to be used as a suppressor violates the NFA and is illegal.

D. *Destructive devices*

DESTRUCTIVE DEVICES
27 C.F.R. § 478.11. **Part A.** Any explosive, incendiary, or poison gas (1) bomb, (2) grenade, (3) rocket having a propellant charge of more than 4 ounces, (4) missile having an explosive or incendiary charge of more than one-quarter ounce, (5) mine, or (6) device similar to any of the devices described in the preceding paragraphs of this definition. **Part B.** Any type of weapon (other than a shotgun or shotgun shell which the Director finds is generally recognized as particularly suitable for sporting purposes) by whatever name known which will, or which may be readily converted to, expel a projectile by the action of an explosive or other propellant, and which has any barrel with a bore of more than one-half inch in diameter. **Part C.** Any combination of parts either designed or intended for use in converting any destructive device described in [part] (A) and (B) of this section and from which a destructive device may be readily assembled.

The term "destructive device" is a legal term given to certain firearms, objects, and munitions that are illegal under the NFA. The "destructive devices" as defined in the statute are effectively broken down into three categories: explosive devices, large caliber weapons, and parts easily convertible into a destructive device.

The first portion of the definition of a destructive device deals with explosive, incendiary and poison gas munitions. The definition specifies that any explosive, incendiary, or poison gas bomb, grenade, mine or similar device is a destructive device. In addition, the definition includes a rocket having a propellant charge of more than four ounces and a missile (projectile) having an explosive or incendiary charge of more than one-quarter ounce. These topics and the regulations thereof are beyond the scope of this book's discussion.

The second section of the definition addresses large caliber weapons and states that any type of weapon that has a bore diameter of more than one-half inch is a destructive device with the exception of shotguns (and shotgun shells) that are suitable for sporting purposes. Thus, any caliber in a rifle or handgun more than .5 inches or .50 caliber is classified as a destructive device. Shotguns are exempt from this prohibition on size unless the ATF rules it is not for "sporting purposes."

How do you know if a shotgun is suitable for sporting purposes? The ATF keeps a list, and has issued rulings classifying specific shotguns as destructive devices because they are not considered to be particularly "suitable for sporting purposes" including the USAS-12, Striker-12, Streetsweeper, and 37/38mm Beanbags. The ATF neither provides any specific definition of what constitutes being "suitable for sporting purposes" nor does it specify the methodology in which it determines what makes a particular shotgun suitable for sporting purposes. Ultimately, one will have to check with the ATF lists to see whether a particular shotgun with a larger bore-diameter is classified as a destructive device or not.

Finally, a destructive device does not need to be a completed and assembled product to fall under the federal definition and regulation under the NFA. Much like machine guns, if a person possesses parts that can be readily assembled into a destructive device, then whether or not the device has actually been constructed is irrelevant—by law it's already a destructive device.

Although these firearms, munitions, and devices are prohibited by the law on its face pursuant to the NFA, a person may nevertheless receive permission to possess them so long as they possess the correct legal authorization. *See* 18 U.S.C. § 921(a)(4); 26 U.S.C. § 5845(f).

E.   *"Any Other Weapons" or AOWs*
The "Any Other Weapons" or AOW category under the NFA pertains to firearms and weapons that may not fit the traditional definition of some of the firearms discussed elsewhere in this book due to the way in which they are manufactured or modified. Under federal law,

an AOW is "any weapon or device capable of being concealed on the person from which a shot can be discharged through the energy of an explosion, a pistol or revolver having a barrel with a smooth bore designed or redesigned to fire a fixed shotgun shell, weapons with combination shotgun and rifle barrels 12 inches or more, less than 18 inches in length, from which only a single discharge can be made from either barrel without manual reloading, and shall include any such weapon which may be readily restored to fire. Such term shall not include a pistol or a revolver having a rifled bore, or rifled bores, or weapons designed, made, or intended to be fired from the shoulder and not capable of firing fixed ammunition." *See* 26 U.S.C. § 5845(e).

1. <u>Concealable weapons and devices</u>

Weapons which are capable of being concealed from which one shot can be discharged are AOWs. This includes such weapons as a pengun, knife gun, or umbrella gun.

Left to right: Concealable weapons and devices include the pen-gun, umbrella gun, knife gun, and wallet gun.

2. <u>Pistols and revolvers having a smooth-bore barrel for firing shotgun shells</u>

Pistols and revolvers that have a smooth bore (no rifling) that are designed to shoot shotgun ammunition are defined as an AOW. The ATF cites firearms such as the H&R Handy Gun or the Ithaca Auto & Burglar Gun as firearms which fall under the AOW category. Note: Handguns with partially rifled barrels such as The Judge do not fall under this category due to the rifling of the barrel.

Left, the H&R Handy Gun; right, the Ithaca Auto & Burglar Gun.

3. <u>Weapons with barrels 12 inches or longer and lengths 18 inches or shorter</u>

The definition of AOW also includes any weapon which has a shotgun or rifle barrel of 12 inches or more but is 18 inches or less in overall length from which only a single discharge can be made from either barrel without manual reloading. The ATF identifies the "Marble Game Getter" as the firearm most commonly associated with this definition (excluding the model with an 18-inch barrel and folding shoulder stock).

4. Pistols and revolvers with vertical handgrips

If a pistol is modified with a vertical grip on the front, it will now be legally classified as an AOW, which requires registration and a tax to be paid. Note, vertical grips are readily available and are legal to own as long as they are not placed on a handgun. The definition of a handgun is a weapon which is intended to be fired by one hand, the addition of the vertical grip makes it so the weapon now is intended to be used with two hands to fire. This modification changes the weapon from a handgun to what is known as an "AOW" and is now a prohibited weapon without the proper documentation.

F. *Antique firearms*

Antique firearms are not regulated by the NFA. We discussed antique firearms in Chapter 2. Note: the ATF states in its NFA handbook that it is important to note that a specific type of fixed ammunition that has been out of production for many years may again become available due to increasing interest in older firearms. Therefore, the classification of a specific NFA firearm as an antique firearm could change if ammunition for the weapon becomes readily available in the ordinary channels of commerce. *See* 26 U.S.C. § 5845(g).

G. *NFA curio firearms and relics*

A firearm classified as either a "curio" or "relic" may be regulated by the NFA depending on the ATF's analysis of the firearm. We also discussed curios and relics in Chapter 2. Persons that collect curios or relics may do so with a special collector's license although one is not required. The impact of an NFA item being classified as a curio or relic is that it allows the item to be transferred interstate to persons possessing a collector's license. The collector's license does not allow the individual to deal in curios or relics, nor does it allow the collector to obtain other firearms interstate as those transactions still require an FFL firearm dealer's license. The ATF maintains a list of firearms that are classified as curios or relics.

H. *After-market gun parts may make your gun illegal*

A number of companies manufacture and sell firearm products or parts that alter the appearance or utility of a firearm (*i.e.* shoulder stocks, forward hand grips, *etc.*). Some of these after-market products can change a normally unregulated firearm into a firearm that is regulated by the NFA. Many law abiding gun owners will simply purchase one of these firearm products or accessories and modify the firearm without knowing they have possibly altered the classification of their firearm.

> ### PRACTICAL LEGAL TIP
>
> Even if you don't own a machine gun today, that doesn't mean you won't be the intended owner of one later. A person could always leave you their NFA items in a will. If this happens, you must file the appropriate paperwork with the ATF as soon as possible, or at least before probate is closed. —*Ed*

Consider the example of a vertical forward grip on a handgun. Vertical forward grips are legal to buy or possess; however, if you actually install one on a handgun, you have manufactured an AOW and it is illegal, unless you comply with the ATF registration and tax requirements. Note: There are other types of braces that are permissible in their proper application, but illegal if the brace alters the classification of the weapon. For example, the Sig Arm Brace is legal to attach to an AR Pistol when used as an arm brace, but illegal when used as a shoulder stock.

IV.   Process and procedure for obtaining NFA items
A.   *Who can own and possess an NFA Item?*
Any person may own and possess an NFA firearm or item as long as they properly register the firearm or item, pay the tax, are not legally disqualified to own or possess firearms, and live in a state that allows possession of NFA items. The ATF also allows for legal entities to own these items such as corporations, partnerships, and trusts, *etc.*

B.   *Steps for buying or manufacturing NFA items*
Whether a person is buying or making (manufacturing) an NFA firearm or item, there are several steps in the process. The transfer or manufacture of an NFA firearm or item requires the filing of an appropriate transfer form with the ATF, payment of any federal-

ly-mandated transfer tax, approval of the transfer by the ATF, and registration of the firearm to the transferee. Only after these steps have occurred may a purchaser legally take possession of the NFA item from the FFL firearms dealer, or may a person legally assemble or manufacture an NFA item. In this section, we will walk through the process, step-by-step, of either purchasing an NFA item that already exists or manufacturing an NFA item.

Steps for buying or transferring an existing NFA item

1. Select and purchase the NFA item from a dealer;
2. Assemble appropriate ATF paperwork (ATF Form 4) by applicant/all responsible persons when applicant is a trust, LLC or corporation, *etc.*, which includes the $200 tax payment ($5 for AOW), photograph and fingerprint card of applicant/all responsible persons (*see* 27 CFR § 479.84; 27 CFR § 479.85);
3. Each applicant/responsible person must notify the chief law enforcement prior to submission of the application to the ATF by forwarding a completed copy of ATF Form 4;
4. Submit all required processing documentation to the ATF for ATF review and approval;
5. ATF sends approval or denial of the application to the dealer with the tax remittance returned in cases of applications that are denied by the ATF (*see* 27 CFR § 479.86);
6. Upon approval, the applicant can now purchase the NFA item from the FFL firearm dealer upon completion of ATF Form 4473 that was discussed in Chapter 3.

Steps for manufacturing an NFA item

1. Select the NFA item to manufacture or modify;
2. Assemble appropriate ATF paperwork (ATF Form 1) by applicant/all responsible persons when applicant is a trust, LLC or corporation, *etc.*, which includes the $200 tax payment ($5 for AOW), photograph and fingerprint card of applicant/all responsible persons (*see* 27 CFR § 479.62; 27 CFR § 479.63);
3. Submit all required processing documentation to the ATF for ATF review and approval;
4. ATF sends approval or denial of the application to the ap-

plicant with the tax remittance returned to the applicant in cases of applications that are denied by the ATF (*see* 27 CFR § 479.64; 27 CFR § 479.65);

5. Upon approval, you may then legally manufacture the NFA item. The item must now be engraved and identified. *See* Section C.

C. *How to engrave and identify a homemade NFA item*

Once you receive ATF approval to manufacture your own NFA item, federal law requires that you engrave, cast, stamp, or otherwise conspicuously place or cause to be engraved, cast, stamped, or placed on the frame, receiver, or barrel of the NFA item the following information:

1. The item's serial number;
2. The item's model (if so designated);
3. Caliber or gauge;
4. The name of the owner whether individual, corporation, or trust; and
5. The city and state where the item was made.

This information must be placed on the item with a minimum depth of .003 inch and in a print size no smaller than $\frac{1}{16}$ inch. *See* 27 CFR § 479.102.

D. *The tax stamp*

Once the ATF has an applicant's materials in hand, they will be reviewed and checked by NFA researchers and an examiner. The application will then either be approved or denied. A denial will be accompanied by an explanation of why the application was denied and how to remedy it, if possible. If the application is approved, the examiner will affix a tax stamp on either a submitted Form 1 or Form 4, and send the newly-stamped form to the applicant.

This tax stamp on the appropriate form is a person's evidence of compliance with the NFA's requirements and is a very important document. A copy should always be kept with the NFA item.

E.   Required documents for NFA items

If you have an NFA item, then you must always have the proper documentation with you to prove that you legally possess the item or it may be a long day with law enforcement. To show you are legal, always keep a copy of your ATF Form 4 or Form 1 (whichever is applicable) with the tax stamp affixed for every NFA item in your possession along with personal identification. If the item is held in a trust or a corporation, then you must possess a copy of the trust or articles of incorporation, and the authorization for possession. Care should be given to make sure these documents name the individuals who are either co-trustees or officers of the corporation.

Practically, individuals should not carry around the original documents as they could be destroyed by wear and tear, rain, or be misplaced, effectively destroying the required evidence of compliance. Photocopies of the stamp and any other pertinent documents are generally enough to satisfy inquisitive law enforcement officials. The more technologically advanced may take pictures on their phone or other mobile device, or save them on a server or cloud database. Keep in mind that if the phone dies or the server cannot be reached, and you have no other way to access the documents, then your proof is gone and you may have a very bad day ahead of you! We recommend keeping photocopies of the ATF form with the tax stamp affixed and appropriate documents to avoid any problems with technology.

Appendix A

Selected Virginia Statutes

Code of Virginia

Title 3.2. Agriculture, Animal Care, and Food
Chapter 65. Comprehensive Animal Care
Article 6. Authority of Local Governing Bodies

§ 3.2-6552. Dogs killing, injuring, or chasing livestock or poultry.
A. It shall be the duty of any animal control officer or other officer who may find a dog in the act of killing or injuring livestock or poultry to seize or kill such dog forthwith whether such dog bears a tag or not. Any person finding a dog committing any of the depredations mentioned in this section shall have the right to kill such dog on sight as shall any owner of livestock or his agent finding a dog chasing livestock on land utilized by the livestock when the circumstances show that such chasing is harmful to the livestock. Any court shall have the power to order the animal control officer or other officer to kill any dog known to be a confirmed livestock or poultry killer, and any dog killing poultry for the third time shall be considered a confirmed poultry killer. The court, through its contempt powers, may compel the owner, custodian, or harborer of the dog to produce the dog.

B. Any animal control officer who has reason to believe that any dog is killing livestock or poultry shall be empowered to seize such dog solely for the purpose of examining such dog in order to determine whether it committed any of the depredations mentioned herein. Any animal control officer or other person who has reason to believe that any dog is killing livestock, or committing any of the depredations mentioned in this section, shall apply to a magistrate serving the locality wherein the dog may be, who shall issue a warrant requiring the owner or custodian, if known, to appear before a general district court at a time and place named therein, at which time evidence shall be heard. If it shall appear that the dog is a livestock killer, or has committed any of the depredations mentioned in this section, the district court shall order that the dog be (i) killed or euthanized immediately by the animal control officer or other officer designated by the court or (ii) removed to another state that does not border on the Commonwealth and prohibited from returning to the Commonwealth. Any dog ordered removed from the Commonwealth that is later found in the Commonwealth shall be ordered by a court to be killed or euthanized immediately.

C. Notwithstanding the provisions of subsection B, if it is determined that the dog has killed or injured only poultry, the district court may, instead of ordering killing, euthanasia, or removal to another state pursuant to this section, order either (a) that the dog be transferred to another owner whom the court deems appropriate and permanently fitted with an identifying microchip registered to that owner or (b) that the dog be fitted with an identifying microchip registered to the owner and confined indoors or in a securely enclosed and locked structure of sufficient height and design to prevent the dog's escape; direct contact with the dog by minors, adults, or other animals; or entry by minors, adults, or other animals. The structure shall be designed to provide the dog with shelter from the elements of nature. When off its owner's property, any dog found to be a poultry killer shall be kept on a leash and muzzled in such a manner as not to cause injury to the dog or interfere with its vision or respiration, but so as to prevent it from biting a person or another animal.

Title 3.2. Agriculture, Animal Care, and Food
Chapter 65. Comprehensive Animal Care
Article 9. Cruelty to Animals

§ 3.2-6570. Cruelty to animals; penalty.
A. Any person who: (i) overrides, overdrives, overloads, tortures, ill-treats, abandons, willfully inflicts inhumane injury or pain not connected with bona fide scientific or medical experimentation, or cruelly or unnecessarily beats, maims, mutilates, or kills any animal, whether belonging to himself or another; (ii) deprives any animal of necessary food, drink, shelter or emergency veterinary treatment; (iii) sores any equine for any purpose or administers drugs or medications to alter or mask such soring for the purpose of sale, show, or exhibition of any kind, unless such administration of drugs or medications is within the context of a veterinary client-patient relationship and solely for therapeutic purposes; (iv) ropes, lassoes,

or otherwise obstructs or interferes with one or more legs of an equine in order to intentionally cause it to trip or fall for the purpose of engagement in a rodeo, contest, exhibition, entertainment, or sport unless such actions are in the practice of accepted animal husbandry or for the purpose of allowing veterinary care; (v) willfully sets on foot, instigates, engages in, or in any way furthers any act of cruelty to any animal; (vi) carries or causes to be carried by any vehicle, vessel or otherwise any animal in a cruel, brutal, or inhumane manner, so as to produce torture or unnecessary suffering; or (vii) causes any of the above things, or being the owner of such animal permits such acts to be done by another is guilty of a Class 1 misdemeanor.

In addition to the penalties provided in this subsection, the court may, in its discretion, require any person convicted of a violation of this subsection to attend an anger management or other appropriate treatment program or obtain psychiatric or psychological counseling. The court may impose the costs of such a program or counseling upon the person convicted.

B. Any person who: (i) tortures, willfully inflicts inhumane injury or pain not connected with bona fide scientific or medical experimentation, or cruelly and unnecessarily beats, maims, mutilates or kills any animal whether belonging to himself or another; (ii) sores any equine for any purpose or administers drugs or medications to alter or mask such soring for the purpose of sale, show, or exhibit of any kind, unless such administration of drugs or medications is under the supervision of a licensed veterinarian and solely for therapeutic purposes; (iii) ropes, lassoes, or otherwise obstructs or interferes with one or more legs of an equine in order to intentionally cause it to trip or fall for the purpose of engagement in a rodeo, contest, exhibition, entertainment, or sport unless such actions are in the practice of accepted animal husbandry or for the purpose of allowing veterinary care; (iv) maliciously deprives any companion animal of necessary food, drink, shelter or emergency veterinary treatment; (v) instigates, engages in, or in any way furthers any act of cruelty to any animal set forth in clauses (i) through (iv) or (vi) causes any of the actions described in clauses (i) through (v), or being the owner of such animal permits such acts to be done by another; and has been within five years convicted of a violation of this subsection or subsection A, is guilty of a Class 6 felony if the current violation or any previous violation of this subsection or sub-section A resulted in the death of an animal or the euthanasia of an animal based on the recommendation of a licensed veterinarian upon determination that such euthanasia was necessary due to the condition of the animal, and such condition was a direct result of a violation of this subsection or subsection A.

C. Nothing in this section shall be construed to prohibit the dehorn-ing of cattle conducted in a reasonable and customary manner.

D. This section shall not prohibit authorized wildlife management activities or hunting, fishing or trapping as regulated under other ti-tles of the Code of Virginia, including Title 29.1, or to farming activ-ities as provided under this title or regulations adopted hereunder.

E. It is unlawful for any person to kill a domestic dog or cat for the purpose of obtaining the hide, fur or pelt of the dog or cat. A viola-tion of this subsection is a Class 1 misdemeanor. A second or subse-quent violation of this subsection is a Class 6 felony.

F. Any person who: (i) tortures, willfully inflicts inhumane injury or pain not connected with bona fide scientific or medical experimen-tation or cruelly and unnecessarily beats, maims or mutilates any dog or cat that is a companion animal whether belonging to him or another; and (ii) as a direct result causes the death of such dog or cat that is a companion animal, or the euthanasia of such animal on the recommendation of a licensed veterinarian upon determina-tion that such euthanasia was necessary due to the condition of the animal, is guilty of a Class 6 felony. If a dog or cat is attacked on its owner's property by a dog so as to cause injury or death, the own-er of the injured dog or cat may use all reasonable and necessary force against the dog at the time of the attack to protect his dog or cat. Such owner may be presumed to have taken necessary and ap-propriate action to defend his dog or cat and shall therefore be pre-sumed not to have violated this subsection. The provisions of this subsection shall not overrule § 3.2-6540, 3.2-6540.1, or 3.2-6552.

G. Any person convicted of violating this section may be prohibited by the court from possession or ownership of companion animals.

Title 9.1. Commonwealth Public Safety
Chapter 1. Department of Criminal Justice Services
Article 3. Criminal Justice Information System

§ 9.1-132. Individual's right of access to and review and correction of information.

A. Any individual who believes that criminal history record information is being maintained about him by the Central Criminal Records Exchange (the "Exchange"), or by the arresting law-enforcement agency in the case of offenses not required to be reported to the Exchange, shall have the right to inspect a copy of his criminal history record information at the Exchange or the arresting law-enforcement agency, respectively, for the purpose of ascertaining the completeness and accuracy of the information. The individual's right to access and review shall not extend to any information or data other than that defined in § 9.1-101.

B. The Board shall adopt regulations with respect to an individual's right to access and review criminal history record information about himself reported to the Exchange or, if not reported to the Exchange, maintained by the arresting law-enforcement agency. The regulations shall provide for (i) public notice of the right of access; (ii) access to criminal history record information by an individual or an attorney-at-law acting for an individual; (iii) the submission of identification; (iv) the places and times for review; (v) review of Virginia records by individuals located in other states; (vi) assistance in understanding the record; (vii) obtaining a copy for purposes of initiating a challenge to the record; (viii) procedures for investigation of alleged incompleteness or inaccuracy; (ix) completion or correction of records if indicated; and (x) notification of the individuals and agencies to whom an inaccurate or incomplete record has been disseminated.

C. If an individual believes information maintained about him is inaccurate or incomplete, he may request the agency having custody or control of the records to purge, modify, or supplement them. Should the agency decline to so act, or should the individual believe the agency's decision to be otherwise unsatisfactory, the individual may make written request for review by the Board. The Board or its designee shall, in each case in which it finds prima facie basis for a complaint, conduct a hearing at which the individual may appear with counsel, present evidence, and examine and cross-examine witnesses. The Board shall issue written findings and conclusions. Should the record in question be found to be inaccurate or incomplete, the criminal justice agency maintaining the information shall purge, modify, or supplement it in accordance with the findings and conclusions of the Board. Notification of purging, modification, or supplementation of criminal history record information shall be promptly made by the criminal justice agency maintaining the previously inaccurate information to any individuals or agencies to which the information in question was communicated, as well as to the individual who is the subject of the records.

D. Criminal justice agencies shall maintain records of all agencies to whom criminal history record information has been disseminated, the date upon which the information was disseminated, and such other record matter for the number of years required by regulations of the Board.

E. Any individual or agency aggrieved by any order or decision of the Board may appeal the order or decision in accordance with the Administrative Process Act (§ 2.2-4000 et seq.).

§ 9.1-135. Civil remedies for violation of this chapter
A. Any person may institute a civil action in the circuit court of the jurisdiction in which the Board has its administrative headquarters, or in the jurisdiction in which any violation is alleged to have occurred:

1. For actual damages resulting from violation of this article or to restrain any such violation, or both.

2. To obtain appropriate equitable relief against any person who has engaged, is engaged, or is about to engage in any acts or practices in violation of Chapter 23 (§ 19.2-387 et seq.) of Title 19.2, this chapter or rules or regulations of the Board.

B. This section shall not be construed as a waiver of the defense of sovereign immunity.

Title 15.2. Counties, Cities and Towns
Chapter 9. General Powers of Local Governments
Article 1. Public Health and Safety; Nuisances

§ 15.2-914. Regulation of child-care services and facilities in certain counties and cities.
Any (i) county that has adopted the urban county executive form of government, (ii) city adjacent to a county that has adopted the urban county executive form of government, or (iii) city which is completely surrounded by such county may by ordinance provide for the regulation and licensing of persons who provide child-care services for compensation and for the regulation and licensing of child-care facilities. "Child-care services" means provision of regular care, protection and guidance to one or more children not related by blood or marriage while such children are separated from their parent, guardian or legal custodian in a dwelling not the residence of the child during a part of the day for at least four days of a calendar week. "Child-care facilities" includes any commercial or residential structure which is used to provide child-care services.

Such local ordinance shall not require the regulation or licensing of any child-care facility that is licensed by the Commonwealth and such ordinance shall not require the regulation or licensing of any facility operated by a religious institution as exempted from licensure by § 63.2-1716.

Such local ordinances shall not be more extensive in scope than comparable state regulations applicable to family day homes. Such local ordinances may regulate the possession and storage of firearms, ammunition, or components or combination thereof at child-care facilities so long as such regulation remains no more extensive in scope than comparable state regulations applicable to family day homes. Local regulations shall not affect the manner of construction or materials to be used in the erection, alteration, repair or use of a residential dwelling.

Such local ordinances may require that persons who provide child-care services shall provide certification from the Central Criminal Records Exchange and a national criminal background check, in accordance with §§ 19.2-389 and 19.2-392.02, that such persons have not been convicted of any offense involving the sexual molestation of children, the physical or sexual abuse or rape of a child or any offense identified in § 63.2-1719, and such ordinances may require that persons who provide child-care services shall provide certification from the central registry of the Department of Social Services that such persons have not been the subject of a founded complaint of abuse or neglect. If an applicant is denied licensure because of any adverse information appearing on a record obtained from the Central Criminal Records Exchange, the national criminal background check, or the Department of Social Services, the applicant shall be provided a copy of the information upon which that denial was based.

§ 15.2-915. Control of firearms; applicability to authorities and local governmental agencies.

A. No locality shall adopt or enforce any ordinance, resolution or motion, as permitted by § 15.2-1425, and no agent of such locality shall take any administrative action, governing the purchase, possession, transfer, ownership, carrying, storage or transporting of firearms, ammunition, or components or combination thereof other than those expressly authorized by statute. For purposes of this section, a statute that does not refer to firearms, ammunition, or components or combination thereof, shall not be construed to provide express authorization.

Nothing in this section shall prohibit a locality from adopting workplace rules relating to terms and conditions of employment of the workforce. However, no locality shall adopt any workplace rule, other than for the purposes of a community services board or behavioral health authority as defined in § 37.2-100, that prevents an employee of that locality from storing at that locality's workplace a lawfully possessed firearm and ammunition in a locked private motor vehicle. Nothing in this section shall prohibit a law-enforcement officer, as defined in § 9.1-101, from acting within the scope of his duties.

The provisions of this section applicable to a locality shall also apply to any authority or to a local governmental entity, including a department or agency, but not including any local or regional jail, juvenile detention facility, or state-governed entity, department, or agency.

B. Any local ordinance, resolution or motion adopted prior to the effective date of this act governing the purchase, possession, transfer, ownership, carrying or transporting of firearms, ammunition, or components or combination thereof, other than those expressly authorized by statute, is invalid.

C. In addition to any other relief provided, the court may award reasonable attorney fees, expenses, and court costs to any person, group, or entity that prevails in an action challenging (i) an ordinance, resolution, or motion as being in conflict with this section or (ii) an administrative action taken in bad faith as being in conflict with this section.

D. For purposes of this section, "workplace" means "workplace of the locality."

§ 15.2-915.2. Regulation of transportation of a loaded rifle or shotgun.

The governing body of any county or city may by ordinance make it unlawful for any person to transport, possess or carry a loaded shotgun or loaded rifle in any vehicle on any public street, road, or highway within such locality. Any violation of such ordinance shall be punishable by a fine of not more than $100. Conservation police officers, sheriffs and all other law-enforcement officers shall enforce the provisions of this section. No ordinance adopted pursuant to this section shall be enforceable unless the governing body adopting such ordinance so notifies the Director of the Department of Game and Inland Fisheries by registered mail prior to May 1 of the year in which such ordinance is to take effect.

The provisions of this section shall not apply to duly authorized law-enforcement officers or military personnel in the performance of their lawful duties, nor to any person who reasonably believes that a loaded rifle or shotgun is necessary for his personal safety in the course of his employment or business.

Title 16.1. Courts Not of Record
Chapter 11. Juvenile and Domestic Relations District Courts
Article 4. Immediate Custody, Arrest, Detention and Shelter Care

§ 16.1-253. Preliminary protective order.

A. Upon the motion of any person or upon the court's own motion, the court may issue a preliminary protective order, after a hearing, if necessary to protect a child's life, health, safety or normal development pending the final determination of any matter before the court. The order may require a child's parents, guardian, legal custodian, other person standing in loco parentis or other family or household member of the child to observe reasonable conditions of behavior for a specified length of time. These conditions shall include any one or more of the following:

1. To abstain from offensive conduct against the child, a family or household member of the child or any person to whom custody of the child is awarded;

2. To cooperate in the provision of reasonable services or programs designed to protect the child's life, health or normal development;

3. To allow persons named by the court to come into the child's home at reasonable times designated by the court to visit the child or inspect the fitness of the home and to determine the physical or emotional health of the child;

4. To allow visitation with the child by persons entitled thereto, as determined by the court;

5. To refrain from acts of commission or omission which tend to endanger the child's life, health or normal development;

6. To refrain from such contact with the child or family or household members of the child, as the court may deem appropriate, including removal of such person from the residence of the child. However, prior to the issuance by the court of an order removing such person from the residence of the child, the petitioner must prove by a preponderance of the evidence that such person's probable future conduct would constitute a danger to the life or health of such child, and that there are no less drastic alternatives which could reasonably and adequately protect the child's life or health pending a final determination on the petition; or

7. To grant the person on whose behalf the order is issued the possession of any companion animal as defined in § 3.2-6500 if such person meets the definition of owner in § 3.2-6500.

B. A preliminary protective order may be issued ex parte upon motion of any person or the court's own motion in any matter before the court, or upon petition. The motion or petition shall be supported by an affidavit or by sworn testimony in person before the judge or intake officer which establishes that the child would be subjected to an imminent threat to life or health to the extent that delay for the provision of an adversary hearing would be likely to result in serious or irremediable injury to the child's life or health. If an ex parte order is issued without an affidavit being presented, the court, in its order, shall state the basis upon which the order was entered, including a summary of the allegations made and the court's findings. Following the issuance of an ex parte order the court shall provide an adversary hearing to the affected parties within the shortest practicable time not to exceed five business days after the issuance of the order.

C. Prior to the hearing required by this section, notice of the hearing shall be given at least 24 hours in advance of the hearing to the guardian ad litem for the child, to the parents, guardian, legal custodian, or other person standing in loco parentis of the child, to any other family or household member of the child to whom the protective order may be directed and to the child if he or she is 12 years of age or older. The notice provided herein shall include (i) the time, date and place for the hearing and (ii) a specific statement of the factual circumstances which allegedly necessitate the issuance of a preliminary protective order.

D. All parties to the hearing shall be informed of their right to counsel pursuant to § 16.1-266.

E. At the hearing the child, his or her parents, guardian, legal custodian or other person standing in loco parentis and any other family or household member of the child to whom notice was given shall have the right to confront and cross-examine all adverse witnesses and evidence and to present evidence on their own behalf.

F. If a petition alleging abuse or neglect of a child has been filed, at the hearing pursuant to this section the court shall determine whether the allegations of abuse or neglect have been proven by a preponderance of the evidence. Any finding of abuse or neglect shall be stated in the court order. However, if, before such a finding is made, a person responsible for the care and custody of the child, the child's guardian ad litem or the local department of social services objects to a finding being made at the hearing, the court shall schedule an adjudicatory hearing to be held within 30 days of the date of the initial preliminary protective order hearing. The adjudicatory hearing shall be held to determine whether the allegations of abuse and neglect have been proven by a preponderance of the evidence. Parties who are present at the hearing shall be given notice of the date set for the adjudicatory hearing and parties who are not present shall be summoned as provided in § 16.1-263. The adjudicatory hearing shall be held and an order may be entered, although a party to the hearing fails to appear and is not represented by counsel, provided personal or substituted service was made on the person, or the court determines that such person cannot be found, after reasonable effort, or in the case of a person who is without the Commonwealth, the person cannot be found or his post office address cannot be ascertained after reasonable effort.

Any preliminary protective order issued shall remain in full force and effect pending the adjudicatory hearing.

G. If at the preliminary protective order hearing held pursuant to this section the court makes a finding of abuse or neglect and a preliminary protective order is issued, a dispositional hearing shall be held pursuant to § 16.1-278.2. The court shall forthwith, but in all cases no later than the end of the business day on which the order was issued, enter and transfer electronically to the Virginia Criminal Information Network the respondent's identifying information and the name, date of birth, sex, and race of each protected person provided to the court. A copy of the preliminary protective order containing any such identifying information shall be forwarded forthwith to the primary law-enforcement agency responsible for service and entry of protective orders. Upon receipt of the order by the primary law-enforcement agency, the agency shall forthwith verify and enter any modification as necessary to the identifying information and other appropriate information required by the Department of State Police into the Virginia Criminal Information Network established and maintained by the Department of State Police pursuant to Chapter 2 (§ 52-12 et seq.) of Title 52 and the order shall be served forthwith on the allegedly abusing person in person as provided in § 16.1-264 and due return made to the court. However, if the order is issued by the circuit court, the clerk of the circuit court shall forthwith forward an attested copy of the order containing the respondent's identifying information and the name, date of birth, sex, and race of each protected person provided to the court to the primary law-enforcement agency providing service and entry of protective orders and upon receipt of the order, the primary law-enforcement agency shall enter the name of the person subject to the order and other appropriate information required by the Department of State Police into the Virginia Criminal Information Network established and maintained by the Department pursuant to Chapter 2 (§ 52-12 et seq.) of Title 52 and the order shall be served forthwith upon the allegedly abusing person in person as provided in § 16.1-264. Upon service, the agency making service shall enter the date and time of service and other appropriate information required by the Department of State Police into the Virginia Criminal Information Network and make due return to the court. The preliminary order shall specify a date for the dispositional hearing. The dispositional hearing shall be scheduled at the time of the hearing pursuant to this section, and shall be held within 60 days of this hearing. If an adjudicatory hearing is requested pursuant to subsection F, the dispositional hearing shall nonetheless be scheduled at the hearing pursuant to this section. All parties present at the hearing shall be given notice of the date and time scheduled for the dispositional hearing; parties who are not present shall be summoned to appear as provided in § 16.1-263.

H. Nothing in this section enables the court to remove a child from the custody of his or her parents, guardian, legal custodian or other person standing in loco parentis, except as provided in § 16.1-278.2, and no order hereunder shall be entered against a person over whom the court does not have jurisdiction.

I. Neither a law-enforcement agency, the attorney for the Commonwealth, a court nor the clerk's office, nor any employee of them, may disclose, except among themselves, the residential address, telephone number, or place of employment of the person protected by the order or that of the family of such person, except to the extent that disclosure is (i) required by law or the Rules of the Supreme Court, (ii) necessary for law-enforcement purposes, or (iii) permitted by the court for good cause.

J. Violation of any order issued pursuant to this section shall constitute contempt of court.

K. The court shall forthwith, but in all cases no later than the end of the business day on which the order was issued, enter and transfer electronically to the Virginia Criminal Information Network the respondent's identifying information and the name, date of birth, sex, and race of each protected person provided to the court. A copy of the preliminary protective order containing any such identifying information shall be forwarded forthwith to the primary law-enforcement agency responsible for service and entry of protective orders. Upon receipt of the order by the primary law-enforcement agency, the agency shall forthwith verify and enter any modification as necessary to the identifying information and other appropriate information required by the Department of State Police into the Virginia Criminal Information Network established and maintained by the Department pursuant to Chapter 2 (§ 52-12 et seq.) of Title 52 and the order shall be served forthwith on the allegedly abusing person in person as provided in § 16.1-264 and due return made to the court. However, if the order is issued by the circuit court, the clerk of the circuit court shall forthwith forward an attested copy of the order containing the respondent's identifying information and the name, date of birth, sex, and race of each protected person provided to the court to the primary law-enforcement agency providing service and entry of protective orders and upon receipt of the order, the primary law-enforcement agency shall enter the name of the person subject to the order and other appropriate information required by the Department of State Police into the Virginia Criminal Information Network established and maintained by the Department pursuant to Chapter 2 (§ 52-12 et seq.) of Title 52 and the order shall be served forthwith on the allegedly abusing person in person as provided in § 16.1-264. Upon service, the agency making service shall enter the date and time of service and other appropriate information required by the Department of State Police into the Virginia Criminal Information Network and make due return to the court. The preliminary order shall specify a date for the full hearing.

Upon receipt of the return of service or other proof of service pursuant to subsection C of § 16.1-264, the clerk shall forthwith forward an attested copy of the preliminary protective order to the primary law-enforcement agency and the agency shall forthwith verify and enter any modification as necessary into the Virginia Criminal Information Network as described above. If the order is later dissolved or modified, a copy of the dissolution or modification order shall also be attested, forwarded forthwith to the primary law-enforcement agency responsible for service and entry of protective orders, and upon receipt of the order by the primary law-enforcement agency, the agency shall forthwith verify and enter any modification as necessary to the identifying information and other appropriate information required by the Department of State Police into the Virginia Criminal Information Network as described above and the order shall be served forthwith and due return made to the court.

L. No fee shall be charged for filing or serving any petition or order pursuant to this section.

§ 16.1-253.1. Preliminary protective orders in cases of family abuse; confidentiality.

A. Upon the filing of a petition alleging that the petitioner is or has been, within a reasonable period of time, subjected to family abuse, the court may issue a preliminary protective order against an allegedly abusing person in order to protect the health and safety of the petitioner or any family or household member of the petitioner. The order may be issued in an ex parte proceeding upon good cause shown when the petition is supported by an affidavit or sworn testimony before the judge or intake officer. Immediate and present danger of family abuse or evidence sufficient to establish probable cause that family abuse has recently occurred shall constitute good cause. Evidence that the petitioner has been subjected to family abuse within a reasonable time and evidence of immediate and present danger of family abuse may be established by a showing that (i) the allegedly abusing person is incarcerated and is to be released from incarceration within 30 days following the petition or has been released from incarceration within 30 days prior to the petition, (ii) the crime for which the allegedly abusing person was convicted and incarcerated involved family abuse against the petitioner, and (iii) the allegedly abusing person has made threatening contact with the petitioner while he was incarcerated, exhibiting a renewed threat to the petitioner of family abuse.

A preliminary protective order may include any one or more of the following conditions to be imposed on the allegedly abusing person:

1. Prohibiting acts of family abuse or criminal offenses that result in injury to person or property.
2. Prohibiting such contacts by the respondent with the petitioner or family or household members of the petitioner as the court deems necessary for the health or safety of such persons.
3. Granting the petitioner possession of the premises occupied by the parties to the exclusion of the allegedly abusing person; however, no such grant of possession shall affect title to any real or personal property.
4. Enjoining the respondent from terminating any necessary utility service to a premises that the petitioner has been granted possession of pursuant to subdivision 3 or, where appropriate, ordering the respondent to restore utility services to such premises.
5. Granting the petitioner temporary possession or use of a motor vehicle owned by the petitioner alone or jointly owned by the parties to the exclusion of the allegedly abusing person; however, no such grant of possession or use shall affect title to the vehicle.
6. Requiring that the allegedly abusing person provide suitable alternative housing for the petitioner and any other family or household member and, where appropriate, requiring the respondent to pay deposits to connect or restore necessary utility services in the alternative housing provided.
7. Granting the petitioner the possession of any companion animal as defined in § 3.2-6500 if such petitioner meets the definition of owner in § 3.2-6500.
8. Any other relief necessary for the protection of the petitioner and family or household members of the petitioner.

B. The court shall forthwith, but in all cases no later than the end of the business day on which the order was issued, enter and transfer electronically to the Virginia Criminal Information Network the respondent's identifying information and the name, date of birth, sex, and race of each protected person provided to the court. A copy of a preliminary protective order containing any such identifying information shall be forwarded forthwith to the primary law-enforcement agency responsible for service and entry of protective orders. Upon receipt of the order by the primary law-enforcement agency, the agency shall forthwith verify and enter any modification as necessary to the identifying information and other appropriate information required by the Department of State Police into the Virginia Criminal Information Network established and maintained by the Department pursuant to Chapter 2 (§ 52-12 et seq.) of Title 52 and the order shall be served forthwith on the allegedly abusing person in person as provided in § 16.1-264 and due return made to the court. However, if the order is issued by the circuit court, the clerk of the circuit court shall forthwith forward an attested copy of the order containing the respondent's identifying information and the name, date of birth, sex, and race of each protected person provided to the court to the primary law-enforcement agency providing service and entry of protective orders and upon receipt of the order, the primary law-enforcement agency shall enter the name of the person subject to the order and other appropriate information required by the Department of State Police into the Virginia Criminal Information Network established and maintained by the Department pursuant to Chapter 2 (§ 52-12 et seq.) of Title 52 and the order shall be served forthwith on the allegedly abusing person in person as provided in § 16.1-264. Upon service, the agency making service shall enter the date and time of service and other appropriate information required by the Department of State Police into the Virginia Criminal Information Network and make due return to the court. The preliminary order shall specify a date for the full hearing. The hearing shall be held within 15 days of the issuance of the preliminary order. If the respondent fails to appear at this hearing because the respondent was not personally served, or if personally served was incarcerated and not transported to the hearing, the court may extend the protective order for a period not to exceed six months. The extended protective order shall be served forthwith on the respondent. However, upon motion of the respondent and for good cause shown, the court may continue the hearing. The preliminary order shall remain in effect until the hearing. Upon request after the order is issued, the clerk shall provide the petitioner with a copy of the order and information regarding the date and time of service. The order shall further specify that either party may at any time file a motion with the court requesting a hearing to dissolve or modify the order. The hearing on the motion shall be given precedence on the docket of the court.

Upon receipt of the return of service or other proof of service pursuant to subsection C of § 16.1-264, the clerk shall forthwith forward an attested copy of the preliminary protective order to the primary law-enforcement agency, and the agency shall forthwith verify and enter any modification as necessary into the Virginia Criminal Information Network as described above. If the order is later dissolved or modified, a copy of the dissolution or modification order shall also be attested, forwarded forthwith to the primary law-enforcement agency responsible for service and entry of protective orders, and upon receipt of the order by the primary law-enforcement agency, the agency shall forthwith verify and enter any modification as necessary to the identifying information and other appropriate information required by the Department of State Police into the Virginia Criminal Information Network as described above and the order shall be served forthwith and due return made to the court.

C. The preliminary order is effective upon personal service on the allegedly abusing person. Except as otherwise provided in § 16.1-253.2, a violation of the order shall constitute contempt of court.

D. At a full hearing on the petition, the court may issue a protective order pursuant to § 16.1-279.1 if the court finds that the petitioner has proven the allegation of family abuse by a preponderance of the evidence.

E. Neither a law-enforcement agency, the attorney for the Commonwealth, a court nor the clerk's office, nor any employee of them, may disclose, except among themselves, the residential address, telephone number, or place of employment of the person protected by the order or that of the family of such person, except to the extent that disclosure is (i) required by law or the Rules of the Supreme Court, (ii) necessary for law-enforcement purposes, or (iii) permitted by the court for good cause.

F. As used in this section, "copy" includes a facsimile copy.

G. No fee shall be charged for filing or serving any petition or order pursuant to this section.

§ 16.1-253.4. Emergency protective orders authorized in certain cases; penalty.

A. Any judge of a circuit court, general district court, juvenile and domestic relations district court or magistrate may issue a written or oral ex parte emergency protective order pursuant to this section in order to protect the health or safety of any person.

B. When a law-enforcement officer or an allegedly abused person asserts under oath to a judge or magistrate, and on that assertion or other evidence the judge or magistrate (i) finds that a warrant for a violation of § 18.2-57.2 has been issued or issues a warrant for violation of § 18.2-57.2 and finds that there is probable danger of further acts of family abuse against a family or household member by the respondent or (ii) finds that reasonable grounds exist to believe that the respondent has committed family abuse and there is probable danger of a further such offense against a family or household member by the respondent, the judge or magistrate shall issue an ex parte emergency protective order, except if the respondent is a minor, an emergency protective order shall not be required, imposing one or more of the following conditions on the respondent:

1. Prohibiting acts of family abuse or criminal offenses that result in injury to person or property;
2. Prohibiting such contacts by the respondent with the allegedly abused person or family or household members of the allegedly abused person, including prohibiting the respondent from being in the physical presence of the allegedly abused person or family or household members of the allegedly abused person, as the judge or magistrate deems necessary to protect the safety of such persons;
3. Granting the family or household member possession of the premises occupied by the parties to the exclusion of the respondent; however, no such grant of possession shall affect title to any real or personal property; and
4. Granting the petitioner the possession of any companion animal as defined in § 3.2-6500 if such petitioner meets the definition of owner in § 3.2-6500.

When the judge or magistrate considers the issuance of an emergency protective order pursuant to clause (i), he shall presume that there is probable danger of further acts of family abuse against a family or household member by the respondent unless the presumption is rebutted by the allegedly abused person.

C. An emergency protective order issued pursuant to this section shall expire at 11:59 p.m. on the third day following issuance. If the expiration occurs on a day that the court is not in session, the emergency protective order shall be extended until 11:59 p.m. on the next day that the juvenile and domestic relations district court is in session. When issuing an emergency protective order under this section, the judge or magistrate shall provide the protected person or the law-enforcement officer seeking the emergency protective order with the form for use in filing petitions pursuant to § 16.1-253.1 and written information regarding protective orders that shall include the telephone numbers of domestic violence agencies and legal referral sources on a form prepared by the Supreme Court. If these forms are provided to a law-enforcement officer, the officer may provide these forms to the protected person when giving the emergency protective order to the protected person. The respondent may at any time file a motion with the court requesting a hearing to dissolve or modify the order issued hereunder. The hearing on the motion shall be given precedence on the docket of the court.

D. A law-enforcement officer may request an emergency protective order pursuant to this section and, if the person in need of protection is physically or mentally incapable of filing a petition pursuant to § 16.1-253.1 or 16.1-279.1, may request the extension of an emergency protective order for an additional period of time not to exceed three days after expiration of the original order. The request for an emergency protective order or extension of an order may be made orally, in person or by electronic means, and the judge of a circuit court, general district court, or juvenile and domestic relations district court or a magistrate may issue an oral emergency protective order. An oral emergency protective order issued pursuant to this section shall be reduced to writing, by the law-enforcement officer requesting the order or the magistrate on a preprinted form approved and provided by the Supreme Court of Virginia. The completed form shall include a statement of the grounds for the order asserted by the officer or the allegedly abused person.

E. The court or magistrate shall forthwith, but in all cases no later than the end of the business day on which the order was issued, enter and transfer electronically to the Virginia Criminal Information Network the respondent's identifying information and the name, date of birth, sex, and race of each protected person provided to the court or magistrate. A copy of an emergency protective order issued pursuant to this section containing any such identifying information shall be forwarded forthwith to the primary law-enforcement agency responsible for service and entry of protective orders. Upon receipt of the order by the primary law-enforcement agency, the agency shall forthwith verify and enter any modification as necessary to the identifying information and other appropriate information required by the Department of State Police into the Virginia Criminal Information Network established and maintained by the Department pursuant to Chapter 2 (§ 52-12 et seq.) of Title 52 and the order shall be served forthwith upon the respondent and due return made to the court. However, if the order is issued by the circuit court, the clerk of the circuit court shall forthwith forward an attested copy of the order containing the respondent's identifying information and the name, date of birth, sex, and race of each protected person provided to the court to the primary law-enforcement agency providing service and entry of protective orders and upon receipt of the order, the primary law-enforcement agency shall enter the name of the person subject to the order and other appropriate information required by the Department of State Police into the Virginia Criminal Network established and maintained by the Department pursuant to Chapter 2 (§ 52-12 et seq.) of Title 52 and the order shall be served forthwith on the respondent. Upon service, the agency making service shall enter the date and time of service and other appropriate information required by the Department of State Police into the Virginia Criminal Information Network and make due return to the court. One copy of the order shall be given to the allegedly abused person when it is issued, and one copy shall be filed with the written report required by subsection D of § 19.2-81.3. The judge or magistrate who issues an oral order pursuant to an electronic request by a law-enforcement officer shall verify the written order to determine whether the officer who reduced it to writing accurately transcribed the contents of the oral order. The original copy shall be filed with the clerk of the juvenile and domestic relations district court within five business days of the issuance of the order. If the order is later dissolved or modified, a copy of the dissolution or modification order shall also be attested, forwarded forthwith to the primary law-enforcement agency responsible for service and entry of protective orders, and upon receipt of the order by the primary law-enforcement agency, the agency shall forthwith verify and enter any modification as necessary to the identifying information and other appropriate information required by the Department of State Police into the Virginia Criminal Information Network as described above and the order shall be served forthwith and due return made to the court. Upon request, the clerk shall provide the allegedly abused person with information regarding the date and time of service.

F. The availability of an emergency protective order shall not be affected by the fact that the family or household member left the premises to avoid the danger of family abuse by the respondent.

G. The issuance of an emergency protective order shall not be considered evidence of any wrongdoing by the respondent.

H. As used in this section, "law-enforcement officer" means (i) any full-time or part-time employee of a police department or sheriff's office which is part of or administered by the Commonwealth or any political subdivision thereof and who is responsible for the prevention and detection of crime and the enforcement of the penal, traffic, or highway laws of the Commonwealth; (ii) any member of an auxiliary police force established pursuant to § 15.2-1731; and (iii) any special conservator of the peace who meets the certification requirements for a law-enforcement officer as set forth in § 15.2-1706. Part-time employees are compensated officers who are not full-time employees as defined by the employing police department or sheriff's office.

I. Neither a law-enforcement agency, the attorney for the Commonwealth, a court nor the clerk's office, nor any employee of them, may disclose, except among themselves, the residential address, telephone number, or place of employment of the person protected by the order or that of the family of such person, except to the extent that disclosure is (i) required by law or the Rules of the Supreme Court, (ii) necessary for law-enforcement purposes, or (iii) permitted by the court for good cause.

J. As used in this section:

"Copy" includes a facsimile copy.

"Physical presence" includes (i) intentionally maintaining direct visual contact with the petitioner or (ii) unreasonably being within 100 feet from the petitioner's residence or place of employment.

K. No fee shall be charged for filing or serving any petition or order pursuant to this section.

L. Except as provided in § 16.1-253.2, a violation of a protective order issued under this section shall constitute contempt of court.

Title 16.1. Courts Not of Record
Chapter 11. Juvenile and Domestic Relations District Courts
Article 9. Disposition

§ 16.1-278.2. Abused, neglected, or abandoned children or children without parental care.
A. Within 60 days of a preliminary removal order hearing held pursuant to § 16.1-252 or a hearing on a preliminary protective order held pursuant to § 16.1-253, a dispositional hearing shall be held if the court found abuse or neglect and (i) removed the child from his home or (ii) entered a preliminary protective order. Notice of the dispositional hearing shall be provided to the child's parent, guardian, legal custodian, or other person standing in loco parentis in accordance with § 16.1-263. The hearing shall be held and a dispositional order may be entered, although a parent, guardian, legal custodian, or person standing in loco parentis fails to appear and is not represented by counsel, provided personal or substituted service was made on the person, or the court determines that such person cannot be found, after reasonable effort, or in the case of a person who is without the Commonwealth, the person cannot be found or his post office address cannot be ascertained after reasonable effort. Notice shall also be provided to the local department of social services, the guardian ad litem and, if appointed, the court-appointed special advocate.

If a child is found to be (a) abused or neglected; (b) at risk of being abused or neglected by a parent or custodian who has been adjudicated as having abused or neglected another child in his care; or (c) abandoned by his parent or other custodian, or without parental care and guardianship because of his parent's absence or physical or mental incapacity, the juvenile court or the circuit court may make any of the following orders of disposition to protect the welfare of the child:

1. Enter an order pursuant to the provisions of § 16.1-278;
2. Permit the child to remain with his parent, subject to such conditions and limitations as the court may order with respect to such child and his parent or other adult occupant of the same dwelling;
3. Prohibit or limit contact as the court deems appropriate between the child and his parent or other adult occupant of the same dwelling whose presence tends to endanger the child's life, health or normal development. The prohibition may exclude any such individual from the home under such conditions as the court may prescribe for a period to be determined by the court but in no event for longer than 180 days from the date of such determination. A hearing shall be held within 150 days to determine further disposition of the matter that may include limiting or prohibiting contact for another 180 days;
4. Permit the local board of social services or a public agency designated by the community policy and management team to place the child, subject to the provisions of § 16.1-281, in suitable family homes, child-caring institutions, residential facilities, or independent living arrangements with legal custody remaining with the parents or guardians. The local board or public agency and the parents or guardians shall enter into an agreement which shall specify the responsibilities of each for the care and control of the child. The board or public agency that places the child shall have the final authority to determine the appropriate placement for the child.

Any order allowing a local board or public agency to place a child where legal custody remains with the parents or guardians as provided in this section shall be entered only upon a finding by the court that reasonable efforts have been made to prevent placement out of the home and that continued placement in the home would be contrary to the welfare of the child; and the order shall so state.

5. After a finding that there is no less drastic alternative, transfer legal custody, subject to the provisions of § 16.1-281, to any of the following:

a. A relative or other interested individual subject to the provisions of subsection A1 of this section;

b. A child welfare agency, private organization or facility that is licensed or otherwise authorized by law to receive and provide care for such child; however, a court shall not transfer legal custody of an abused or neglected child to an agency, organization or facility out of the Commonwealth without the approval of the Commissioner of Social Services; or

c. The local board of social services of the county or city in which the court has jurisdiction or, at the discretion of the court, to the local board of the county or city in which the child has residence if other than the county or city in which the court has jurisdiction. The local board shall accept the child for care and custody, provided that it has been given reasonable notice of the pendency of the case and an opportunity to be heard. However, in an emergency in the county or city in which the court has jurisdiction, the local board may be required to accept a child for a period not to exceed 14 days without prior notice or an opportunity to be heard if the judge entering the placement order describes the emergency and the need for such temporary placement in the order. Nothing in this section shall prohibit the commitment of a child to any local board of social services in the Commonwealth when the local board consents to the commitment. The board to which the child is committed shall have the final authority to determine the appropriate placement for the child.

Any order authorizing removal from the home and transferring legal custody of a child to a local board of social services as provided in this section shall be entered only upon a finding by the court that reasonable efforts have been made to prevent removal and that continued placement in the home would be contrary to the welfare of the child; and the order shall so state.

6. Transfer legal custody pursuant to subdivision 5 of this section and order the parent to participate in such services and programs or to refrain from such conduct as the court may prescribe; or

7. Terminate the rights of the parent pursuant to § 16.1-283.

A1. Any order transferring custody of the child to a relative or other interested individual pursuant to subdivision A 5 a shall be entered only upon a finding, based upon a preponderance of the evidence, that the relative or other interested individual is one who, after an investigation as directed by the court, (i) is found by the court to be willing and qualified to receive and care for the child; (ii) is willing to have a positive, continuous relationship with the child; (iii) is committed to providing a permanent, suitable home for the child; and (iv) is willing and has the ability to protect the child from abuse and neglect; and the order shall so state. The court's order transferring custody to a relative or other interested individual should further provide for, as appropriate, any terms or conditions which would promote the child's interest and welfare; ongoing provision of social services to the child and the child's custodian; and court review of the child's placement.

B. If the child has been placed in foster care, at the dispositional hearing the court shall review the foster care plan for the child filed in accordance with § 16.1-281 by the local department of social services, a public agency designated by the community policy and management team which places a child through an agreement with the parents or guardians where legal custody remains with the parents or guardians, or child welfare agency.

C. Any preliminary protective orders entered on behalf of the child shall be reviewed at the dispositional hearing and may be incorporated, as appropriate, in the dispositional order.

D. A dispositional order entered pursuant to this section is a final order from which an appeal may be taken in accordance with § 16.1-296.

§ 16.1-279.1. Protective order in cases of family abuse.

A. In cases of family abuse, including any case involving an incarcerated or recently incarcerated respondent against whom a preliminary protective order has been issued pursuant to § 16.1-253.1, the court may issue a protective order to protect the health and safety of the petitioner and family or household members of the petitioner. A protective order issued under this section may include any one or more of the following conditions to be imposed on the respondent:

1. Prohibiting acts of family abuse or criminal offenses that result in injury to person or property;
2. Prohibiting such contacts by the respondent with the petitioner or family or household members of the petitioner as the court deems necessary for the health or safety of such persons;
3. Granting the petitioner possession of the residence occupied by the parties to the exclusion of the respondent; however, no such grant of possession shall affect title to any real or personal property;
4. Enjoining the respondent from terminating any necessary utility service to the residence to which the petitioner was granted possession pursuant to subdivision 3 or, where appropriate, ordering the respondent to restore utility services to that residence;
5. Granting the petitioner temporary possession or use of a motor vehicle owned by the petitioner alone or jointly owned by the parties to the exclusion of the respondent and enjoining the respondent from terminating any insurance, registration, or taxes on the motor vehicle and directing the respondent to maintain the insurance, registration, and taxes, as appropriate; however, no such grant of possession or use shall affect title to the vehicle;
6. Requiring that the respondent provide suitable alternative housing for the petitioner and, if appropriate, any other family or household member and where appropriate, requiring the respondent to pay deposits to connect or restore necessary utility services in the alternative housing provided;
7. Ordering the respondent to participate in treatment, counseling or other programs as the court deems appropriate;
8. Granting the petitioner the possession of any companion animal as defined in § 3.2-6500 if such petitioner meets the definition of owner in § 3.2-6500; and
9. Any other relief necessary for the protection of the petitioner and family or household members of the petitioner, including a provision for temporary custody or visitation of a minor child.

A1. If a protective order is issued pursuant to subsection A, the court may also issue a temporary child support order for the support of any children of the petitioner whom the respondent has a legal obligation to support. Such order shall terminate upon the determination of support pursuant to § 20-108.1.

B. The protective order may be issued for a specified period of time up to a maximum of two years. The protective order shall expire at 11:59 p.m. on the last day specified or at 11:59 p.m. on the last day of the two-year period if no date is specified. Prior to the expiration of the protective order, a petitioner may file a written motion requesting a hearing to extend the order. Proceedings to extend a protective order shall be given precedence on the docket of the court. If the petitioner was a family or household member of the respondent at the time the initial protective order was issued, the court may extend the protective order for a period not longer than two years to protect the health and safety of the petitioner or persons who are family or household members of the petitioner at the time the request for an extension is made. The extension of the protective order shall expire at 11:59 p.m. on the last day specified or at 11:59 p.m. on the last day of the two-year period if no date is specified. Nothing herein shall limit the number of extensions that may be requested or issued.

C. A copy of the protective order shall be served on the respondent and provided to the petitioner as soon as possible. The court, including a circuit court if the circuit court issued the order, shall forthwith, but in all cases no later than the end of the business day on which the order was issued, enter and transfer electronically to the Virginia Criminal Information Network the respondent's identifying information and the name, date of birth, sex, and race of each protected person provided to the court and shall forthwith forward the attested copy of the protective order containing any such identifying information to the primary law-enforcement agency responsible for service and entry of protective orders. Upon receipt of the order by the primary law-enforcement agency, the agency shall forthwith verify and enter any modification as necessary to the identifying information and other appropriate information required by the Department of State Police into the Virginia Criminal Information Network established and maintained by the Department pursuant to Chapter 2 (§ 52-12 et seq.) of Title 52 and the order shall be served forthwith upon the respondent and due return made to the court. Upon service, the agency making service shall enter the date and time of service and other appropriate information required by the Department of State Police into the Virginia Criminal Information Network and make due return to the court. If the order is later dissolved or modified, a copy of the dissolution or modification order shall also be attested, forwarded forthwith to the primary law-enforcement agency responsible for service and entry of protective orders, and upon receipt of the order by the primary law-enforcement agency, the agency shall forthwith verify and enter any modification as necessary to the identifying information and other appropriate information required by the Department of State Police into the Virginia Criminal Information Network as described above and the order shall be served forthwith and due return made to the court.

D. Except as otherwise provided in § 16.1-253.2, a violation of a protective order issued under this section shall constitute contempt of court.

E. The court may assess costs and attorneys' fees against either party regardless of whether an order of protection has been issued as a result of a full hearing.

F. Any judgment, order or decree, whether permanent or temporary, issued by a court of appropriate jurisdiction in another state, the United States or any of its territories, possessions or Commonwealths, the District of Columbia or by any tribal court of appropriate jurisdiction for the purpose of preventing violent or threatening acts or harassment against or contact or communication with or physical proximity to another person, including any of the conditions specified in subsection A, shall be accorded full faith and credit and enforced in the Commonwealth as if it were an order of the Commonwealth, provided reasonable notice and opportunity to be heard were given by the issuing jurisdiction to the person against whom the order is sought to be enforced sufficient to protect such person's due process rights and consistent with federal law. A person entitled to protection under such a foreign order may file the order in any juvenile and domestic relations district court by filing with the court an attested or exemplified copy of the order. Upon such a filing, the clerk shall forthwith forward an attested copy of the order to the primary law-enforcement agency responsible for service and entry of protective orders which shall, upon receipt, enter the name of the person subject to the order and other appropriate information required by the Department of State Police into the Virginia Criminal Information Network established and maintained by the Department pursuant to Chapter 2 (§ 52-12 et seq.) of Title 52. Where practical, the court may transfer information electronically to the Virginia Criminal Information Network.

Upon inquiry by any law-enforcement agency of the Commonwealth, the clerk shall make a copy available of any foreign order filed with that court. A law-enforcement officer may, in the performance of his duties, rely upon a copy of a foreign protective order or other suitable evidence which has been provided to him by any source and may also rely upon the statement of any person protected by the order that the order remains in effect.

G. Either party may at any time file a written motion with the court requesting a hearing to dissolve or modify the order. Proceedings to dissolve or modify a protective order shall be given precedence on the docket of the court.

H. As used in this section:

"Copy" includes a facsimile copy; and

"Protective order" includes an initial, modified or extended protective order.

I. Neither a law-enforcement agency, the attorney for the Commonwealth, a court nor the clerk's office, nor any employee of them, may disclose, except among themselves, the residential address, telephone number, or place of employment of the person protected by the order or that of the family of such person, except to the extent that disclosure is (i) required by law or the Rules of the Supreme Court, (ii) necessary for law-enforcement purposes, or (iii) permitted by the court for good cause.

J. No fee shall be charged for filing or serving any petition or order pursuant to this section.

Title 18.2. Crimes and Offenses Generally
Chapter 1. In General
Article 3. Classification of Criminal Offenses and Punishment

§ 18.2-10. Punishment for conviction of felony; penalty.
The authorized punishments for conviction of a felony are:

(a) For Class 1 felonies, death, if the person so convicted was 18 years of age or older at the time of the offense and is not determined to be mentally retarded pursuant to § 19.2-264.3:1.1, or imprisonment for life and, subject to subdivision (g), a fine of not more than $100,000. If the person was under 18 years of age at the time of the offense or is determined to be mentally retarded pursuant to § 19.2-264.3:1.1, the punishment shall be imprisonment for life and, subject to subdivision (g), a fine of not more than $100,000.

(b) For Class 2 felonies, imprisonment for life or for any term not less than 20 years and, subject to subdivision (g), a fine of not more than $100,000.

(c) For Class 3 felonies, a term of imprisonment of not less than five years nor more than 20 years and, subject to subdivision (g), a fine of not more than $100,000.

(d) For Class 4 felonies, a term of imprisonment of not less than two years nor more than 10 years and, subject to subdivision (g), a fine of not more than $100,000.

(e) For Class 5 felonies, a term of imprisonment of not less than one year nor more than 10 years, or in the discretion of the jury or the court trying the case without a jury, confinement in jail for not more than 12 months and a fine of not more than $2,500, either or both.

(f) For Class 6 felonies, a term of imprisonment of not less than one year nor more than five years, or in the discretion of the jury or the court trying the case without a jury, confinement in jail for not more than 12 months and a fine of not more than $2,500, either or both.

(g) Except as specifically authorized in subdivision (e) or (f), or in Class 1 felonies for which a sentence of death is imposed, the court shall impose either a sentence of imprisonment together with a fine, or imprisonment only. However, if the defendant is not a natural person, the court shall impose only a fine.

For any felony offense committed (i) on or after January 1, 1995, the court may, and (ii) on or after July 1, 2000, shall, except in cases in which the court orders a suspended term of confinement of at least six months, impose an additional term of not less than six months nor more than three years, which shall be suspended conditioned upon successful completion of a period of post-release supervision pursuant to § 19.2-295.2 and compliance with such other terms as the sentencing court may require. However, such additional term may only be imposed when the sentence includes an active term of incarceration in a correctional facility.

For a felony offense prohibiting proximity to children as described in subsection A of § 18.2-370.2, the sentencing court is authorized to impose the punishment set forth in that section in addition to any other penalty provided by law.

§ 18.2-11. Punishment for conviction of misdemeanor.
The authorized punishments for conviction of a misdemeanor are:
    (a) For Class 1 misdemeanors, confinement in jail for not more than twelve months and a fine of not more than $2,500, either or both.
    (b) For Class 2 misdemeanors, confinement in jail for not more than six months and a fine of not more than $1,000, either or both.
    (c) For Class 3 misdemeanors, a fine of not more than $500.
    (d) For Class 4 misdemeanors, a fine of not more than $250.

For a misdemeanor offense prohibiting proximity to children as described in subsection A of § 18.2-370.2, the sentencing court is authorized to impose the punishment set forth in subsection B of that section in addition to any other penalty provided by law.

Title 18.2. Crimes and Offenses Generally
Chapter 4. Crimes Against the Person
Article 1. Homicide

§ 18.2-31. Capital murder defined; punishment.

The following offenses shall constitute capital murder, punishable as a Class 1 felony:

1. The willful, deliberate, and premeditated killing of any person in the commission of abduction, as defined in § 18.2-48, when such abduction was committed with the intent to extort money or a pecuniary benefit or with the intent to defile the victim of such abduction;

2. The willful, deliberate, and premeditated killing of any person by another for hire;

3. The willful, deliberate, and premeditated killing of any person by a prisoner confined in a state or local correctional facility as defined in § 53.1-1, or while in the custody of an employee thereof;

4. The willful, deliberate, and premeditated killing of any person in the commission of robbery or attempted robbery;

5. The willful, deliberate, and premeditated killing of any person in the commission of, or subsequent to, rape or attempted rape, forcible sodomy or attempted forcible sodomy or object sexual penetration;

6. The willful, deliberate, and premeditated killing of a law-enforcement officer as defined in § 9.1-101, a fire marshal appointed pursuant to § 27-30 or a deputy or an assistant fire marshal appointed pursuant to § 27-36, when such fire marshal or deputy or assistant fire marshal has police powers as set forth in §§ 27-34.2 and 27-34.2:1, an auxiliary police officer appointed or provided for pursuant to §§ 15.2-1731 and 15.2-1733, an auxiliary deputy sheriff appointed pursuant to § 15.2-1603, or any law-enforcement officer of another state or the United States having the power to arrest for a felony under the laws of such state or the United States, when such killing is for the purpose of interfering with the performance of his official duties;

7. The willful, deliberate, and premeditated killing of more than one person as a part of the same act or transaction;

8. The willful, deliberate, and premeditated killing of more than one person within a three-year period;

9. The willful, deliberate, and premeditated killing of any person in the commission of or attempted commission of a violation of § 18.2-248, involving a Schedule I or II controlled substance, when such killing is for the purpose of furthering the commission or attempted commission of such violation;

10. The willful, deliberate, and premeditated killing of any person by another pursuant to the direction or order of one who is engaged in a continuing criminal enterprise as defined in subsection I of § 18.2-248;

11. The willful, deliberate, and premeditated killing of a pregnant woman by one who knows that the woman is pregnant and has the intent to cause the involuntary termination of the woman's pregnancy without a live birth;

12. The willful, deliberate, and premeditated killing of a person under the age of fourteen by a person age twenty-one or older;

13. The willful, deliberate, and premeditated killing of any person by another in the commission of or attempted commission of an act of terrorism as defined in § 18.2-46.4;

14. The willful, deliberate, and premeditated killing of a justice of the Supreme Court, a judge of the Court of Appeals, a judge of a circuit court or district court, a retired judge sitting by designation or under temporary recall, or a substitute judge appointed under § 16.1-69.9:1 when the killing is for the purpose of interfering with his official duties as a judge; and

15. The willful, deliberate, and premeditated killing of any witness in a criminal case after a subpoena has been issued for such witness by the court, the clerk, or an attorney, when the killing is for the purpose of interfering with the person's duties in such case.

If any one or more subsections, sentences, or parts of this section shall be judged unconstitutional or invalid, such adjudication shall not affect, impair, or invalidate the remaining provisions thereof but shall be confined in its operation to the specific provisions so held unconstitutional or invalid.

§ 18.2-32. First and second degree murder defined; punishment.
Murder, other than capital murder, by poison, lying in wait, imprisonment, starving, or by any willful, deliberate, and premeditated killing, or in the commission of, or attempt to commit, arson, rape, forcible sodomy, inanimate or animate object sexual penetration,

robbery, burglary or abduction, except as provided in § 18.2-31, is murder of the first degree, punishable as a Class 2 felony.

All murder other than capital murder and murder in the first degree is murder of the second degree and is punishable by confinement in a state correctional facility for not less than five nor more than forty years.

Title 18.2. Crimes and Offenses Generally
Chapter 4. Crimes Against the Person
Article 3. Kidnapping and Related Offenses

§ 18.2-47. Abduction and kidnapping defined; punishment.
A. Any person who, by force, intimidation or deception, and without legal justification or excuse, seizes, takes, transports, detains or secretes another person with the intent to deprive such other person of his personal liberty or to withhold or conceal him from any person, authority or institution lawfully entitled to his charge, shall be deemed guilty of "abduction."

B. Any person who, by force, intimidation or deception, and without legal justification or excuse, seizes, takes, transports, detains or secretes another person with the intent to subject him to forced labor or services shall be deemed guilty of "abduction." For purposes of this subsection, the term "intimidation" shall include destroying, concealing, confiscating, withholding, or threatening to withhold a passport, immigration document, or other governmental identification or threatening to report another as being illegally present in the United States.

C. The provisions of this section shall not apply to any law-enforcement officer in the performance of his duty. The terms "abduction" and "kidnapping" shall be synonymous in this Code. Abduction for which no punishment is otherwise prescribed shall be punished as a Class 5 felony.

D. If an offense under subsection A is committed by the parent of the person abducted and punishable as contempt of court in any proceeding then pending, the offense shall be a Class 1 misdemeanor in addition to being punishable as contempt of court. However, such offense, if committed by the parent of the person abducted and punishable as contempt of court in any proceeding then pending and the person abducted is removed from the Commonwealth by the abducting parent, shall be a Class 6 felony in addition to being punishable as contempt of court.

Title 18.2. Crimes and Offenses Generally
Chapter 4. Crimes Against the Person
Article 4. Assaults and Bodily Woundings

§ 18.2-52. Malicious bodily injury by means of any caustic substance or agent or use of any explosive or fire.
If any person maliciously causes any other person bodily injury by means of any acid, lye or other caustic substance or agent or use of any explosive or fire, he shall be guilty of a felony and shall be punished by confinement in a state correctional facility for a period of not less than five years nor more than thirty years. If such act is done unlawfully but not maliciously, the offender shall be guilty of a Class 6 felony.

§ 18.2-56.2. Allowing access to firearms by children; penalty.
A. It shall be unlawful for any person to recklessly leave a loaded, unsecured firearm in such a manner as to endanger the life or limb of any child under the age of fourteen. Any person violating the provisions of this subsection shall be guilty of a Class 3 misdemeanor.

B. It shall be unlawful for any person knowingly to authorize a child under the age of twelve to use a firearm except when the child is under the supervision of an adult. Any person violating this subsection shall be guilty of a Class 1 misdemeanor. For purposes of this subsection, "adult" shall mean a parent, guardian, person standing in loco parentis to the child or a person twenty-one years or over who has the permission of the parent, guardian, or person standing in loco parentis to supervise the child in the use of a firearm.

§ 18.2-57.01. Pointing laser at law-enforcement officer unlawful; penalty.
If any person, knowing or having reason to know another person is a law-enforcement officer as defined in § 18.2-57, a probation or parole officer appointed pursuant to § 53.1-143, a correctional officer as defined in § 53.1-1, or a person employed by the Depart-

ment of Corrections directly involved in the care, treatment or supervision of inmates in the custody of the Department engaged in the performance of his public duties as such, intentionally projects at such other person a beam or a point of light from a laser, a laser gun sight, or any device that simulates a laser, shall be guilty of a Class 2 misdemeanor.

Title 18.2. Crimes and Offenses Generally
Chapter 4. Crimes Against the Person
Article 5. Robbery

§ 18.2-58. Robbery; penalty.

If any person commit robbery by partial strangulation, or suffocation, or by striking or beating, or by other violence to the person, or by assault or otherwise putting a person in fear of serious bodily harm, or by the threat or presenting of firearms, or other deadly weapon or instrumentality whatsoever, he shall be guilty of a felony and shall be punished by confinement in a state correctional facility for life or any term not less than five years.

Title 18.2. Crimes and Offenses Generally
Chapter 4. Crimes Against the Person
Article 6. Extortion and Other Threats

§ 18.2-60.3. Stalking; penalty.

A. Any person, except a law-enforcement officer, as defined in § 9.1-101, and acting in the performance of his official duties, and a registered private investigator, as defined in § 9.1-138, who is regulated in accordance with § 9.1-139 and acting in the course of his legitimate business, who on more than one occasion engages in conduct directed at another person with the intent to place, or when he knows or reasonably should know that the conduct places that other person in reasonable fear of death, criminal sexual assault, or bodily injury to that other person or to that other person's family or household member is guilty of a Class 1 misdemeanor. If the person contacts or follows or attempts to contact or follow the person at whom the conduct is directed after being given actual notice that the person does not want to be contacted or followed, such actions shall be prima facie evidence that the person intended to place that other person, or reasonably should have known that the other person was placed, in reasonable fear of death, criminal sexual assault, or bodily injury to himself or a family or household member.

B. Any person who is convicted of a second offense of subsection A occurring within five years of a prior conviction of such an offense under this section or for a substantially similar offense under the law of any other jurisdiction is guilty of a Class 6 felony.

C. A person may be convicted under this section irrespective of the jurisdiction or jurisdictions within the Commonwealth wherein the conduct described in subsection A occurred, if the person engaged in that conduct on at least one occasion in the jurisdiction where the person is tried. Evidence of any such conduct that occurred outside the Commonwealth may be admissible, if relevant, in any prosecution under this section provided that the prosecution is based upon conduct occurring within the Commonwealth.

D. Upon finding a person guilty under this section, the court shall, in addition to the sentence imposed, issue an order prohibiting contact between the defendant and the victim or the victim's family or household member.

E. The Department of Corrections, sheriff or regional jail director shall give notice prior to the release from a state correctional facility or a local or regional jail of any person incarcerated upon conviction of a violation of this section, to any victim of the offense who, in writing, requests notice, or to any person designated in writing by the victim. The notice shall be given at least 15 days prior to release of a person sentenced to a term of incarceration of more than 30 days or, if the person was sentenced to a term of incarceration of at least 48 hours but no more than 30 days, 24 hours prior to release. If the person escapes, notice shall be given as soon as practicable following the escape. The victim shall keep the Department of Corrections, sheriff or regional jail director informed of the current mailing address and telephone number of the person named in the writing submitted to receive notice.

All information relating to any person who receives or may receive notice under this subsection shall remain confidential and shall not be made available to the person convicted of violating this section.

For purposes of this subsection, "release" includes a release of the offender from a state correctional facility or a local or regional jail (i) upon completion of his term of incarceration or (ii) on probation or parole.

No civil liability shall attach to the Department of Corrections nor to any sheriff or regional jail director or their deputies or employees for a failure to comply with the requirements of this subsection.

F. For purposes of this section:

"Family or household member" has the same meaning as provided in § 16.1-228.

Title 18.2. Crimes and Offenses Generally
Chapter 4. Crimes Against the Person
Article 7. Criminal Sexual Assault

§ 18.2-61. Rape.
A. If any person has sexual intercourse with a complaining witness, whether or not his or her spouse, or causes a complaining witness, whether or not his or her spouse, to engage in sexual intercourse with any other person and such act is accomplished (i) against the complaining witness's will, by force, threat or intimidation of or against the complaining witness or another person; or (ii) through the use of the complaining witness's mental incapacity or physical helplessness; or (iii) with a child under age 13 as the victim, he or she shall be guilty of rape.

B. A violation of this section shall be punishable, in the discretion of the court or jury, by confinement in a state correctional facility for life or for any term not less than five years; and in addition:
　　1. For a violation of clause (iii) of subsection A where the offender is more than three years older than the victim, if done in the commission of, or as part of the same course of conduct as, or as part of a common scheme or plan as a violation of (i) subsection A of § 18.2-47 or § 18.2-48, (ii) § 18.2-89, 18.2-90, or 18.2-91, or (iii) § 18.2-51.2, the punishment shall include a mandatory minimum term of confinement of 25 years; or
　　2. For a violation of clause (iii) of subsection A where it is alleged in the indictment that the offender was 18 years of age or

older at the time of the offense, the punishment shall include a mandatory minimum term of confinement for life.

The mandatory minimum terms of confinement prescribed for violations of this section shall be served consecutively with any other sentence. If the term of confinement imposed for any violation of clause (iii) of subsection A, where the offender is more than three years older than the victim, is for a term less than life imprisonment, the judge shall impose, in addition to any active sentence, a suspended sentence of no less than 40 years. This suspended sentence shall be suspended for the remainder of the defendant's life, subject to revocation by the court.

There shall be a rebuttable presumption that a juvenile over the age of 10 but less than 12, does not possess the physical capacity to commit a violation of this section. In any case deemed appropriate by the court, all or part of any sentence imposed for a violation under this section against a spouse may be suspended upon the defendant's completion of counseling or therapy, if not already provided, in the manner prescribed under § 19.2-218.1 if, after consideration of the views of the complaining witness and such other evidence as may be relevant, the court finds such action will promote maintenance of the family unit and will be in the best interest of the complaining witness.

C. Upon a finding of guilt under this section, when a spouse is the complaining witness in any case tried by the court without a jury, the court, without entering a judgment of guilt, upon motion of the defendant who has not previously had a proceeding against him for violation of this section dismissed pursuant to this subsection and with the consent of the complaining witness and the attorney for the Commonwealth, may defer further proceedings and place the defendant on probation pending completion of counseling or therapy, if not already provided, in the manner prescribed under § 19.2-218.1. If the defendant fails to so complete such counseling or therapy, the court may make final disposition of the case and proceed as otherwise provided. If such counseling is completed as prescribed under § 19.2-218.1, the court may discharge the defendant and dismiss the proceedings against him if, after consideration of the views of the complaining witness and such other evidence as may be relevant, the court finds such action will promote maintenance of the family unit and be in the best interest of the complaining witness.

Title 18.2. Crimes and Offenses Generally
Chapter 5. Crimes Against Property
Article 5. Trespass to Realty

§ 18.2-119. Trespass after having been forbidden to do so; penalties.
If any person without authority of law goes upon or remains upon the lands, buildings or premises of another, or any portion or area thereof, after having been forbidden to do so, either orally or in writing, by the owner, lessee, custodian, or the agent of any such person, or other person lawfully in charge thereof, or after having been forbidden to do so by a sign or signs posted by or at the direction of such persons or the agent of any such person or by the holder of any easement or other right-of-way authorized by the instrument creating such interest to post such signs on such lands, structures, premises or portion or area thereof at a place or places where it or they may be reasonably seen, or if any person, whether he is the owner, tenant or otherwise entitled to the use of such land, building or premises, goes upon, or remains upon such land, building or premises after having been prohibited from doing so by a court of competent jurisdiction by an order issued pursuant to §§ 16.1-253, 16.1-253.1, 16.1-253.4, 16.1-278.2 through 16.1-278.6, 16.1-278.8, 16.1-278.14, 16.1-278.15, 16.1-279.1, 19.2-152.8, 19.2-152.9 or § 19.2-152.10 or an ex parte order issued pursuant to § 20-103, and after having been served with such order, he shall be guilty of a Class 1 misdemeanor. This section shall not be construed to affect in any way the provisions of §§ 18.2-132 through 18.2-136.

§ 18.2-154. Shooting at or throwing missiles, etc., at train, car, vessel, etc.; penalty.
Any person who maliciously shoots at, or maliciously throws any missile at or against, any train or cars on any railroad or other transportation company or any vessel or other watercraft, or any motor vehicle or other vehicles when occupied by one or more persons, whereby the life of any person on such train, car, vessel, or other watercraft, or in such motor vehicle or other vehicle, may be put in

peril, is guilty of a Class 4 felony. In the event of the death of any such person, resulting from such malicious shooting or throwing, the person so offending is guilty of murder in the second degree. However, if the homicide is willful, deliberate, and premeditated, he is guilty of murder in the first degree.

If any such act is committed unlawfully, but not maliciously, the person so offending is guilty of a Class 6 felony and, in the event of the death of any such person, resulting from such unlawful act, the person so offending is guilty of involuntary manslaughter.

If any person commits a violation of this section by maliciously or unlawfully shooting, with a firearm, at a conspicuously marked law-enforcement, fire, or emergency medical services vehicle, the sentence imposed shall include a mandatory minimum term of imprisonment of one year to be served consecutively with any other sentence.

Title 18.2. Crimes and Offenses Generally
Chapter 7. Crimes Involving Health and Safety
Article 1. Drugs

§ 18.2-250. Possession of controlled substances unlawful.
A. It is unlawful for any person knowingly or intentionally to possess a controlled substance unless the substance was obtained directly from, or pursuant to, a valid prescription or order of a practitioner while acting in the course of his professional practice, or except as otherwise authorized by the Drug Control Act (§ 54.1-3400 et seq.).

Upon the prosecution of a person for a violation of this section, ownership or occupancy of premises or vehicle upon or in which a controlled substance was found shall not create a presumption that such person either knowingly or intentionally possessed such controlled substance.

(a) Any person who violates this section with respect to any controlled substance classified in Schedule I or II of the Drug Control Act shall be guilty of a Class 5 felony, except that any person other than an inmate of a penal institution as defined in § 53.1-1 or in the custody of an employee thereof who violates this section with respect to a cannabimimetic agent is guilty of a Class 1 misdemeanor.

(b) Any person other than an inmate of a penal institution as defined in § 53.1-1 or in the custody of an employee thereof, who violates this section with respect to a controlled substance classified in Schedule III shall be guilty of a Class 1 misdemeanor.

(b1) Violation of this section with respect to a controlled substance classified in Schedule IV shall be punishable as a Class 2 misdemeanor.

(b2) Violation of this section with respect to a controlled substance classified in Schedule V shall be punishable as a Class 3 misdemeanor.

(c) Violation of this section with respect to a controlled substance classified in Schedule VI shall be punishable as a Class 4 misdemeanor.

B. The provisions of this section shall not apply to members of state, federal, county, city or town law-enforcement agencies, jail officers, or correctional officers, as defined in § 53.1-1, certified as handlers of dogs trained in the detection of controlled substances when possession of a controlled substance or substances is necessary in the performance of their duties.

§ 18.2-250.1. Possession of marijuana unlawful.
A. It is unlawful for any person knowingly or intentionally to possess marijuana unless the substance was obtained directly from, or pursuant to, a valid prescription or order of a practitioner while acting in the course of his professional practice, or except as otherwise authorized by the Drug Control Act (§ 54.1-3400 et seq.).

Upon the prosecution of a person for violation of this section, ownership or occupancy of the premises or vehicle upon or in which marijuana was found shall not create a presumption that such person either knowingly or intentionally possessed such marijuana.

Any person who violates this section is guilty of a misdemeanor and shall be confined in jail not more than 30 days and fined not more than $500, either or both; any person, upon a second or subsequent conviction of a violation of this section, is guilty of a Class 1 misdemeanor.

B. The provisions of this section shall not apply to members of state, federal, county, city, or town law-enforcement agencies, jail officers, or correctional officers, as defined in § 53.1-1, certified as handlers of dogs trained in the detection of controlled substances when possession of marijuana is necessary for the performance of their duties.

C. In any prosecution under this section involving marijuana in the form of cannabidiol oil or THC-A oil as those terms are defined in § 54.1-3408.3, it shall be an affirmative defense that the individual possessed such oil pursuant to a valid written certification issued by a practitioner in the course of his professional practice pursuant to § 54.1-3408.3 for treatment or to alleviate the symptoms of (i) the individual's intractable epilepsy or (ii) if such individual is the parent or legal guardian of a minor, such minor's intractable epilepsy. If the individual files the valid written certification with the court at least 10 days prior to trial and causes a copy of such written certification to be delivered to the attorney for the Commonwealth, such written certification shall be prima facie evidence that such oil was possessed pursuant to a valid written certification.

§ 18.2-251. Persons charged with first offense may be placed on probation; conditions; substance abuse screening, assessment treatment and education programs or services; drug tests; costs and fees; violations; discharge.
Whenever any person who has not previously been convicted of any offense under this article or under any statute of the United States or of any state relating to narcotic drugs, marijuana, or stimulant, depressant, or hallucinogenic drugs, or has not previously had a proceeding against him for violation of such an offense dismissed as provided in this section, pleads guilty to or enters a plea of not guilty to possession of a controlled substance under § 18.2-250 or to possession of marijuana under § 18.2-250.1, the court, upon such plea if the facts found by the court would justify a finding of guilt, without entering a judgment of guilt and with the consent of the accused, may defer further proceedings and place him on probation upon terms and conditions.

As a term or condition, the court shall require the accused to undergo a substance abuse assessment pursuant to § 18.2-251.01 or 19.2-299.2, as appropriate, and enter treatment and/or education program or services, if available, such as, in the opinion of the court, may be best suited to the needs of the accused based upon consideration of the substance abuse assessment. The program or services may be located in the judicial district in which the charge is brought or in any other judicial district as the court may provide. The services shall be provided by (i) a program licensed by the Department of Behavioral Health and Developmental Services, by a similar program which is made available through the Department of Corrections, (ii) a local community-based probation services agency established pursuant to § 9.1-174, or (iii) an ASAP program certified by the Commission on VASAP.

The court shall require the person entering such program under the provisions of this section to pay all or part of the costs of the program, including the costs of the screening, assessment, testing, and treatment, based upon the accused's ability to pay unless the person is determined by the court to be indigent.

As a condition of probation, the court shall require the accused (i) to successfully complete treatment or education program or services, (ii) to remain drug and alcohol free during the period of probation and submit to such tests during that period as may be necessary and appropriate to determine if the accused is drug and alcohol free, (iii) to make reasonable efforts to secure and maintain employment, and (iv) to comply with a plan of at least 100 hours of community service for a felony and up to 24 hours of community service for a misdemeanor. Such testing shall be conducted by personnel of the supervising probation agency or personnel of any program or agency approved by the supervising probation agency.

The court shall, unless done at arrest, order the accused to report to the original arresting law-enforcement agency to submit to fingerprinting.

Upon violation of a term or condition, the court may enter an adjudication of guilt and proceed as otherwise provided. Upon fulfillment of the terms and conditions, the court shall discharge the person and dismiss the proceedings against him. Discharge and dismissal under this section shall be without adjudication of guilt and is a conviction only for the purposes of applying this section in subsequent proceedings.

Notwithstanding any other provision of this section, whenever a court places an individual on probation upon terms and conditions pursuant to this section, such action shall be treated as a conviction for purposes of §§ 18.2-259.1, 22.1-315, and 46.2-390.1, and the driver's license forfeiture provisions of those sections shall be imposed. The provisions of this paragraph shall not be applicable to any offense for which a juvenile has had his license suspended or denied pursuant to § 16.1-278.9 for the same offense.

Title 18.2. Crimes and Offenses Generally
Chapter 7. Crimes Involving Health and Safety
Article 4. Dangerous Use of Firearms or Other Weapons

§ 18.2-279. Discharging firearms or missiles within or at building or dwelling house; penalty.
If any person maliciously discharges a firearm within any building when occupied by one or more persons in such a manner as to endanger the life or lives of such person or persons, or maliciously shoots at, or maliciously throws any missile at or against any dwelling house or other building when occupied by one or more persons, whereby the life or lives of any such person or persons may be put in peril, the person so offending is guilty of a Class 4 felony. In the event of the death of any person, resulting from such malicious shooting or throwing, the person so offending is guilty of murder in the second degree. However, if the homicide is willful, deliberate and premeditated, he is guilty of murder in the first degree.

If any such act be done unlawfully, but not maliciously, the person so offending is guilty of a Class 6 felony; and, in the event of the death of any person resulting from such unlawful shooting or throwing, the person so offending is guilty of involuntary manslaughter. If any person willfully discharges a firearm within or shoots at any school building whether occupied or not, he is guilty of a Class 4 felony.

§ 18.2-280. Willfully discharging firearms in public places.
A. If any person willfully discharges or causes to be discharged any firearm in any street in a city or town, or in any place of public business or place of public gathering, and such conduct results in bodily injury to another person, he shall be guilty of a Class 6 felony. If such conduct does not result in bodily injury to another person, he shall be guilty of a Class 1 misdemeanor.

B. If any person willfully discharges or causes to be discharged any firearm upon the buildings and grounds of any public, private or religious elementary, middle or high school, he shall be guilty of a Class 4 felony, unless he is engaged in a program or curriculum sponsored by or conducted with permission of a public, private or religious school.

C. If any person willfully discharges or causes to be discharged any firearm upon any public property within 1,000 feet of the property line of any public, private or religious elementary, middle or high school property he shall be guilty of a Class 4 felony, unless he is engaged in lawful hunting.

D. This section shall not apply to any law-enforcement officer in the performance of his official duties nor to any other person whose said willful act is otherwise justifiable or excusable at law in the protection of his life or property, or is otherwise specifically authorized by law.

E. Nothing in this statute shall preclude the Commonwealth from electing to prosecute under any other applicable provision of law instead of this section.

§ 18.2-281. Setting spring gun or other deadly weapon.
It shall be unlawful for any person to set or fix in any manner any firearm or other deadly weapon so that it may be discharged or activated by a person coming in contact therewith or with any string, wire, spring, or any other contrivance attached thereto or designed to activate such weapon remotely. Any person violating this section shall be guilty of a Class 6 felony.

§ 18.2-282. Pointing, holding, or brandishing firearm, air or gas operated weapon or object similar in appearance; penalty.
A. It shall be unlawful for any person to point, hold or brandish any firearm or any air or gas operated weapon or any object similar in appearance, whether capable of being fired or not, in such manner as to reasonably induce fear in the mind of another or hold a firearm or any air or gas operated weapon in a public place in such a manner as to reasonably induce fear in the mind of another of being shot or injured. However, this section shall not apply to any person engaged in excusable or justifiable self-defense. Persons

violating the provisions of this section shall be guilty of a Class 1 misdemeanor or, if the violation occurs upon any public, private or religious elementary, middle or high school, including buildings and grounds or upon public property within 1,000 feet of such school property, he shall be guilty of a Class 6 felony.

B. Any police officer in the performance of his duty, in making an arrest under the provisions of this section, shall not be civilly liable in damages for injuries or death resulting to the person being arrested if he had reason to believe that the person being arrested was pointing, holding, or brandishing such firearm or air or gas operated weapon, or object that was similar in appearance, with intent to induce fear in the mind of another.

C. For purposes of this section, the word "firearm" means any weapon that will or is designed to or may readily be converted to expel single or multiple projectiles by the action of an explosion of a combustible material. The word "ammunition," as used herein, shall mean a cartridge, pellet, ball, missile or projectile adapted for use in a firearm.

§ 18.2-283. Carrying dangerous weapon to place of religious worship.
If any person carry any gun, pistol, bowie knife, dagger or other dangerous weapon, without good and sufficient reason, to a place of worship while a meeting for religious purposes is being held at such place he shall be guilty of a Class 4 misdemeanor.

§ 18.2-283.1. Carrying weapon into courthouse.
It shall be unlawful for any person to possess in or transport into any courthouse in this Commonwealth any (i) gun or other weapon designed or intended to propel a missile or projectile of any kind, (ii) frame, receiver, muffler, silencer, missile, projectile or ammunition designed for use with a dangerous weapon and (iii) any other dangerous weapon, including explosives, stun weapons as defined in § 18.2-308.1, and those weapons specified in subsection A of § 18.2-308. Any such weapon shall be subject to seizure by a law-enforcement officer. A violation of this section is punishable as a Class 1 misdemeanor.

The provisions of this section shall not apply to any police officer, sheriff, law-enforcement agent or official, conservation police officer, conservator of the peace, magistrate, court officer, judge, or city or county treasurer while in the conduct of such person's official duties.

§ 18.2-286. Shooting in or across road or in street.
If any person discharges a firearm, crossbow or bow and arrow in or across any road, or within the right-of-way thereof, or in a street of any city or town, he shall, for each offense, be guilty of a Class 4 misdemeanor.

The provisions of this section shall not apply to firing ranges or shooting matches maintained, and supervised or approved, by law-enforcement officers and military personnel in performance of their lawful duties.

§ 18.2-287.01. Carrying weapon in air carrier airport terminal.
It shall be unlawful for any person to possess or transport into any air carrier airport terminal in the Commonwealth any (i) gun or other weapon designed or intended to propel a missile or projectile of any kind, (ii) frame, receiver, muffler, silencer, missile, projectile or ammunition designed for use with a dangerous weapon, and (iii) any other dangerous weapon, including explosives, stun weapons as defined in § 18.2-308.1, and those weapons specified in subsection A of § 18.2-308. Any such weapon shall be subject to seizure by a law-enforcement officer. A violation of this section is punishable as a Class 1 misdemeanor. Any weapon possessed or transported in violation of this section shall be forfeited to the Commonwealth and disposed of as provided in § 19.2-386.28.

The provisions of this section shall not apply to any police officer, sheriff, law-enforcement agent or official, conservation police officer, conservator of the peace employed by the air carrier airport, or retired law-enforcement officer qualified pursuant to subsection C of § 18.2-308.016, nor shall the provisions of this section apply to any passenger of an airline who, to the extent otherwise permitted by law, transports a lawful firearm, weapon, or ammunition into or out of an air carrier airport terminal for the sole purposes, respectively, of (i) presenting such firearm, weapon, or ammunition to U.S. Customs agents in advance of an international flight, in order to comply with federal law, (ii) checking such firearm, weapon, or ammunition with his luggage, or (iii) retrieving such firearm, weapon, or ammunition from the baggage claim area.

Any other statute, rule, regulation, or ordinance specifically addressing the possession or transportation of weapons in any airport in the Commonwealth shall be invalid, and this section shall control.

Title 18.2. Crimes and Offenses Generally
Chapter 7. Crimes Involving Health and Safety
Article 5. Uniform Machine Gun Act

§ 18.2-288. Machine Gun & Crime of Violence Definitions.
When used in this article:
(1) "Machine gun" applies to any weapon which shoots or is designed to shoot automatically more than one shot, without manual reloading, by a single function of the trigger.
(2) "Crime of violence" applies to and includes any of the following crimes or an attempt to commit any of the same, namely, murder, manslaughter, kidnapping, rape, mayhem, assault with intent to maim, disable, disfigure or kill, robbery, burglary, housebreaking, breaking and entering and larceny.
(3) "Person" applies to and includes firm, partnership, association or corporation.

§ 18.2-289. Use of machine gun for crime of violence.
Possession or use of a machine gun in the perpetration or attempted perpetration of a crime of violence is hereby declared to be a Class 2 felony.

§ 18.2-290. Use of machine gun for aggressive purpose.
Unlawful possession or use of a machine gun for an offensive or aggressive purpose is hereby declared to be a Class 4 felony.

§ 18.2-291. Aggressive Purpose Definition.

Possession or use of a machine gun shall be presumed to be for an offensive or aggressive purpose:

(1) When the machine gun is on premises not owned or rented for bona fide permanent residence or business occupancy by the person in whose possession the machine gun may be found;

(2) When the machine gun is in the possession of, or used by, a person who has been convicted of a crime of violence in any court of record, state or federal, of the United States of America, its territories or insular possessions;

(3) When the machine gun has not been registered as required in § 18.2-295; or

(4) When empty or loaded shells which have been or are susceptible of use in the machine gun are found in the immediate vicinity thereof.

§ 18.2-292. Presence is prima facie evidence of Machine Gun use.

The presence of a machine gun in any room, boat or vehicle shall be prima facie evidence of the possession or use of the machine gun by each person occupying the room, boat, or vehicle where the weapon is found.

§ 18.2-293.1. Machine Gun Act Does Not Prohibit.

Nothing contained in this article shall prohibit or interfere with:

(1) The possession of a machine gun for scientific purposes, or the possession of a machine gun not usable as a weapon and possessed as a curiosity, ornament, or keepsake; and

(2) The possession of a machine gun for a purpose manifestly not aggressive or offensive.

Provided, however, that possession of such machine guns shall be subject to the provisions of § 18.2-295.

§ 18.2-295. Registration of machine guns.

Every machine gun in this Commonwealth shall be registered with the Department of State Police within twenty-four hours after its acquisition or, in the case of semi-automatic weapons which are converted, modified or otherwise altered to become machine guns, within twenty-four hours of the conversion, modification or alteration. Blanks for registration shall be prepared by the Superintendent of State Police, and furnished upon application. To comply with this section the application as filed shall be notarized and shall show the model and serial number of the gun, the name, address and occupation of the person in possession, and from whom and the purpose for which, the gun was acquired or altered. The Superintendent of State Police shall upon registration required in this section forthwith furnish the registrant with a certificate of registration, which shall be valid as long as the registrant remains the same. Certificates of registration shall be retained by the registrant and produced by him upon demand by any peace officer. Failure to keep or produce such certificate for inspection shall be a Class 3 misdemeanor, and any peace officer, may without warrant, seize the machine gun and apply for its confiscation as provided in § 18.2-296. Upon transferring a registered machine gun, the transferor shall forthwith notify the Superintendent in writing, setting forth the date of transfer and name and address of the transferee. Failure to give the required notification shall constitute a Class 3 misdemeanor. Registration data shall not be subject to inspection by the public.

Title 18.2. Crimes and Offenses Generally
Chapter 7. Crimes Involving Health and Safety
Article 6. "Sawed-Off" Shotgun and "Sawed-Off" Rifle Act

§ 18.2-299. "Sawed-Off' Shotgun and "Sawed-Off" Rifle Definitions.
When used in this article:

"Sawed-off shotgun" means any weapon, loaded or unloaded, originally designed as a shoulder weapon, utilizing a self-contained cartridge from which a number of ball shot pellets or projectiles may be fired simultaneously from a smooth or rifled bore by a single function of the firing device and which has a barrel length of less than 18 inches for smooth bore weapons and 16 inches for rifled weapons. Weapons of less than .225 caliber shall not be included.

"Sawed-off rifle" means a rifle of any caliber, loaded or unloaded, which expels a projectile by action of an explosion of a combustible material and is designed as a shoulder weapon with a barrel or barrels length of less than 16 inches or which has been modified to an overall length of less than 26 inches.

"Crime of violence" applies to and includes any of the following crimes or an attempt to commit any of the same, namely, murder, manslaughter, kidnapping, rape, mayhem, assault with intent to maim, disable, disfigure or kill, robbery, burglary, housebreaking, breaking and entering and larceny.

"Person" applies to and includes firm, partnership, association or corporation.

§ 18.2-300. Possession or use of "sawed-off" shotgun or rifle.
A. Possession or use of a "sawed-off" shotgun or "sawed-off" rifle in the perpetration or attempted perpetration of a crime of violence is a Class 2 felony.

B. Possession or use of a "sawed-off" shotgun or "sawed-off" rifle for any other purpose, except as permitted by this article and official use by those persons permitted possession by § 18.2-303, is a Class 4 felony.

§ 18.2-303. Exemptions to the "sawed-off" shotgun and rifle
The provisions of this article shall not be applicable to:
> (1) The manufacture for, and sale of, "sawed-off" shotguns or "sawed-off" rifles to the armed forces or law-enforcement officers of the United States or of any state or of any political subdivision thereof, or the transportation required for that purpose; and
> (2) "Sawed-off" shotguns, "sawed-off" rifles and automatic arms issued to the National Guard of Virginia by the United States or such arms used by the United States Army or Navy or in the hands of troops of the national guards of other states or territories of the United States passing through Virginia, or such arms as may be provided for the officers of the State Police or officers of penal institutions.

§ 18.2-303.1. "Sawed-off" shotgun & rifle Act does not prohibit.
Nothing contained in this article shall prohibit or interfere with the possession of a "sawed-off" shotgun or "sawed-off" rifle for scientific purposes, the possession of a "sawed-off" shotgun or "sawed-off" rifle possessed in compliance with federal law or the possession of a "sawed-off" shotgun or "sawed-off" rifle not usable as a firing weapon and possessed as a curiosity, ornament, or keepsake.

Title 18.2. Crimes and Offenses Generally
Chapter 7. Crimes Involving Health and Safety
Article 6.1. Concealed Weapons and Concealed Handgun Permits

§ 18.2-307.1. Concealed Weapon Definitions.
As used in this article, unless the context requires a different meaning:

"Ballistic knife" means any knife with a detachable blade that is propelled by a spring-operated mechanism.

"Handgun" means any pistol or revolver or other firearm, except a machine gun, originally designed, made, and intended to fire a projectile by means of an explosion of a combustible material from one or more barrels when held in one hand.

"Law-enforcement officer" means those individuals defined as a law-enforcement officer in § 9.1-101, law-enforcement agents of the armed forces of the United States and the Naval Criminal Investigative Service, and federal agents who are otherwise authorized to carry weapons by federal law. "Law-enforcement officer" also means any sworn full-time law-enforcement officer employed by a law-enforcement agency of the United States or any state or political subdivision thereof, whose duties are substantially similar to those set forth in § 9.1-101.

"Lawfully admitted for permanent residence" means the status of having been lawfully accorded the privilege of residing permanently in the United States as an immigrant in accordance with the immigration laws, such status not having changed.

"Personal knowledge" means knowledge of a fact that a person has himself gained through his own senses, or knowledge that was gained by a law-enforcement officer or prosecutor through the performance of his official duties.

"Spring stick" means a spring-loaded metal stick activated by pushing a button that rapidly and forcefully telescopes the weapon to several times its original length.

§ 18.2-308. Carrying concealed weapons; exceptions; penalty.

A. If any person carries about his person, hidden from common observation, (i) any pistol, revolver, or other weapon designed or intended to propel a missile of any kind by action of an explosion of any combustible material; (ii) any dirk, bowie knife, switchblade knife, ballistic knife, machete, razor, slingshot, spring stick, metal knucks, or blackjack; (iii) any flailing instrument consisting of two or more rigid parts connected in such a manner as to allow them to swing freely, which may be known as a nun chahka, nun chuck, nunchaku, shuriken, or fighting chain; (iv) any disc, of whatever configuration, having at least two points or pointed blades which is designed to be thrown or propelled and which may be known as a throwing star or oriental dart; or (v) any weapon of like kind as those enumerated in this subsection, he is guilty of a Class 1 misdemeanor. A second violation of this section or a conviction under this section subsequent to any conviction under any substantially similar ordinance of any county, city, or town shall be punishable as a Class 6 felony, and a third or subsequent such violation shall be punishable as a Class 5 felony. For the purpose of this section, a weapon shall be deemed to be hidden from common observation when it is observable but is of such deceptive appearance as to disguise the weapon's true nature. It shall be an affirmative defense to a violation of clause (i) regarding a handgun, that a person had been issued, at the time of the offense, a valid concealed handgun permit.

B. This section shall not apply to any person while in his own place of abode or the curtilage thereof.

C. Except as provided in subsection A of § 18.2-308.012, this section shall not apply to:
    1. Any person while in his own place of business;
    2. Any law-enforcement officer, or retired law-enforcement officer pursuant to § 18.2-308.016, wherever such law-enforcement officer may travel in the Commonwealth;
    3. Any person who is at, or going to or from, an established shooting range, provided that the weapons are unloaded and securely wrapped while being transported;
    4. Any regularly enrolled member of a weapons collecting organization who is at, or going to or from, a bona fide weapons exhibition, provided that the weapons are unloaded and securely

wrapped while being transported;

5. Any person carrying such weapons between his place of abode and a place of purchase or repair, provided the weapons are unloaded and securely wrapped while being transported;

6. Any person actually engaged in lawful hunting, as authorized by the Board of Game and Inland Fisheries, under inclement weather conditions necessitating temporary protection of his firearm from those conditions, provided that possession of a handgun while engaged in lawful hunting shall not be construed as hunting with a handgun if the person hunting is carrying a valid concealed handgun permit;

7. Any attorney for the Commonwealth or assistant attorney for the Commonwealth, wherever such attorney may travel in the Commonwealth;

8. Any person who may lawfully possess a firearm and is carrying a handgun while in a personal, private motor vehicle or vessel and such handgun is secured in a container or compartment in the vehicle or vessel;

9. Any enrolled participant of a firearms training course who is at, or going to or from, a training location, provided that the weapons are unloaded and securely wrapped while being transported; and

10. Any judge or justice of the Commonwealth, wherever such judge or justice may travel in the Commonwealth.

D. This section shall also not apply to any of the following individuals while in the discharge of their official duties, or while in transit to or from such duties:

1. Carriers of the United States mail;

2. Officers or guards of any state correctional institution;

3. Conservators of the peace, except that a judge or justice of the Commonwealth, an attorney for the Commonwealth, or an assistant attorney for the Commonwealth may carry a concealed handgun pursuant to subdivisions C 7 and 10. However, the following conservators of the peace shall not be permitted to carry a concealed handgun without obtaining a permit as provided in this article: (i) notaries public; (ii) registrars; (iii) drivers, operators, or other persons in charge of any motor vehicle carrier of passengers for hire; or (iv) commissioners in chancery;

4. Noncustodial employees of the Department of Corrections

designated to carry weapons by the Director of the Department of Corrections pursuant to § 53.1-29; and

5. Harbormaster of the City of Hopewell.

§ 18.2-308.01. Carrying a concealed handgun with a permit.

A. The prohibition against carrying a concealed handgun in clause (i) of subsection A of § 18.2-308 shall not apply to a person who has a valid concealed handgun permit issued pursuant to this article. The person issued the permit shall have such permit on his person at all times during which he is carrying a concealed handgun and shall display the permit and a photo identification issued by a government agency of the Commonwealth or by the U.S. Department of Defense or U.S. State Department (passport) upon demand by a law-enforcement officer. A person to whom a nonresident permit is issued shall have such permit on his person at all times when he is carrying a concealed handgun in the Commonwealth and shall display the permit on demand by a law-enforcement officer. A person whose permit is extended due to deployment shall carry with him and display, upon request of a law-enforcement officer, a copy of the documents required by subsection B of § 18.2-308.010.

B. Failure to display the permit and a photo identification upon demand by a law-enforcement officer shall be punishable by a $25 civil penalty, which shall be paid into the state treasury. Any attorney for the Commonwealth of the county or city in which the alleged violation occurred may bring an action to recover the civil penalty. A court may waive such penalty upon presentation to the court of a valid permit and a government-issued photo identification. Any law-enforcement officer may issue a summons for the civil violation of failure to display the concealed handgun permit and photo identification upon demand.

C. The granting of a concealed handgun permit pursuant to this article shall not thereby authorize the possession of any handgun or other weapon on property or in places where such possession is otherwise prohibited by law or is prohibited by the owner of private property.

§ 18.2-308.02. Application for a concealed handgun permit; Virginia resident or domiciliary.

A. Any person 21 years of age or older may apply in writing to the clerk of the circuit court of the county or city in which he resides, or if he is a member of the United States armed forces, the county or city in which he is domiciled, for a five-year permit to carry a concealed handgun. There shall be no requirement regarding the length of time an applicant has been a resident or domiciliary of the county or city. The application shall be made under oath before a notary or other person qualified to take oaths and shall be made only on a form prescribed by the Department of State Police, in consultation with the Supreme Court, requiring only that information necessary to determine eligibility for the permit. No information or documentation other than that which is allowed on the application in accordance with this section may be requested or required by the clerk or the court.

B. The court shall require proof that the applicant has demonstrated competence with a handgun and the applicant may demonstrate such competence by one of the following, but no applicant shall be required to submit to any additional demonstration of competence, nor shall any proof of demonstrated competence expire:

1. Completing any hunter education or hunter safety course approved by the Department of Game and Inland Fisheries or a similar agency of another state;
2. Completing any National Rifle Association firearms safety or training course;
3. Completing any firearms safety or training course or class available to the general public offered by a law-enforcement agency, junior college, college, or private or public institution or organization or firearms training school utilizing instructors certified by the National Rifle Association or the Department of Criminal Justice Services;
4. Completing any law-enforcement firearms safety or training course or class offered for security guards, investigators, special deputies, or any division or subdivision of law enforcement or security enforcement;
5. Presenting evidence of equivalent experience with a firearm through participation in organized shooting competition or current military service or proof of an honorable discharge from any branch of the armed services;
6. Obtaining or previously having held a license to carry a firearm in the Commonwealth or a locality thereof, unless such license has been revoked for cause;

7. Completing any firearms training or safety course or class, including an electronic, video, or online course, conducted by a state-certified or National Rifle Association-certified firearms instructor;
8. Completing any governmental police agency firearms training course and qualifying to carry a firearm in the course of normal police duties; or
9. Completing any other firearms training which the court deems adequate.

A photocopy of a certificate of completion of any of the courses or classes; an affidavit from the instructor, school, club, organization, or group that conducted or taught such course or class attesting to the completion of the course or class by the applicant; or a copy of any document that shows completion of the course or class or evidences participation in firearms competition shall constitute evidence of qualification under this subsection.

C. The making of a materially false statement in an application under this article shall constitute perjury, punishable as provided in § 18.2-434.

D. The clerk of court shall withhold from public disclosure the applicant's name and any other information contained in a permit application or any order issuing a concealed handgun permit, except that such information shall not be withheld from any law-enforcement officer acting in the performance of his official duties or from the applicant with respect to his own information. The prohibition on public disclosure of information under this subsection shall not apply to any reference to the issuance of a concealed handgun permit in any order book before July 1, 2008; however, any other concealed handgun records maintained by the clerk shall be withheld from public disclosure.

E. An application is deemed complete when all information required to be furnished by the applicant, including the fee for a concealed handgun permit as set forth in § 18.2-308.03, is delivered to and received by the clerk of court before or concomitant with the conduct of a state or national criminal history records check.

§ 18.2-308.03. Fees for concealed handgun permits.

A. The clerk shall charge a fee of $10 for the processing of an application or issuing of a permit, including his costs associated with the consultation with law-enforcement agencies. The local law-enforcement agency conducting the background investigation may charge a fee not to exceed $35 to cover the cost of conducting an investigation pursuant to this article. The $35 fee shall include any amount assessed by the U.S. Federal Bureau of Investigation for providing criminal history record information, and the local law-enforcement agency shall forward the amount assessed by the U.S. Federal Bureau of Investigation to the State Police with the fingerprints taken from any nonresident applicant. The State Police may charge a fee not to exceed $5 to cover its costs associated with processing the application. The total amount assessed for processing an application for a permit shall not exceed $50, with such fees to be paid in one sum to the person who receives the application. Payment may be made by any method accepted by that court for payment of other fees or penalties. No payment shall be required until the application is received by the court as a complete application.

B. (Effective until July 1, 2018) No fee shall be charged for the issuance of such permit to a person who has retired from service (i) as a magistrate in the Commonwealth; (ii) as a special agent with the Alcoholic Beverage Control Board or as a law-enforcement officer with the Department of State Police, the Department of Game and Inland Fisheries, or a sheriff or police department, bureau, or force of any political subdivision of the Commonwealth, after completing 15 years of service or after reaching age 55; (iii) as a law-enforcement officer with the U.S. Federal Bureau of Investigation, Bureau of Alcohol, Tobacco and Firearms, Secret Service Agency, Drug Enforcement Administration, United States Citizenship and Immigration Services, U.S. Customs and Border Protection, Department of State Diplomatic Security Service, U.S. Marshals Service, or Naval Criminal Investigative Service, after completing 15 years of service or after reaching age 55; (iv) as a law-enforcement officer with any police or sheriff's department within the United States, the District of Columbia, or any of the territories of the United States, after completing 15 years of service; (v) as a law-enforcement officer with any combination of the agencies listed in clauses (ii) through (iv), after completing 15 years of service; (vi) as a designated boarding team member or boarding officer of the United States Coast

Guard, after completing 15 years of service or after reaching age 55; or (vii) as a correctional officer as defined in § 53.1-1 after completing 15 years of service.

B. (Effective July 1, 2018) No fee shall be charged for the issuance of such permit to a person who has retired from service (i) as a magistrate in the Commonwealth; (ii) as a special agent with the Virginia Alcoholic Beverage Control Authority or as a law-enforcement officer with the Department of State Police, the Department of Game and Inland Fisheries, or a sheriff or police department, bureau, or force of any political subdivision of the Commonwealth, after completing 15 years of service or after reaching age 55; (iii) as a law-enforcement officer with the U.S. Federal Bureau of Investigation, Bureau of Alcohol, Tobacco and Firearms, Secret Service Agency, Drug Enforcement Administration, United States Citizenship and Immigration Services, U.S. Customs and Border Protection, Department of State Diplomatic Security Service, U.S. Marshals Service, or Naval Criminal Investigative Service, after completing 15 years of service or after reaching age 55; (iv) as a law-enforcement officer with any police or sheriff's department within the United States, the District of Columbia, or any of the territories of the United States, after completing 15 years of service; (v) as a law-enforcement officer with any combination of the agencies listed in clauses (ii) through (iv), after completing 15 years of service; (vi) as a designated boarding team member or boarding officer of the United States Coast Guard, after completing 15 years of service or after reaching age 55; or (vii) as a correctional officer as defined in § 53.1-1 after completing 15 years of service.

§ 18.2-308.04. Processing of the application and issuance of a concealed handgun permit.

A. The clerk of court shall enter on the application the date on which the application and all other information required to be submitted by the applicant is received.

B. Upon receipt of the completed application, the court shall consult with either the sheriff or police department of the county or city and receive a report from the Central Criminal Records Exchange.

C. The court shall issue the permit via United States mail and notify the State Police of the issuance of the permit within 45 days of receipt of the completed application unless it is determined that the applicant is disqualified. Any order denying issuance of the permit shall be in accordance with § 18.2-308.08. If the applicant is later found by the court to be disqualified after a five-year permit has been issued, the permit shall be revoked.

D. A court may authorize the clerk to issue concealed handgun permits, without judicial review, to applicants who have submitted complete applications, for whom the criminal history records check does not indicate a disqualification and, after consulting with either the sheriff or police department of the county or city, about which application there are no outstanding questions or issues. The court clerk shall be immune from suit arising from any acts or omissions relating to the issuance of concealed handgun permits without judicial review pursuant to this section unless the clerk was grossly negligent or engaged in willful misconduct. This section shall not be construed to limit, withdraw, or overturn any defense or immunity already existing in statutory or common law, or to affect any cause of action accruing prior to July 1, 2010.

E. The permit to carry a concealed handgun shall specify only the following information: name, address, date of birth, gender, height, weight, color of hair, color of eyes, and signature of the permittee; the signature of the judge issuing the permit, of the clerk of court who has been authorized to sign such permits by the issuing judge, or of the clerk of court who has been authorized to issue such permits pursuant to subsection D; the date of issuance; and the expiration date. The permit to carry a concealed handgun shall be no larger than two inches wide by three and one-fourth inches long and shall be of a uniform style prescribed by the Department of State Police.

§ 18.2-308.05. Issuance of a *de facto* permit.
If the court has not issued the permit or determined that the applicant is disqualified within 45 days of the date of receipt noted on the application, the clerk shall certify on the application that the 45-day period has expired, and mail or send via electronic mail a copy of the certified application to the applicant within five business days of the expiration of the 45-day period. The certified application shall serve as a de facto permit, which shall expire 90 days after issuance, and shall be recognized as a valid concealed hand-

gun permit when presented with a valid government-issued photo identification pursuant to subsection A of § 18.2-308.01, until the court issues a five-year permit or finds the applicant to be disqualified. If the applicant is found to be disqualified after the de facto permit is issued, the applicant shall surrender the de facto permit to the court and the disqualification shall be deemed a denial of the permit and a revocation of the de facto permit.

§ 18.2-308.06. Nonresident concealed handgun permits.
A. Nonresidents of the Commonwealth 21 years of age or older may apply in writing to the Virginia Department of State Police for a five-year permit to carry a concealed handgun. Every applicant for a nonresident concealed handgun permit shall submit two photographs of a type and kind specified by the Department of State Police for inclusion on the permit and shall submit fingerprints on a card provided by the Department of State Police for the purpose of obtaining the applicant's state or national criminal history record. As a condition for issuance of a concealed handgun permit, the applicant shall submit to fingerprinting by his local or state law-enforcement agency and provide personal descriptive information to be forwarded with the fingerprints through the Central Criminal Records Exchange to the U.S. Federal Bureau of Investigation for the purpose of obtaining criminal history record information regarding the applicant and obtaining fingerprint identification information from federal records pursuant to criminal investigations by state and local law-enforcement agencies. The application shall be made under oath before a notary or other person qualified to take oaths on a form provided by the Department of State Police, requiring only that information necessary to determine eligibility for the permit. If the permittee is later found by the Department of State Police to be disqualified, the permit shall be revoked and the person shall return the permit after being so notified by the Department of State Police. The permit requirement and restriction provisions of subsection C of § 18.2-308.02 and § 18.2-308.09 shall apply, mutatis mutandis, to the provisions of this subsection.

B. The applicant shall demonstrate competence with a handgun by one of the following:
    1. Completing a hunter education or hunter safety course approved by the Virginia Department of Game and Inland Fisheries or a similar agency of another state;

2. Completing any National Rifle Association firearms safety or training course;

3. Completing any firearms safety or training course or class available to the general public offered by a law-enforcement agency, junior college, college, or private or public institution or organization or firearms training school utilizing instructors certified by the National Rifle Association or the Department of Criminal Justice Services or a similar agency of another state;

4. Completing any law-enforcement firearms safety or training course or class offered for security guards, investigators, special deputies, or any division or subdivision of law enforcement or security enforcement;

5. Presenting evidence of equivalent experience with a firearm through participation in organized shooting competition approved by the Department of State Police or current military service or proof of an honorable discharge from any branch of the armed services;

6. Obtaining or previously having held a license to carry a firearm in the Commonwealth or a locality thereof, unless such license has been revoked for cause;

7. Completing any firearms training or safety course or class, including an electronic, video, or on-line course, conducted by a state-certified or National Rifle Association-certified firearms instructor;

8. Completing any governmental police agency firearms training course and qualifying to carry a firearm in the course of normal police duties; or

9. Completing any other firearms training that the Virginia Department of State Police deems adequate.

A photocopy of a certificate of completion of any such course or class; an affidavit from the instructor, school, club, organization, or group that conducted or taught such course or class attesting to the completion of the course or class by the applicant; or a copy of any document that shows completion of the course or class or evidences participation in firearms competition shall satisfy the requirement for demonstration of competence with a handgun.

C. The Department of State Police may charge a fee not to exceed $100 to cover the cost of the background check and issuance of the permit. Any fees collected shall be deposited in a special account to be used to offset the costs of administering the nonresident concealed handgun permit program.

D. The permit to carry a concealed handgun shall contain only the following information: name, address, date of birth, gender, height, weight, color of hair, color of eyes, and photograph of the permittee; the signature of the Superintendent of the Virginia Department of State Police or his designee; the date of issuance; and the expiration date.

E. The Superintendent of the State Police shall promulgate regulations, pursuant to the Administrative Process Act (§ 2.2-4000 et seq.), for the implementation of an application process for obtaining a nonresident concealed handgun permit.

§ 18.2-308.08. Denial of a concealed handgun permit; appeal.

A. Only a circuit court judge may deny issuance of a concealed handgun permit to a Virginia resident or domiciliary who has applied for a permit pursuant to § 18.2-308.04. Any order denying issuance of a concealed handgun permit shall state the basis for the denial of the permit, including, if applicable, any reason under § 18.2-308.09 that is the basis of the denial, and the clerk shall provide notice, in writing, upon denial of the application, of the applicant's right to an ore tenus hearing and the requirements for perfecting an appeal of such order.

B. Upon request of the applicant made within 21 days, the court shall place the matter on the docket for an ore tenus hearing. The applicant may be represented by counsel, but counsel shall not be appointed, and the rules of evidence shall apply. The final order of the court shall include the court's findings of fact and conclusions of law.

C. Any person denied a permit to carry a concealed handgun by the circuit court may present a petition for review to the Court of Appeals. The petition for review shall be filed within 60 days of the expiration of the time for requesting an ore tenus hearing, or if an ore tenus hearing is requested, within 60 days of the entry of the final order of the circuit court following the hearing. The petition shall be accompanied by a copy of the original papers filed in the circuit court, including a copy of the order of the circuit court denying the permit. Subject to the provisions of subsection B of § 17.1-410, the decision of the Court of Appeals or judge shall be final. Notwithstanding any other provision of law, if the decision to deny the permit is reversed upon appeal, taxable costs incurred by the person shall be paid by the Commonwealth.

§ 18.2-308.09. Disqualifications for a concealed handgun permit.
The following persons shall be deemed disqualified from obtaining a permit:

1. An individual who is ineligible to possess a firearm pursuant to § 18.2-308.1:1, 18.2-308.1:2, or 18.2-308.1:3 or the substantially similar law of any other state or of the United States.

2. An individual who was ineligible to possess a firearm pursuant to § 18.2-308.1:1 and who was discharged from the custody of the Commissioner pursuant to § 19.2-182.7 less than five years before the date of his application for a concealed handgun permit.

3. An individual who was ineligible to possess a firearm pursuant to § 18.2-308.1:2 and whose competency or capacity was restored pursuant to § 64.2-2012 less than five years before the date of his application for a concealed handgun permit.

4. An individual who was ineligible to possess a firearm under § 18.2-308.1:3 and who was released from commitment less than five years before the date of this application for a concealed handgun permit.

5. An individual who is subject to a restraining order, or to a protective order and prohibited by § 18.2-308.1:4 from purchasing, possessing, or transporting a firearm.

6. An individual who is prohibited by § 18.2-308.2 from possessing or transporting a firearm, except that a permit may be obtained in accordance with subsection C of that section.

7. An individual who has been convicted of two or more misdemeanors within the five-year period immediately preceding the application, if one of the misdemeanors was a Class 1 misdemeanor, but the judge shall have the discretion to deny a permit for two or more misdemeanors that are not Class 1. Traffic infractions and misdemeanors set forth in Title 46.2 shall not be considered for purposes of this disqualification.

8. An individual who is addicted to, or is an unlawful user or distributor of, marijuana, synthetic cannabinoids, or any controlled substance.

9. An individual who has been convicted of a violation of § 18.2-266 or a substantially similar local ordinance, or of public drunkenness, or of a substantially similar offense under the laws of any other state, the District of Columbia, the United States, or its territories within the three-year period immediately preceding the application, or who is a habitual drunkard as determined pursuant to § 4.1-333.

10. An alien other than an alien lawfully admitted for permanent residence in the United States.

11. An individual who has been discharged from the armed forces of the United States under dishonorable conditions.

12. An individual who is a fugitive from justice.

13. An individual who the court finds, by a preponderance of the evidence, based on specific acts by the applicant, is likely to use a weapon unlawfully or negligently to endanger others. The sheriff, chief of police, or attorney for the Commonwealth may submit to the court a sworn, written statement indicating that, in the opinion of such sheriff, chief of police, or attorney for the Commonwealth, based upon a disqualifying conviction or upon the specific acts set forth in the statement, the applicant is likely to use a weapon unlawfully or negligently to endanger others. The statement of the sheriff, chief of police, or the attorney for the Commonwealth shall be based upon personal knowledge of such individual or of a deputy sheriff, police officer, or assistant attorney for the Commonwealth of the specific acts, or upon a written statement made under oath before a notary public of a competent person having personal knowledge of the specific acts.

14. An individual who has been convicted of any assault, assault and battery, sexual battery, discharging of a firearm in violation of § 18.2-280 or 18.2-286.1 or brandishing of a firearm in violation of § 18.2-282 within the three-year period immediately preceding the application.

15. An individual who has been convicted of stalking.

16. An individual whose previous convictions or adjudications of delinquency were based on an offense that would have been at the time of conviction a felony if committed by an adult under the laws of any state, the District of Columbia, the United States or its territories. For purposes of this disqualifier, only convictions occurring within 16 years following the later of the date of (i) the conviction or adjudication or (ii) release from any

incarceration imposed upon such conviction or adjudication shall be deemed to be "previous convictions." Disqualification under this subdivision shall not apply to an individual with previous adjudications of delinquency who has completed a term of service of no less than two years in the Armed Forces of the United States and, if such person has been discharged from the Armed Forces of the United States, received an honorable discharge.

17. An individual who has a felony charge pending or a charge pending for an offense listed in subdivision 14 or 15.

18. An individual who has received mental health treatment or substance abuse treatment in a residential setting within five years prior to the date of his application for a concealed handgun permit.

19. An individual not otherwise ineligible pursuant to this article, who, within the three-year period immediately preceding the application for the permit, was found guilty of any criminal offense set forth in Article 1 (§ 18.2-247 et seq.) or former § 18.2-248.1:1 or of a criminal offense of illegal possession or distribution of marijuana, synthetic cannabinoids, or any controlled substance, under the laws of any state, the District of Columbia, or the United States or its territories.

20. An individual, not otherwise ineligible pursuant to this article, with respect to whom, within the three-year period immediately preceding the application, upon a charge of any criminal offense set forth in Article 1 (§ 18.2-247 et seq.) or former § 18.2-248.1:1 or upon a charge of illegal possession or distribution of marijuana, synthetic cannabinoids, or any controlled substance under the laws of any state, the District of Columbia, or the United States or its territories, the trial court found that the facts of the case were sufficient for a finding of guilt and disposed of the case pursuant to § 18.2-251 or the substantially similar law of any other state, the District of Columbia, or the United States or its territories.

§ 18.2-308.010. Renewal of concealed handgun permit.

A.1. Persons who previously have held a concealed handgun permit shall be issued, upon application as provided in § 18.2-308.02, a new five-year permit unless it is found that the applicant is subject to any of the disqualifications set forth in § 18.2-308.09. Persons who previously have been issued a concealed handgun permit pursuant to this article shall not be required to appear in person to apply for a new five-year permit pursuant to this section, and the application for the new permit may be submitted via the United States mail. The circuit court that receives the application shall promptly notify an applicant if the application is incomplete or if the fee submitted for the permit pursuant to § 18.2-308.03 is incorrect.

2. If a new five-year permit is issued while an existing permit remains valid, the new five-year permit shall become effective upon the expiration date of the existing permit, provided that the application is received by the court at least 90 days but no more than 180 days prior to the expiration of the existing permit.

3. Any order denying issuance of the new permit shall be in accordance with subsection A of § 18.2-308.08.

B. If a permit holder is a member of the Virginia National Guard, armed forces of the United States, or the Armed Forces Reserves of the United States, and his five-year permit expires during an active-duty military deployment outside of the permittee's county or city of residence, such permit shall remain valid for 90 days after the end date of the deployment. In order to establish proof of continued validity of the permit, such a permittee shall carry with him and display, upon request of a law-enforcement officer, a copy of the permittee's deployment orders or other documentation from the permittee's commanding officer that order the permittee to travel outside of his county or city of residence and that indicate the start and end date of such deployment.

§ 18.2-308.011. Replacement permits.
A. The clerk of a circuit court that issued a valid concealed handgun permit shall, upon presentation of the valid permit and proof of a new address of residence by the permit holder, issue a replacement permit specifying the permit holder's new address. The clerk of court shall forward the permit holder's new address of residence to the State Police. The State Police may charge a fee not to exceed $5, and the clerk of court issuing the replacement permit may charge a fee not to exceed $5. The total amount assessed for processing a replacement permit pursuant to this subsection shall not exceed $10, with such fees to be paid in one sum to the person who receives the information for the replacement permit.

B. The clerk of a circuit court that issued a valid concealed handgun permit shall, upon submission of a notarized statement by the permit holder that the permit was lost or destroyed or that the permit holder has undergone a legal name change, issue a replacement permit. The replacement permit shall have the same expiration date as the permit that was lost, destroyed, or issued to the permit holder under a previous name. The clerk shall issue the replacement permit within 10 business days of receiving the notarized statement and may charge a fee not to exceed $5.

§ 18.2-308.012. Prohibited conduct.

A. Any person permitted to carry a concealed handgun who is under the influence of alcohol or illegal drugs while carrying such handgun in a public place is guilty of a Class 1 misdemeanor. Conviction of any of the following offenses shall be prima facie evidence, subject to rebuttal, that the person is "under the influence" for purposes of this section: manslaughter in violation of § 18.2-36.1, maiming in violation of § 18.2-51.4, driving while intoxicated in violation of § 18.2-266, public intoxication in violation of § 18.2-388, or driving while intoxicated in violation of § 46.2-341.24. Upon such conviction that court shall revoke the person's permit for a concealed handgun and promptly notify the issuing circuit court. A person convicted of a violation of this subsection shall be ineligible to apply for a concealed handgun permit for a period of five years.

B. (Effective until July 1, 2018) No person who carries a concealed handgun onto the premises of any restaurant or club as defined in § 4.1-100 for which a license to sell and serve alcoholic beverages for on-premises consumption has been granted by the Virginia Alcoholic Beverage Control Board under Title 4.1 may consume an alcoholic beverage while on the premises. A person who carries a concealed handgun onto the premises of such a restaurant or club and consumes alcoholic beverages is guilty of a Class 2 misdemeanor. However, nothing in this subsection shall apply to a federal, state, or local law-enforcement officer.

B. (Effective July 1, 2018) No person who carries a concealed handgun onto the premises of any restaurant or club as defined in § 4.1-100 for which a license to sell and serve alcoholic beverages for on-premises consumption has been granted by the Virginia Alcoholic Beverage Control Authority under Title 4.1 may consume an alcoholic beverage while on the premises. A person who carries a concealed handgun onto the premises of such a restaurant or club and consumes alcoholic beverages is guilty of a Class 2 misdemeanor. However, nothing in this subsection shall apply to a federal, state, or local law-enforcement officer.

§ 18.2-308.013. Suspension or revocation of permit.

A. Any person convicted of an offense that would disqualify that person from obtaining a permit under § 18.2-308.09 or who violates subsection C of § 18.2-308.02 shall forfeit his permit for a concealed handgun and surrender it to the court. Upon receipt by the Central Criminal Records Exchange of a record of the arrest, conviction, or occurrence of any other event that would disqualify a person from obtaining a concealed handgun permit under § 18.2-308.09, the Central Criminal Records Exchange shall notify the court having issued the permit of such disqualifying arrest, conviction, or other event. Upon receipt of such notice of a conviction, the court shall revoke the permit of a person disqualified pursuant to this subsection, and shall promptly notify the State Police and the person whose permit was revoked of the revocation.

B. An individual who has a felony charge pending or a charge pending for an offense listed in subdivision 14 or 15 of § 18.2-308.09, holding a permit for a concealed handgun, may have the permit suspended by the court before which such charge is pending or by the court that issued the permit.

C. The court shall revoke the permit of any individual for whom it would be unlawful to purchase, possess, or transport a firearm under § 18.2-308.1:2 or 18.2-308.1:3, and shall promptly notify the State Police and the person whose permit was revoked of the revocation.

§ 18.2-308.014. Reciprocity.

A. A valid concealed handgun or concealed weapon permit or license issued by another state shall authorize the holder of such permit or license who is at least 21 years of age to carry a concealed handgun in the Commonwealth, provided (i) the issuing authority provides the means for instantaneous verification of the validity of all such permits or licenses issued within that state, accessible 24 hours a day if available; (ii) the permit or license holder carries a photo identification issued by a government agency of any state or by the U.S. Department of Defense or U.S. Department of State and displays the permit or license and such identification upon demand by a law-enforcement officer; and (iii) the permit or license holder has not previously had a Virginia concealed handgun permit revoked. The Superintendent of State Police shall enter into agreements for reciprocal recognition with such other states that require an agreement to be in place before such state will recognize a Virginia concealed handgun permit as valid in such state. The Attorney General shall provide the Superintendent with any legal assistance or advice necessary for the Superintendent to perform his duties set forth in this subsection. If the Superintendent determines that another state requires that an agreement for reciprocal recognition be executed by the Attorney General or otherwise formally approved by the Attorney General as a condition of such other state's entering into an agreement for reciprocal recognition, the Attorney General shall (a) execute such agreement or otherwise formally approve such agreement and (b) return to the Superintendent the executed agreement or, in a form deemed acceptable by such other state, documentation of his formal approval of such agreement within 30 days after the Superintendent notifies the Attorney General, in writing, that he is required to execute or otherwise formally approve such agreement.

B. For the purposes of participation in concealed handgun reciprocity agreements with other jurisdictions, the official government-issued law-enforcement identification card issued to an active-duty law-enforcement officer in the Commonwealth who is exempt from obtaining a concealed handgun permit under this article shall be deemed a concealed handgun permit.

§ 18.2-308.016. (Effective October 1, 2016, until July 1, 2018) Retired law-enforcement officers; carrying a concealed handgun.

A. Except as provided in subsection A of § 18.2-308.012, § 18.2-308 shall not apply to:

    1. Any State Police officer retired from the Department of State Police, any officer retired from the Division of Capitol Police, any local law-enforcement officer, auxiliary police officer or animal control officer retired from a police department or sheriff's office within the Commonwealth, any special agent retired

from the State Corporation Commission or the Virginia Alcoholic Beverage Control Board, any employee with internal investigations authority designated by the Department of Corrections pursuant to subdivision 11 of § 53.1-10 retired from the Department of Corrections, any conservation police officer retired from the Department of Game and Inland Fisheries, any Virginia Marine Police officer retired from the Law Enforcement Division of the Virginia Marine Resources Commission, any campus police officer appointed under Article 3 (§ 23.1-809 et seq.) of Chapter 8 of Title 23.1 retired from a campus police department, any retired member of the enforcement division of the Department of Motor Vehicles appointed pursuant to § 46.2-217, and any retired investigator of the security division of the Virginia Lottery, other than an officer or agent terminated for cause, (i) with a service-related disability; (ii) following at least 10 years of service with any such law-enforcement agency, commission, board, or any combination thereof; (iii) who has reached 55 years of age; or (iv) who is on long-term leave from such law-enforcement agency or board due to a service-related injury, provided such officer carries with him written proof of consultation with and favorable review of the need to carry a concealed handgun issued by the chief law-enforcement officer of the last such agency from which the officer retired or the agency that employs the officer or, in the case of special agents, issued by the State Corporation Commission or the Virginia Alcoholic Beverage Control Board. A copy of the proof of consultation and favorable review shall be forwarded by the chief, Commission, or Board to the Department of State Police for entry into the Virginia Criminal Information Network. The chief law-enforcement officer shall not without cause withhold such written proof if the retired law-enforcement officer otherwise meets the requirements of this section. An officer set forth in clause (iv) who receives written proof of consultation to carry a concealed handgun shall surrender such proof of consultation upon return to work or upon termination of employment with the law-enforcement agency. Notice of the surrender shall be forwarded to the Department of State Police for entry into the Virginia Criminal Information Network. However, if such officer retires on disability because of the service-related injury, and would be eligible under clause (i) for written proof of consultation to carry a concealed handgun, he may retain the previously issued written proof of consultation.

2. Any person who is eligible for retirement with at least 20 years of service with a law-enforcement agency, commission, or board mentioned in subdivision 1 who has resigned in good standing from such law-enforcement agency, commission, or board to accept a position covered by a retirement system that is authorized under Title 51.1, provided such person carries with him written proof of consultation with and favorable review of the need to carry a concealed handgun issued by the chief law-enforcement officer of the agency from which he resigned or, in the case of special agents, issued by the State Corporation Commission or the Virginia Alcoholic Beverage Control Board. A copy of the proof of consultation and favorable review shall be forwarded by the chief, Commission, or Board to the Department of State Police for entry into the Virginia Criminal Information Network. The chief law-enforcement officer shall not without cause withhold such written proof if the law-enforcement officer otherwise meets the requirements of this section.

3. Any State Police officer who is a member of the organized reserve forces of any of the Armed Services of the United States or National Guard, while such officer is called to active military duty, provided such officer carries with him written proof of consultation with and favorable review of the need to carry a concealed handgun issued by the Superintendent of State Police. The proof of consultation and favorable review shall be valid as long as the officer is on active military duty and shall expire when the officer returns to active law-enforcement duty. The issuance of the proof of consultation and favorable review shall be entered into the Virginia Criminal Information Network. The Superintendent of State Police shall not without cause withhold such written proof if the officer is in good standing and is qualified to carry a weapon while on active law-enforcement duty.

B. For purposes of complying with the federal Law Enforcement Officers Safety Act of 2004, a retired or resigned law-enforcement officer who receives proof of consultation and review pursuant to this section shall have the opportunity to annually participate, at the retired or resigned law-enforcement officer's expense, in the same training and testing to carry firearms as is required of active law-enforcement officers in the Commonwealth. If such retired or resigned law-enforcement officer meets the training and qualification standards, the chief law-enforcement officer shall issue the retired or resigned officer certification, valid one year from the date of issuance, indicating that the retired or resigned officer has met the standards of the agency to carry a firearm.

C. A retired or resigned law-enforcement officer who receives proof of consultation and review pursuant to this section may annually participate and meet the training and qualification standards to carry firearms as is required of active law-enforcement officers in the Commonwealth. If such retired or resigned law-enforcement officer meets the training and qualification standards, the chief law-enforcement officer shall issue the retired or resigned officer certification, valid one year from the date of issuance, indicating that the retired or resigned officer has met the standards of the Commonwealth to carry a firearm. A copy of the certification indicating that the retired or resigned officer has met the standards of the Commonwealth to carry a firearm shall be forwarded by the chief, Commission, or Board to the Department of State Police for entry into the Virginia Criminal Information Network.

D. For all purposes, including for the purpose of applying the reciprocity provisions of § 18.2-308.014, any person granted the privilege to carry a concealed handgun pursuant to this section, while carrying the proof of consultation and favorable review required, shall be deemed to have been issued a concealed handgun permit.

Title 18.2. Crimes and Offenses Generally
Chapter 7. Crimes Involving Health and Safety
Article 7. Other Illegal Weapons

§ 18.2-308.1. Possession of firearm, stun weapon, or other weapon on school property prohibited; penalty.
A. If any person knowingly possesses any (i) stun weapon as defined in this section; (ii) knife, except a pocket knife having a folding metal blade of less than three inches; or (iii) weapon, including a weapon of like kind, designated in subsection A of § 18.2-308, other than a firearm; upon (a) the property of any public, private or religious elementary, middle or high school, including buildings and grounds; (b) that portion of any property open to the public and

then exclusively used for school-sponsored functions or extracurricular activities while such functions or activities are taking place; or (c) any school bus owned or operated by any such school, he shall be guilty of a Class 1 misdemeanor.

B. If any person knowingly possesses any firearm designed or intended to expel a projectile by action of an explosion of a combustible material while such person is upon (i) any public, private or religious elementary, middle or high school, including buildings and grounds; (ii) that portion of any property open to the public and then exclusively used for school-sponsored functions or extracurricular activities while such functions or activities are taking place; or (iii) any school bus owned or operated by any such school, he shall be guilty of a Class 6 felony.

C. If any person knowingly possesses any firearm designed or intended to expel a projectile by action of an explosion of a combustible material within a public, private or religious elementary, middle or high school building and intends to use, or attempts to use, such firearm, or displays such weapon in a threatening manner, such person shall be guilty of a Class 6 felony and sentenced to a mandatory minimum term of imprisonment of five years to be served consecutively with any other sentence.

The exemptions set out in §§ 18.2-308 and 18.2-308.016 shall apply, mutatis mutandis, to the provisions of this section. The provisions of this section shall not apply to (i) persons who possess such weapon or weapons as a part of the school's curriculum or activities; (ii) a person possessing a knife customarily used for food preparation or service and using it for such purpose; (iii) persons who possess such weapon or weapons as a part of any program sponsored or facilitated by either the school or any organization authorized by the school to conduct its programs either on or off the school premises; (iv) any law-enforcement officer, or retired law-enforcement officer qualified pursuant to subsection C of § 18.2-308.016; (v) any person who possesses a knife or blade which he uses customarily in his trade; (vi) a person who possesses an unloaded firearm that is in a closed container, or a knife having a metal blade, in or upon a motor vehicle, or an unloaded shotgun or rifle in a firearms rack in or upon a motor vehicle; (vii) a person who has a valid concealed handgun permit and possesses a concealed handgun while in a motor vehicle in a parking lot, traffic circle, or other means of vehicular ingress or egress to the school; or (viii) an armed security officer, licensed pursuant to Article 4 (§ 9.1-138 et seq.) of Chapter 1 of Title 9.1, hired by a private or religious school for the protection of students and employees as authorized by such school. For the purposes of this paragraph, "weapon" includes a knife having a metal blade of three inches or longer and "closed container" includes a locked vehicle trunk.

As used in this section:

"Stun weapon" means any device that emits a momentary or pulsed output, which is electrical, audible, optical or electromagnetic in nature and which is designed to temporarily incapacitate a person.

§ 18.2-308.1:1. Purchase, possession or transportation of firearms by persons acquitted by reason of insanity; penalty.
A. It shall be unlawful for any person acquitted by reason of insanity and committed to the custody of the Commissioner of Behavioral Health and Developmental Services, pursuant to Chapter 11.1 (§ 19.2-182.2 et seq.) of Title 19.2, on a charge of treason, any felony or any offense punishable as a misdemeanor under Title 54.1 or a Class 1 or Class 2 misdemeanor under this title, except those misdemeanor violations of (i) Article 2 (§ 18.2-266 et seq.) of Chapter 7 of this title, (ii) Article 2 (§ 18.2-415 et seq.) of Chapter 9 of this title, or (iii) § 18.2-119, or (iv) an ordinance of any county, city, or town similar to the offenses specified in (i), (ii), or (iii), to knowingly and intentionally purchase, possess, or transport any firearm. A violation of this subsection shall be punishable as a Class 1 misdemeanor.

B. Any person so acquitted may, upon discharge from the custody of the Commissioner, petition the general district court in the city or county in which he resides to restore his right to purchase, possess or transport a firearm. A copy of the petition shall be mailed or delivered to the attorney for the Commonwealth for the jurisdiction where the petition was filed who shall be entitled to respond and represent the interests of the Commonwealth. The court shall conduct a hearing if requested by either party. If the court determines, after receiving and considering evidence concerning the circumstances regarding the disability referred to in subsection A and the person's criminal history, treatment record, and reputation as developed through character witness statements, testimony, or other character evidence, that the person will not be likely to act in a manner dangerous to public safety and that the granting of the relief would not be contrary to the public interest, the court shall grant the petition. Any person denied relief by the general district court may petition the circuit court for a de novo review of the denial. Upon a grant of relief in any court, the court shall enter a written order granting the petition, in which event the provisions of subsection A do not apply. The clerk of court shall certify and forward forthwith to the Central Criminal Records Exchange, on a form provided by the Exchange, a copy of any such order.

C. As used in this section, "treatment record" shall include copies of health records detailing the petitioner's psychiatric history, which shall include the records pertaining to the commitment or adjudication that is the subject of the request for relief pursuant to this section.

§ 18.2-308.1:2. Purchase, possession or transportation of firearm by persons adjudicated legally incompetent or mentally incapacitated; penalty.

A. It shall be unlawful for any person who has been adjudicated (i) legally incompetent pursuant to former § 37.1-128.02 or former § 37.1-134, (ii) mentally incapacitated pursuant to former § 37.1-128.1 or former § 37.1-132 or (iii) incapacitated pursuant to Chapter 20 (§ 64.2-2000 et seq.) of Title 64.2 to purchase, possess, or transport any firearm. A violation of this subsection shall be punishable as a Class 1 misdemeanor.

B. Any person whose competency or capacity has been restored pursuant to former § 37.1-134.1, former § 37.2-1012, or § 64.2-2012 may petition the general district court in the city or county in which he resides to restore his right to purchase, possess or transport a firearm. A copy of the petition shall be mailed or delivered to the attorney for the Commonwealth for the jurisdiction where the petition was filed who shall be entitled to respond and represent the interests of the Commonwealth. The court shall conduct a hearing if requested by either party. If the court determines, after receiving and considering evidence concerning the circumstances regarding the disability referred to in subsection A and the person's criminal history, treatment record, and reputation as developed through character witness statements, testimony, or other character evidence, that the person will not be likely to act in a manner dangerous to public safety and that the granting of the relief would not be contrary to the public interest, the court shall grant the petition. Any person denied relief by the general district court may petition the circuit court for a de novo review of the denial. Upon a grant of relief in any court, the court shall enter a written order granting the petition, in which event the provisions of subsection A do not apply. The clerk of court shall certify and forward forthwith to the Central Criminal Records Exchange, on a form provided by the Exchange, a copy of any such order.

C. As used in this section, "treatment record" shall include copies of health records detailing the petitioner's psychiatric history, which shall include the records pertaining to the commitment or adjudication that is the subject of the request for relief pursuant to this section.

§ 18.2-308.1:3. Purchase, possession or transportation of firearm by persons involuntarily admitted or ordered to outpatient treatment; penalty.

A. It shall be unlawful for any person involuntarily admitted to a facility or ordered to mandatory outpatient treatment pursuant to § 19.2-169.2, involuntarily admitted to a facility or ordered to mandatory outpatient treatment as the result of a commitment hearing pursuant to Article 5 (§ 37.2-814 et seq.) of Chapter 8 of Title 37.2, or who was the subject of a temporary detention order pursuant to § 37.2-809 and subsequently agreed to voluntary admission pursuant to § 37.2-805 to purchase, possess or transport a firearm. A violation of this subsection shall be punishable as a Class 1 misdemeanor.

B. Any person prohibited from purchasing, possessing or transporting firearms under this section may, at any time following his release from involuntary admission to a facility, his release from an order of mandatory outpatient treatment, or his release from voluntary admission pursuant to § 37.2-805 following the issuance of a temporary detention order, petition the general district court in the city or county in which he resides to restore his right to purchase, possess or transport a firearm. A copy of the petition shall be mailed or delivered to the attorney for the Commonwealth for the jurisdiction where the petition was filed who shall be entitled to respond and represent the interests of the Commonwealth. The court shall conduct a hearing if requested by either party. If the court determines, after receiving and considering evidence concerning the circumstances regarding the disabilities referred to in subsection A and the person's criminal history, treatment record, and reputation as developed through character witness statements, testimony, or other character evidence, that the person will not likely act in a manner dangerous to public safety and that granting the relief would not be contrary to the public interest, the court shall grant the petition. Any person denied relief by the general district court may petition the circuit court for a de novo review of the denial. Upon a grant of relief in any court, the court shall enter a written order granting the petition, in which event the provisions of subsection A do not apply. The clerk of court shall certify and forward forthwith to the Central Criminal Records Exchange, on a form provided by the Exchange, a copy of any such order.

C. As used in this section, "treatment record" shall include copies of health records detailing the petitioner's psychiatric history, which shall include the records pertaining to the commitment or adjudication that is the subject of the request for relief pursuant to this section.

§ 18.2-308.1:4. Purchase or transportation of firearm by persons subject to protective orders; penalties.

A. It is unlawful for any person who is subject to (i) a protective order entered pursuant to § 16.1-253.1, 16.1-253.4, 16.1-278.2, 16.1-279.1, 19.2-152.8, 19.2-152.9, or 19.2-152.10; (ii) an order issued pursuant to subsection B of § 20-103; (iii) an order entered pursuant to subsection E of § 18.2-60.3; (iv) a preliminary protective order entered pursuant to subsection F of § 16.1-253 where a petition alleging abuse or neglect has been filed; or (v) an order issued by a tribunal of another state, the United States or any of its territories, possessions, or commonwealths, or the District of Columbia pursuant to a statute that is substantially similar to those cited in clauses (i), (ii), (iii), or (iv) to purchase or transport any firearm while the order is in effect. Any person with a concealed handgun permit shall be prohibited from carrying any concealed firearm, and shall surrender his permit to the court entering the order, for the duration of any protective order referred to herein. A violation of this subsection is a Class 1 misdemeanor.

B. In addition to the prohibition set forth in subsection A, it is unlawful for any person who is subject to a protective order entered pursuant to § 16.1-279.1 or an order issued by a tribunal of another state, the United States or any of its territories, possessions, or commonwealths, or the District of Columbia pursuant to a statute that is substantially similar to § 16.1-279.1 to knowingly possess any firearm while the order is in effect, provided that for a period of 24 hours after being served with a protective order in accordance with subsection C of § 16.1-279.1 such person may continue to possess and, notwithstanding the provisions of subsection A, transport any firearm possessed by such person at the time of service for the purposes of selling or transferring any such firearm to any person who is not otherwise prohibited by law from possessing such firearm. A violation of this subsection is a Class 6 felony.

§ 18.2-308.1:5. Purchase or transportation of firearm by persons convicted of certain drug offenses prohibited.

Any person who, within a 36-consecutive-month period, has been convicted of two misdemeanor offenses under subsection B of former § 18.2-248.1:1, § 18.2-250 or 18.2-250.1 shall be ineligible to purchase or transport a handgun. However, upon expiration of a period of five years from the date of the second conviction and provided the person has not been convicted of any such offense within that period, the ineligibility shall be removed.

§ 18.2-308.2. Possession or transportation of firearms, firearms ammunition, stun weapons, explosives or concealed weapons by convicted felons; penalties; petition for permit; when issued.

A. It shall be unlawful for (i) any person who has been convicted of a felony; (ii) any person adjudicated delinquent as a juvenile 14 years of age or older at the time of the offense of murder in violation of § 18.2-31 or 18.2-32, kidnapping in violation of § 18.2-47, robbery by the threat or presentation of firearms in violation of § 18.2-58, or rape in violation of § 18.2-61; or (iii) any person under the age of 29 who was adjudicated delinquent as a juvenile 14 years of age or older at the time of the offense of a delinquent act which would be a felony if committed by an adult, other than those felonies set forth in clause (ii), whether such conviction or adjudication occurred under the laws of the Commonwealth, or any other state, the District of Columbia, the United States or any territory thereof, to knowingly and intentionally possess or transport any firearm or ammunition for a firearm, any stun weapon as defined by § 18.2-308.1, or any explosive material, or to knowingly and intentionally carry about his person, hidden from common observation, any weapon described in subsection A of § 18.2-308. However, such person may possess in his residence or the curtilage thereof a stun weapon as defined by § 18.2-308.1. Any person who violates this section shall be guilty of a Class 6 felony. However, any person who violates this section by knowingly and intentionally possessing or transporting any firearm and who was previously convicted of a violent felony as defined in § 17.1-805 shall be sentenced to a mandatory minimum term of imprisonment of five years. Any person who violates this section by knowingly and intentionally possessing or transporting any firearm and who was previously convicted of any other felony within the prior 10 years shall be sentenced to a mandatory minimum term of imprisonment of two years. The mandatory minimum terms of imprisonment prescribed for violations of this section shall be served consecutively with any other sentence.

B. The prohibitions of subsection A shall not apply to (i) any person who possesses a firearm, ammunition for a firearm, explosive material or other weapon while carrying out his duties as a member of the Armed Forces of the United States or of the National Guard of Virginia or of any other state, (ii) any law-enforcement officer in the performance of his duties, (iii) any person who has been pardoned or whose political disabilities have been removed pursuant to Article V, Section 12 of the Constitution of Virginia provided the Governor, in the document granting the pardon or removing the person's political disabilities, may expressly place conditions upon the reinstatement of the person's right to ship, transport, possess or receive firearms, (iv) any person whose right to possess firearms or ammunition has been restored under the law of another state subject to conditions placed upon the reinstatement of the person's right to ship, transport, possess, or receive firearms by such state, or (v) any person adjudicated delinquent as a juvenile who has completed a term of service of no less than two years in the Armed Forces of the United States and, if such person has been discharged from the Armed Forces of the United States, received an honorable discharge and who is not otherwise prohibited under clause (i) or (ii) of subsection A.

C. Any person prohibited from possessing, transporting, or carrying a firearm, ammunition for a firearm, or a stun weapon under subsection A may petition the circuit court of the jurisdiction in which he resides or, if the person is not a resident of the Commonwealth, the circuit court of any county or city where such person was last convicted of a felony or adjudicated delinquent of a disqualifying offense pursuant to subsection A, for a permit to possess or carry a firearm, ammunition for a firearm, or a stun weapon; however, no person who has been convicted of a felony shall be qualified to petition for such a permit unless his civil rights have been restored by the Governor or other appropriate authority. A copy of the petition shall be mailed or delivered to the attorney for the Commonwealth for the jurisdiction where the petition was filed who shall be entitled to respond and represent the interests of the Commonwealth. The court shall conduct a hearing if requested by either party. The court may, in its discretion and for good cause shown, grant such petition and issue a permit. The provisions of this section relating to firearms, ammunition for a firearm, and stun weapons shall not apply to any person who has been granted a permit pursuant to this subsection.

C1. Any person who was prohibited from possessing, transporting or carrying explosive material under subsection A may possess, transport or carry such explosive material if his right to possess, transport or carry explosive material has been restored pursuant to federal law.

D. For the purpose of this section:

"Ammunition for a firearm" means the combination of a cartridge, projectile, primer, or propellant designed for use in a firearm other than an antique firearm as defined in § 18.2-308.2:2.

"Explosive material" means any chemical compound mixture, or device, the primary or common purpose of which is to function by explosion; the term includes, but is not limited to, dynamite and other high explosives, black powder, pellet powder, smokeless gun powder, detonators, blasting caps and detonating cord but shall not include fireworks or permissible fireworks as defined in § 27-95.

§ 18.2-308.2:01. Possession or transportation of certain firearms by certain persons.

A. It shall be unlawful for any person who is not a citizen of the United States or who is not a person lawfully admitted for permanent residence to knowingly and intentionally possess or transport any assault firearm or to knowingly and intentionally carry about his person, hidden from common observation, an assault firearm.

B. It shall be unlawful for any person who is not a citizen of the United States and who is not lawfully present in the United States to knowingly and intentionally possess or transport any firearm or to knowingly and intentionally carry about his person, hidden from common observation, any firearm. A violation of this section shall be punishable as a Class 6 felony.

C. For purposes of this section, "assault firearm" means any semi-automatic center-fire rifle or pistol that expels single or multiple projectiles by action of an explosion of a combustible material and is equipped at the time of the offense with a magazine which will hold more than 20 rounds of ammunition or designed by the manufacturer to accommodate a silencer or equipped with a folding stock.

§ 18.2-308.2:1. Prohibiting the selling, etc., of firearms to certain persons.

Any person who sells, barters, gives or furnishes, or has in his possession or under his control with the intent of selling, bartering, giving or furnishing, any firearm to any person he knows is prohibited from possessing or transporting a firearm pursuant to § 18.2-308.1:1, 18.2-308.1:2, 18.2-308.1:3, 18.2-308.2, subsection B of § 18.2-308.2:01, or § 18.2-308.7 shall be guilty of a Class 4 felony. However, this prohibition shall not be applicable when the person convicted of the felony, adjudicated delinquent or acquitted by reason of insanity has (i) been issued a permit pursuant to subsection C of § 18.2-308.2 or been granted relief pursuant to subsection B of § 18.2-308.1:1, or § 18.2-308.1:2 or 18.2-308.1:3 (ii) been pardoned or had his political disabilities removed in accordance with subsection B of § 18.2-308.2 or (iii) obtained a permit to ship, transport, possess or receive firearms pursuant to the laws of the United States.

§ 18.2-308.2:2. Criminal history record information check required for the transfer of certain firearms.

A. Any person purchasing from a dealer a firearm as herein defined shall consent in writing, on a form to be provided by the Department of State Police, to have the dealer obtain criminal history record information. Such form shall include only the written consent; the name, birth date, gender, race, citizenship, and social security number and/or any other identification number; the number of firearms by category intended to be sold, rented, traded, or transferred; and answers by the applicant to the following questions: (i) has the applicant been convicted of a felony offense or found guilty or adjudicated delinquent as a juvenile 14 years of age or older at the time of the offense of a delinquent act that would be a felony if committed by an adult; (ii) is the applicant subject to a court order restraining the applicant from harassing, stalking, or threatening the applicant's child or intimate partner, or a child of such partner, or is the applicant subject to a protective order; and (iii) has the applicant ever been acquitted by reason of insanity and prohibited from purchasing, possessing or transporting a firearm pursuant to § 18.2-308.1:1 or any substantially similar law of any other jurisdiction, been adjudicated legally incompetent, mentally incapacitated or adjudicated an incapacitated person and prohibited from purchasing a firearm pursuant to § 18.2-308.1:2 or any substantially similar law of any other jurisdiction, or been involuntarily admitted to an inpatient facility or involuntarily ordered to outpatient mental health treatment and prohibited from purchasing a firearm pursuant to § 18.2-308.1:3 or any substantially similar law of any other jurisdiction.

B. 1. No dealer shall sell, rent, trade or transfer from his inventory any such firearm to any other person who is a resident of Virginia until he has (i) obtained written consent and the other information on the consent form specified in subsection A, and provided the Department of State Police with the name, birth date, gender, race, citizenship, and social security and/or any other identification number and the number of firearms by category intended to be sold, rented, traded or transferred and (ii) requested criminal history record information by a telephone call to or other communication authorized by the State Police and is authorized by subdivision 2 to complete the sale or other such transfer. To establish personal identification and residence in Virginia for purposes of this section, a dealer must require any prospective purchaser to present one photo-identification form issued by a governmental agency of the Commonwealth or by the United States Department of Defense that demonstrates that the prospective purchaser resides in Virginia. For the purposes of this section and establishment of residency for firearm purchase, residency of a member of the armed forces shall include both the state in which the member's permanent duty post is located and any nearby state in which the member resides and from which he commutes to the permanent duty post. A member of the armed forces whose photo identification issued by the Department of Defense does not have a Virginia address may establish his Virginia residency with such photo identification and either permanent orders assigning the purchaser to a duty post, including the Pentagon, in Virginia or the purchaser's Leave and Earnings Statement. When the photo identification presented to a dealer by the prospective purchaser is a driver's license or other photo identification issued by the Department of Motor Vehicles, and such identification form contains a date of issue, the dealer shall not, except for a renewed driver's license or other photo identification issued by the Department of Motor Vehicles, sell or otherwise transfer a firearm to the prospective purchaser until 30 days after the date of issue of an original or duplicate driver's license unless the prospective purchaser also presents a copy of his Virginia Department of Motor Vehicles driver's record showing that the original date of issue of the driver's license was more than 30 days prior to the attempted purchase.

In addition, no dealer shall sell, rent, trade, or transfer from his inventory any assault firearm to any person who is not a citizen of the United States or who is not a person lawfully admitted for permanent residence.

Upon receipt of the request for a criminal history record information check, the State Police shall (a) review its criminal history record information to determine if the buyer or transferee is prohibited from possessing or transporting a firearm by state or federal law, (b) inform the dealer if its record indicates that the buyer or transferee is so prohibited, and (c) provide the dealer with a unique reference number for that inquiry.

2. The State Police shall provide its response to the requesting dealer during the dealer's request, or by return call without delay. If the criminal history record information check indicates the prospective purchaser or transferee has a disqualifying criminal record or has been acquitted by reason of insanity and committed to the custody of the Commissioner of Behavioral Health and Developmental Services, the State Police shall have until the end of the dealer's next business day to advise the dealer if its records indicate the buyer or transferee is prohibited from possessing or transporting a firearm by state or federal law. If not so advised by the end of the dealer's next business day, a dealer who has fulfilled the requirements of subdivision 1 may immediately complete the sale or transfer and shall not be deemed in violation of this section with respect to such sale or transfer. In case of electronic failure or other circumstances beyond the control of the State Police, the dealer shall be advised immediately of the reason for such delay and be given an estimate of the length of such delay. After such notification, the State Police shall, as soon as possible but in no event later than the end of the dealer's next business day, inform the requesting dealer if its records indicate the buyer or transferee is prohibited from possessing or transporting a firearm by state or federal law. A dealer who fulfills the requirements of subdivision 1 and is told by the State Police that a response will not be available by the end of the dealer's next business day may immediately complete the sale or transfer and shall not be deemed in violation of this section with respect to such sale or transfer.

3. Except as required by subsection D of § 9.1-132, the State Police shall not maintain records longer than 30 days, except for multiple handgun transactions for which records shall be maintained for 12 months, from any dealer's request for a criminal history record information check pertaining to a buyer or transferee who is not found to be prohibited from possessing and transporting a firearm under state or federal law. However, the log on requests made may be maintained for a period of 12 months, and such log shall consist of the name of the purchaser, the dealer identification number, the unique approval number and the transaction date.

4. On the last day of the week following the sale or transfer of any firearm, the dealer shall mail or deliver the written consent form required by subsection A to the Department of State Police. The State Police shall immediately initiate a search of all available crimi-

nal history record information to determine if the purchaser is pro-hibited from possessing or transporting a firearm under state or federal law. If the search discloses information indicating that the buyer or transferee is so prohibited from possessing or transporting a firearm, the State Police shall inform the chief law-enforcement officer in the jurisdiction where the sale or transfer occurred and the dealer without delay.

5. Notwithstanding any other provisions of this section, rifles and shotguns may be purchased by persons who are citizens of the Unit-ed States or persons lawfully admitted for permanent residence but residents of other states under the terms of subsections A and B upon furnishing the dealer with one photo-identification form is-sued by a governmental agency of the person's state of residence and one other form of identification determined to be acceptable by the Department of Criminal Justice Services.

6. For the purposes of this subsection, the phrase "dealer's next business day" shall not include December 25.

C. No dealer shall sell, rent, trade or transfer from his inventory any firearm, except when the transaction involves a rifle or a shotgun and can be accomplished pursuant to the provisions of subdivision B 5 to any person who is not a resident of Virginia unless he has first obtained from the Department of State Police a report indicat-ing that a search of all available criminal history record information has not disclosed that the person is prohibited from possessing or transporting a firearm under state or federal law. The dealer shall obtain the required report by mailing or delivering the written con-sent form required under subsection A to the State Police within 24 hours of its execution. If the dealer has complied with the pro-visions of this subsection and has not received the required report from the State Police within 10 days from the date the written con-sent form was mailed to the Department of State Police, he shall not be deemed in violation of this section for thereafter completing the sale or transfer.

D. Nothing herein shall prevent a resident of the Commonwealth, at his option, from buying, renting or receiving a firearm from a dealer in Virginia by obtaining a criminal history record information check through the dealer as provided in subsection C.

E. If any buyer or transferee is denied the right to purchase a firearm under this section, he may exercise his right of access to and review and correction of criminal history record information under § 9.1-132 or institute a civil action as provided in § 9.1-135, provided any such action is initiated within 30 days of such denial.

F. Any dealer who willfully and intentionally requests, obtains, or seeks to obtain criminal history record information under false pretenses, or who willfully and intentionally disseminates or seeks to disseminate criminal history record information except as authorized in this section shall be guilty of a Class 2 misdemeanor.

G. For purposes of this section:

"Actual buyer" means a person who executes the consent form required in subsection B or C, or other such firearm transaction records as may be required by federal law.

"Antique firearm" means:
1. Any firearm (including any firearm with a matchlock, flintlock, percussion cap, or similar type of ignition system) manufactured in or before 1898;
2. Any replica of any firearm described in subdivision 1 of this definition if such replica (i) is not designed or redesigned for using rimfire or conventional centerfire fixed ammunition or (ii) uses rimfire or conventional centerfire fixed ammunition that is no longer manufactured in the United States and that is not readily available in the ordinary channels of commercial trade;
3. Any muzzle-loading rifle, muzzle-loading shotgun, or muzzle-loading pistol that is designed to use black powder, or a black powder substitute, and that cannot use fixed ammunition. For purposes of this subdivision, the term "antique firearm" shall not include any weapon that incorporates a firearm frame or receiver, any firearm that is converted into a muzzle-loading weapon, or any muzzle-loading weapon that can be readily converted to fire fixed ammunition by replacing the barrel, bolt, breech-block, or any combination thereof; or
4. Any curio or relic as defined in this subsection.

"Assault firearm" means any semi-automatic center-fire rifle or pistol which expels single or multiple projectiles by action of an explosion of a combustible material and is equipped at the time of the offense with a magazine which will hold more than 20 rounds of ammunition or designed by the manufacturer to accommodate a silencer or equipped with a folding stock.

"Curios or relics" means firearms that are of special interest to collectors by reason of some quality other than is associated with firearms intended for sporting use or as offensive or defensive weapons. To be recognized as curios or relics, firearms must fall within one of the following categories:
1. Firearms that were manufactured at least 50 years prior to the current date, which use rimfire or conventional centerfire fixed ammunition that is no longer manufactured in the United States and that is not readily available in the ordinary channels of commercial trade, but not including replicas thereof;
2. Firearms that are certified by the curator of a municipal, state, or federal museum that exhibits firearms to be curios or relics of museum interest; and
3. Any other firearms that derive a substantial part of their monetary value from the fact that they are novel, rare, bizarre, or because of their association with some historical figure, period, or event. Proof of qualification of a particular firearm under this category may be established by evidence of present value and evidence that like firearms are not available except as collectors' items, or that the value of like firearms available in ordinary commercial channels is substantially less.

"Dealer" means any person licensed as a dealer pursuant to 18 U.S.C. § 921 et seq.

"Firearm" means any handgun, shotgun, or rifle that will or is designed to or may readily be converted to expel single or multiple projectiles by action of an explosion of a combustible material.

"Handgun" means any pistol or revolver or other firearm originally designed, made and intended to fire single or multiple projectiles by means of an explosion of a combustible material from one or more barrels when held in one hand.

"Lawfully admitted for permanent residence" means the status of having been lawfully accorded the privilege of residing permanently in the United States as an immigrant in accordance with the immigration laws, such status not having changed.

H. The Department of Criminal Justice Services shall promulgate regulations to ensure the identity, confidentiality and security of all records and data provided by the Department of State Police pursuant to this section.

I. (Effective October 1, 2016) The provisions of this section shall not apply to (i) transactions between persons who are licensed as firearms importers or collectors, manufacturers or dealers pursuant to 18 U.S.C. § 921 et seq.; (ii) purchases by or sales to any law-enforcement officer or agent of the United States, the Commonwealth or any local government, or any campus police officer appointed under Article 3 (§ 23.1-809 et seq.) of Chapter 8 of Title 23.1; or (iii) antique firearms, curios or relics.

J. The provisions of this section shall not apply to restrict purchase, trade or transfer of firearms by a resident of Virginia when the resident of Virginia makes such purchase, trade or transfer in another state, in which case the laws and regulations of that state and the United States governing the purchase, trade or transfer of firearms shall apply. A National Instant Criminal Background Check System (NICS) check shall be performed prior to such purchase, trade or transfer of firearms.

J1. All licensed firearms dealers shall collect a fee of $2 for every transaction for which a criminal history record information check is required pursuant to this section, except that a fee of $5 shall be collected for every transaction involving an out-of-state resident. Such fee shall be transmitted to the Department of State Police by the last day of the month following the sale for deposit in a special fund for use by the State Police to offset the cost of conducting criminal history record information checks under the provisions of this section.

K. Any person willfully and intentionally making a materially false statement on the consent form required in subsection B or C or on such firearm transaction records as may be required by federal law, shall be guilty of a Class 5 felony.

L. Except as provided in § 18.2-308.2:1, any dealer who willfully and intentionally sells, rents, trades or transfers a firearm in violation of this section shall be guilty of a Class 6 felony.

L1. Any person who attempts to solicit, persuade, encourage, or entice any dealer to transfer or otherwise convey a firearm other than to the actual buyer, as well as any other person who willfully and intentionally aids or abets such person, shall be guilty of a Class 6 felony. This subsection shall not apply to a federal law-enforcement officer or a law-enforcement officer as defined in § 9.1-101, in the performance of his official duties, or other person under his direct supervision.

M. Any person who purchases a firearm with the intent to (i) resell or otherwise provide such firearm to any person who he knows or has reason to believe is ineligible to purchase or otherwise receive from a dealer a firearm for whatever reason or (ii) transport such firearm out of the Commonwealth to be resold or otherwise provided to another person who the transferor knows is ineligible to purchase or otherwise receive a firearm, shall be guilty of a Class 4 felony and sentenced to a mandatory minimum term of imprisonment of one year. However, if the violation of this subsection involves such a transfer of more than one firearm, the person shall be sentenced to a mandatory minimum term of imprisonment of five years. The prohibitions of this subsection shall not apply to the purchase of a firearm by a person for the lawful use, possession, or transport thereof, pursuant to § 18.2-308.7, by his child, grandchild, or individual for whom he is the legal guardian if such child, grandchild, or individual is ineligible, solely because of his age, to purchase a firearm.

N. Any person who is ineligible to purchase or otherwise receive or possess a firearm in the Commonwealth who solicits, employs or assists any person in violating subsection M shall be guilty of a Class 4 felony and shall be sentenced to a mandatory minimum term of imprisonment of five years.

O. Any mandatory minimum sentence imposed under this section shall be served consecutively with any other sentence.

P. All driver's licenses issued on or after July 1, 1994, shall carry a letter designation indicating whether the driver's license is an original, duplicate or renewed driver's license.

Q. Prior to selling, renting, trading, or transferring any firearm owned by the dealer but not in his inventory to any other person, a dealer may require such other person to consent to have the dealer obtain criminal history record information to determine if such other person is prohibited from possessing or transporting a firearm by state or federal law. The Department of State Police shall establish policies and procedures in accordance with 28 C.F.R. § 25.6 to permit such determinations to be made by the Department of State Police, and the processes established for making such determinations shall conform to the provisions of this section.

§ 18.2-308.3. Use or attempted use of restricted ammunition in commission or attempted commission of crimes prohibited; penalty.
A. When used in this section:

"Restricted firearm ammunition" applies to bullets, projectiles or other types of ammunition that are: (i) coated with or contain, in whole or in part, polytetrafluoroethylene or a similar product, (ii) commonly known as "KTW" bullets or "French Arcanes," or (iii) any cartridges containing bullets coated with a plastic substance with other than lead or lead alloy cores, jacketed bullets with other than lead or lead alloy cores, or cartridges of which the bullet itself is wholly comprised of a metal or metal alloy other than lead. This definition shall not be construed to include shotgun shells or solid plastic bullets.

B. It shall be unlawful for any person to knowingly use or attempt to use restricted firearm ammunition while committing or attempting to commit a crime. Violation of this section shall constitute a separate and distinct felony and any person found guilty thereof shall be guilty of a Class 5 felony.

§ 18.2-308.5. Manufacture, import, sale, transfer or possession of plastic firearm prohibited.
It shall be unlawful for any person to manufacture, import, sell, transfer or possess any plastic firearm. As used in this section,

"plastic firearm" means any firearm, including machine guns and sawed-off shotguns as defined in this chapter, containing less than 3.7 ounces of electromagnetically detectable metal in the barrel, slide, cylinder, frame or receiver of which, when subjected to inspection by X-ray machines commonly used at airports, does not generate an image that accurately depicts its shape. A violation of this section shall be punishable as a Class 5 felony.

§ 18.2-308.7. Possession or transportation of certain firearms by persons under the age of 18; penalty.

It shall be unlawful for any person under 18 years of age to knowingly and intentionally possess or transport a handgun or assault firearm anywhere in the Commonwealth. For the purposes of this section, "handgun" means any pistol or revolver or other firearm originally designed, made and intended to fire single or multiple projectiles by means of an explosion of a combustible material from one or more barrels when held in one hand and "assault firearm" means any (i) semi-automatic centerfire rifle or pistol which expels single or multiple projectiles by action of an explosion of a combustible material and is equipped at the time of the offense with a magazine which will hold more than 20 rounds of ammunition or designed by the manufacturer to accommodate a silencer or equipped with a folding stock or (ii) shotgun with a magazine which will hold more than seven rounds of the longest ammunition for which it is chambered. A violation of this section shall be a Class 1 misdemeanor.

This section shall not apply to:

1. Any person (i) while in his home or on his property; (ii) while in the home or on the property of his parent, grandparent, or legal guardian; or (iii) while on the property of another who has provided prior permission, and with the prior permission of his parent or legal guardian if the person has the landowner's written permission on his person while on such property;
2. Any person who, while accompanied by an adult, is at, or going to and from, a lawful shooting range or firearms educational class, provided that the weapons are unloaded while being transported;
3. Any person actually engaged in lawful hunting or going to and from a hunting area or preserve, provided that the weapons are unloaded while being transported; and

4. Any person while carrying out his duties in the Armed Forces of the United States or the National Guard of this Commonwealth or any other state.

§ 18.2-308.8. Importation, sale, possession or transfer of Striker 12's prohibited; penalty.

It shall be unlawful for any person to import, sell, possess or transfer the following firearms: the Striker 12, commonly called a "streetsweeper," or any semi-automatic folding stock shotgun of like kind with a spring tension drum magazine capable of holding twelve shotgun shells. A violation of this section shall be punishable as a Class 6 felony.

§ 18.2-309. Furnishing certain weapons to minors; penalty.

A. If any person sells, barters, gives or furnishes, or causes to be sold, bartered, given or furnished, to any minor a dirk, switchblade knife or bowie knife, having good cause to believe him to be a minor, such person shall be guilty of a Class 1 misdemeanor.

B. If any person sells, barters, gives or furnishes, or causes to be sold, bartered, given or furnished, to any minor a handgun, having good cause to believe him to be a minor, such person shall be guilty of a Class 6 felony. This subsection shall not apply to any transfer made between family members or for the purpose of engaging in a sporting event or activity.

§ 18.2-311. Prohibiting the selling or having in possession blackjacks, etc.

If any person sells or barters, or exhibits for sale or for barter, or gives or furnishes, or causes to be sold, bartered, given or furnished, or has in his possession, or under his control, with the intent of selling, bartering, giving or furnishing, any blackjack, brass or metal knucks, any disc of whatever configuration having at least two points or pointed blades which is designed to be thrown or propelled and which may be known as a throwing star or oriental dart, switchblade knife, ballistic knife as defined in § 18.2-307.1, or like weapons, such person is guilty of a Class 4 misdemeanor. The having in one's possession of any such weapon shall be prima facie evidence, except in the case of a conservator of the peace, of his intent to sell, barter, give or furnish the same.

8

.999

Title 18.2. Crimes and Offenses Generally
Chapter 7. Crimes Involving Health and Safety
Article 8. Miscellaneous Dangerous Conduct

§ 18.2-312. Illegal use of tear gas, phosgene and other gases.
If any person maliciously release or cause or procure to be released in any private home, place of business or place of public gathering any tear gas, mustard gas, phosgene gas or other noxious or nauseating gases or mixtures of chemicals designed to, and capable of, producing vile or injurious or nauseating odors or gases, and bodily injury results to any person from such gas or odor, the offending person shall be guilty of a Class 3 felony.

If such act be done unlawfully, but not maliciously, the offending person shall be guilty of a Class 6 felony.

Nothing herein contained shall prevent the use of tear gas or other gases by police officers or other peace officers in the proper performance of their duties, or by any person or persons in the protection of person, life or property.

§ 18.2-324. Throwing or depositing certain substances upon highway; removal of such substances.
No person shall throw or deposit or cause to be deposited upon any highway any glass bottle, glass, nail, tack, wire, can, or any other substance likely to injure any person or animal, or damage any vehicle upon such highway, nor shall any person throw or deposit or cause to be deposited upon any highway any soil, sand, mud, gravel or other substances so as to create a hazard to the traveling public. Any person who drops, or permits to be dropped or thrown, upon any highway any destructive, hazardous or injurious material shall immediately remove the same or cause it to be removed. Any person removing a wrecked or damaged vehicle from a highway shall remove any glass or other injurious substance dropped upon the highway from such vehicle. Any persons violating the provisions of this section shall be guilty of a Class 1 misdemeanor.

This section shall not apply to the use, by a law-enforcement officer while in the discharge of official duties, of any device designed to deflate tires. The Division of Purchase and Supply shall, pursuant to § 2.2-1112, set minimum standards for such devices and shall give notice of such standards to law-enforcement offices in the Commonwealth. No such device shall be used which does not meet or exceed the standards.

Title 18.2. Crimes and Offenses Generally
Chapter 8. Crimes Involving Morals and Decency
Article 5. Obscenity and Related Offenses

§ 18.2-388. Profane swearing and intoxication in public; penalty; transportation of public inebriates to detoxification center.
If any person profanely curses or swears or is intoxicated in public, whether such intoxication results from alcohol, narcotic drug or other intoxicant or drug of whatever nature, he shall be deemed guilty of a Class 4 misdemeanor. In any area in which there is located a court-approved detoxification center a law-enforcement officer may authorize the transportation, by police or otherwise, of public inebriates to such detoxification center in lieu of arrest; however, no person shall be involuntarily detained in such center.

Title 18.2. Crimes and Offenses Generally
Chapter 9. Crimes Against Peace and Order
Article 8. Unlawful Paramilitary Activity

§ 18.2-433.1. Definitions.
As used in this article:

"Civil disorder" means any public disturbance within the United States or any territorial possessions thereof involving acts of violence by assemblages of three or more persons, which causes an immediate danger of or results in damage or injury to the property or person of any other individual.

"Explosive or incendiary device" means (i) dynamite and all other forms of high explosives, (ii) any explosive bomb, grenade, missile, or similar device, or (iii) any incendiary bomb or grenade, fire bomb, or similar device, including any device which consists of or includes a breakable container including a flammable liquid or compound, and a wick composed of any material which, when ignited, is capable of igniting such flammable liquid or compound, and can be carried or thrown by one individual acting alone.

"Firearm" means any weapon that will or is designed to or may readily be converted to expel single or multiple projectiles by the action of an explosion of a combustible material; or the frame or receiver of any such weapon.

"Law-enforcement officer" means any officer as defined in § 9.1-101 or any such officer or member of the armed forces of the United States, any state, any political subdivision of a state, or the District of Columbia, and such term shall specifically include, but shall not be limited to, members of the National Guard, as defined in § 101(c) of Title 10, United States Code, members of the organized militia of any state or territory of the United States, the Commonwealth of Puerto Rico, or the District of Columbia, not included within the definition of National Guard as defined by such § 101(c), and members of the Armed Forces of the United States.

Title 19.2. Criminal Procedure
Chapter 9.1. Protective Orders

§ 19.2-152.8. Emergency protective orders authorized.
A. Any judge of a circuit court, general district court, juvenile and domestic relations district court or magistrate may issue a written or oral ex parte emergency protective order pursuant to this section in order to protect the health or safety of any person.

B. When a law-enforcement officer or an alleged victim asserts under oath to a judge or magistrate that such person is being or has been subjected to an act of violence, force, or threat and on that assertion or other evidence the judge or magistrate finds that (i) there is probable danger of a further such act being committed by the respondent against the alleged victim or (ii) a petition or warrant for the arrest of the respondent has been issued for any criminal offense resulting from the commission of an act of violence, force, or threat, the judge or magistrate shall issue an ex parte emergency protective order imposing one or more of the following conditions on the respondent:
    1. Prohibiting acts of violence, force, or threat or criminal offenses resulting in injury to person or property;
    2. Prohibiting such contacts by the respondent with the alleged victim or the alleged victim's family or household members, including prohibiting the respondent from being in the physical

presence of the alleged victim or the alleged victim's family or household members, as the judge or magistrate deems necessary to protect the safety of such persons;

3. Such other conditions as the judge or magistrate deems necessary to prevent (i) acts of violence, force, or threat, (ii) criminal offenses resulting in injury to person or property, or (iii) communication or other contact of any kind by the respondent; and

4. Granting the petitioner the possession of any companion animal as defined in § 3.2-6500 if such petitioner meets the definition of owner in § 3.2-6500.

C. An emergency protective order issued pursuant to this section shall expire at 11:59 p.m. on the third day following issuance. If the expiration occurs on a day that the court is not in session, the emergency protective order shall be extended until 11:59 p.m. on the next day that the court which issued the order is in session. The respondent may at any time file a motion with the court requesting a hearing to dissolve or modify the order. The hearing on the motion shall be given precedence on the docket of the court.

D. A law-enforcement officer may request an emergency protective order pursuant to this section and, if the person in need of protection is physically or mentally incapable of filing a petition pursuant to § 19.2-152.9 or 19.2-152.10, may request the extension of an emergency protective order for an additional period of time not to exceed three days after expiration of the original order. The request for an emergency protective order or extension of an order may be made orally, in person or by electronic means, and the judge of a circuit court, general district court, or juvenile and domestic relations district court or a magistrate may issue an oral emergency protective order. An oral emergency protective order issued pursuant to this section shall be reduced to writing, by the law-enforcement officer requesting the order or the magistrate, on a preprinted form approved and provided by the Supreme Court of Virginia. The completed form shall include a statement of the grounds for the order asserted by the officer or the alleged victim of such crime.

E. The court or magistrate shall forthwith, but in all cases no later than the end of the business day on which the order was issued, enter and transfer electronically to the Virginia Criminal Information Network the respondent's identifying information and the name, date of birth, sex, and race of each protected person provided to the court or magistrate. A copy of an emergency protective order issued pursuant to this section containing any such identifying information shall be forwarded forthwith to the primary law-enforcement agency responsible for service and entry of protective orders. Upon receipt of the order by the primary law-enforcement agency, the agency shall forthwith verify and enter any modification as necessary to the identifying information and other appropriate information required by the Department of State Police into the Virginia Criminal Information Network established and maintained by the Department pursuant to Chapter 2 (§ 52-12 et seq.) of Title 52 and the order shall be served forthwith upon the respondent and due return made to the court. However, if the order is issued by the circuit court, the clerk of the circuit court shall forthwith forward an attested copy of the order containing the respondent's identifying information and the name, date of birth, sex, and race of each protected person provided to the court to the primary law-enforcement agency providing service and entry of protective orders and upon receipt of the order, the primary law-enforcement agency shall enter the name of the person subject to the order and other appropriate information required by the Department of State Police into the Virginia Criminal Information Network established and maintained by the Department pursuant to Chapter 2 (§ 52-12 et seq.) of Title 52 and the order shall be served forthwith upon the respondent. Upon service, the agency making service shall enter the date and time of service and other appropriate information required into the Virginia Criminal Information Network and make due return to the court. One copy of the order shall be given to the alleged victim of such crime. The judge or magistrate who issues an oral order pursuant to an electronic request by a law-enforcement officer shall verify the written order to determine whether the officer who reduced it to writing accurately transcribed the contents of the oral order. The original copy shall be filed with the clerk of the appropriate district court within five business days of the issuance of the order. If the order is later dissolved or modified, a copy of the dissolution or modification order shall also be attested, forwarded forthwith to the primary law-enforcement agency responsible for service and entry of protective orders, and upon receipt of the order by the primary law-enforcement agency, the agency shall forthwith verify and enter any modification as necessary to the identifying information and other appropriate information required by the Department of State Police into the Virginia Criminal Information Network as described above and the order shall be served forthwith and due return made to the court. Upon request, the clerk shall provide the alleged victim of such crime with information regarding the date and time of service.

F. The issuance of an emergency protective order shall not be considered evidence of any wrongdoing by the respondent.

G. As used in this section, a "law-enforcement officer" means any (i) person who is a full-time or part-time employee of a police department or sheriff's office which is part of or administered by the Commonwealth or any political subdivision thereof and who is responsible for the prevention and detection of crime and the enforcement of the penal, traffic or highway laws of the Commonwealth and (ii) member of an auxiliary police force established pursuant to § 15.2-1731. Part-time employees are compensated officers who are not full-time employees as defined by the employing police department or sheriff's office.

H. Neither a law-enforcement agency, the attorney for the Commonwealth, a court nor the clerk's office, nor any employee of them, may disclose, except among themselves, the residential address, telephone number, or place of employment of the person protected by the order or that of the family of such person, except to the extent that disclosure is (i) required by law or the Rules of the Supreme Court, (ii) necessary for law-enforcement purposes, or (iii) permitted by the court for good cause.

I. As used in this section:

"Copy" includes a facsimile copy.

"Physical presence" includes (i) intentionally maintaining direct visual contact with the petitioner or (ii) unreasonably being within 100 feet from the petitioner's residence or place of employment.

J. No fee shall be charged for filing or serving any petition pursuant to this section.

K. No emergency protective order shall be issued pursuant to this section against a law-enforcement officer for any action arising out of the lawful performance of his duties.

§ 19.2-152.9. Preliminary protective orders.

A. Upon the filing of a petition alleging that (i) the petitioner is or has been, within a reasonable period of time, subjected to an act of violence, force, or threat, or (ii) a petition or warrant has been issued for the arrest of the alleged perpetrator for any criminal offense resulting from the commission of an act of violence, force, or threat, the court may issue a preliminary protective order against the alleged perpetrator in order to protect the health and safety of the petitioner or any family or household member of the petitioner. The order may be issued in an ex parte proceeding upon good cause shown when the petition is supported by an affidavit or sworn testimony before the judge or intake officer. Immediate and present danger of any act of violence, force, or threat or evidence sufficient to establish probable cause that an act of violence, force, or threat has recently occurred shall constitute good cause.

A preliminary protective order may include any one or more of the following conditions to be imposed on the respondent:

1. Prohibiting acts of violence, force, or threat or criminal offenses that may result in injury to person or property;

2. Prohibiting such other contacts by the respondent with the petitioner or the petitioner's family or household members as the court deems necessary for the health and safety of such persons;

3. Such other conditions as the court deems necessary to prevent (i) acts of violence, force, or threat, (ii) criminal offenses that may result in injury to person or property, or (iii) communication or other contact of any kind by the respondent; and

4. Granting the petitioner the possession of any companion animal as defined in § 3.2-6500 if such petitioner meets the definition of owner in § 3.2-6500.

B. The court shall forthwith, but in all cases no later than the end of the business day on which the order was issued, enter and transfer electronically to the Virginia Criminal Information Network the respondent's identifying information and the name, date of birth, sex, and race of each protected person provided to the court. A copy of a preliminary protective order containing any such identifying information shall be forwarded forthwith to the primary law-enforcement agency responsible for service and entry of protective orders. Upon receipt of the order by the primary law-enforcement agency, the agency shall forthwith verify and enter any modification as necessary to the identifying information and other appropriate information required by the Department of State Police into the Virginia Criminal Information Network established and maintained by the Department pursuant to Chapter 2 (§ 52-12 et seq.) of Title 52 and the order shall be served forthwith on the alleged perpetrator in person as provided in § 16.1-264, and due return made to the court. However, if the order is issued by the circuit court, the clerk of the circuit court shall forthwith forward an attested copy of the order containing the respondent's identifying information and the name, date of birth, sex, and race of each protected person provided to the court to the primary law-enforcement agency providing service and entry of protective orders and upon receipt of the order, the primary law-enforcement agency shall enter the name of the person subject to the order and other appropriate information required by the Department of State Police into the Virginia Criminal Information Network established and maintained by the Department pursuant to Chapter 2 (§ 52-12 et seq.) of Title 52 and the order shall be served forthwith on the alleged perpetrator in person as provided in § 16.1-264. Upon service, the agency making service shall enter the date and time of service and other appropriate information required by the Department of State Police into the Virginia Criminal Information Network and make due return to the court. The preliminary order shall specify a date for the full hearing. The hearing shall be held within 15 days of the issuance of the preliminary order. If the respondent fails to appear at this hearing because the respondent was not personally served, the court may extend the protective order for a period not to exceed six months. The extended protective order shall be served as soon as possible on the respondent. However, upon motion of the respondent and for good cause shown, the court may continue the hearing. The preliminary order shall remain in effect until the hearing. Upon request after the order is issued, the clerk shall provide the petitioner with a copy of the order and information regarding the date and time of service. The order shall further specify that either party may at any time file a motion with the court requesting a hearing to dissolve or modify the order. The hearing on the motion shall be given precedence on the docket of the court.

Upon receipt of the return of service or other proof of service pursuant to subsection C of § 16.1-264, the clerk shall forthwith forward an attested copy of the preliminary protective order to primary law-enforcement agency and the agency shall forthwith verify and enter any modification as necessary into the Virginia Criminal Information Network as described above. If the order is later dissolved or modified, a copy of the dissolution or modification order shall also be attested, forwarded forthwith to the primary law-enforcement agency responsible for service and entry of protective orders, and upon receipt of the order by the primary law-enforcement agency, the agency shall forthwith verify and enter any modification as necessary to the identifying information and other appropriate information required by the Department of State Police into the Virginia Criminal Information Network as described above and the order shall be served forthwith and due return made to the court.

C. The preliminary order is effective upon personal service on the alleged perpetrator. Except as otherwise provided, a violation of the order shall constitute contempt of court.

D. At a full hearing on the petition, the court may issue a protective order pursuant to § 19.2-152.10 if the court finds that the petitioner has proven the allegation that the petitioner is or has been, within a reasonable period of time, subjected to an act of violence, force, or threat by a preponderance of the evidence.

E. No fees shall be charged for filing or serving petitions pursuant to this section.

F. Neither a law-enforcement agency, the attorney for the Commonwealth, a court nor the clerk's office, nor any employee of them, may disclose, except among themselves, the residential address, telephone number, or place of employment of the person protected by the order or that of the family of such person, except to the extent that disclosure is (i) required by law or the Rules of the Supreme Court, (ii) necessary for law-enforcement purposes, or (iii) permitted by the court for good cause.

G. As used in this section, "copy" includes a facsimile copy.

§ 19.2-152.10. Protective order.

A. The court may issue a protective order pursuant to this chapter to protect the health and safety of the petitioner and family or household members of a petitioner upon (i) the issuance of a petition or warrant for, or a conviction of, any criminal offense resulting from the commission of an act of violence, force, or threat or (ii) a hearing held pursuant to subsection D of § 19.2-152.9. A protective order issued under this section may include any one or more of the following conditions to be imposed on the respondent:

1. Prohibiting acts of violence, force, or threat or criminal offenses that may result in injury to person or property;

2. Prohibiting such contacts by the respondent with the petitioner or family or household members of the petitioner as the court deems necessary for the health or safety of such persons;

3. Any other relief necessary to prevent (i) acts of violence, force, or threat, (ii) criminal offenses that may result in injury to person or property, or (iii) communication or other contact of any kind by the respondent; and

4. Granting the petitioner the possession of any companion animal as defined in § 3.2-6500 if such petitioner meets the definition of owner in § 3.2-6500.

B. The protective order may be issued for a specified period of time up to a maximum of two years. The protective order shall expire at 11:59 p.m. on the last day specified or at 11:59 p.m. on the last day of the two-year period if no date is specified. Prior to the expiration of the protective order, a petitioner may file a written motion requesting a hearing to extend the order. Proceedings to extend a protective order shall be given precedence on the docket of the court. The court may extend the protective order for a period not longer than two years to protect the health and safety of the petitioner or persons who are family or household members of the petitioner at the time the request for an extension is made. The extension of the protective order shall expire at 11:59 p.m. on the last day specified or at 11:59 p.m. on the last day of the two-year period if no date is specified. Nothing herein shall limit the number of extensions that may be requested or issued.

C. A copy of the protective order shall be served on the respondent and provided to the petitioner as soon as possible. The court, including a circuit court if the circuit court issued the order, shall forthwith, but in all cases no later than the end of the business day on which the order was issued, enter and transfer electronically to the Virginia Criminal Information Network the respondent's identifying information and the name, date of birth, sex, and race of each protected person provided to the court and shall forthwith forward the attested copy of the protective order and containing any such identifying information to the primary law-enforcement agency responsible for service and entry of protective orders. Upon receipt of the order by the primary law-enforcement agency, the agency shall forthwith verify and enter any modification as necessary to the identifying information and other appropriate information required by the Department of State Police into the Virginia Criminal Information Network established and maintained by the Department pursuant to Chapter 2 (§ 52-12 et seq.) of Title 52 and the order shall be served forthwith upon the respondent and due return made to the court. Upon service, the agency making service shall enter the date and time of service and other appropriate information required into the Virginia Criminal Information Network and make due return to the court. If the order is later dissolved or modified, a copy of the dissolution or modification order shall also be attested, forwarded forthwith to the primary law-enforcement agency responsible for service and entry of protective orders, and upon receipt of the order by the primary law-enforcement agency, the agency shall forthwith verify and enter any modification as necessary to the identifying information and other appropriate information required by the Department of State Police into the Virginia Criminal Information Network as described above and the order shall be served forthwith and due return made to the court.

D. Except as otherwise provided, a violation of a protective order issued under this section shall constitute contempt of court.

E. The court may assess costs and attorneys' fees against either party regardless of whether an order of protection has been issued as a result of a full hearing.

F. Any judgment, order or decree, whether permanent or temporary, issued by a court of appropriate jurisdiction in another state, the United States or any of its territories, possessions or Commonwealths, the District of Columbia or by any tribal court of appropriate jurisdiction for the purpose of preventing violent or threatening acts or harassment against or contact or communication with or physical proximity to another person, including any of the conditions specified in subsection A, shall be accorded full faith and credit and enforced in the Commonwealth as if it were an order of the Commonwealth, provided reasonable notice and opportunity to be heard were given by the issuing jurisdiction to the person against whom the order is sought to be enforced sufficient to protect such person's due process rights and consistent with federal law. A person entitled to protection under such a foreign order may file the order in any appropriate district court by filing with the court, an attested or exemplified copy of the order. Upon such a filing, the clerk shall forthwith forward an attested copy of the order to the primary law-enforcement agency responsible for service and entry of protective orders which shall, upon receipt, enter the name of the person subject to the order and other appropriate information required by the Department of State Police into the Virginia Criminal Information Network established and maintained by the Department pursuant to Chapter 2 (§ 52-12 et seq.) of Title 52. Where practical, the court may transfer information electronically to the Virginia Criminal Information Network.

Upon inquiry by any law-enforcement agency of the Commonwealth, the clerk shall make a copy available of any foreign order filed with that court. A law-enforcement officer may, in the performance of his duties, rely upon a copy of a foreign protective order or other suitable evidence which has been provided to him by any source and may also rely upon the statement of any person protected by the order that the order remains in effect.

G. Either party may at any time file a written motion with the court requesting a hearing to dissolve or modify the order. Proceedings to modify or dissolve a protective order shall be given precedence on the docket of the court.

H. Neither a law-enforcement agency, the attorney for the Commonwealth, a court nor the clerk's office, nor any employee of them, may disclose, except among themselves, the residential address, telephone number, or place of employment of the person protected by the order or that of the family of such person, except to the extent that disclosure is (i) required by law or the Rules of the Supreme Court, (ii) necessary for law-enforcement purposes, or (iii) permitted by the court for good cause.

I. No fees shall be charged for filing or serving petitions pursuant to this section.

J. As used in this section:

"Copy" includes a facsimile copy; and

"Protective order" includes an initial, modified or extended protective order.

Title 19.2. Criminal Procedure
Chapter 11. Proceedings on Question of Insanity

§ 19.2-169.2. Disposition when defendant found incompetent.
A. Upon finding pursuant to subsection E of § 19.2-169.1 that the defendant, including a juvenile transferred pursuant to § 16.1-269.1, is incompetent, the court shall order that the defendant receive treatment to restore his competency on an outpatient basis or, if the court specifically finds that the defendant requires inpatient hospital treatment, at a hospital designated by the Commissioner of Behavioral Health and Developmental Services as appropriate for treatment of persons under criminal charge. Any psychiatric records and other information that have been deemed relevant and submitted by the attorney for the defendant pursuant to subsection C of § 19.2-169.1 and any reports submitted pursuant to subsection D of § 19.2-169.1 shall be made available to the director of the community services board or behavioral health authority or his designee or to the director of the treating inpatient facility or his designee within 96 hours of the issuance of the court order requiring treatment to restore the defendant's competency. If the 96-hour period expires on a Saturday, Sunday, or other legal holiday, the 96 hours shall be extended to the next day that is not a Saturday, Sunday, or legal holiday.

B. If, at any time after the defendant is ordered to undergo treatment under subsection A of this section, the director of the community services board or behavioral health authority or his designee or the director of the treating inpatient facility or his designee believes the defendant's competency is restored, the director or his designee shall immediately send a report to the court as prescribed in subsection D of § 19.2-169.1. The court shall make a ruling on the defendant's competency according to the procedures specified in subsection E of § 19.2-169.1.

C. The clerk of court shall certify and forward forthwith to the Central Criminal Records Exchange, on a form provided by the Exchange, a copy of an order for treatment issued pursuant to subsection A.

Title 19.2. Criminal Procedure
Chapter 23.1. Expungement of Criminal Records

§ 19.2-392.2. Expungement of police and court records.
A. If a person is charged with the commission of a crime or any offense defined in Title 18.2, and
    1. Is acquitted, or
    2. A *nolle prosequi* is taken or the charge is otherwise dismissed, including dismissal by accord and satisfaction pursuant to § 19.2-151, he may file a petition setting forth the relevant facts and requesting expungement of the police records and the court records relating to the charge.

B. If any person whose name or other identification has been used without his consent or authorization by another person who has been charged or arrested using such name or identification, he may file a petition with the court disposing of the charge for relief pursuant to this section. Such person shall not be required to pay any fees for the filing of a petition under this subsection. A petition filed under this subsection shall include one complete set of the petitioner's fingerprints obtained from a law-enforcement agency.

C. The petition with a copy of the warrant or indictment if reasonably available shall be filed in the circuit court of the county or city in which the case was disposed of by acquittal or being otherwise dismissed and shall contain, except where not reasonably available, the date of arrest and the name of the arresting agency. Where this information is not reasonably available, the petition shall state the reason for such unavailability. The petition shall further state the specific criminal charge to be expunged, the date of final disposition of the charge as set forth in the petition, the petitioner's date of birth, and the full name used by the petitioner at the time of arrest.

D. A copy of the petition shall be served on the attorney for the Commonwealth of the city or county in which the petition is filed. The attorney for the Commonwealth may file an objection or answer to the petition or may give written notice to the court that he does not object to the petition within 21 days after it is served on him.

E. The petitioner shall obtain from a law-enforcement agency one complete set of the petitioner's fingerprints and shall provide that agency with a copy of the petition for expungement. The law-enforcement agency shall submit the set of fingerprints to the Central Criminal Records Exchange (CCRE) with a copy of the petition for expungement attached. The CCRE shall forward under seal to the court a copy of the petitioner's criminal history, a copy of the source documents that resulted in the CCRE entry that the petitioner wishes to expunge, and the set of fingerprints. Upon completion of the hearing, the court shall return the fingerprint card to the petitioner. If no hearing was conducted, upon the entry of an order of expungement or an order denying the petition for expungement, the court shall cause the fingerprint card to be destroyed unless, within 30 days of the date of the entry of the order, the petitioner requests the return of the fingerprint card in person from the clerk of the court or provides the clerk of the court a self-addressed, stamped envelope for the return of the fingerprint card.

F. After receiving the criminal history record information from the CCRE, the court shall conduct a hearing on the petition. If the court finds that the continued existence and possible dissemination of information relating to the arrest of the petitioner causes or may cause circumstances which constitute a manifest injustice to the petitioner, it shall enter an order requiring the expungement of the police and court records, including electronic records, relating to the charge. Otherwise, it shall deny the petition. However, if the petitioner has no prior criminal record and the arrest was for a misdemeanor violation, the petitioner shall be entitled, in the absence of good cause shown to the contrary by the Commonwealth, to expungement of the police and court records relating to the charge, and the court shall enter an order of expungement. If the attorney for the Commonwealth of the county or city in which the petition is filed (i) gives written notice to the court pursuant to subsection D that he does not object to the petition and (ii) when the charge to be expunged is a felony, stipulates in such written notice that the continued existence and possible dissemination of information relating to the arrest of the petitioner causes or may cause circumstances which constitute a manifest injustice to the petitioner, the court may enter an order of expungement without conducting a hearing.

G. The Commonwealth shall be made party defendant to the proceeding. Any party aggrieved by the decision of the court may appeal, as provided by law in civil cases.

H. Notwithstanding any other provision of this section, when the charge is dismissed because the court finds that the person arrested or charged is not the person named in the summons, warrant, indictment or presentment, the court dismissing the charge shall, upon motion of the person improperly arrested or charged, enter an order requiring expungement of the police and court records relating to the charge. Such order shall contain a statement that the dismissal and expungement are ordered pursuant to this subsection and shall be accompanied by the complete set of the petitioner's fingerprints filed with his petition. Upon the entry of such order, it shall be treated as provided in subsection K.

I. Notwithstanding any other provision of this section, when a person has been granted an absolute pardon for the commission of a crime that he did not commit, he may file in the circuit court of the county or city in which the conviction occurred a petition setting forth the relevant facts and requesting expungement of the police records and the court records relating to the charge and conviction, and the court shall enter an order requiring expungement of the police and court records relating to the charge and conviction. Such order shall contain a statement that the expungement is ordered pursuant to this subsection. Upon the entry of such order, it shall be treated as provided in subsection K.

J. Upon receiving a copy of a writ vacating a conviction pursuant to § 19.2-327.5 or 19.2-327.13, the court shall enter an order requiring expungement of the police and court records relating to the charge and conviction. Such order shall contain a statement that the expungement is ordered pursuant to this subsection. Upon the entry of the order, it shall be treated as provided in subsection K.

K. Upon the entry of an order of expungement, the clerk of the court shall cause a copy of such order to be forwarded to the Department of State Police, which shall, pursuant to rules and regulations adopted pursuant to § 9.1-134, direct the manner by which the appropriate expungement or removal of such records shall be effected.

L. Costs shall be as provided by § 17.1-275, but shall not be recoverable against the Commonwealth. If the court enters an order of expungement, the clerk of the court shall refund to the petitioner such costs paid by the petitioner.

M. Any order entered where (i) the court or parties failed to strictly comply with the procedures set forth in this section or (ii) the court enters an order of expungement contrary to law, shall be voidable upon motion and notice made within three years of the entry of such order.

Title 20. Domestic Relations
Chapter 6. Divorce, Affirmation and Annulment

§ 20-103. Court may make orders pending suit for divorce, custody or visitation, etc.
A. In suits for divorce, annulment and separate maintenance, and in proceedings arising under subdivision A 3 or subsection L of § 16.1-241, the court having jurisdiction of the matter may, at any time pending a suit pursuant to this chapter, in the discretion of such court, make any order that may be proper (i) to compel a spouse to pay any sums necessary for the maintenance and support of the petitioning spouse, including (a) an order that the other spouse provide health care coverage for the petitioning spouse, unless it is shown that such coverage cannot be obtained, or (b) an order that a party pay secured or unsecured debts incurred jointly or by either party, (ii) to enable such spouse to carry on the suit, (iii) to prevent

either spouse from imposing any restraint on the personal liberty of the other spouse, (iv) to provide for the custody and maintenance of the minor children of the parties, including an order that either party or both parties provide health care coverage or cash medical support, or both, for the children, (v) to provide support, calculated in accordance with § 20-108.2, for any child of the parties to whom a duty of support is owed and to pay or continue to pay support for any child over the age of 18 who meets the requirements set forth in subsection C of § 20-124.2, (vi) for the exclusive use and possession of the family residence during the pendency of the suit, (vii) to preserve the estate of either spouse, so that it be forthcoming to meet any decree which may be made in the suit, (viii) to compel either spouse to give security to abide such decree, or (ix)(a) to compel a party to maintain any existing policy owned by that party insuring the life of either party or to require a party to name as a beneficiary of the policy the other party or an appropriate person for the exclusive use and benefit of the minor children of the parties and (b) to allocate the premium cost of such life insurance between the parties, provided that all premiums are billed to the policyholder. Nothing in clause (ix) shall be construed to create an independent cause of action on the part of any beneficiary against the insurer or to require an insurer to provide information relating to such policy to any person other than the policyholder without the written consent of the policyholder. The parties to any petition where a child whose custody, visitation, or support is contested shall show proof that they have attended within the 12 months prior to their court appearance or that they shall attend within 45 days thereafter an educational seminar or other like program conducted by a qualified person or organization approved by the court except that the court may require the parties to attend such seminar or program in uncontested cases only if the court finds good cause. The seminar or other program shall be a minimum of four hours in length and shall address the effects of separation or divorce on children, parenting responsibilities, options for conflict resolution and financial responsibilities. Once a party has completed one educational seminar or other like program, the required completion of additional programs shall be at the court's discretion. Parties under this section shall include natural or adoptive parents of the child, or any person with a legitimate interest as defined in § 20-124.1. The fee charged a party for participation in such program shall be based on the party's ability to pay; however, no fee in excess of $50 may be charged. Whenever possible, before participating in mediation or alternative dispute resolution to address custody, visitation or support, each party shall have attended the educational seminar or other like program. The court may grant an exemption from attendance of such program for good cause shown or if there is no program reasonably available. Other than statements or admissions by a party admitting criminal activity or child abuse, no statement or admission by a party in such seminar or program shall be admissible into evidence in any subsequent proceeding.

A1. Any award or order made by the court pursuant to subsection A shall be paid from the post-separation income of the obligor unless the court, for good cause shown, orders otherwise. Upon the request of either party, the court may identify and state in such order or award the specific source from which the financial obligation imposed is to be paid.

B. In addition to the terms provided in subsection A, upon a showing by a party of reasonable apprehension of physical harm to that party by such party's family or household member as that term is defined in § 16.1-228, and consistent with rules of the Supreme Court of Virginia, the court may enter an order excluding that party's family or household member from the jointly owned or jointly rented family dwelling. In any case where an order is entered under this paragraph, pursuant to an ex parte hearing, the order shall not exclude a family or household member from the family dwelling for a period in excess of 15 days from the date the order is served, in person, upon the person so excluded. The order may provide for an extension of time beyond the 15 days, to become effective automatically. The person served may at any time file a written motion in the clerk's office requesting a hearing to dissolve or modify the order. Nothing in this section shall be construed to prohibit the court from extending an order entered under this subsection for such longer period of time as is deemed appropriate, after a hearing on notice to the parties. If the party subject to the order fails to appear at this hearing, the court may extend the order for a period not to exceed six months.

C. In cases other than those for divorce in which a custody or visitation arrangement for a minor child is sought, the court may enter an order providing for custody, visitation or maintenance pending the suit as provided in subsection A. The order shall be directed to either parent or any person with a legitimate interest who is a party to the suit.

D. Orders entered pursuant to this section which provide for custody or visitation arrangements pending the suit shall be made in accordance with the standards set out in Chapter 6.1 (§ 20-124.1 et seq.). Orders entered pursuant to subsection B shall be certified by the clerk and forwarded as soon as possible to the local police department or sheriff's office which shall, on the date of receipt, enter the name of the person subject to the order and other appropriate information required by the Department of State Police into the Virginia crime information network system established and maintained by the Department of State Police pursuant to Chapter 2 (§ 52-12 et seq.) of Title 52. If the order is later dissolved or modified, a copy of the dissolution or modification shall also be certified, forwarded and entered in the system as described above.

E. An order entered pursuant to this section shall have no presumptive effect and shall not be determinative when adjudicating the underlying cause.

Title 29.1. Game, Inland Fisheries and Boating
Chapter 1. Administration of Game and Inland Fisheries
Article 1. General Provisions

§ 29.1-100. Definitions.
As used in and for the purposes of this title only, or in any of the regulations of the Board, unless the context clearly requires a different meaning:

"Bag or creel limit" means the quantity of game, fish or fur-bearing animals that may be taken, caught, or possessed during a period fixed by the Board.

"Board" means the Board of Game and Inland Fisheries.

"Closed season" means that period of time fixed by the Board during which wild animals, birds or fish may not be taken, captured, killed, pursued, hunted, trapped or possessed.

"Conservation police officers" means supervising officers, and regular and special conservation police officers.

"Department" means the Department of Game and Inland Fisheries.

"Director" means the Director of the Department of Game and Inland Fisheries.

"Firearm" means any weapon that will or is designed to or may readily be converted to expel single or multiple projectiles by the action of an explosion of a combustible material.

"Fishing" means taking, capturing, killing, or attempting to take, capture or kill any fish in and upon the inland waters of this Commonwealth.

"Fur-bearing animals" includes beaver, bobcat, fisher, fox, mink, muskrat, opossum, otter, raccoon, skunk, and weasel.

"Game" means wild animals and wild birds that are commonly hunted for sport or food.

"Game animals" means deer (including all Cervidae), bear, rabbit, fox, squirrel, bobcat and raccoon.

"Game fish" means trout (including all Salmonidae), all of the sunfish family (including largemouth bass, smallmouth bass and spotted bass, rock bass, bream, bluegill and crappie), walleye or pike perch, white bass, chain pickerel or jackfish, muskellunge, and northern pike, wherever such fish are found in the waters of this Commonwealth and rockfish or striped bass where found above tidewaters or in streams which are blocked from access from tidewaters by dams.

"Hunting and trapping" includes the act of or the attempted act of taking, hunting, trapping, pursuing, chasing, shooting, snaring or netting birds or animals, and assisting any person who is hunting, trapping or attempting to do so regardless of whether birds or animals are actually taken; however, when hunting and trapping are allowed, reference is made to such acts as being conducted by lawful means and in a lawful manner. The Board of Game and Inland

Fisheries may authorize by regulation the pursuing or chasing of wild birds or wild animals during any closed hunting season where persons have no intent to take such birds or animals.

"Lawful," "by law," or "law" means the statutes of this Commonwealth or regulations adopted by the Board which the Director is empowered to enforce.

"Migratory game birds" means doves, ducks, brant, geese, swan, coot, gallinules, sora and other rails, snipe, woodcock and other species of birds on which open hunting seasons are set by federal regulations.

"Muzzleloading pistol" means a firearm originally designed, made or intended to fire a projectile (bullet) from one or more barrels when held in one hand and that is loaded from the muzzle or forward end of the cylinder.

"Muzzleloading rifle" means a firearm firing a single projectile that is loaded along with the propellant from the muzzle of the gun.

"Muzzleloading shotgun" means a firearm with a smooth bore firing multiple projectiles that are loaded along with the propellant from the muzzle of the gun.

"Nonmigratory game birds" means grouse, bobwhite quail, turkey and all species of birds introduced into the Commonwealth by the Board.

"Nuisance species" means blackbirds, coyotes, crows, cowbirds, feral swine, grackles, English sparrows, starlings, or those species designated as such by regulations of the Board, and those species found committing or about to commit depredation upon ornamental or shade trees, agricultural crops, wildlife, livestock or other property or when concentrated in numbers and manners as to constitute a health hazard or other nuisance. However, the term nuisance does not include (i) animals designated as endangered or threatened pursuant to §§ 29.1-563, 29.1-564, and 29.1-566, (ii) animals classified as game or fur-bearing animals, and (iii) those species protected by state or federal law.

"Open season" means that period of time fixed by the Board during which wild animals, wild birds and fish may be taken, captured, killed, pursued, trapped or possessed.

"Pistol" means a weapon originally designed, made, and intended to fire a projectile (bullet) from one or more barrels when held in one hand, and having one or more chambers as an integral part of or permanently aligned with the bore and a short stock at an angle to and extending below the line of the bore that is designed to be gripped by one hand.

"Possession" means the exercise of control of any wild animal, wild bird, fish or fur-bearing animal, or any part of the carcass thereof.

"Properly licensed person" means a person who, while engaged in hunting, fishing or trapping, or in any other activity permitted under this title, in and upon the lands and inland waters of this Commonwealth, has upon his person all the licenses, permits and stamps required by law.

"Regulation" means a regulation duly adopted by the Board pursuant to the authority vested by the provisions of this title.

"Revolver" means a projectile weapon of the pistol type, having a breechloading chambered cylinder arranged so that the cocking of the hammer or movement of the trigger rotates it and brings the next cartridge in line with the barrel for firing.

"Rifle" means a weapon designed or redesigned, made or remade, and intended to be fired from the shoulder, and designed or redesigned and made or remade to use the energy of the explosive in a fixed metallic cartridge to fire only a single projectile through a rifled bore for each single pull of the trigger.

"Shotgun" means a weapon designed or redesigned, made or remade, and intended to be fired from the shoulder, and designed or redesigned and made or remade to use the energy of the explosive in a fixed shotgun shell to fire through a smooth bore or rifled shotgun barrel either a number of ball shot or a single projectile for each single pull of the trigger.

"Transportation" means the transportation, either upon the person or by any other means, of any wild animal or wild bird or fish.

"Wildlife" means all species of wild animals, wild birds and freshwater fish in the public waters of this Commonwealth.

Title 29.1. Game, Inland Fisheries and Boating
Chapter 5. Wildlife and Fish Laws
Article 2. Hunting and Trapping

§ 29.1-512. Closed season on other species.
There shall be a continuous closed hunting season on all birds and wild animals which are not nuisance species as defined in § 29.1-100, except as provided by law.

§ 29.1-529. Killing of deer, elk or bear damaging fruit trees, crops, livestock, or personal property; wildlife creating a hazard to aircraft or motor vehicles.
A. Whenever deer, elk or bear are damaging fruit trees, crops, livestock or personal property utilized for commercial agricultural production in the Commonwealth, the owner or lessee of the lands on which such damage is done shall immediately report the damage to the Director or his designee for investigation. If after investigation the Director or his designee finds that deer or bear are responsible for the damage, he shall authorize in writing the owner, lessee or any other person designated by the Director or his designee to kill such deer or bear when they are found upon the land upon which the damages occurred. However, the Director or his designee shall have the option of authorizing nonlethal control measures rather than authorizing the killing of elk or bear, provided that such measures occur within a reasonable period of time; and whenever deer cause damage on parcels of land of five acres or less, except when such acreage is used for commercial agricultural production, the Director or his designee shall have discretion as to whether to issue a written authorization to kill the deer. The Director or his designee may limit such authorization by specifying in writing the number of animals to be killed and duration for which the authorization is effective and may in proximity to residential areas and under other appropriate circumstances limit or prohibit the authorization between 11:00 p.m. and one-half hour before sunrise of the following day. The Director or his designees issuing these authorizations shall

specify in writing that only antlerless deer shall be killed, unless the Director or his designee determines that there is clear and convincing evidence that the damage was done by deer with antlers. Any owner or lessee of land who has been issued a written authorization shall not be issued an authorization in subsequent years unless he can demonstrate to the satisfaction of the Director or his designee that during the period following the prior authorization, the owner or his designee has hunted bear or deer on the land for which he received a previous authorization.

B. Subject to the provisions of subsection A, the Director or his designee may issue a written authorization to kill deer causing damage to residential plants, whether ornamental, noncommercial agricultural, or other types of residential plants. The Director may charge a fee not to exceed actual costs. The holder of this written authorization shall be subject to local ordinances, including those regulating the discharge of firearms.

C. Whenever wildlife is creating a hazard to the operation of any aircraft or to the facilities connected with the operation of aircraft, the person or persons responsible for the safe operation of the aircraft or facilities shall report such fact to the Director or his designee for investigation. If after investigation the Director or his designee finds that wildlife is creating a hazard, he shall authorize such person or persons or their representatives to kill wildlife when the wildlife is found to be creating such a hazard. As used in this subsection, the term "wildlife" shall not include any federally protected species.

D. Whenever deer are creating a hazard to the operation of motor vehicle traffic within the corporate limits of any city or town, the operator of a motor vehicle or chief law-enforcement officer of the city or town may report such fact to the Director or his designee for investigation. If after investigation the Director or his designee finds that deer are creating a hazard within such city or town, he may authorize responsible persons, or their representatives, to kill the deer when they are found to be creating such a hazard.

E. Whenever deer are damaging property in a locality in which deer herd population reduction has been recommended in the current Deer Management Plan adopted by the Board, the owner or lessee of the lands on which such damage is being done may report such damage to the Director or his designee for investigation. If after investigation the Director or his designee finds that deer are responsible for the damage, he may authorize in writing the owner, lessee or any other person designated by the Director or his designee to kill such deer when they are found upon the land upon which the damages occurred. The Director or his designee also may limit such authorization by specifying in writing the number of animals to be killed and the period of time for which the authorization is effective. The requirement in subsection A of this section, that an owner or lessee of land demonstrate that during the period following the prior authorization deer or bear have been hunted on his land, shall not apply to any locality that conducts a deer population control program authorized by the Department.

F. The Director or his designee may revoke or refuse to reissue any authorization granted under this section when it has been shown by a preponderance of the evidence that an abuse of the authorization has occurred. Such evidence may include a complaint filed by any person with the Department alleging that an abuse of the written authorization has occurred. Any person aggrieved by the issuance, denial or revocation of a written authorization can appeal the decision to the Department of Game and Inland Fisheries. Any person convicted of violating any provision of the hunting and trapping laws and regulations shall be entitled to receive written authorization to kill deer or bear. However, such person shall not (i) be designated as a shooter nor (ii) carry out the authorized activity for a person who has received such written authorization for a period of at least two years and up to five years following his most recent conviction for violating any provision of the hunting and trapping laws and regulations. In determining the appropriate length of this restriction, the Director shall take into account the nature and severity of the most recent violation and of any past violations of the hunting and trapping laws and regulations by the applicant. No person shall be designated as a shooter under this section during a period when such person's hunting license or privileges to hunt have been suspended or revoked.

G. The Director or his designee may authorize, subject to the provisions of this section, the killing of deer over bait within the political boundaries of any city or town, or any county with a special late

antlerless season, in the Commonwealth when requested by a certified letter from the governing body of such locality.

H. The parts of any deer or bear killed pursuant to this section or
wildlife killed pursuant to subsection C shall not be used for the
purposes of taxidermy, mounts, or any public display unless authorized by the Director or his designee. However, the meat of any
such animal may be used for human consumption. The carcass and
any unused meat of any such animal shall be disposed of within 24
hours of being killed. Any person who violates any provision of this
subsection is guilty of a Class 3 misdemeanor.

I. It is unlawful to willfully and intentionally impede any person who
is engaged in the lawful killing of a bear or deer pursuant to written
authorization issued under this section. Any person convicted of a
violation of this subsection is guilty of a Class 3 misdemeanor.

Title 29.1. Game, Inland Fisheries and Boating
Chapter 7. Boating Laws
Article 1. Boat Registration and Identification

§ 29.1-700. Definitions.
As used in this chapter, unless the context clearly requires a different meaning:

"Motorboat" means any vessel propelled by machinery whether or
not the machinery is the principal source of propulsion.

"No wake" means operation of a motorboat at the slowest possible
speed required to maintain steerage and headway.

"Operate" means to navigate or otherwise control the movement
of a motorboat or a vessel.

"Owner" means a person, other than a lien holder, having the property in or title to a motorboat. The term includes a person entitled
to the use or possession of a motorboat subject to an interest in
another person, reserved or created by agreement and securing
payment of performance of an obligation, but the term excludes a
lessee under a lease not intended as security.

"Personal watercraft" means a motorboat less than sixteen feet in length which uses an inboard motor powering a jet pump, as its primary motive power and which is designed to be operated by a person sitting, standing, or kneeling on, rather than in the conventional manner of sitting or standing inside, the vessel.

"Vessel" means every description of watercraft, other than a seaplane on the water, used or capable of being used as a means of transportation on water.

"Waters of the Commonwealth" means any public waters within the territorial limits of the Commonwealth, the adjacent marginal sea and the high seas when navigated as a part of a journey or ride to or from the Virginia shore.

Title 29.1. Game, Inland Fisheries and Boating
Chapter 7. Boating Laws
Article 2.1. Virginia Uniform Certificate of Title for Watercraft Act

§ 29.1-733.2. Definitions.
The definitions in this section do not apply to any Virginia or federal law governing licensing, numbering, or registration if the same term is used in that law. As used in this article, unless the context requires a different meaning: ·

"Abandoned watercraft" means a watercraft that is left unattended on private property for more than 10 days without the consent of the property's owner, regardless of whether it was brought onto the private property with the consent of the owner or person in control of the private property.

"Agreement" means the same as that term is defined in subdivision (b)(3) of § 8.1A-201.

"Barge" means a watercraft that is not self-propelled or fitted for propulsion by sail, paddle, oar, or similar device.

"Builder's certificate" means a certificate of the facts of the build of a vessel described in 46 C.F.R. § 67.99, as amended.

"Buyer" means a person that buys or contracts to buy a watercraft.

"Buyer in ordinary course of business" means the same as that term is defined in subdivision (b)(9) of § 8.1A-201.

"Cancel," with respect to a certificate of title, means to make the certificate ineffective.

"Certificate of origin" means a record created by a manufacturer or importer as the manufacturer's or importer's proof of identity of a watercraft. The term includes a manufacturer's certificate or statement of origin and an importer's certificate or statement of origin. The term does not include a builder's certificate.

"Certificate of title" means a record, created by the Department under this article or by a governmental agency of another jurisdiction under the law of that jurisdiction that is designated as a certificate of title by the Department or agency and is evidence of ownership of a watercraft.

"Conspicuous" means the same as that term is defined in subdivision (b)(10) of § 8.1A-201.

"Consumer goods" means the same as that term is defined in subdivision (a)(23) of § 8.9A-102.

"Dealer" means any watercraft dealer as defined in § 29.1-801.

"Debtor" means the same as that term is defined in subdivision (a) (28) of § 8.9A-102.

"Documented vessel" means a watercraft covered by a certificate of documentation issued pursuant to 46 U.S.C. § 12105, as amended. The term does not include a foreign-documented vessel.

"Electronic" means relating to technology having electrical, digital, magnetic, wireless, optical, electromagnetic, or similar capabilities.

"Electronic certificate of title" means a certificate of title consisting of information that is stored solely in an electronic medium and is retrievable in perceivable form.

"Foreign-documented vessel" means a watercraft whose owner-ship is recorded in a registry maintained by a country other than the United States that identifies each person that has an ownership interest in a watercraft and includes a unique alphanumeric designation for the watercraft.

"Good faith" means honesty in fact and the observance of reasonable commercial standards of fair dealing.

"Hull damaged" means compromised with respect to the integrity of a watercraft's hull by a collision, allision, lightning strike, fire, explosion, running aground, or similar occurrence, or the sinking of a watercraft in a manner that creates a significant risk to the integrity of the watercraft's hull.

"Hull identification number" means the alphanumeric designation assigned to a watercraft pursuant to 33 C.F.R. Part 181, as amended.

"Knowledge" means the same as that term is defined in § 8.1A-202.

"Lease" means the same as that term is defined in subdivision (1) (j) of § 8.2A-103.

"Lessor" means the same as that term is defined in subdivision (1) (p) of § 8.2A-103.

"Lien creditor," with respect to a watercraft, means:
1. A creditor that has acquired a lien on the watercraft by attachment, levy, or the like;
2. An assignee for benefit of creditors from the time of assignment;
3. A trustee in bankruptcy from the date of the filing of the petition; or
4. A receiver in equity from the time of appointment.

"Notice" means the same as that term is defined in § 8.1A-202.

"Owner" means a person that has legal title to a watercraft.

"Owner of record" means the owner indicated in the files of the

Department or, if the files indicate more than one owner, the one first indicated.

"Person" means an individual, corporation, business trust, estate, trust, statutory trust, partnership, limited liability company, association, joint venture, public corporation, government or governmental subdivision, agency or instrumentality, or any other legal or commercial entity.

"Purchase" means to take by sale, lease, mortgage, pledge, consensual lien, security interest, gift, or any other voluntary transaction that creates an interest in a watercraft.

"Purchaser" means a person that takes by purchase.

"Record" means information that is inscribed on a tangible medium or that is stored in an electronic or other medium and is retrievable in perceivable form.

"Registration number" means the alphanumeric designation for a vessel issued pursuant to 46 U.S.C. § 12301, as amended.

"Representative" means the same as that term is defined in subdivision (b)(33) of § 8.1A-201.

"Sale" means the same as that term is defined in § 8.2-106.

"Secured party," with respect to a watercraft, means a person:
 1. In whose favor a security interest is created or provided for under a security agreement, whether or not any obligation to be secured is outstanding;
 2. That is a consignor under Title 8.9A; or
 3. That holds a security interest arising under § 8.2-401 or 8.2-505, subsection (3) of § 8.2-711, or subsection (5) of § 8.2A-508.

"Secured party of record" means the secured party whose name is indicated as the name of the secured party in the files of the Department or, if the files indicate more than one secured party, the one first indicated.

"Security agreement" means the same as that term is defined in subdivision (a)(74) of § 8.9A-102.

"Security interest" means an interest in a watercraft that secures payment or performance of an obligation if the interest is created by contract or arises under § 8.2-401 or 8.2-505, subsection (3) of § 8.2-711, or subsection (5) of § 8.2A-508. The term includes any interest of a consignor in a watercraft in a transaction that is subject to Title 8.9A. The term does not include the special property interest of a buyer of a watercraft on identification of that watercraft to a contract for sale under § 8.2-401, but a buyer also may acquire a security interest by complying with Title 8.9A. Except as otherwise provided in § 8.2-505, the right of a seller or lessor of a watercraft under Title 8.2 or Title 8.2A to retain or acquire possession of the watercraft is not a security interest, but a seller or lessor also may acquire a security interest by complying with Title 8.9A. The retention or reservation of title by a seller of a watercraft notwithstanding shipment or delivery to the buyer under § 8.2-401 is limited in effect to a reservation of a security interest. Whether a transaction in the form of a lease creates a security interest is determined by § 8.1A-304.

"Seller" means the same as that term is defined in subdivision (1)(o) of § 8.2A-103.

"Send" means the same as that term is defined in subdivision (b)(36) of § 8.1A-201.

"Sign" means, with present intent to authenticate or adopt a record, to:
    1. Make or adopt a tangible symbol; or
    2. Attach to or logically associate with the record an electronic symbol, sound, or process.

"State" means a state of the United States, the District of Columbia, Puerto Rico, the United States Virgin Islands, or any territory or insular possession subject to the jurisdiction of the United States.

"State of principal use" means the state on whose waters a watercraft is or will be used, operated, navigated, or employed more than on the waters of any other state during a calendar year.

"Title brand" means a designation of previous damage, use, or condition that shall be indicated on a certificate of title.

"Transfer of ownership" means a voluntary or involuntary conveyance of an interest in a watercraft.

"Value" means the same as that term is defined in § 8.1A-204.

"Watercraft" means any vessel that is used or capable of being used as a means of transportation on water and is propelled by machinery, whether or not the machinery is the principal source of propulsion, except:
1. A seaplane;
2. An amphibious vehicle for which a certificate of title is issued pursuant to Chapter 6 (§ 46.2-600 et seq.) of Title 46.2 or a similar statute of another state;
3. A vessel that measures 18 feet or less in length along the centerline and is propelled by sail;
4. A vessel that operates only on a permanently fixed, manufactured course and whose movement is restricted to or guided by means of a mechanical device to which the vessel is attached or by which the vessel is controlled;
5. A stationary floating structure that:
    a. Does not have and is not designed to have a mode of propulsion of its own;
    b. Is dependent for utilities upon a continuous utility hookup to a source originating on shore; and
    c. Has a permanent, continuous hookup to a shoreside sewage system;
6. A vessel owned by the United States, a state, or a foreign government or a political subdivision of any of them;
7. A vessel used solely as a lifeboat on another vessel; or
8. A vessel that has a valid marine document issued by the United States Coast Guard.

"Written certificate of title" means a certificate of title consisting of information inscribed on a tangible medium.

Title 37.2. Behavioral Health and Developmental Services
Chapter 8. Emergency Custody and Voluntary and Involuntary Civil Admissions
Article 2. Voluntary Admission

§ 37.2-805. Voluntary admission.

Any state facility shall admit any person requesting admission who has been (i) screened by the community services board or behavioral health authority that serves the county or city where the person resides or, if impractical, where the person is located, (ii) examined by a physician on the staff of the state facility, and (iii) deemed by the board or authority and the state facility physician to be in need of treatment, training, or habilitation in a state facility. Upon motion of the treating physician, a family member or personal representative of the person, or the community services board serving the county or city where the facility is located, the county or city where the person resides, or the county or city where the person receives treatment, a hearing shall be held prior to the release date of any person who has been the subject of a temporary detention order and voluntarily admitted himself in accordance with subsection B of § 37.2-814 to determine whether such person should be ordered to mandatory outpatient treatment pursuant to subsection D of § 37.2-817 upon his release if such person, on at least two previous occasions within 36 months preceding the date of the hearing, has been (a) the subject of a temporary detention order and voluntarily admitted himself in accordance with subsection B of § 37.2-814 or (b) involuntarily admitted pursuant to § 37.2-817. A district court judge or special justice shall hold the hearing within 72 hours after receiving the motion for a mandatory outpatient treatment order; however, if the 72-hour period expires on a Saturday, Sunday, or legal holiday, the hearing shall be held by the close of business on the next day that is not a Saturday, Sunday, or legal holiday.

Title 37.2. Behavioral Health and Developmental Services
Chapter 8. Emergency Custody and Voluntary and Involuntary Civil Admissions
Article 4. Emergency Custody and Involuntary Temporary Detention

§ 37.2-809. Involuntary temporary detention; issuance and execution of order.

A. For the purposes of this section:

"Designee of the local community services board" means an examiner designated by the local community services board who (i) is skilled in the assessment and treatment of mental illness, (ii) has completed a certification program approved by the Department, (iii) is able to provide an independent examination of the person, (iv) is not related by blood or marriage to the person being evaluated, (v) has no financial interest in the admission or treatment of the person being evaluated, (vi) has no investment interest in the facility detaining or admitting the person under this article, and (vii) except for employees of state hospitals and of the U.S. Department of Veterans Affairs, is not employed by the facility.

"Employee" means an employee of the local community services board who is skilled in the assessment and treatment of mental illness and has completed a certification program approved by the Department.

"Investment interest" means the ownership or holding of an equity or debt security, including shares of stock in a corporation, interests or units of a partnership, bonds, debentures, notes, or other equity or debt instruments.

B. A magistrate shall issue, upon the sworn petition of any responsible person, treating physician, or upon his own motion and only after an evaluation conducted in-person or by means of a two-way electronic video and audio communication system as authorized in § 37.2-804.1 by an employee or a designee of the local community services board to determine whether the person meets the criteria for temporary detention, a temporary detention order if it appears from all evidence readily available, including any recommendation from a physician or clinical psychologist treating the person, that the person (i) has a mental illness and that there exists a substantial likelihood that, as a result of mental illness, the person will, in the near future, (a) cause serious physical harm to himself or others as evidenced by recent behavior causing, attempting, or threatening harm and other relevant information, if any, or (b) suffer serious harm due to his lack of capacity to protect himself from harm or to provide for his basic human needs; (ii) is in need of hospitalization or treatment; and (iii) is unwilling to volunteer or incapable of volunteering for hospitalization or treatment. The magistrate shall also consider, if available, (a) information provided by the person who initiated emergency custody and (b) the recommendations of any treating or examining physician licensed in Virginia either verbally or in writing prior to rendering a decision. Any temporary detention order entered pursuant to this section shall provide for the disclosure of medical records pursuant to § 37.2-804.2. This subsection shall not preclude any other disclosures as required or permitted by law.

C. When considering whether there is probable cause to issue a temporary detention order, the magistrate may, in addition to the petition, consider (i) the recommendations of any treating or examining physician or psychologist licensed in Virginia, if available, (ii) any past actions of the person, (iii) any past mental health treatment of the person, (iv) any relevant hearsay evidence, (v) any medical records available, (vi) any affidavits submitted, if the witness is unavailable and it so states in the affidavit, and (vii) any other information available that the magistrate considers relevant to the determination of whether probable cause exists to issue a temporary detention order.

D. A magistrate may issue a temporary detention order without an emergency custody order proceeding. A magistrate may issue a temporary detention order without a prior evaluation pursuant to subsection B if (i) the person has been personally examined within the previous 72 hours by an employee or a designee of the local community services board or (ii) there is a significant physical, psychological, or medical risk to the person or to others associated with conducting such evaluation.

E. An employee or a designee of the local community services board shall determine the facility of temporary detention in accordance with the provisions of § 37.2-809.1 for all individuals detained pursuant to this section. An employee or designee of the local community services board may change the facility of temporary detention and may designate an alternative facility for temporary detention at any point during the period of temporary detention if it is determined that the alternative facility is a more appropriate facility for temporary detention of the individual given the specific security, medical, or behavioral health needs of the person. In cases in which the facility of temporary detention is changed following transfer of custody to an initial facility of temporary custody, transportation of the individual to the alternative facility of temporary detention shall be provided in accordance with the provisions of § 37.2-810. The initial facility of temporary detention shall be identified on the preadmission screening report and indicated on the temporary detention order; however, if an employee or designee of the local community services board designates an alternative facility, that employee or designee shall provide written notice forthwith, on a form developed by the Executive Secretary of the Supreme Court of Virginia, to the clerk of the issuing court of the name and address of the alternative facility. Subject to the provisions of § 37.2-809.1, if a facility of temporary detention cannot be identified by the time of the expiration of the period of emergency custody pursuant to § 37.2-808, the individual shall be detained in a state facility for the treatment of individuals with mental illness and such facility shall be indicated on the temporary detention order. Except as provided in § 37.2-811 for inmates requiring hospitalization in accordance with subdivision A 2 of § 19.2-169.6, the person shall not be detained in a jail or other place of confinement for persons charged with criminal offenses and shall remain in the custody of law enforcement until the person is either detained within a secure facility or custody has been accepted by the appropriate personnel designated by either the initial facility of temporary detention identified in the temporary detention order or by the alternative facility of temporary detention designated by the employee or designee of the local community services board pursuant to this subsection. The person detained or in custody pursuant to this section shall be given a written summary of the temporary detention procedures and the statutory protections associated with those procedures.

F. Any facility caring for a person placed with it pursuant to a temporary detention order is authorized to provide emergency medical and psychiatric services within its capabilities when the facility determines that the services are in the best interests of the person within its care. The costs incurred as a result of the hearings and by the facility in providing services during the period of temporary detention shall be paid and recovered pursuant to § 37.2-804. The maximum costs reimbursable by the Commonwealth pursuant to this section shall be established by the State Board of Medical Assistance Services based on reasonable criteria. The State Board of Medical Assistance Services shall, by regulation, establish a reasonable rate per day of inpatient care for temporary detention.

G. The employee or the designee of the local community services board who is conducting the evaluation pursuant to this section shall determine, prior to the issuance of the temporary detention order, the insurance status of the person. Where coverage by a third party payor exists, the facility seeking reimbursement under this section shall first seek reimbursement from the third party payor. The Commonwealth shall reimburse the facility only for the balance of costs remaining after the allowances covered by the third party payor have been received.

H. The duration of temporary detention shall be sufficient to allow for completion of the examination required by § 37.2-815, preparation of the preadmission screening report required by § 37.2-816, and initiation of mental health treatment to stabilize the person's psychiatric condition to avoid involuntary commitment where possible, but shall not exceed 72 hours prior to a hearing. If the 72-hour period herein specified terminates on a Saturday, Sunday, legal holiday, or day on which the court is lawfully closed, the person may be detained, as herein provided, until the close of business on the next day that is not a Saturday, Sunday, legal holiday, or day on which the court is lawfully closed. The person may be released, pursuant to § 37.2-813, before the 72-hour period herein specified has run.

I. If a temporary detention order is not executed within 24 hours of its issuance, or within a shorter period as is specified in the order, the order shall be void and shall be returned unexecuted to the office of the clerk of the issuing court or, if the office is not open, to any magistrate serving the jurisdiction of the issuing court. Subsequent orders may be issued upon the original petition within 96 hours after the petition is filed. However, a magistrate must again obtain the advice of an employee or a designee of the local community services board prior to issuing a subsequent order upon the original petition. Any petition for which no temporary detention order or other process in connection therewith is served on the subject of the petition within 96 hours after the petition is filed shall be void and shall be returned to the office of the clerk of the issuing court.

J. The Executive Secretary of the Supreme Court of Virginia shall establish and require that a magistrate, as provided by this section, be available seven days a week, 24 hours a day, for the purpose of performing the duties established by this section. Each community services board shall provide to each general district court and magistrate's office within its service area a list of its employees and designees who are available to perform the evaluations required herein.

K. For purposes of this section, a health care provider or designee of a local community services board or behavioral health authority shall not be required to encrypt any email containing information or medical records provided to a magistrate unless there is reason to believe that a third party will attempt to intercept the email.

L. If the employee or designee of the community services board who is conducting the evaluation pursuant to this section recommends that the person should not be subject to a temporary detention order, such employee or designee shall (i) inform the petitioner, the person who initiated emergency custody if such person is present, and an onsite treating physician of his recommendation; (ii) promptly inform such person who initiated emergency custody that the community services board will facilitate communication between the person and the magistrate if the person disagrees with recommendations of the employee or designee of the community services board who conducted the evaluation and the person who initiated emergency custody so requests; and (iii) upon prompt request made by the person who initiated emergency custody, arrange for such person who initiated emergency custody to communicate with the magistrate as soon as is practicable and prior to the expiration of the period of emergency custody. The magistrate shall consider any information provided by the person who initiated emergency custody and any recommendations of the treating or examining physician and the employee or designee of the community services board who conducted the evaluation and consider such information and recommendations in accordance with subsection B in making his determination to issue a temporary detention order. The individual who is the subject of emergency custody shall remain in the custody of law enforcement or a designee of law enforcement and shall not be released from emergency custody until communication with the magistrate pursuant to this subsection has concluded and the magistrate has made a determination regarding issuance of a temporary detention order.

M. For purposes of this section, "person who initiated emergency custody" means any person who initiated the issuance of an emergency custody order pursuant to § 37.2-808 or a law-enforcement officer who takes a person into custody pursuant to subsection G of § 37.2-808.

Title 37.2. Behavioral Health and Developmental Services
Chapter 8. Emergency Custody and Voluntary and Involuntary Civil Admissions
Article 5. Involuntary Admissions

§ 37.2-814. Commitment hearing for involuntary admission; written explanation; right to counsel; rights of petitioner.
A. The commitment hearing for involuntary admission shall be held after a sufficient period of time has passed to allow for completion of the examination required by § 37.2-815, preparation of the pre-admission screening report required by § 37.2-816, and initiation of mental health treatment to stabilize the person's psychiatric condition to avoid involuntary commitment where possible, but shall be held within 72 hours of the execution of the temporary detention order as provided for in § 37.2-809; however, if the 72-hour period herein specified terminates on a Saturday, Sunday, legal holiday, or day on which the court is lawfully closed, the person may be detained, as herein provided, until the close of business on the next day that is not a Saturday, Sunday, legal holiday, or day on which the court is lawfully closed.

B. At the commencement of the commitment hearing, the district court judge or special justice shall inform the person whose involuntary admission is being sought of his right to apply for voluntary admission for inpatient treatment as provided for in § 37.2-805 and shall afford the person an opportunity for voluntary admission. The district court judge or special justice shall advise the person whose involuntary admission is being sought that if the person chooses to be voluntarily admitted pursuant to § 37.2-805, such person will be prohibited from possessing, purchasing, or transporting a firearm pursuant to § 18.2-308.1:3. The judge or special justice shall ascertain if the person is then willing and capable of seeking voluntary admission for inpatient treatment. In determining whether a person is capable of consenting to voluntary admission, the judge or special justice may consider evidence regarding the person's past compliance or noncompliance with treatment. If the judge or special justice finds that the person is capable and willingly accepts voluntary admission for inpatient treatment, the judge or special justice shall require him to accept voluntary admission for a minimum period of treatment not to exceed 72 hours. After such minimum period of treatment, the person shall give the facility 48 hours' notice prior to leaving the facility. During this notice period, the person shall not be discharged except as provided in § 37.2-837, 37.2-838, or 37.2-840. The person shall be subject to the transportation provisions as provided in § 37.2-829 and the requirement for preadmission screening by a community services board as provided in § 37.2-805.

C. If a person is incapable of accepting or unwilling to accept voluntary admission and treatment, the judge or special justice shall inform the person of his right to a commitment hearing and right to counsel. The judge or special justice shall ascertain if the person whose admission is sought is represented by counsel, and, if he is not represented by counsel, the judge or special justice shall appoint an attorney to represent him. However, if the person requests an opportunity to employ counsel, the judge or special justice shall give him a reasonable opportunity to employ counsel at his own expense.

D. A written explanation of the involuntary admission process and the statutory protections associated with the process shall be given to the person, and its contents shall be explained by an attorney prior to the commitment hearing. The written explanation shall describe, at a minimum, the person's rights to (i) retain private counsel or be represented by a court-appointed attorney, (ii) present any defenses including independent evaluation and expert testimony or the testimony of other witnesses, (iii) be present during the hearing and testify, (iv) appeal any order for involuntary admission to the circuit court, and (v) have a jury trial on appeal. The judge or special justice shall ascertain whether the person whose involuntary admission is sought has been given the written explanation required herein.

E. To the extent possible, during or before the commitment hearing, the attorney for the person whose involuntary admission is sought shall interview his client, the petitioner, the examiner described in § 37.2-815, the community services board staff, and any other material witnesses. He also shall examine all relevant diagnostic and other reports, present evidence and witnesses, if any, on his client's behalf, and otherwise actively represent his client in the proceedings. A health care provider shall disclose or make available all such reports, treatment information, and records concerning his client to the attorney, upon request. The role of the attorney shall be to represent the wishes of his client, to the extent possible.

F. The petitioner shall be given adequate notice of the place, date, and time of the commitment hearing. The petitioner shall be entitled to retain counsel at his own expense, to be present during the hearing, and to testify and present evidence. The petitioner shall be encouraged but shall not be required to testify at the hearing, and the person whose involuntary admission is sought shall not be released solely on the basis of the petitioner's failure to attend or testify during the hearing.

Title 54.1. Professions and Occupations
Chapter 42. Dealers in Firearms

§ 54.1-4201.2. Firearm transactions by persons other than dealers; voluntary background checks.
A. The Department of State Police shall be available at every firearms show held in the Commonwealth to make determinations in accordance with the procedures set out in § 18.2-308.2:2 of whether a prospective purchaser or transferee is prohibited under state or federal law from possessing a firearm. The Department of State Police shall establish policies and procedures in accordance with 28 C.F.R. § 25.6 to permit such determinations to be made by the Department of State Police.

Unless otherwise required by state or federal law, any party involved in the transaction may decide whether or not to have such a determination made.

The Department of State Police may charge a reasonable fee for the determination.

B. The promoter, as defined in § 54.1-4201.1, shall give the Department of State Police notice of the time and location of a firearms show at least 30 days prior to the show. The promoter shall provide the Department of State Police with adequate space, at no charge, to conduct such prohibition determinations. The promoter shall ensure that a notice that such determinations are available is prominently displayed at the show.

C. No person who sells or transfers a firearm at a firearms show after receiving a determination from the Department of State Police that the purchaser or transferee is not prohibited by state or federal law from possessing a firearm shall be liable for selling or transferring a firearm to such person.

D. The provisions of § 18.2-308.2:2, including definitions, procedures, and prohibitions, shall apply, mutatis mutandis, to the provisions of this section.

APPENDIX B

SELECTED FEDERAL FORMS

ATF Form 4473, page 1

U.S. Department of Justice Bureau of Alcohol, Tobacco, Firearms and Explosives	OMB No. 1140-0020 **Firearms Transaction Record**

	Transferor's/Seller's Transaction Serial Number *(If any)*
WARNING: You may not receive a firearm if prohibited by Federal or State law. The information you provide will be used to determine whether you are prohibited from receiving a firearm. Certain violations of the Gun Control Act, 18 U.S.C. 921 et. seq., are punishable by up to 10 years imprisonment and/or up to a $250,000 fine.	

Read the Notices, Instructions, and Definitions on this form. Prepare in original only at the licensed premises *("licensed premises" includes business temporarily conducted from a qualifying gun show or event in the same State in which the licensed premises is located)* unless the transaction qualifies under 18 U.S.C. 922(c). All entries must be handwritten in ink. **"PLEASE PRINT."**

Section A - Must Be Completed Personally By Transferee/Buyer

1. Transferee's/Buyer's Full Name *(If legal name contains an initial only, record "IO" after the initial. If no middle initial or name, record "NMN".)*
Last Name *(Including suffix (e.g., Jr, Sr, II, III))* | First Name | Middle Name

2. Current State of Residence and Address **(U.S. Postal abbreviations are acceptable. Cannot be a post office box.)**
Number and Street Address | City | County | State | ZIP Code

3. Place of Birth: U.S. City and State **-OR-** Foreign Country | 4. Height Ft. In. | 5. Weight *(Lbs.)* | 6. Sex □ Male □ Female | 7. Birth Date Month Day Year

8. Social Security Number *(Optional, but will help prevent misidentification)* | 9. Unique Personal Identification Number *(UPIN)* if applicable *(See Instructions for Question 9.)*

10.a. Ethnicity: □ Hispanic or Latino □ Not Hispanic or Latino
10.b. Race *(In addition to ethnicity, select one or more race in 10.b. Both 10.a. and 10.b. must be answered.)* □ American Indian or Alaska Native □ Asian □ Black or African American □ Native Hawaiian or Other Pacific Islander □ White

11. Answer the following questions by checking or marking "yes" or "no" in the boxes to the right of the questions.

		Yes	No
a.	Are you the actual transferee/buyer of the firearm(s) listed on this form? **Warning: You are not the actual transferee/buyer if you are acquiring the firearm(s) on behalf of another person. If you are not the actual transferee/buyer, the licensee cannot transfer the firearm(s) to you.** *Exception: If you are picking up a repaired firearm(s) for another person, you are not required to answer 11.a. and may proceed to question 11.b. (See Instructions for Question 11.a.)*	□	□
b.	Are you under indictment or information in any court for a **felony**, or any other crime for which the judge could imprison you for more than one year? *(See Instructions for Question 11.b.)*	□	□
c.	Have you ever been convicted in any court of a **felony**, or any other crime for which the judge could have imprisoned you for more than one year, even if you received a shorter sentence including probation? *(See Instructions for Question 11.c.)*	□	□
d.	Are you a fugitive from justice? *(See Instructions for Question 11.d.)*	□	□
e.	Are you an unlawful user of, or addicted to, marijuana or any depressant, stimulant, narcotic drug, or any other controlled substance? **Warning: The use or possession of marijuana remains unlawful under Federal law regardless of whether it has been legalized or decriminalized for medicinal or recreational purposes in the state where you reside.**	□	□
f.	Have you ever been adjudicated as a mental defective **OR** have you ever been committed to a mental institution? *(See Instructions for Question 11.f.)*	□	□
g.	Have you been discharged from the Armed Forces under **dishonorable** conditions?	□	□
h.	Are you subject to a court order restraining you from harassing, stalking, or threatening your child or an intimate partner or child of such partner? *(See Instructions for Question 11.h.)*	□	□
i.	Have you ever been **convicted** in any court of a misdemeanor crime of domestic violence? *(See Instructions for Question 11.i.)*	□	□

12.a. Country of Citizenship: *(Check/List more than one, if applicable. Nationals of the United States may check U.S.A.)* □ United States of America *(U.S.A)* □ Other Country/Countries (Specify):

		Yes	No
12.b.	Have you ever renounced your United States citizenship?	□	□
12.c.	Are you an alien **illegally** or **unlawfully** in the United States?	□	□
12.d.1.	Are you an alien who has been admitted to the United States under a nonimmigrant visa? *(See Instructions for Question 12.d.)*	□	□
12.d.2.	If "yes", do you fall within any of the exceptions stated in the instructions? □ N/A	□	□

13. If you are an alien, record your U.S.-Issued Alien or Admission number *(AR#, USCIS#, or I94#)*:

Previous Editions Are Obsolete Page 1 of 6	**Transferee/Buyer Continue to Next Page** **STAPLE IF PAGES BECOME SEPARATED**	ATF Form 4473 (5300.9) Revised October 2016

ATF Form 4473, page 2

I certify that my answers in Section A are true, correct, and complete. I have read and understand the Notices, Instructions, and Definitions on ATF Form 4473. I understand that answering "yes" to question 11.a. if I am not the actual transferee/buyer is a crime punishable as a felony under Federal law, and may also violate State and/or local law. I understand that a person who answers "yes" to any of the questions 11.b. through 11.i and/or 12.b. through 12.c. is prohibited from purchasing or receiving a firearm. I understand that a person who answers "yes" to question 12.d.1. is prohibited from receiving or possessing a firearm, unless the person answers "yes" to question 12.d.2. and provides the documentation required in 18.c. I also understand that making any false oral or written statement, or exhibiting any false or misrepresented identification with respect to this transaction, is a crime punishable as a felony under Federal law, and may also violate State and/or local law. I further understand that the repetitive purchase of firearms for the purpose of resale for livelihood and profit without a Federal firearms license is a violation of Federal law. *(See Instructions for Question 14.)*

14. Transferee's/Buyer's Signature	15. Certification Date

Section B - Must Be Completed By Transferor/Seller	
16. Type of firearm(s) to be transferred *(check or mark all that apply)*: ☐ Handgun ☐ Long Gun *(rifles or shotguns)* ☐ Other Firearm *(frame, receiver, etc. See Instructions for Question 16.)*	17. If transfer is at a qualifying gun show or event: Name of Function: _____ City, State: _____

18.a. Identification *(e.g., Virginia Driver's license (VA DL) or other valid government-issued photo identification.)* *(See Instructions for Question 18.a.)*

Issuing Authority and Type of Identification	Number on Identification	Expiration Date of Identification *(if any)*		
		Month	Day	Year

18.b. Supplemental Government Issued Documentation *(if identification document does not show current residence address)* *(See Instructions for Question 18.b.)*

18.c. Exception to the Nonimmigrant Alien Prohibition: If the transferee/buyer answered "YES" to 12.d.2. the transferor/seller must record the type of documentation showing the exception to the prohibition and attach a copy to this ATF Form 4473. *(See Instructions for Question 18.c.)*

Questions 19, 20, or 21 Must Be Completed Prior To The Transfer Of The Firearm(s) *(See Instructions for Questions 19, 20 and 21.)*	
19.a. Date the transferee's/buyer's identifying information in Section A was transmitted to NICS or the appropriate State agency: Month Day Year	19.b. The NICS or State transaction number *(if provided)* was:
19.c. The response initially (first) provided by NICS or the appropriate State agency was: ☐ Proceed ☐ Delayed ☐ Denied *[The firearm(s) may be transferred on* ☐ Cancelled *_____ if State law permits (optional)]*	19.d. The following response(s) was/were later received from NICS or the appropriate State agency: ☐ Proceed _____ *(date)* ☐ Overturned ☐ Denied _____ *(date)* ☐ Cancelled _____ *(date)* ☐ No response was provided within 3 business days.

19.e. *(Complete if applicable.)* After the firearm was transferred, the following response was received from NICS or the appropriate State agency on: _____ *(date)*. ☐ Proceed ☐ Denied ☐ Cancelled

19.f. The name and Brady identification number of the NICS examiner. *(Optional)* _____ *(name)* _____ *(number)*	19.g. Name of FFL Employee Completing NICS check. *(Optional)*

20. ☐ No NICS check was required because a background check was completed during the NFA approval process on the individual who will receive the NFA firearm(s), as reflected on the approved NFA application. *(See Instructions for Question 20.)*

21. ☐ No NICS check was required because the transferee/buyer has a valid permit from the State where the transfer is to take place, which qualifies as an exemption to NICS. *(See Instructions for Question 21.)*

Issuing State and Permit Type	Date of Issuance *(if any)*	Expiration Date *(if any)*	Permit Number *(if any)*

Section C - Must Be Completed Personally By Transferee/Buyer
If the transfer of the firearm(s) takes place on a different day from the date the transferee/buyer signed Section A, the transferee/buyer must complete Section C immediately prior to the transfer of the firearm(s). *(See Instructions for Question 22 and 23.)*
I certify that my answers to the questions in Section A of this form are still true, correct, and complete.

22. Transferee's/Buyer's Signature	23. Recertification Date

Transferor/Seller Continue to Next Page
STAPLE IF PAGES BECOME SEPARATED

ATF Form 4473 (5300.9)
Revised October 2016

ATF Form 4473, page 3

Section D - Must Be Completed By Transferor /Seller Even If The Firearm(s) is Not Transferred

24. Manufacturer and Importer (If any) (If the manufacturer and importer are different, the FFL must include both.)	25. Model (If Designated)	26. Serial Number	27. Type (See Instructions for Question 27.)	28. Caliber or Gauge
1.				
2.				
3.				
4.				

REMINDER - By the Close of Business Complete ATF Form 3310.4 For Multiple Purchases of Handguns Within 5 Consecutive Business Days

29. Total Number of Firearms Transferred (Please handwrite by printing e.g., zero, one, two, three, etc. **Do not use numerals.**)	30. Check if any part of this transaction is a pawn redemption. ☐ Line Number(s) From Question 24 Above:
31. For Use by Licensee (See Instructions for Question 31.)	32. Check if this transaction is to facilitate a private party transfer. ☐ (See Instructions for Question 32.)

33. Trade/corporate name and address of transferor/seller and Federal Firearm License Number (Must contain at least first three and last five digits of FFL Number X-XX-XXXXX.) (Hand stamp may be used.)

The Person Transferring The Firearm(s) Must Complete Questions 34-37.
For Denied/Cancelled Transactions, the Person Who Completed Section B Must Complete Questions 34-36.

I certify that: (1) I have read and understand the Notices, Instructions, and Definitions on this ATF Form 4473; (2) the information recorded in Sections B and D is true, correct, and complete; and (3) this entire transaction record has been completed at my licensed business premises ("licensed premises" includes business temporarily conducted from a qualifying gun show or event in the same State in which the licensed premises is located) unless this transaction has met the requirements of 18 U.S.C. 922(c). Unless this transaction has been denied or cancelled, I further certify on the basis of — (1) the transferee's/buyer's responses in Section A (and Section C, if applicable); (2) my verification of the identification recorded in question 18 (and my re-verification at the time of transfer, if Section C was completed); and (3) State or local law applicable to the firearms business — it is my belief that it is not unlawful for me to sell, deliver, transport, or otherwise dispose of the firearm(s) listed on this form to the person identified in Section A.

34. Transferor's/Seller's Name (Please print)	35. Transferor's/Seller's Signature	36. Transferor's/Seller's Title	37. Date Transferred

NOTICES, INSTRUCTIONS, AND DEFINITIONS

Purpose of the Form: The information and certification on this form are designed so that a person licensed under 18 U.S.C. 923 may determine if he/she may lawfully sell or deliver a firearm to the person identified in Section A, and to alert the transferee/buyer of certain restrictions on the receipt and possession of firearms. The transferor/seller of a firearm must determine the lawfulness of the transaction and maintain proper records of the transaction. Consequently, the transferor/seller must be familiar with the provisions of 18 U.S.C. 921-931 and the regulations in 27 CFR Parts 478 and 479. In determining the lawfulness of the sale or delivery of a rifle or shotgun to a resident of another State, the transferor/seller is presumed to know the applicable State laws and published ordinances in both the transferor's/seller's State and the transferee's/buyer's State. (See ATF Publication 5300.5, State Laws and Published Ordinances.)

Generally, ATF Form 4473 must be completed at the licensed business premises when a firearm is transferred over-the-counter. Federal law, 18 U.S.C. 922(c), allows a licensed importer, manufacturer, or dealer to sell a firearm to a nonlicensee who does not appear in person at the licensee's business premises only if the transferee/buyer meets certain requirements. These requirements are set forth in section 922(c), 27 CFR 478.96(b), and ATF Procedure 2013-2.

After the transferor/seller has completed the firearms transaction, he/she must make the completed, original ATF Form 4473 (which includes the Notices, General Instructions, and Definitions), and any supporting documents, part of his/her permanent records. Such Forms 4473 must be retained for at least 20 years and after that period may be submitted to ATF. Filing may be chronological (by date of disposition), alphabetical (by name of purchaser), or numerical (by transaction serial number), as long as all of the transferor's/seller's completed Forms 4473 are filed in the same manner.

FORMS 4473 FOR DENIED/CANCELLED TRANSFERS MUST BE RETAINED: If the transfer of a firearm is denied/cancelled by NICS, or if for any other reason the transfer is not completed after a NICS check is initiated, the licensee must retain the ATF Form 4473 in his/her records for at least 5 years. Forms 4473 with respect to which a sale, delivery, or transfer did not take place shall be separately retained in alphabetical (by name of transferee) or chronological (by date of transferee's certification) order.

If the transferor/seller or the transferee/buyer discovers that an ATF Form 4473 is incomplete or improperly completed after the firearm was transferred, and the transferor/seller or the transferee/buyer wishes to correct the omission(s) or error(s), photocopy the inaccurate form and make any necessary additions or revisions to the photocopy. The transferor/seller should only make changes to Sections B and D. The transferee/buyer should only make changes to Section A and C. Whoever made the changes should initial and date the changes. The corrected photocopy should be attached to the original Form 4473 and retained as part of the transferor's/seller's permanent records.

Exportation of Firearms: The State or Commerce Departments may require a firearms exporter to obtain a license prior to export. **Warning:** Any person who exports a firearm without proper authorization may be fined not more than $1,000,000 and/or imprisoned for not more than 20 years. See 22 U.S.C. 2778(c).

Section A

The transferee/buyer must personally complete Section A of this form and certify (sign) that the answers are true, correct, and complete. However, if the transferee/buyer is unable to read and/or write, the answers (other than the signature) may be completed by another person, excluding the transferor/seller. Two persons (other than the transferor/seller) must then sign as witnesses to the transferee's/buyer's answers and signature/certification in question 14.

Page 3 of 6

ATF Form 4473 (5300.9)
Revised October 2016

ATF Form 4, page 1

U.S. Department of Justice
Bureau of Alcohol, Tobacco, Firearms and Explosives

OMB No. 1140-0014 (06/30/2019)

Application for Tax Paid Transfer and Registration of Firearm

ATF Control Number

National Firearms Act Branch
SUBMIT in DUPLICATE to: Bureau of Alcohol, Tobacco, Firearms and Explosives, P.O. Box 530298, Atlanta, GA 30353-0298

1. Type of Transfer *(Check one)*
☐ $5   ☐ $200

Submit the appropriate tax payment with the application. The tax may be paid by credit or debit card, check, or money order. Please complete item 20. Upon approval of the application, we will affix and cancel the required National Firearms Act stamp. *(See instructions 2b, 2i and 3)*

2a. Transferee's Name and Address *(Include trade name, if any) (See instruction 2d)*

☐ INDIVIDUAL   ☐ TRUST or LEGAL ENTITY

2b. County

3a. Transferor's Name and Address *(Include trade name, if any) (Executors: see instruction 2k)*

3b. e-mail address *(optional)*

3c. Transferor's Telephone *(Area Code and Number)*

3d. If Applicable: Decedent's Name, Address, and Date of Death

3e. Number, Street, City, State and Zip Code of Residence *(or Firearms Business Premises)* If Different from Item 3a.

The above-named and undersigned transferor hereby makes application as required by Section 5812 of the National Firearms Act to transfer and register the firearm described below to the transferee.

4. Description of Firearm *(Complete items a through h) (See instruction 2m)*

a. Name and Address of Maker, Manufacturer and/or Importer of Firearm	b. Type of Firearm *(See definitions)*	c. Caliber or Gauge	d. Model
			e. Of Barrel:
			f. Overall:
		Length *(Inches)*	g. Serial Number

h. Additional Description or Data Appearing on Firearm *(Attach additional sheet if necessary)*

5. Transferee's Federal Firearms License *(If any)* *(Give complete 15-digit number) (See instruction 2c)*

| First 6 digits | 2 digits | 2 digits | 5 digits |

6. Transferee's Special (Occupational) Tax Status *(If any)*
a. Employer Identification Number   b. Class

7. Transferor's Federal Firearms License *(If any)*

| First 6 digits | 2 digits | 2 digits | 5 digits |

8. Transferor's Special (Occupational) Tax Status *(If any)*
a. Employer Identification Number   b. Class

Under Penalties of Perjury, I Declare that I have examined this application, and to the best of my knowledge and belief it is true, correct and complete, and that the transfer of the described firearm to the transferee and receipt and possession of it by the transferee are not prohibited by the provisions of Title 18, United States Code, Chap 44; Title 26, United States Code, Chap 53; or any provisions of State or local law.

9. Signature of Transferor *(Or authorized official)*

10. Name and Title of Authorized Official *(Print or type)*   11. Date

The Space Below is for the use of the Bureau of Alcohol, Tobacco, Firearms and Explosives

By Authority of The Director, This Application Has Been Examined, and the Transfer and Registration of the Firearm Described Herein and the Interstate Movement of that Firearm, When Applicable to the Transferee are:

Stamp Denomination

☐ Approved *(With the following conditions, if any)*   ☐ Disapproved *(For the following reasons)*

Signature of Authorized ATF Official   Date

Previous Editions are Obsolete   ATF Copy   ATF E-Form 4 (5320.4) Revised May 2016

ATF Form 4, page 2

Transferee Certification

12. Law Enforcement Notification *(See instruction 2f)*

The transferee is to provide notification of the proposed acquisition and possession of the firearm described on this Form 4 by providing a copy of the completed form to the chief law enforcement officer in the agency identified below.

Agency or Department Name | Name and Title of Official

Address (Street address or P.O. Box, City, State and Zip Code) to which sent (mailed or delivered))

Information for the Chief Law Enforcement Officer

This form provides notification of the transferee's intent to acquire and possess a National Firearms Act (NFA) firearm. No action on your part is required. However, should you have information that may disqualify this person from acquiring or possessing a firearm, please contact the NFA Branch at (304) 616-4500 or NFA @atf.gov. A "Yes" answer to items 14.a through 14.h or 16.a or 16.b could disqualify a person from acquiring or possessing a firearm. Also, ATF will not approve an application if the transfer or possession of the firearm is in violation of State or local law.

13. Transferee Necessity Statement *(See instruction 2e)*

I, _____ , have a reasonable necessity to possess the machinegun, short-barreled rifle,
(Name and Title of Transferee)
short-barreled shotgun, or destructive device described on this application for the following reason(s) _____

and my possession of the device or weapon would be consistent with public safety (18 U.S.C. § 922(b) (4) and 27 CFR § 4 /8.98).

Transferee Questions (Complete Only When Transferee is An Individual)

14. Answer questions 14.a. through 14.h. Answer questions 16 through 17 if applicable. For any "Yes" answer the transferee shall provide details on a separate sheet. *(See instruction 7b and definitions)*

		Yes	No	15. Photograph
a.	Are you under indictment or information in any court for a felony, or any other crime, for which the judge could imprison you for more than one year? *(See definition 1m)*			
b.	Have you ever been convicted in any court for a felony, or any other crime, for which the judge could have imprisoned you for more than one year, even if you received a shorter sentence including probation? *(See definition 1n)*			Affix Recent Photograph Here *(Approximately 2" x 2")* *(See instruction 2g)*
c.	Are you a fugitive from justice? *(See definitions 1s)*			
d.	Are you an unlawful user of, or addicted to, marijuana or any depressant, stimulant, narcotic drug, or any other controlled substance? **Warning: The use or possession of marijuana remains unlawful under Federal law regardless of whether it has been legalized or decriminalized for medicinal or recreational purposes in the state where you reside.**			
e.	Have you ever been adjudicated as a mental defective OR have you ever been committed to a mental institution? *(See definitions 1n and 1o)*			
f.	Have you been discharged from the Armed Forces under dishonorable conditions?			
g.	Are you subject to a court order restraining you from harassing, stalking, or threatening your child or an intimate partner or child of such partner? *(See definition 1p)*			
h.	Have you ever been convicted in any court of a misdemeanor crime of domestic violence? *(See definition 1q)*			

16a. Country of Citizenship. *(Check/List more than one, if applicable. Nationals of the United States may check U.S.A.) (See definition 1r)*
☐ United States of America   ☐ Other Country/Countries *(specify):* _____

		Yes	No
b.	Have you ever renounced your United States citizenship?		
c.	Are you an alien illegally or unlawfully in the United States?		
d.1.	Are you an alien who has been admitted to the United States under a nonimmigrant visa?		
d.2.	If "yes", do you fall within any of the exceptions stated in the instructions? Attach the documentation to the application ☐ N/A		

17. If you are an alien, record your U.S.-Issued Alien or Admission number (AR#, USCIS#, or 194#):

CERTIFICATION: Under penalties imposed by 18 U.S.C. § 924 and 26 U.S.C. § 5861, I certify that, upon submission of this form to ATF, a completed copy of this form will be directed to the chief law enforcement officer (CLEO) shown in item 12, that the statements, as applicable, contained in this certification, and any attached documents in support thereof, are true and correct to the best of my knowledge and belief. NOTE: See instructions 2.d(2) and 2.d(3) for the items to be completed depending on the type of transferee.

Signature of Transferee | Date
ATF Copy

ATF E-Form 4 (5320.4)
Revised May 2016

ATF Form 4, page 3

18. Number of Responsible Persons *(see definitions)* associated with the transferee trust or legal entity _____

19. Provide the full name (printed or typed) below for each Responsible Person associated with the applicant trust or legal entity (if there are more Responsible Persons than can be listed on the form, attach a separate sheet listing the additional Responsible Person(s)). Please note that a completed Form 5320.23, National Firearms Act (NFA) Responsible Person Questionnaire, must be submitted with the Form 4 application for each Responsible Person.

Full Name _____ Full Name _____

20. **Method of Payment** *(Check one) (See instruction 2i)* (if paying by credit/debit card, complete the sections below)

◯ Check *(Enclosed)* ◯ Cashier's Check or Money Order *(Enclosed)* ◯ Visa ◯ Mastercard ◯ American Express ◯ Discover ◯ Diners Club

Credit/Debit Card Number *(No dashes)* | Name as Printed on the Credit/Debit Card | Expiration Date *(Month & year)*

Credit/Debit Card Billing Address: Address: | City: | State: | Zip Code:

Total Amount: $

I Authorize ATF to Charge my Credit/Debit Card the Tax Amount.

Signature of Cardholder _____   Date _____

Your credit/debit card will be charged the above stated amount upon receipt of the application. The charge will be reflected on your credit/debit card statement. In the event your application is NOT approved, the above amount will be credited to the credit/debit card noted above.

Important Information for Currently Registered Firearms
If you are the current registrant of the firearm described on this form, please note the following information.

Estate Procedures: For procedures regarding the transfer of firearms in an estate resulting from the death of the registrant identified in item 2a, the executor should contact the NFA Branch, Bureau of Alcohol, Tobacco, Firearms and Explosives, 244 Needy Road, Martinsburg, WV 25405.

Change of Address: Unless currently licensed under the Gun Control Act, the registrant shall notify the NFA Branch, Bureau of Alcohol, Tobacco, Firearms, and Explosives, 244 Needy Road, Martinsburg, WV 25405, in writing, of any change to the address in item 2a.

Change of Description: The registrant shall notify the NFA Branch, Bureau of Alcohol, Tobacco, Firearms and Explosives, 244 Needy Road, Martinsburg, WV 25405, in writing, of any change to the description of the firearm(s) in item 4.

Interstate Movement: If the firearm identified in item 4 is a **machinegun, short-barreled rifle, short-barreled shotgun,** or **destructive device,** the registrant may be required by 18 U.S.C. § 922(a)(4) to obtain permission from ATF prior to any transportation in interstate or foreign commerce. ATF E-Form 5320.20 can be used to request this permission.

Restrictions on Possession: Any restriction *(see approval block on face of form)* on the possession of the firearm identified in item 4 continues with the further transfer of the firearm.

Persons Prohibited from Possessing Firearms: If the registrant becomes prohibited from possessing a firearm, please contact the NFA Branch for procedures on how to dispose of the firearm.

Proof of Registration: A person possessing a firearm registered as required by the NFA shall retain proof of registration which shall be made available to any ATF officer upon request.

Paperwork Reduction Act Notice
This form meets the clearance requirements of the Paperwork Reduction Act of 1995. The information you provide is used in applying to transfer serviceable firearms taxpaid. Data is used to identify transferor, transferee, and firearm, and to ensure legality for transfer under Federal, State and local laws. The furnishing of this information is mandatory (26 U.S.C. § 5812).

The estimated average burden associated with this collection of information is 3.78 hours per respondent or recordkeeper, depending on individual circumstances. Comments concerning the accuracy of this burden estimate and suggestion for reducing this burden should be addressed to Reports Management Officer, Information Technology Coordination Staff, Bureau of Alcohol, Tobacco, Firearms and Explosives, Washington, DC 20226.

An agency may not conduct or sponsor, and a person is not required to respond to, a collection of information unless it displays a currently valid OMB control number.

ATF Copy

ATF E-Form 4 (5320.4)
Revised May 2016

ATF Form 1, page 1

OMB No. 1140-0011 (06/30/2019)

U.S. Department of Justice
Bureau of Alcohol, Tobacco, Firearms and Explosives

Application to Make and Register a Firearm

ATF Control Number

To: National Firearms Act Branch, Bureau of Alcohol, Tobacco, Firearms and Explosives, P.O. Box 530298, Atlanta, GA 30353-0298

(Submit in duplicate. See instructions attached.)

As required by Sections 5821(b), 5822, and 5841 of the National Firearms Act, Title 26 U.S.C., Chapter 53, the undersigned hereby submits application to make and register the firearm described below.

2. Application is made by: ○ INDIVIDUAL ○ TRUST or LEGAL ENTITY ○ GOVERNMENT ENTITY 3a. Trade name *(If any)*	1. Type of Application *(Check one)* ○ a. Tax Paid. Submit your tax payment of $200 with the application. The tax may be paid by credit or debit card, check, or money order. Please complete item 17. Upon approval of the application, we will affix and cancel the required National Firearms Act Stamp. *(See instruction 2c and 3)*

3b. Applicant's name and mailing address *(Type or print below and between the dots) (See instruction 2d)*

• •

○ b. Tax Exempt because firearm is being made on behalf of the United States, or any department, independent establishment, or agency thereof.

3c. If P.O. Box is shown above, street address must be given here

○ c. Tax Exempt because firearm is being made by or on behalf of any State or possession of the United States, or any political subdivision thereof, or any official police organization of such a government entity engaged in criminal investigations.

3d. County	3e. Telephone area code and number	3f. e-mail address (optional)

4 Description of Firearm *(complete items a through k) (See instruction 2j)*

a. Name and Address of Original Manufacturer and/or Importer of Firearm *(if any)*	b. Type of Firearm to be made *(See definition 1c) If a destructive device, complete item 4)*	c. Caliber or Gauge *(Specify one)*	d. Model
			e. Of Barrel: f. Overall Length *(Inches)*
			g. Serial Number

h. Additional Description *(Include all numbers and other identifying data to include maker's name, city and state which will appear on the firearm) (use additional sheet if necessary)*	i. State Why You Intend To Make Firearm *(Use additional sheet if necessary)*

j. Type of destructive device (check one box): ○ Firearm ○ Explosives *(if the Explosives box is checked, complete item 5 and see instruction 2l)*

If an explosive type destructive device, identify the type of explosive(s): _____

k. Is this firearm being reactivated? ○ Yes ○ No *(See definition 1k)*

5. Applicant's Federal Firearms License *(If any)* or Explosives License or Permit Number	6. Special *(Occupational)* Tax Status *(If applicable) (See definitions)*
(Give complete 15-digit Number)	a. Employer Identification Number | b. Class

Under Penalties of Perjury, I Declare that I have examined this application, including accompanying documents, and to the best of my knowledge and belief it is true, accurate and complete and the making and possession of the firearm described above would not constitute a violation of Title 18, U.S.C., Chapter 44, Title 26, U.S.C., Chapter 53; or any provisions of State or local law.

7. Signature of Applicant	8. Name and Title of Authorized Official	9. Date

The space below is for the use of the Bureau of Alcohol, Tobacco, Firearms, and Explosives

By authority of the Director, Bureau of Alcohol, Tobacco, Firearms and Explosives, this application has been examined and the applicant's making and registration of the firearms described above is:

☐ Approved *(With the following conditions, if any)*   ☐ Disapproved *(For the following reasons)*

Authorized ATF Official	Date

Previous Editions are Obsolete

ATF Copy

ATF E-Form 1 (5320.1) Revised May 2016

ATF Form 1, page 2

MAKER'S CERTIFICATION *(not completed by a GOVERNMENT ENTITY)*

10. Law Enforcement Notification *(See instruction 2g)*

Each applicant is to provide notification of the proposed making and possession of the firearm described on this Form 1 by providing a copy of the completed form to the chief law enforcement officer in the agency identified below:

Agency or Department Name	Name and Title of Official

Address (Street address or P.O. Box, City, State and Zip Code) to which sent (mailed or delivered)

Information for the Chief Law Enforcement Officer

This form provides notification of the applicant's intent to make and register a National Firearms Act (NFA) firearm. No action on your part is required. However, should you have information that may disqualify this person from making or possessing a firearm, please contact the NFA Branch at (304) 616-4500 or NFA@atf.gov. A "Yes" answer to items 11.a through 11.h or 13.b or 13.c could disqualify a person from acquiring or possessing a firearm. Also, ATF will not approve an application if the making or possession of the firearm is in violation of State or local law.

Maker's Questions *(complete only when the maker is an individual)*

A maker who is an individual must complete this Section.

11. Answer questions 11.a. through 11.h. Answer questions 13 and 14, if applicable. For any "Yes" answer the applicant shall provide details on a separate sheet. *(See instruction 7c and definitions)*

	Yes	No	12. Photograph
a. Are you under indictment or information in any court for a felony, or any other crime, for which the judge could imprison you for more than one year? *(See definition 1n)*	O	O	
b. Have you ever been convicted in any court for a felony, or any other crime, for which the judge could have imprisoned you for more than one year, even if you received a shorter sentence including probation? *(See definition 1n)*	O	O	Affix Recent Photograph Here
c. Are you a fugitive from justice? *(See definition 1t)*	O	O	*(Approximately 2" x 2")*
d. Are you an unlawful user of, or addicted to, marijuana or any depressant, stimulant, narcotic drug, or any other controlled substance? **Warning: The use or possession of marijuana remains unlawful under Federal law regardless of whether it has been legalized or decriminalized for medicinal or recreational purposes in the state where you reside.**	O	O	*(See instruction 2e)*
e. Have you ever been adjudicated as a mental defective **OR** have you ever been committed to a mental institution? *(See definition 1o and 1p)*	O	O	
f. Have you been discharged from the Armed Forces under **dishonorable** conditions?	O	O	
g. Are you subject to a court order restraining you from harassing, stalking, or threatening your child or an intimate partner or child of such a partner? *(See definition 1q)*	O	O	
h. Have you ever been convicted in any court of a misdemeanor crime of domestic violence? *(See definition 1r)*	O	O	

13a. Country of Citizenship: *(Check/List more than one, if applicable. Nationals of the United States may check U.S.A.) (See definition 1s)*

    O United States of America   O Other Country/Countries *(specify)*: _____

	Yes	No
b. Have you ever renounced your United States citizenship?	O	O
c. Are you an alien illegally or unlawfully in the United States?	O	O
d.1. Are you an alien who has been admitted to the United States under a nonimmigrant visa?	O	O
d.2. If "yes", do you fall within any of the exceptions stated in the instructions? Attach the documentation to the application	O N/A	O	O

14. If you are an alien, record your U.S.-Issued Alien or Admission number (AR#, USCIS#, or 194#): _____

CERTIFICATION: Under penalties imposed by 18 U.S.C. § 924 and 26 U.S.C. § 5861, I certify that, upon submission of this form to ATF, a completed copy of this form will be directed to the chief law enforcement officer (CLEO) shown in item 10, that the statements, as applicable, contained in this certification, and any attached documents in support thereof, are true and correct to the best of my knowledge and belief. NOTE: See instructions 2.d(2) and 2.d(3) for the items to be completed depending on the type of applicant.

Signature of Maker	Date

ATF Copy

ATF E-Form 1 (5320.1)
Revised May 2016

ATF Form 1, page 3

15. Number of Responsible Persons *(see definitions)* associated with the applicant trust or legal entity _____

16. Provide the full name (printed or typed) below for each Responsible Person associated with the applicant trust or legal entity (if there are more Responsible Persons than can be listed on the form, attach a separate sheet listing the additional Responsible Person(s)). Please note that a completed Form 5320.23, National Firearms Act (NFA) Responsible Person Questionnaire, must be submitted with the Form 1 application for each Responsible Person.

Full Name   Full Name

_____   _____

_____   _____

_____   _____

---

17. **Method of Payment** *(Check one) (See instruction 2h) (if paying by credit/debit card, complete the sections below)*

☐ Check *(Enclosed)*	☐ Cashier's Check or Money Order *(Enclosed)*	☐ Visa	☐ Mastercard	☐ American Express	☐ Discover	☐ Diners Club

Credit/Debit Card Number *(No dashes)*	Name as Printed on the Credit/Debit Card	Expiration Date *(Month & year)*

Credit/Debit Card Billing Address:	Address:		
	City:	State:	Zip Code:

Total Amount:
$

I Authorize ATF to Charge my Credit/Debit Card the Above Amount.

_____   _____
                    Signature of Cardholder   Date

Your credit/debit card will be charged the above stated amount upon receipt of your application. The charge will be reflected on your credit/debit card statement.
In the event your application is NOT approved, the above amount will be credited to the credit/debit card noted above.

Important Information for Currently Registered Firearms

If you are the current registrant of the firearm described on this form, please note the following information.

Estate Procedures: For procedures regarding the transfer of firearms in an estate resulting from the death of the registrant identified in item 3b, the executor should contact the NFA Branch, Bureau of ATF, 244 Needy Road, Martinsburg, WV 25405.

Interstate Movement: If the firearm identified in item 4 is a **machinegun, short-barreled rifle, short-barreled shotgun,** or **destructive device,** the registrant may be required by 18 U.S.C. § 922(a)(4) to obtain permission from ATF prior to any transportation in interstate or foreign commerce. ATF E-Form 5320.20 can be used to request this permission.

Change of Description or Address: The registrant shall notify the NFA Branch, Bureau of Alcohol, Tobacco, Firearms and Explosives, 244 Needy Road, Martinsburg, WV 25405, in writing, of any change to the description of the firearm in Item 4, or any change to the address of the registrant.

Restrictions on Possession: Any restriction *(see approval block on face of form)* on the possession of the firearm identified in item 4 continues with the further transfer of the firearm.

Persons Prohibited from Possessing Firearms: If the registrant becomes prohibited from possessing a firearm, please contact the NFA Branch for procedures on how to dispose of the firearm.

Proof of Registration: A person possessing a firearm registered as required by the NFA shall retain proof of registration which shall be made available to any ATF officer upon request.

Paperwork Reduction Act Notice

This form is in accordance with the Paperwork Reduction Act of 1995. The information you provide is used to establish that the applicant's making and possession of the firearm would be in conformance with Federal, State, and local law. The data is used as proof of lawful registration of a firearm to the manufacturer. The furnishing of this information is mandatory *(26 U.S.C. § 5822)*.

The estimated average burden associated with this collection of information is 4.0 hours per respondent or recordkeeper, depending on individual circumstances. Comments concerning the accuracy of this burden estimate and suggestion for reducing this burden should be addressed to Reports Management Officer, Information Technology Coordination Staff, Bureau of Alcohol, Tobacco, Firearms and Explosives, Washington, DC 20226.

An agency may not conduct or sponsor, and a person is not required to respond to, a collection of information unless it displays a currently valid OMB control number.

ATF Copy   ATF E-Form 1 (5320.1)
                                                         Revised May 2016

ATF Form 5320.23, page 1

U.S. Department of Justice
Bureau of Alcohol, Tobacco, Firearms and Explosives

OMB No. 1140-0107 (06/30/2019)

National Firearms Act *(NFA)*
Responsible Person Questionnaire

Complete the form in duplicate. The ATF copy of the form, with fingerprints on Form FD-258 and photograph, will be submitted with the ATF Form 1, 4, or 5 (to the address shown on the specific form) and the other copy will be directed to the responsible person's chief law enforcement officer. *(See Instructions)*

1. Please check the appropriate box to indicate with which ATF form this questionnaire will be submitted.
   ☐ ATF Form 1   ☐ ATF Form 4   ☐ ATF Form 5

2. Name and Address of Applicant or Transferee *(as shown on the ATF Form 1, 4 or 5) (see instruction 2)*

3a. Name and Home Address of Responsible Person

3b. Telephone *(Area code and Number)*

3c. e-mail address *(optional)*

3d. Other names used *(including maiden name)*

4a. Type of Firearm *(see definition 5)*

3e. Photograph

4b. Name and Address of Maker, Manufacturer and/or Importer of Firearm

Affix recent Photograph Here

(Approximately 2" x 2")
(See instruction 3b)

4c. Firearm Model | 4d. Caliber or Gauge | 4e. Firearm Serial Number

5. Law Enforcement Notification *(See instruction 5)*

As a responsible person (see definition 4) of the trust or legal entity identified in Item 2 of this form, I am required to provide notification of the proposed making or acquisition and possession of the firearm described in item 4 of this form by providing a copy of the completed form to the chief law enforcement officer (CLEO) in the agency identified below:

Agency or Department Name

Name and Title of Official

Address (Street address or P.O. Box, City, State and Zip Code) to which sent (mailed or delivered)

Information for the Chief Law Enforcement Officer

This form provides notification of the maker or transferee's intent to make or acquire and possess a National Firearms Act (NFA) firearm. No action on your part is required. However, should you have information that may disqualify this person from making or possessing a firearm, please contact the NFA Branch at (304) 616-4500 or NFA@atf.gov. A "Yes" answer to items 6b or item 7b or 7c could disqualify a person from acquiring or possessing a firearm. Also, ATF may not approve an application if the transfer or possession of the firearm would be in violation of State or local law.

ATF Copy

ATF E-Form 5320.23
Revised May 2016

ATF Form 5320.23, page 2

6. Answer questions 6.a through 6.h. Answer questions 7 and 8 if applicable. For any "Yes" answer the transferee shall provide details on a separate sheet. *(See definitions 8-12)*	Yes	No
a. Are you under indictment or information in any court for a felony, or any other crime, for which the judge could imprison you for more than one year? *(See definition 8)*	O	O
b. Have you ever been convicted in any court for a felony, or any other crime, for which the judge could have imprisoned you for more than one year, even if you received a shorter sentence including probation? *(See definition 8)*	O	O
c. Are you a fugitive from justice? *(See definition 13)*	O	O
d. Are you an unlawful user of, or addicted to, marijuana or any depressant, stimulant, narcotic drug, or any other controlled substance? **Warning: The use or possession of marijuana remains unlawful under Federal law regardless of whether is has been legalized or decriminalized for medicinal or recreational purposes in the state where you reside.**	O	O
e. Have you ever been adjudicated as a mental defective OR have you ever been committed to a mental institution? *(See definitions 9 and 10)*	O	O
f. Have you been discharged from the Armed Forces under **dishonorable** conditions?	O	O
g. Are you subject to a court order restraining you from harassing, stalking, or threatening your child or an intimate partner or child of such partner? *(See definition 11)*	O	O
h. Have you ever been convicted in any court of a misdemeanor crime of domestic violence? *(See definition 14)*	O	O

7a. Country of Citizenship: (Check/List more than one, if applicable. Nationals of the United States may check U.S.A.) *(See definition 12)*

O United States of America   O Other Country/Countries (specify): _____

	Yes	No
b. Have you ever renounced your United States citizenship?	O	O
c. Are you an alien illegally or unlawfully in the United States?	O	O
d.1. Are you an alien who has been admitted to the United States under a nonimmigrant visa?	O	O
d.2. If "yes", do you fall within any of the exceptions stated in the instructions? Attach the documentation to the questionnaire O N/A	O	O

8. If you are an alien, record your U.S. -Issued Alien or Admission number (AR#, USCIS#, or 194#):

CERTIFICATION: Under penalties imposed by 18 U.S.C. § 924 and 26 U.S.C. § 5861, I certify that, upon submission of this form to ATF, a completed copy of this form will be directed to the chief law enforcement officer (CLEO) shown in item 5, that the statements contained in this certification, and any attached documents in support thereof, are true and correct to the best of my knowledge and belief.

_____   _____
Signature of Responsible Person   Date

Instructions

1. Completion: Each responsible person (see definition 4) of a trust or legal entity seeking to make or acquire a National Firearms Act *(NFA)* firearm shall complete this form in duplicate. (see instruction 9)
   a. Each responsible person must submit his/her fingerprints and photograph with this form *(see below)*.
   b. Please note that this form is not required when the applicant on Form 1, 4 or 5 is an individual.
2. Item 2- Enter the name, trade name *(if any)* and address of the trust or legal entity identified on the Form 1 (items 3a and b); Form 4 *(item 2a)*; or Form 5 *(item 2a)*
3. Item 3- Responsible Person information
   a. Provide the information for the responsible person in items 3a through 3e.
   b. Item 3e - Photograph: The responsible person shall attach, in item 3e on the ATF copy of the form only, a 2-inch by 2-inch frontal view photograph taken within one year prior to the date of the filing of the form. Item 3c is obscured on the CLEO copy.
4. Firearm information
   a. Type of NFA firearm: see definition 5 and as identified in item 4b of Form 1, 4, or 5
   b. Name of maker, manufacturer and/or importer: as identified in item 4a of Form 1, 4, or 5
   c. Firearm Model: identified in item 4d of Form 1, 4, or 5
   d. Caliber or Gauge: identified in item 4c of Form 1, 4 or 5
   e. Firearm Serial Number: identified in item 4g of Form 1, 4 or 5. Item 4e is obscured on the CLEO copy.
5. Item 5- Law Enforcement Notification: Each responsible person must provide a notification on this form of the proposed making or acquisition of an NFA firearm to his/her chief law enforcement officer having jurisdiction where the responsible person is located. The chief law enforcement officer is considered to be the Chief of Police; the Sheriff; the Head of the State Police; or a State or local district attorney or prosecutor.
6. Complete items 6 through 8
7. Fingerprints: The responsible person shall submit, in duplicate with the ATF copy of this form, his or her fingerprints on FBI Form FD-258 and the fingerprints must be clear for accurate classification and taken by someone properly equipped to take them. No fingerprints are required with the copy of the form sent to the chief law enforcement officer.
8. State or Local Permit: If the State in which the responsible person resides requires the responsible person to have a State or Local permit or licensee, a copy of the permit or license must be submitted with this form.
9. Disposition: The ATF copy of the form, with the fingerprints and photograph, shall be submitted with the ATF Form 1, 4 or 5. The other copy shall be directed to the responsible person's chief law enforcement officer identified in item 5 of this form.
10. Sign and date the form. The signature must be original.

ATF Copy

ATF E-Form 5320.23
Revised May 2016

ATF Form 5320.23, page 3

U.S. Department of Justice
Bureau of Alcohol, Tobacco, Firearms and Explosives

OMB No. 1140-0107 (06/30/2019)

National Firearms Act *(NFA)*
Responsible Person Questionnaire

Complete the form in duplicate. The ATF copy of the form, with fingerprints on Form FD-258 and photograph, will be submitted with the ATF Form 1, 4, or 5 (to the address shown on the specific form) and the other copy will be directed to the responsible person's chief law enforcement officer. *(See Instructions)*

1. Please check the appropriate box to indicate with which ATF form this questionnaire will be submitted.

   ◯ ATF Form 1   ◯ ATF Form 4   ◯ ATF Form 5

2. Name and Address of Applicant or Transferee *(as shown on the ATF Form 1, 4 or 5) (see instruction 2)*

3a. Name and Home Address of Responsible Person	3b. Telephone *(Area code and Number)*
	3c. e-mail address *(optional)*
	3d. Other names used *(including maiden name)*

4a. Type of Firearm *(see definition 5)*

4b. Name and Address of Maker, Manufacturer and/or Importer of Firearm

4c. Firearm Model	4d. Caliber or Gauge	

5. Law Enforcement Notification *(See instruction 5)*

As a responsible person (see definition 4) of the trust or legal entity identified in Item 2 of this form, I am required to provide notification of the proposed making or acquisition and possession of the firearm described in item 4 of this form by providing a copy of the completed form to the chief law enforcement officer (CLEO) in the agency identified below:

Agency or Department Name   Name and Title of Official

Address (Street address or P.O. Box, City, State and Zip Code) to which sent (mailed or delivered)

Information for the Chief Law Enforcement Officer

This form provides notification of the maker or transferee's intent to make or acquire and possess a National Firearms Act (NFA) firearm. No action on your part is required. However, should you have information that may disqualify this person from making or possessing a firearm, please contact the NFA Branch at (304) 616-4500 or NFA@atf.gov. A "Yes" answer to items 6h or item 7b or 7c could disqualify a person from acquiring or possessing a firearm. Also, ATF may not approve an application if the transfer or possession of the firearm would be in violation of State or local law.

CLEO Copy

ATF E-Form 5320.23
Revised May 2016

ATF Form 5320.23, page 4

6. Answer questions 6.a through 6.h. Answer questions 7 and 8 if applicable. For any "Yes" answer the transferee shall provide details on a separate sheet. *(See definitions 8-12)*

	Yes	No
a. Are you under indictment or information in any court for a felony, or any other crime, for which the judge could imprison you for more than one year? *(See definition 8)*	O	O
b. Have you ever been convicted in any court for a felony, or any other crime, for which the judge could have imprisoned you for more than one year, even if you received a shorter sentence including probation? *(See definition 8)*	O	O
c. Are you a fugitive from justice? *(See definition 13)*	O	O
d. Are you an unlawful user of, or addicted to, marijuana or any depressant, stimulant, narcotic drug, or any other controlled substance? **Warning: The use or possession of marijuana remains unlawful under Federal law regardless of whether is has been legalized or decriminalized for medicinal or recreational purposes in the state where you reside.**	O	O
e. Have you ever been adjudicated as a mental defective **OR** have you ever been committed to a mental institution? *(See definitions 9 and 10)*	O	O
f. Have you been discharged from the Armed Forces under **dishonorable** conditions?	O	O
g. Are you subject to a court order restraining you from harassing, stalking, or threatening your child or an intimate partner or child of such partner? *(See definition 11)*	O	O
h. Have you ever been convicted in any court of a misdemeanor crime of domestic violence? *(See definition 14)*	O	O

7a. Country of Citizenship: *(Check/List more than one, if applicable. Nationals of the United States may check U.S.A.) (See definition 12)*

     O United States of America   O Other Country/Countries (specify): _____

	Yes	No
h. Have you ever renounced your United States citizenship?	O	O
c. Are you an alien illegally or unlawfully in the United States?	O	O
d.1. Are you an alien who has been admitted to the United States under a nonimmigrant visa?	O	O
d.2. If "yes", do you fall within any of the exceptions stated in the instructions? Attach the documentation to the questionnaire O N/A	O	O

8. If you are an alien, record your U.S. -Issued Alien or Admission number (AR#, USCIS#, or 194#): _____

CERTIFICATION: Under penalties imposed by 18 U.S.C. § 924 and 26 U.S.C. § 5861, I certify that, upon submission of this form to ATF, a completed copy of this form will be directed to the chief law enforcement officer (CLEO) shown in item 5, that the statements contained in this certification, and any attached documents in support thereof, are true and correct to the best of my knowledge and belief.

_____   _____
Signature of Responsible Person   Date

Instructions

1. Completion: Each responsible person (see definition 4) of a trust or legal entity seeking to make or acquire a National Firearms Act *(NFA)* firearm shall complete this form in duplicate. (see instruction 9)
   a. Each responsible person must submit his/her fingerprints and photograph with this form *(see below)*.
   b. Please note that this form is not required when the applicant on Form 1, 4 or 5 is an individual.
2. Item 2- Enter the name, trade name *(if any)* and address of the trust or legal entity identified on the Form 1 *(items 3a and b)*; Form 4 *(item 2a)*; or Form 5 *(item 2a)*
3. Item 3- Responsible Person information
   a. Provide the information for the responsible person in items 3a through 3e.
   b. Item 3e - Photograph: The responsible person shall attach, in item 3e on the ATF copy of the form only, a 2-inch by 2-inch frontal view photograph taken within one year prior to the date of the filing of the form. Item 3c is obscured on the CLEO copy.
4. Firearm information
   a. Type of NFA firearm: see definition 5 and as identified in item 4b of Form 1, 4, or 5
   b. Name of maker, manufacturer and/or importer: as identified in item 4a of Form 1, 4, or 5
   c. Firearm Model: identified in item 4d of Form 1, 4, or 5
   d. Caliber or Gauge: identified in item 4c of Form 1, 4 or 5
   e. Firearm Serial Number: identified in item 4g of Form 1, 4 or 5. Item 4e is obscured on the CLEO copy.
5. Item 5- Law Enforcement Notification: Each responsible person must provide a notification on this form of the proposed making or acquisition of an NFA firearm to his/her chief law enforcement officer having jurisdiction where the responsible person is located. The chief law enforcement officer is considered to be the Chief of Police; the Sheriff; the Head of the State Police; or a State or local district attorney or prosecutor.
6. Complete items 6 through 8
7. Fingerprints: The responsible person shall submit, in duplicate with the ATF copy of this form, his or her fingerprints on FBI Form FD-258 and the fingerprints must be clear for accurate classification and taken by someone properly equipped to take them. No fingerprints are required with the copy of the form sent to the chief law enforcement officer.
8. State or Local Permit: If the State in which the responsible person resides requires the responsible person to have a State or Local permit or licensee, a copy of the permit or license must be submitted with this form.
9. Disposition: The ATF copy of the form, with the fingerprints and photograph, shall be submitted with the ATF Form 1, 4 or 5. The other copy shall be directed to the responsible person's chief law enforcement officer identified in item 5 of this form.
10. Sign and date the form. The signature must be original.

                              CLEO Copy   ATF E-Form 5320.23
                                                                    Revised May 2016

ABOUT THE ATTORNEY AUTHORS

ED RILEY
CO-AUTHOR

Ed Riley is a Virginia trial lawyer & U.S. Law Shield independent program attorney. He has dedicated his entire 25 plus year career to defending clients before Virginia courts. During that time, he has successfully represented thousands of clients and has argued over 200 criminal & civil jury trials in both federal and state courts across the Commonwealth of Virginia. Ed maintains the highest national "AV preeminent" rating with Martindale-Hubbell for legal ability and ethical standards. He is also routinely recognized by his peers as one of the Legal Elite as published by Virginia Business Magazine and has been consecutively selected for inclusion in the annual Virginia Super Lawyers publications by Thomson Reuters. He is a graduate of the University of Virginia and the University of Richmond's T.C. Williams School of Law. His involvement within the legal community is extensive as he chairs or co-chairs various Virginia legal organizations. Ed also regularly serves as a criminal law commentator for local media outlets and regularly lectures on criminal law to other lawyers and judges.

MITCH WELLS
CO-AUTHOR

Mitch Wells is a Virginia criminal law attorney with the law firm of Riley & Wells in Richmond and is a U.S. Law Shield independent program lawyer. Mitch began his professional career in 1994 serving as a Virginia State Trooper. In that capacity, he investigated numerous gun cases, received special weapons & self-defense training, and was a general instructor during his eight year tenure with the Virginia State Police. He is a graduate of Virginia Military Institute, Virginia Commonwealth University, and William & Mary School of Law. Over the last decade, Mitch has successfully represented thousands of clients before the Virginia courts and has been repeatedly recognized for his legal skill, ability, achievement and ethics by numerous legal publications. He maintains an "AV Preeminent" rating from Martindale-Hubbell and a rating of "Superb" from AVVO, each organization's highest legal rating for ethical standards and legal ability, Prior to entering private practice, Mitch served as an Assistant Virginia Attorney General and was a judicial law clerk to the Honorable Robert E. Payne, Judge, for the U.S. District Court in the Eastern District of Virginia.